Americans View Their

Dust Bowl

Experience

University Press of Colorado

Americans View Their
Dust Bowl
Experience

edited by

JOHN R. WUNDER,

FRANCES W. KAYE,

and

VERNON CARSTENSEN

Published by the University Press of Colorado
5589 Arapahoe Avenue, Suite 206C
Boulder, Colorado 80303

The University Press of Colorado is a cooperative publishing enterprise supported, in part, by Adams State College, Colorado State University, Fort Lewis College, Mesa State College, Metropolitan State College of Denver, University of Colorado, University of Northern Colorado, University of Southern Colorado, and Western State College of Colorado.

The paper used in this publication meets the minimum requirements of the American National Standard for Information Sciences—Permanence of Paper for Printed Library Materials. ANSI Z39.48-1992

Library of Congress Cataloging-in-Publication Data

Americans view their Dust Bowl experience / edited by John R. Wunder,
 Frances W. Kaye, and Vernon Carstensen.
   p.   cm.
   Includes bibliographical references and index.
   ISBN 0-87081-507-5 (cloth : alk. paper) — 0-87081-648-9 (pbk. : alk. paper)
   1. Great Plains—History—20th century—Sources. 2. Great Plains—Economic
conditions—Sources. 2. Great Plains—Rural conditions—Sources. 4. Depressions—
1929—Great Plains—Sources. 5. Droughts—Great Plains—History—20th Century—
Sources. I. Wunder, John R. II. Kaye, Frances W. III. Carstensen, Vernon Rosco,
1907–.
F595.A55
978'.03—dc21   98-26105
                                                                    CIP

10 09 08 07 06 05 04 03 02 01   10 9 8 7 6 5 4 3 2 1

Photograph on title page and part openings: "Black Blizzards," courtesy Southwest Collection, Texas Tech University

Contents

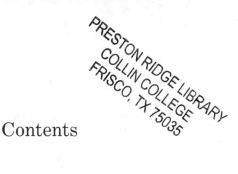

Preface

This book began thirty-plus years ago. Prior to 1960, the American Historical Association (AHA) published a number of document-based monographs, and Vernon Carstensen, then a professor of history at the University of Wisconsin–Madison, was invited to prepare documents and a narrative reflecting on the nature of the Dust Bowl experience. He did so promptly, but in the interim the AHA discontinued the series.

When John Wunder accepted an appointment at the University of Nebraska–Lincoln, Vernon Carstensen (VC to his students) sent the documents, his editorial comments, and his unpublished essay on the film *The Plow That Broke the Plains* to his former student. VC reasoned that because Wunder was now director of the Center for Great Plains Studies, the center might find the material of interest. Wunder thought his mentor's work had significant merit, and he sought the advice of the editor of the *Great Plains Quarterly*, Frances Kaye. Kaye agreed with Wunder and suggested that the documents and comments be supplemented with articles already published in the *Quarterly* and other articles selected from other journals. In due course, five *Quarterly* articles were selected for inclusion, along with two articles from *North Dakota History* and one article each from *Annals of Iowa, Nebraska History, Agricultural History, South Dakota History,* and *Montana, Magazine of Western History.*

Wunder informed VC about Kaye's and his proposal to pull together a special volume about how Americans interpret their Dust Bowl experiences. He was delighted, but he told them his name should not be included on the title page. This request, although meritorious, seemed unreasonable to Wunder and Kaye. To not acknowledge Vernon Carstensen's very important contribution would constitute, it seemed to them, academic fraud. So they overruled VC—a bold decision by student Wunder. Kaye and Wunder also agreed to explain explicitly who had contributed what to the volume.

Americans View Their Dust Bowl Experience is the product of the talents of three persons. The documents were compiled and briefly introduced by Vernon Carstensen, who also wrote the chapter *"The Plow That Broke the Plains*: Film Legacy of the Great Depression." John Wunder wrote the introduction, edited the documents, wrote a conclusion to the Carstensen chapter, supplied the subheadings in chapters lacking such consistency, and wrote the summaries connecting the book sections. Fran Kaye edited four *Great Plains Quarterly* articles and edited the entire manuscript.

John Wunder and Fran Kaye wish to acknowledge several persons who assisted in the preparation of this volume. Both believe the legacy of land historians and now environmental historians was crucial to the evolution of this manuscript. John Wunder studied with Vernon Carstensen and Malcolm Rohrbough, both of whom emphasized the importance of understanding the nature of land and the relationship of humans to the land. Vernon Carstensen, who after his retirement resided at his home in Seattle, Washington, recently died. He did see the manuscript before his death and was pleased with it. His sons, Fred and Peter Carstensen, have approved the publishing of this last academic work of their father.

Fran Kaye studied with Paul Gates at Cornell University, known as Mr. Gates to his students. Kaye wishes to acknowledge her debt to Mr. Gates for his pathbreaking ideas and ever-active scholarly life. Paul Gates continues to contribute his thoughts to the environmental history of this continent.

There are two primary purposes for compiling this book. One is to let American people speak to the general public about the Dust Bowl in basic, understandable ways. The other is to provide secondary teachers and college professors with a dynamic story for students to enjoy. The title of the book is also designed to recognize the outstanding teaching career of Thomas Pressly, professor emeritus at the University of Washington. It is a play on the title of Pressly's very successful book, *Americans View Their Civil War.*

The staff of the Center for Great Plains Studies, especially Linda Ratcliffe, must be acknowledged for their help in assembling this manuscript. Lori Gourama, Sharon Bays, and Gretchen Walker assisted the editors in typing and making corrections. Emily Levine, a Great Plains Studies major and graduate of the University of Nebraska–Lincoln (UNL), helped to identify missing notes, documents, and bibliographical entries, and Jay H. Buckley, a Ph.D. student in history at UNL, compiled the bibliography. Michael Shambaugh-Miller and Robert Watrel, Ph.D. students in geography at UNL, created the maps. Without the help of all of these people, this volume would not have been developed.

The editors also wish to pay tribute to the men, women, and children who lived in the Great Plains during the Dust Bowl years. It is through their experiences that the documents and articles in this volume come alive.

John R. Wunder and Frances W. Kaye
University of Nebraska–Lincoln, May 1998

Reprint Acknowledgments

*We are grateful to the following journals for
permission to reprint the articles listed below*

AGRICULTURAL HISTORY, Center for Agricultural History and Rural Studies, Iowa State University

John E. Miller, "Restrained, Respectable Radicals: The South Dakota Farm Holiday," *Agricultural History* 59 (July 1985):429–447.

ANNALS OF IOWA, State Historical Society of Iowa

Originally published as Rodney D. Karr, "Farmer Rebels in Plymouth County, Iowa, 1932–1933," *Annals of Iowa* 47 (Winter 1985):637–645. Copyright 1985 State Historical Society of Iowa.

GREAT PLAINS QUARTERLY, Center for Great Plains Studies, University of Nebraska

Brad Lookingbill, " 'A God-forsaken Place': Folk Eschatology and the Dust Bowl," *Great Plains Quarterly* 14 (Fall 1994):273–286.

Harry C. McDean, "Dust Bowl Historiography," *Great Plains Quarterly* 6 (Spring 1986):117–126.

William C. Pratt, "Rethinking the Farm Revolt of the 1930s," *Great Plains Quarterly* 8 (Summer 1988):131–144.

Dorothy Schwieder and Deborah Fink, "Plains Women: Rural Life in the 1930s," *Great Plains Quarterly* 8 (Spring 1988):79–88.

Donald Worster, "The Dirty Thirties: A Study in Agricultural Capitalism," *Great Plains Quarterly* 6 (Spring 1986):107–116.

MONTANA, MAGAZINE OF WESTERN HISTORY, Montana State Historical Society

Charles Vindex, "Radical Rule in Montana," *Montana, Magazine of Western History* 18 (Winter 1968):2–18.

NEBRASKA HISTORY, Nebraska State Historical Society

John L. Shover, "The Farm Holiday Movement in Nebraska," *Nebraska History* 43 (March 1962):53–78.

NORTH DAKOTA HISTORY, State Historical Society of North Dakota

James W. Dodd, "Resolutions, Programs, and Policies of the North Dakota Farmers' Holiday Association, 1932–1937," *North Dakota History* 28 (April–June 1961):107–117.

Larry Remele, "The North Dakota Farm Strike of 1932," *North Dakota History* 41 (Fall 1974):5–18.

SOUTH DAKOTA HISTORY, South Dakota State Historical Society

Allan Mathews, "Agrarian Radicals: The United Farmers League of South Dakota," *South Dakota History* 3 (Fall 1973):408–421. Copyright © 1973 by the South Dakota Historical Society.

We are grateful to the following newspapers, magazines, and publishers for permission to reprint selected articles: the Associated Press, *Atlantic Monthly, The Nation, New Republic*, the *New York Times*, and *Time Magazine* of Time Life Syndication; and to the following archives for permission to reproduce their photographs: the Nebraska State Historical Society (Photographic Archives), Lincoln, Nebraska, and the Southwest Collection, Texas Tech University, Lubbock, Texas.

Americans View Their

Dust Bowl

Experience

I

Introduction

John R. Wunder

The Dust Bowl experience was a seminal event for at least two generations of Americans, whose lives it shaped or reshaped. The experience was felt especially by those directly involved in agriculture in
portions of the Mississippi Valley—the farmers of Iowa, Minnesota,
Missouri, and Arkansas—and it deeply touched the farmers and ranchers of the American Great Plains—the agriculturalists of North and
South Dakota, Wyoming and Montana, Nebraska and Colorado, Kansas and Oklahoma, and New Mexico and the Texas Panhandle. The
1930s in the heartland were difficult times.

This book is about those Americans of the Dust Bowl. The book
seeks to foster an understanding of the physical and mental dimensions of the disaster. Through original documents of the times, it offers a glimpse into the human response to the Dust Bowl. The first
section of the book includes contemporary accounts of the plight of
farmers. Dust Bowl distress and anger, farmer strikes, and the farmers' march on Washington are captured in memoirs and news reports
of the times. The human response to this environmental catastrophe
is next observed in letters of self-doubt, attempts to find solutions in
science, and reflections on religious faith.

This volume also includes analyses of the Dust Bowl by historians, and they, too, focus on the human dimension of this environmental disaster. The first articles concern the personal responses of men, women, and children to their predicaments. The different ways men and women sought to cope with the Dust Bowl, the fact that some farmers had to pursue extralegal activities, and the way religion tried to explain the disaster are probed. The history of farmer strikes, the Farm Holiday Movement, and the United Farmers League are described; the use of the media to provide political explanations is also discussed. Finally, three historiographical articles explain the different dimensions of the Dust Bowl and the farm revolts during the 1930s. Thus, both the documents and the articles search for explanations and answers to such basic questions as why did the Dust Bowl happen, why did Americans react as they did, and how did the Dust Bowl affect those who actually witnessed it, as well as their children and grandchildren.

The first inkling of trouble came in the late 1920s. Prices for farm products steadily dropped. When drought conditions began to appear in several areas, many farmers had little, if any, capital reserves. Some farmers, such as a Harrisburg, Arkansas, family of five who slept on the floor of a one-room shanty, battled starvation. They survived on rabbits or by stealing a neighbor's hog. Others were very angry about the economic squeeze and the seeming government indifference.

Indeed, the government sometimes appeared to make the problems worse. Take Iowan Sam Krotter's difficulties, for example. In spite of his observation that "the most hopeful animal in the world" is the farmer, even Krotter began to doubt whether he could survive. Iowa and federal laws requiring tuberculin tests for milk cows were steadily resisted by Iowa farmers. Krotter's jersey calf had been subjected to a test, and the calf became sick and, eventually, worthless. Farmers saw themselves as being shafted; if their herds were deemed infected by the test—a test most farmers saw as defective—they suffered a loss of two-thirds of their investment.

The cow war emerged from this distrust and from a showdown between farmers and government agents at William Butterbrodt's farm near West Branch, Iowa, the birthplace of President Herbert Hoover.

In a show of force, organized farmers threw veterinarians and the sheriff off the Butterbrodt homestead. The cow war accelerated.

As is the case with social upheavals and unexpected events, people who in normal times appear abnormal suddenly seem rational. Take the case of Norman Baker, hypnotist, cancer curer, and manufacturer of calliopes, who took to the radio to defend the farmers in the cow war. Baker stirred up the pot of confusion, anger, and frustration. A frightened Governor Dan Turner called out the National Guard, around 1,400 strong. Everyone—1,000 farmers, the National Guard troops, and the Bakerites—converged on the Eversman farm a few miles north of Burlington, Iowa. It was a standoff. Vaccinations occurred, but the farmers rubbed the cows' lumps so they couldn't be detected, and Iowans paid $100,000 for the National Guard's holiday. This situation was an omen in 1932.

The next two years were complicated by extreme drought, government paralysis, and farmer panic. Milo Reno organized the Farmers' Holiday Association, which spread throughout the northern Plains and the Midwest. Farmers took a manifesto and agreed to hold their products off the market until prices rose to cover production costs and to protect each other from those who would confiscate their land, equipment, animals, crops, and belongings.

Farmers went on strike in Plymouth County, Iowa. Milk trucks became a focal point because they carried milk produced by farmers who were not honoring the strike. The strike had little effect on the market and only increased farmers' frustrations. Some farmers broke off from the Farmers' Holiday Association and other farmers' organizations and started their own local groups, which favored immediate direct action. In Nebraska, trucks seized from a farmer by a Newman Grove company were forcefully taken back by a group of farmers. When a tenant farmer near Petersburg died and his $400 mortgage was not paid by his two sons, the bank foreclosed and ordered an auction of the farm and the equipment. Farmers marched on the farm and intimidated those at the sale so that only a total of $7.10 was bid at the entire auction.

Committees of Action throughout Nebraska experienced some short-term successes and generated a great deal of reaction. They were called the "Soviets" of Nebraska, and the state was compared to 1917 Communist Russia. Businesspeople and the Catholic Church were prominent in their opposition to the farmers; on at least one occasion they used force to drive out farmers intent on rigging an auction. Above all, farmers wanted to avoid being "put on the road," losing everything to a bank or creditor. Banding together seemed to help soothe and sometimes placate those fears.

In 1932, farmers' groups decided to march on Washington, D.C., to explain their plight to Congress. Other groups had recently marched on Washington, with very mixed results. A contingency of Western farmers was to meet in Madison County, Nebraska, and go on to Washington. Not related but called at the same time were a hunger march by the Communist Party and a renewal of the Bonus Army March by unemployed veterans in the East. Washington, D.C., girded itself for confrontation.

There were problems along the way. The marchers were harassed in many ways. Housing and food were denied. In Wilmington, Delaware, police violently attacked the marchers, and Washington, D.C., proved an inhospitable host. The farmers' march broke up, an unmitigated failure.

If they could not petition the government, what remained for the desperate farmers? Violence? Extralegal activities? The violence came in short, unexpected bursts. Chicago schoolteachers set the stage in April 1933 by demanding back salaries and storming City Council headquarters and the banks. In Le Mars, Iowa, District Judge Charles C. Bradley was dragged from his courtroom and nearly hung by a mob because he refused to stop foreclosures on farms. Violence occurred at an auction in Primghar, Iowa, and at a foreclosure near Denison, Iowa. Iowa Governor Clyde Herring blamed hoodlums and urban Communists for these activities, and Iowa's farmers laughed.

The weather, however, was no laughing matter. Drought, heat waves, and dust storms converged on the Great Plains. In April 1931, a dust storm reached the Pacific Ocean, and an even greater dust storm extended to the Atlantic Ocean in May 1934. New Yorkers saw some of the 300 million tons of Plains topsoil that was airborne drift past their windows; the dust was so thick that streetlamps had to be lit during the daytime. As one weatherman commented, it was an amazing time of "opacity." The *Deutschland,* a German ship off the Canadian coast, reported a dust storm at sea.

Farmers were in despair. They joked in macabre fashion about taking their Vitamin K—dust—each morning. They were forced to harvest thistles to feed their cattle. Even photographers, like Margaret Bourke-White, found dust a formidable foe. The dust storms caused deaths, including a young Hays, Kansas, boy found suffocated after he had been lost in the dust. Still a resilient lot, farmers, like Caroline Henderson of the Oklahoma Panhandle, persisted. She wrote of the dust everywhere, of how she thought she was supposed to pretend things were okay, and of wanting to be optimistic. But there were ominous signs. People in her community were leaving, even the wealthy, long-term settlers. There were simply no crops and no markets. She realized that farmers were a minority and concluded that the country no longer cared about them.

Henderson remained committed to farming. She and her husband, Will, changed their farming habits and accepted government conservation efforts. They experimented with livestock and crops. They resisted taking relief while worrying about their loss of individualism. And they tried to contain their anger at those farmers who gave up or who refused to try new ways to solve the problems created by the Dust Bowl.

Through it all, what was desperately needed was rain. Farmers tried machines, offered prayers, and fought to retain a faith in America, their religion, and their land. The new U.S. president, Franklin Delano Roosevelt, visited North Dakota and admitted his ignorance about the problems caused by the lack of rain. He promised to try to help solve the farming dilemma, and, miraculously, he brought rain.

So, in the end, the evolution of new farming sciences, a renewed American economy secured by federal government intervention, and a means of sustaining the life blood of the farmer—water—ended the greatest crisis those in the heartland had experienced in the twentieth century.

Any historical assessment of the Dust Bowl must consider the human factors. Gender is an important differentiation. Many women in Nebraska and South Dakota, for example, responded to the crisis with innovations, such as producing new farm products and taking new jobs, and by limiting their child bearing. Many men and some women in Iowa, Nebraska, and the Dakotas became politically radicalized. Their desperation dictated a political response.

Prior to the 1930s, troubles on the Plains had led farmers to be attracted to Populism, the Socialist Party, and the Non-Partisan League. The 1930s brought a renewal of the Non-Partisan League, the Farmers' Union, the Farmers' Holiday Association, the United Farmers League, the Communist Party, the Farmers National Committee for Action, and the Farmer-Labor Party. Even the Ku Klux Klan entered the political fray.

Throughout the economic, environmental, and political turmoil, answers were sought: Why had this crisis happened? The media had explanations. Radical newspapers, such as the *Producers News* of Plentywood, Montana, described business leaders as "greedy Kaisers" and farmers as "selfless patriots," and its publishers eventually touted communism as the solution. The federal government under Roosevelt sought to explain the crisis to the American people through film. *The Plow That Broke the Plains* offered the controversial explanation that the government itself was primarily to blame because it had encouraged new farmers to attack the unbroken sod of the interior Plains as if another world war necessitated doing so.

Historians do not agree about why the Dust Bowl occurred. Explanations range from viewing the Dust Bowl as a purely natural disaster or as the product of farmers' ignorance about the environment and their misuse of technology to the theory that the application of environmentally unsound capitalism destroyed the farmers' traditional relationship to the land or that failed federal government policies and the happenstance combination of the right kinds of soils, new dryland farming techniques, world economic incentives, and a migratory labor force converged at one place during one time—the Great Plains in the 1930s.

There is probably no clearcut answer, although some possibilities ring more true than others. One can state with certainty that there are no simple solutions to prevent future Dust Bowls. Given the nature of the delicate Plains environment, it is crucial that the lessons learned from the Dust Bowl experience be absorbed by all, lest we be destined to repeat one of the world's worst environmental calamities.

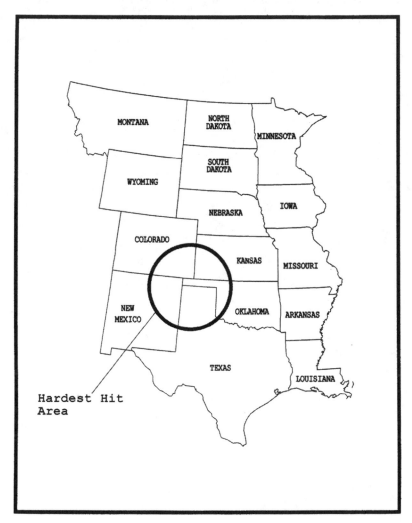

General map of the Dust Bowl region. Map by John R. Wunder and Michael Shambaugh-Miller.

Selected Bibliography

For further information about the Dust Bowl and the Great Depression in the Great Plains and the Midwest, consult the following basic works:

Allen, Frederick Lewis, *Since Yesterday: The Nineteen Thirties in America* (New York: Bantam Books, 1940).

Andryszewski, Tricia, *The Dust Bowl: Disaster on the Plains* (Brookfield, Conn.: Millbrook Press, 1993).

Bennett, Hugh Hammond, *Soil Conservation* (New York: McGraw-Hill, 1939).

Bonnifield, Paul, *The Dust Bowl: Men, Dirt and Depression* (Albuquerque: University of New Mexico Press, 1979).

Brink, Wellington, *Big Hugh: The Father of Conservation* (New York: Macmillan, 1951).

Chandler, Lester V., *America's Greatest Depression, 1929–1941* (New York: Harper and Row, 1970).

Chase, Stuart, *Richland, Poorland: A Study of Waste in the Natural Resources of America* (New York: McGraw-Hill, 1936).

Conrad, David Eugene, *The Forgotten Farmers: The Story of Sharecroppers in the New Deal* (Urbana: University of Illinois Press, 1965).

Faulkner, Edward H., *Plowman's Folly* (Norman: University of Oklahoma Press, 1943).

Galbraith, John Kenneth, *The Great Crash, 1929* (Boston: Houghton Mifflin, 1972).

Ganzel, Bill, *Dust Bowl Descent* (Lincoln: University of Nebraska Press, 1984).

Hargreaves, Mary W.M., *Dry Farming in the Northern Great Plains, 1900–1925* (Cambridge: Harvard University Press, 1957).

Hudson, Lois Phillips, *Reapers of the Dust: A Prairie Chronicle* (St. Paul: Minnesota Historical Society Press, 1984).

Humphreys, William Jackson, *Rain Making and Other Weather Vagaries* (Baltimore: Williams and Wilkins, 1926).

Hurt, R. Douglas, *The Dust Bowl: An Agricultural and Social History* (Chicago: Nelson-Hall, 1981).

Jacks, Graham Vernon, and Robert Orr Whyte, *Vanishing Lands: A World Survey of Soil Erosion* (New York: Doubleday, Doran, 1939).

Johnson, Vance, *Heaven's Tableland: The Dust Bowl Story* (New York: Farrar, Straus, 1947).

Kramer, Dale, *The Wild Jackasses: The American Farmer in Revolt* (New York: Hastings House, 1956).

Lauber, Patricia, *Dust Bowl: The Story of Man on the Great Plains* (New York: Coward-McCann, 1958).

Lord, Russell, *Behold Our Land* (Boston: Houghton Mifflin, 1938).

Low, Ann Marie, *Dust Bowl Diary* (Lincoln: University of Nebraska Press, 1984).

Malin, James, "Dust Storms: Part One, 1850–1860," *Kansas Historical Quarterly* 14 (May 1946):129–144; "Dust Storms: Part Two, 1861–1880," *Kansas Historical Quarterly* 14 (August 1946):265–296; "Dust Storms: Part Three, 1881–1900—Concluded," *Kansas Historical Quarterly* 14 (November 1946):391–413; and *The Grassland of North America: Prolegomena to Its History* (Lawrence, Kansas: The Author, 1947).

McWilliams, Carey, *Ill Fares the Land: Migrants and Migratory Labor in the United States* (Boston: Little, Brown, 1942).

Mitchell, Broadus, *Depression Decade: From New Era Through New Deal, 1929–1941* (New York: Rinehart, 1947).

Osburn, Fairfield, *Our Plundered Planet* (Boston: Little, Brown, 1948).

Parks, William Robert, *Soil Conservation Districts in Action* (Ames: Iowa State College Press, 1952).

Riney-Kehrberg, Pamela, *Rooted in Dust: Surviving Drought and Depression in Southwestern Kansas* (Lawrence: University Press of Kansas, 1994).

Saloutos, Theodore, and John D. Hicks, *Agricultural Discontent in the Middle West, 1900–1939* (Madison: University of Wisconsin Press, 1951).

Sears, Paul B., *Deserts on the March* (Norman: University of Oklahoma Press, 1935).

Shannon, David, ed., *The Great Depression* (Englewood Cliffs, N.J.: Prentice-Hall, 1960).

Shover, John L., *Cornbelt Rebellion: The Farmers' Holiday Association* (Urbana: University of Illinois Press, 1956).

Smith, Henry Nash, "Rain Follows the Plow: The Notion of Increased Rainfall for the Great Plains, 1844–1880," *Huntington Library Quarterly* 10 (February 1947):169–193.

Snyder, Robert L., *Pare Lorentz and the Documentary Film* (Norman: University of Oklahoma Press, 1968).

Steinbeck, John, *The Grapes of Wrath* (New York: Viking Press, 1939).

Svobida, Lawrence, *An Empire of Dust* (Caldwell, Idaho: Caxton Printers, 1940).

Tannehill, Ivan Ray, *Drought: Its Causes and Effects* (Princeton: Princeton University Press, 1947).

Warrick, Richard A., *Drought on the Great Plains: A Case Study on Climate and Society in the USA* (Worcester, Mass.: Clark University, Center for Technology, Environment, and Development, 1980).

Wecter, Dixon, *The Age of the Great Depression, 1929–1941* (New York: Macmillan, 1948).

White, Roland A., *Milo Reno: Farmers' Union Pioneer, the Story of a Man and a Movement* (Iowa City: Athens Press, 1941).

Worster, Donald, *Dust Bowl: The Southern Plains in the 1930s* (New York: Oxford University Press, 1979).

II

Contemporary Accounts

THE PLIGHT OF THE FARMERS IN THE GREAT DEPRESSION, 1931–1936

The collapse of farm prices after 1929 at first seemed to numb and then even to paralyze farmers, many of whom had hoped Herbert Hoover's Farm Board would raise prices. When relief did not come, strident voices began to be heard. In 1931 and 1932, Iowa witnessed what appeared to be a full-scale revolt against constituted authority when farmers in Cedar County refused to have their cows tested for tuberculosis and chased veterinarians and deputy sheriffs off their farms. The state militia was called out to enforce the law, and after much difficulty it was successful.

In summer 1932, Milo Reno called for a "farm holiday" in which farmers would hold their produce off the market unless they were paid at least for the cost of production. In western Iowa, Nebraska, North Dakota, Minnesota, and Wisconsin, there were farm strikes and violence. Meanwhile, farmers hit on a device through which to frustrate farm foreclosure auctions by what came to be called penny, or Sears-Roebuck, auctions.

Deuel County Farmers' Holiday Association. (Courtesy Nebraska State Historical Society.)

If a creditor lent a farmer money and took a mortgage on chattels or the farm or both, and if the farmer did not pay according to the terms of the loan, under the law the creditor could take steps to collect from the farmer. Doing so involved a court order under which the property was offered for sale by the sheriff at a public auction. Under a theory long held in law, a public auction, advertised in advance, was the best and fairest way of obtaining a fair price for what was offered for sale. It was assumed that all interested bidders would be present and that open competition would assure a fair market price.

In the past, ways had been found to inhibit free bidding at some auctions. Indeed, a century earlier the claim or squatter associations in the Midwest had used force or threats of force to prevent anyone but members of their associations from bidding on lands occupied by association members when those lands were offered for sale at public auctions. Once a court had ordered that a farm or a farmer's chattels had to be sold to satisfy an honest debt and the auction had started, the auction had to go on, and the highest bid took what was offered for sale. No one knows who first thought of rigging the farm auctions by simply having farmers show up in large numbers to prevent, by force if necessary, any bids other than those they themselves offered.

The first such penny auction farm sale probably took place in Iowa in 1931, and the practice quickly spread. Large numbers of farmers attended sales and refused to permit anyone else to bid. They would bid a few cents or a few dollars on personal property or farmland, and if they succeeded in preventing other bids, the sale was legally completed. The requirements of the law had been met, and ownership would then pass to the new owners, who returned the chattels or farm title to the bankrupt farmer who was now free of debt. Nothing amused a crowd of farmers more than an auctioneer's efforts to encourage someone to raise the bid on a horse from two cents to three cents. A noose hanging prominently in sight of the auction came to be the symbol of the penny, or Sears-Roebuck, sales.

Such open violation of the law could not be permitted to continue. Sheriffs added deputies to help maintain order at farm auctions, and violence occurred. Sometimes the state militia was called out. Such events led directly to threats to hang a judge at Le Mars, Iowa, and to martial law in Plymouth County, Iowa, in April 1933.

The Farm Holiday movement, farm strikes, penny sales, and martial law in the Midwest and Great Plains all helped to speed Congress to adopt the first Agricultural Adjustment Act and other laws intended to raise farm prices and stop forced farm sales. These acts of the New Deal did reduce farm violence in the summer of 1933. The farmers, although still desperate, no longer felt completely without hope.

EARLY DUST BOWL DISTRESS
AND ANGER, 1931–1932

This brief, melancholy report, reflecting the consequences of both poverty and drought, might have been read as a dark shadow of the wider disasters ahead for many farmers of the Great Plains.

ARKANSANS CLOG
ROADS SEEKING AID

"SHARE CROPPERS," DROUGHT
VICTIMS, GET FLOUR, LARD, AND PORK
FROM RED CROSS DEPOTS.

MARKED TREE, Ark., Jan. 26—Roads clogged with wagons and buggies, not automobiles, and men and women walking, with sacks of flour on their shoulders and pails of lard in their hands, tell a graphic story of what the drought has done to parts of Arkansas.

It is the same picture nearly everywhere in the eastern section of the State, which is the heart of the drought area.

These are the "share croppers," as they are called, on their way to the nearest Red Cross relief office or going back to their homes with the meager rations thus provided.

Nearly always it is a sack of flour, and either a pail of lard or a little package of plain salt pork. These are prescribed by the Red Cross.

It may be lard one week and meat the next, because even from the $2 a week and 50 cents for each child given them, they sometimes find it possible to save out a little meat one week and lard the next, so they alternate, one week taking lard and the next meat.

They are walking or riding in wagons and buggies because they either have sold their automobiles, if they ever had any, or they do not have the money to operate them.

The small villages are not bothered so much with an automobile parking problem, because the old-fashioned hitching rack has returned.

For the most part these destitute people who are dependent upon the Red Cross for food are a philosophical lot. Hardships are not new to them. Most of them are resigned to their condition and are uncomplaining.

The homes of these "share croppers" contain the drama and the tragedy of the drought aftermath. Many of them live in shacks built of logs or in dilapidated board houses. They have little furniture, perhaps a bed, two or three chairs, and a stove in one room and a rickety table and stove in the kitchen. Many are less fortunate than this.

L. G. Minton, a lawyer at Harrisburg, told of visiting one family of five where all were living in one room, sleeping on the floor and with a fireplace made of mud.

Despite the seriousness of their plight, some families refuse or hesitate to seek aid.

Rabbits are plentiful and many persons are virtually living on them. Along the highways and in the woods skirting them are seen men with rifles on their shoulders, out hunting rabbits.

In some of the larger cities farmers stand on street corners with rabbits hanging over their shoulders, offering them for sale to the townspeople.

Small thefts and robberies have increased noticeably, officers say.

A half dozen men are in jail at Harrisburg charged with stealing hogs. Chicken thefts are numerous.

New York Times, January 27, 1931

*   *   *

A full account of the "cow war" in Cedar County, Iowa, is found in Frank D. Dileva, "Frantic Farmers Fight Law," *Annals of Iowa* 32 (Fall 1953):81–109. Briefer accounts appear in John L. Shover, *Cornbelt Rebellion: The Farmers' Holiday Association* (Urbana: University of Illinois Press, 1956), pp. 128–132; and Dale Kramer, *The Wild Jack-*

asses: *The American Farmer in Revolt* (New York: Hastings House, 1956), pp. 207–219. These disturbances were not a direct response to the Depression, but they reflect something of the desperation and perhaps the irrationality of farmers pressed beyond endurance. As the following article suggests, even under these circumstances not all farmers lost their wry sense of humor.

GET AWAY FROM THOSE COWS
Walter Davenport

In the years to come, when today's children in southeastern Iowa feel called upon to tell their grandchildren about the good old days, Sam Krotter's calf will have taken its place in fireside history. Perhaps its likeness will be struck off to appear on the stationery of Farmers' Union, and the Sons and Daughters of the Cow War will wear tiny golden effigies of it on their coats. Anyway it will have joined such legendary animals as Mrs. O'Leary's Chicago cow and the Jabberwock and be an even better story than it is now.

This calf, born of a popeyed Jersey that had been tuberculin-tested by the state veterinarians (with the help of two companies of militia), was a trial to its mother from the very beginning, coming into this harassed world equipped with two perfectly developed horns and spurs like a fighting chicken. Unhappily, Mr. Krotter, a dues-paying and speech-making member of the Farmers' Protective Association of Iowa, was so flabbergasted that he forgot to have the creature's picture taken.

It was so small that the flies missed it and it had to be belled so that it might be located when visitors arrived. It is not easy to name the worst of its unfavorable features and characteristics, although Mr. Krotter leans toward the beast's voice. Day and night without ceasing, he assured me, it "bellowed like a hard-runnin' congressman" and the dominant note in that awful wail was concentrated anguish. Four preachers looked and listened and declared unhesitatingly that Satan had insinuated himself into that calf's immediate family.

There were other curious features, some of the most interesting of which may not be set down here owing to their delicate nature; but we may record that it had teeth like a shark with which it had chewed a sizable chunk out of the leg of Mrs. Krotter and sheared an ear off the Krotter dog.

"Another thing," said Mr. Krotter. "It was an idiot. No sense at all."

"And what became of it?" I asked.

"Oh, nothing much," he sighed. "It just naturally joined the National Guard."

Gravely Mr. Krotter consulted his enormous watch, being one of the few farmers who still had watches, and warned me that it was time to be going on down the street if I proposed to attend the meeting with him. As we walked he explained that the meeting, held in Muscatine, Iowa, had been called more or less unofficially by members of the Farmers' Protective Association and the Farmers' Union with a scattering of members of other farm alliances.

THE MOST HOPEFUL ANIMAL

The object of the meeting was not specifically mentioned in the call: not that it was necessary. Any gathering of farmers in Iowa could be expected to produce floods of hot oratory about the Cow War and the government.

"You will find that the speakers are very indignant," said Mr. Krotter. "But you will also find that outside of everybody agreeing that we ought to carry our indignation to the polls and get rid of all officeholders who won't agree with us that tuberculin tests are unreliable, dangerous, and a darned nuisance, we will do nothing but disagree. And you will find out why the politicians can go on kidding us farmers from election to election and get away with it. The farmer is always hoping. He's the most hopeful animal in the world. He hopes for everything from weather on to crops. He hopes the market will hold up and he hopes the politicians are telling the truth. If he finds that the market breaks down he hopes it will do better next year. And if the politicians don't make good he hopes they will later. Just the hopingest man you ever saw.

"Matter of fact, about all the farmer's got is hope. For years they've been telling him he is the backbone of our country and for a while he believed it. But it's got so now that he just hopes he is. Corn, wheat, hogs, cows, and hay fall down on us but the old hope field gets bigger and bigger until it's our biggest crop. Got paper and pencil? All right, get them out and take down a few very indignant hopes."

And Mr. Krotter's summation of what the meeting would produce was exactly right. I heard the Cow War reviewed from its first rumblings to its whistling climax and left the hall more than ever convinced that the most incurable of all individualists, the most difficult to organize, the most defenseless against the political and commercial exploiter is the farmer, the natural lone-hander.

But it was a grand review of the Cow War, reminding you of army reunions.

About two or three years ago the state of Iowa decided to go into cattle inspection in a big way, particularly regarding the tuberculin test for milk cows. The state law is much the same as the Federal law of 1906. Before that the inspection of cows for tuberculosis was more or less perfunctory; for political reasons (the Iowa farmer representing a great preponderance of the state's vote) the farmer wasn't pressed too hard.

A POOR TIME FOR PURITY

But a certain alarm began to fasten itself upon the farmer himself when it was observed that an increasing number of cattle slaughtered for beef were being rejected by government inspectors as unfit for food. Out of this growing concern came the somewhat belated decision of the state authorities—the Iowa Department of Agriculture—to inspect all the cattle in the state and learn just how healthy or unhealthy they were. The United States Bureau of Animal Industry, too, had been urging a drive, to say nothing of a constant fire from the medical associations who were crying that from twenty-five to thirty per cent of all tuberculosis in children was traceable directly to milk from infected cows.

Unhappily this drive had to be undertaken at a time when the farmer's morale was ebbing. Hard times were upon him. So-called relief legislation had not appeared or had lost whatever potency it may have had by the time it reached the farm. The Farm Board's efforts to stabilize prices had come to naught; about the only thing pegged was the despondency of the farmer. And now the confused man was to have his cattle inspected and perhaps condemned by strangers whom he did not trust and in whose tricks of science he had no faith. A fine time to invade the barnyard.

Nevertheless the business of locating tuberculosis in the cows went on rather smoothly during all of 1930. There were protests and grumblings to be sure, but they were the individual words of individualists. But the number of infected cattle was impressively large— 17,420. Of this number 1,221 were so thoroughly diseased that they went for fertilizer or tankage. The others were destroyed, although a part of the carcasses were pronounced available for food, for which the owners received low-grade beef prices.

In that year—1930—the owners of cattle found to be tuberculous, and therefore slaughtered, received from that sort of salvage an average of $38.28 per animal. In addition to this the owner of such cattle received indemnity from the state and from the Federal government. How the sum is arrived at is simple. The animal is appraised—not without some argument, either. But once the figure is fixed, the salvage return from the packer is deducted. Then the remainder is divided three ways. One third is paid by the Federal government and one third by the state. The other third is the owner's loss.

This loss constitutes a very important cause of the Cow War. For one reason or another the return that the farmer got for a condemned animal was slowly diminishing. It may have been that the state, experiencing the same treasury cramps that had stricken other states, was paring down its evaluation scale. And it was evident, too, that the packers were given less for the salvable portions of the animal. Instead of the average $38.28 they had paid in 1930, it was $28.37 in 1931.

Such, anyway, was the background early in 1931 when the state veterinarians under Dr. Peter Malcolm arrived in the southeastern part of the state with their tuberculin and syringes. It is likely that they had postponed these counties, hoping that time would make them less scornful of urban laws and more amenable to general government.

TOUGH CUSTOMERS

A hardy lot, these southeastern Iowans. A large German influence pervades them. Well matched with the Teuton blood is the Irish. With a nice, even consistency the farmers of this part of the state— excellent farmers, whose well-kept fences, buildings, and livestock proclaim their quality—have been opposed to outside influences. They resisted the draft in 1917, although those finally taken from the farms turned out to be capable soldiers. They hooted the Liberty Bond and Victory Bond barkers, not only refusing to buy but now and then chasing the would-be sellers out of the county. Just "aginners," according to Mr. Krotter. And very unsatisfactory clients for strangers with strange formulas.

Furthermore these southeastern Iowa farmers were pretty well organized—unusually well for individualists. With very few exceptions they were members of the Farmers' Protective Association or of the Farmers' Union. They condemned the tests as inaccurate and inconclusive and the veterinarians as ignorant, unsanitary, and agents of the packers. They claimed that tuberculin (the injected fluid) ruined innocent cattle—drying them up, infecting those that had been clean and, if the tested cow did thereafter produce a calf, the calf was quite likely to be either a weakling or, like Mr. Krotter's curio, a monstrosity.

Nevertheless there was the law; and the state veterinarians, their feelings outraged by the unkind things the farmers had been saying about them, announced that the cows were going to be tested or the reason would be made public.

Whereupon they entered Cedar County, advancing upon the farm of Mr. William Butterbrodt, a few miles from West Branch where, fifty-seven years ago, Mr. Herbert Clark Hoover was born.

Mr. Butterbrodt objected with vehemence; his denunciation of tests, veterinarians, experts, and the government being seconded vigorously by a large gathering of neighbors who had rallied to his cow barns bearing the Stars and Stripes and armed with stout sticks, brooms, and, here and there, a pitchfork. Sheriffs, deputy sheriffs, constables, bailiffs, wardens, selectmen, and a few plain cops appeared with reassuring words for Mr. Butterbrodt and his friends. If, they said, there was no resistance there would be no trouble. And Mr. Butterbrodt, being quick to turn an answer, replied that if there was not trouble there would be no resistance. And anyway he was not going to have his cows bothered.

THE NEW WAR ON THE PLAINS

Whereat Mr. Butterbrodt, whose record for peace and obedience to law was as spotless as his reputation as a farmer, was arrested along with several others.

And the Cow War was on!

In the meantime, the hard-working Dan Turner, governor of Iowa, was coming down with circle-describing jitters. He announced that the law ought to be obeyed. When it became apparent that the farmers of the southeast did not agree with him, he hastened to Iowa City to confer with members of the Protective Association. After much loud talking he returned home saying that the law simply had to be obeyed. And presently, after several hundred farmers had thrown sixty-five officers of the law off the farm of Mr. Jake Lenker and had chased the veterinarians so far that several of them were reported lost, he proclaimed that the law was going to be obeyed.

And with one long agonized shudder he called out the National Guard.

Another well-known citizen of Iowa had injected himself into the brawl. He not only had a prime grievance of his own against the authorities but owned a radio broadcasting station from which he denounced all and sundry with the exception of the farmers, who, he hoped, might rally to his own peculiar contest against the rules and regulations.

His name is Norman Baker. He was the proprietor of a hospital in Muscatine wherein he professed to cure cancer. Of course the American Medical Association did not agree with him and after a terrific

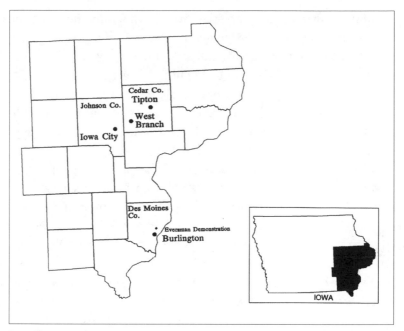

Iowa farmers take action and declare strike, 1932. Map by Robert Watrel.

dispute during which both sides called names (the A.M.A. labeling him a dangerous quack and Baker setting down the A.M.A. as the American Meat-cutters' Association) the state of Iowa enjoined him from accepting any more cancer sufferers. Whereupon he left his hospital, spit on his hands, and went to war too.

A VOLUNTEER WARRIOR

Baker was not as successful with cancer as he had been previously as a hypnotist in a small-time road show, as a mail-order portrait artist, and as a manufacturer of calliopes for circuses and carnivals. But while his radio license lasted, until the Federal Radio Commission banished him, he flooded the salubrious Iowa air with defenses of himself and propaganda for the embattled farmers, to say nothing of pulverizing denunciations of organized medicine, vivisectionists, vaccinationists, the American Telephone and Telegraph Company, the trusts, Parent-Teacher organizations, public-welfare work and workers, public health bureaus, the Red Cross, school-nursing programs, public-school systems, and on and on and on.

If, said he, tuberculin tests must be made why annoy the cow? Why not take samples of the animal's milk and test that? When he was told that this was a highly unsatisfactory procedure he merely denied it, and when Mr. Baker denied something he was done with it. When asked how he would subject the bulls to the milk test he ignored it. And he was equally set in his ignorings.

But nothing was going to deter Mr. Baker in his championship of the farm side of the Cow War. With his radio station silenced, he started a newspaper—*The Midwest Free Press*—and through friends in Washington (which included Senator Smith Wildman Bookhart) was honored by having President Hoover press the gold button which, by wire, started his presses churning. Therein he not only advocated his own platform, the nature of which may be gathered from what has already been set down here about him, but cherished the aims of the farmers.

Now I did not find that the farmers of southeastern Iowa were enthusiastic about Mr. Baker, not nearly as enthusiastic about him as he was about them, anyway. But so long as he cared to be on their side, and so long as he did not attempt to inject his person into the conduct of their affairs, they welcomed him—as a propaganda adjunct.

Such, then, was the situation when on one of the most beautiful days of last September a battalion of National Guard infantry, equipped with orders to be very careful lest they hurt somebody and thereby make matters worse, stepped off the train at Tipton, Iowa, with half of the country gathered around to "see the parade." They were received variously.

Salvos of giggles from the assembled ladies and a scattering of barnyard noises from the men marked the reception; but for some reason none of the vegetables, eggs, corncobs, and other farm tokens which the civilian population had fetched with it were hurled. There was plenty of wit broadcast, of course. And all of it was of the strictly personal and occasionally embarrassing variety.

A bit later in the afternoon, perhaps encouraged and emboldened by a few shots of brisk young corn, one of the young farmers, having failed to entice any of his friends into battle with him, suddenly stepped

up to a lieutenant and knocked him cold with a windmill wallop. Then
just as swiftly he stepped back into the crowd, doubtless feeling much
better, and was lost in the general shuffle.

But, taking it by and large, no important engagement took place
until the troops and the veterinarians arrived at the farm of Mr. Jake
Eversman. That there was to be trouble was indicated by the many
little incidents which had preceded that great mobilization. There
was, for example, the rout of five or six infantrymen by a lady who
explained later that she was not inspired by a desire to protect her
husband's cows but that she hadn't "taken the trouble to raise four
girls up to an age when they would be some good in the world to
have them simpering through the door at a lot of silly-looking soldiers." Whereat the lady had taken her broom and after scattering
her four daughters with one learned swing of it, charged the admiring
warriors, who took promptly to their heels and did not halt until their
enemy had run out of breath, some two hundred yards up the road.

TAKEN FOR A WALK

Little incivilities like that. There were occasional rumors, too, that
the farm folk were not above a bit of bigtown duplicity. For example,
soldiers who sought to spend their off-duty hours roaming higher and
yon through country roads, absorbing the peace of the fields and woods,
were known to return to camp in most unmilitary disarray, including
a black eye or a few teeth gone or a nose out of alignment. What seems
to have happened in a few cases is that the innocently strolling guards-
man would have his attention distracted from the beauties of Mother
Earth by a girl who, apparently, was doing only what he was doing—
taking a walk.

Mr. Krotter assures me that such sirens were town girls and not
daughters of the farm, because "our girls ain't given to taking life that
easy." Moreover, say Mr. Krotter, "When a farmer's daughter ain't
got chores to do, which ain't often, she does not take a walk but sits
down."

Anyway, thus a few National Guardsmen were lured into lonely
stretches, poor fellows, where they were set upon and thoroughly gone

over by men who had wickedly used the girl for their decoy. At least that was the explanation of such of the soldiers who cared to make any explanation at all.

These and similarly annoying brushes between the enemies culminated in the Eversman demonstration, two miles north of Burlington. It having been announced the day before that Mr. Eversman's cows were to be tested whether he favored it or not, a thousand men, women, and children assembled on his lush acres in family lots to do what they could to disconcert the foe. That no gun play was introduced into the clashes was due largely to the coolness and able control of the Protective Association's officers—Messrs. Eversman, E. C. Mitchel, Jake Lenker, and C. L. McKinnon. Iowa should not neglect to thank these resolute farmers for their firm authority.

THE CALL TO BATTLE

The farmers arrived first on the field, fetching with them large hampers of food, tents, their favorite dogs, a number of musical instruments—accordions, cornets, tubas, saxophones, tambourines, and fiddles—to sweeten the occasion. A large barn dance was arranged by the ladies, and here and there the gentlemen were observed playing pinochle, rummy, and casino. Others not thus occupied—men and women—sauntered down the road to the fair grounds where Brigadier General Park A. Finley and Major Will J. Hays were supervising the discipline of 1,400 troops, infantry, and cavalry.

The troops were being drilled in close order and as skirmishers. Likewise, and far more impressive to the large gallery of farmers, they were being sent through bayonet drill—long point, short point, and jab-shooting their bright blades into dummies.

At the appointed hour, the bugles fanfared, and the battalion, company, and platoon leaders began to utter sharp barks. The troops fell in, maneuvered smartly into a column of squads, and advanced, route-step, upon the Eversman farm, flanked by a half-dozen determined veterinarians whose manner made it clear that no more fooling would be tolerated. And closing in behind the regiment came the gallery, making no effort to conceal its admiration. All sorts of advice and suggestions were flung at the soldiers—"Hey, you're out of step," "Where's the war, buddy?" and "Don't be afraid, lieutenant; we won't let the cow bite you."

There was not room for everybody at the Eversman barns, so only five troops of cavalry and one hundred infantrymen entered. Ringing speeches against cattle tests were being made by Mr. Baker and Protective Association officials, and while the infantry was being parked in strategic positions a small boy tied his dog to a beehive, thereby precipitating a near panic. A bee stung the dog and the dog upset the hive. The bees thereupon fell upon the throng, farmers and soldiers indiscriminately. For a while it seemed that the occasion was going to lose dignity.

But a little order was restored and the business of testing the cows proceeded. No resistance was put up by the farmers. In fact, so little verbal protest arose that the authorities began to suspect that all was not as well as it seemed. And this apprehension took on bulk as they realized that, although the crowds at the scenes of inspection were growing larger and larger, the resistance was dwindling and the number of reacting cows diminishing. When the tuberculin is injected into the animal, the veterinarian is prepared to wait forty-eight to seventy-two hours before inspecting his work. If, in that time, an inflamed lump has appeared at the point of injection, the cow is pronounced infected. But it was curious that the sinister lumps were becoming so rare. Was it possible that the inspections had arrived at a cleaner, purer sector where cows were healthier? Or was there something wrong with this new batch of tuberculin?

And then it came to the veterinarians. These crowds had come to the farms to celebrate, not to do battle. They had taken up a new or freshly revived sport—cow massaging. If, after the tuberculin has been injected into your cow, you massage the spot where the bacilli entered the beast, there will be no lump. Of course you've got to rub briskly and the cow is apt to be unappreciative. But if you are a determined person, fond of your cow, you can do it; and your friends will be very glad to lend a hand or so.

WEARY OF WAR

This, then, was what was going on. How long or how frequently the farmers had been massaging the telltale lumps away, nobody knows. But it explains to a certain degree why the resistance of the farmers died away, and ruins to an equal extent the contention of the authorities that the farmers were at last listening to reason. Naturally, the massaging was not infallible. Some cows will develop lumps however vigorously you massage or with what.

Anyway the Battle of Eversman's Farm marked the high tide of the war. By this time the state was getting a little tired of the war. It had always been more or less a political issue, although largely local. Now the foes of Governor Turner, whose lot had been a most unhappy one, began to go statistical. The governor had pledged himself to an administration of economy and already the state troops had run up a bill of $100,000. Nobody knew precisely how far the tests had gone and how many tuberculous cows had escaped detection, and the farmers whose cows had been subjected to the test had a long array of brand-new grievances.

Hundreds of them were telling their legislators, who were anxious for their good will; their bankers, who craved interest money; and merchants, who yearned for a little business, that they had lost too much money through condemnation or that their tested cows were no longer revenue producers. How much truth and untruth there was to all this is no easier to ascertain than it would be if one were to seek the facts from the legislator, the baker, or the merchant. The state department of agriculture announced that Iowa had now more than 2,000,000 accredited cows—cows that had been tested and found healthy. But the farmers replied that these were merely figures, signifying nothing. Many accredited cows, they added, were that and nothing more, having been ruined as milk producers. There is no apparent end to the argument. And Iowa generally is wondering what it got for all that money spent.

"I'll tell you what we'll do," said C. L. McKinnon, vice president of the Farmers' Protective Association of Iowa. "We're so sure that these tests are inaccurate, that infected cows do not necessarily react to tuberculin and that non-tuberculous animals may be ruined by the injection, that we will cooperate with the authorities in an experiment on fifty cows. Let us take twenty-five accredited animals from any county and twenty-five that did react to the test, and slaughter them.

"Then let us subject the carcasses to the usual post-mortem examination and a laboratory test. If we do not find more tuberculosis in the non-reactors than in the reactors, the association will foot the bill. We will pay for the tests and for the cattle. But if our contention is right, we will expect the Department of Agriculture to pay for the experiment.

"The Department may say that this is nonsense; but that certainly is no answer. Such is our proposition. And we have no money to waste. We're farmers."

Mr. McKinnon and his associates cite many instances of the alleged inadequacy and fallibility of tuberculin tests, but the one which the farmers will cite most frequently—saying that much depends upon who one is whether one's cows are confiscated on the word of a veterinarian—is that of United States Senator Glass' heifer.

On Senator Glass' Virginia farm, the animal was tested by a veterinarian from the United States Department of Agriculture. It reacted and was declared tuberculous. Under the law, the heifer should have been destroyed, but Senator Glass refused to have it slaughtered. No militia was called out, nor was the senator arrested. The government withdrew with proper deference and the senator isolated the heifer.

However, the animal injured itself some time later and had to be killed. Whereat its carcass was turned over to Dr. Elmer Lash of the Federal Bureau of Animal Industry and a group of equally capable veterinarians. Their report to the Department of Agriculture, which was duly recorded in print, was that the animal "disclosed no symptoms whatsoever of tuberculosis or any other disease." And just to make sure, the slaughtered animal's glands were subjected to microscopic examination and chemical analysis in commercial laboratories. But no disease was found.

DOUBT, AND MORE DOUBT

The state of Iowa has manifested no willingness to accept Mr. McKinnon's fifty-cow suggestion, preferring to cite the thousands of instances where the reacting cow did have tuberculosis and referring all doubters to many authorities (Dr. Charles H. Mayo, of Rochester, Minnesota, for example). They will show you, too, affidavits from farmers who doubted and kept on doubting until they witnessed the slaughter of their reacting cows and beheld in the carcasses the proofs of the veterinarians' claims.

Moreover, the state offers you the words of Dr. Marion Dorset, chief of the biochemical division of the United States Department of Agriculture, who insists that tuberculin does not do the healthy cow any harm at all nor injure a tuberculous one. It merely indicates the presence of the disease in the infected animal. And when the indications are present, after the injection, the cow should be slaughtered for the sake of the health of the public, say Dr. Dorset.

All of which, says Mr. Sam Krotter, may be true—or may not be.

"Anyway," said he, "you've got a couple of opinions—one from each side. But government opinion or no government opinion, this ain't exactly the time to tell the farmers that the government doesn't agree with them. They know that already. About the only thing they can do in return is not to agree with the government."

Anyway it was a great war.

Collier's, 89 (February 27, 1932):10–11, 44, 46

THE FARMERS GO ON STRIKE, 1932–1933

Milo Reno was the stormy leader of the Iowa Farmers' Union from 1921 until his death in 1936. Born in 1866 in Wapello County, Iowa, he had been a wanderer, an Iowa farmhand, and an occasional preacher until he catapulted into state and national prominence during the early 1920s as a spokesman for Iowa farmers. He advocated that farmers determine the value of their products in the same way labor unions, industries, and bankers did, but this proposal—one advocated by many farmers' leaders before him—found little real support until 1932. In May 1932, he led the organization of the Farmers' Holiday Association at a large meeting of farmers in Des Moines and was elected the group's president. The movement spread quickly to adjoining states.

WHY THE FARMERS HOLIDAY?
Milo Reno

In presenting to the listeners of KFNF the Farmers' National Holiday program, it is necessary to, as briefly as possible, review the causes which have led up to the most amazing and confounding situation in the history of the world—people starving in a land with an abundance of food; naked, because of a surplus of clothing; people bankrupt in the richest nation in the world.

This situation did not just happen. It is not because of an act of Providence! But is the result of a conspiracy as destructive and damnable as has ever occurred in this history of mankind.

Its correction can only be accomplished through heroic measures; a patriotic determination to faithfully carry out the objective for which this government was formed—a guarantee of life, liberty, and the pursuit of happiness for the citizens of this Republic.

In 1920 as a result of the world's war, debts of all nations engaged therein were multiplied many times, vast fortunes were made, with the power that attends the accumulation of great wealth. The conspirators against the peace and tranquility of this Republic determined upon an unwarranted and drastic deflation that began with agriculture and that in eighteen months had destroyed thirty billion dollars of farm values.

Farm organizations pled with Congress for the correction of the situation that was strangling American agriculture, was destroying America's farm homes, and which could only mean the final destruction of the foundation principles upon which this Government rests.

Many measures were proposed, alibis carefully prepared to excuse the pernicious program of the money lords of the nation, but the requests and prayers of the American farmer for economic equality were ignored.

In 1924, a pernicious program of propaganda, designed to excuse the do-nothing policy of those responsible for legislation was begun, leading the public to believe that the farmer himself was to blame; that he had not received the consideration that he was evidently entitled to; that he was so contrary that he would not co-operate with his fellow farmer; that the farm leadership was selfish, envious, and jealous of each other to the extent that they could not agree upon a definite, positive legislative program; and that, if the farm leaders would get together, lay aside their differences of opinion, their organization jealousies, and agree upon an agricultural program, how happy they would be to concede it.

The farm leadership of the United States met the challenge, and, in response to a call sent out by the National Farmers' Union, a meeting was held in Des Moines, Iowa, on the 12th day of May 1925, in which 24 farm groups were represented. In this memorable conference, the Corn Belt committee was formed and a legislative program adopted, which embodied the McNary-Haugen bill. Splendid men were selected from all farm organizations, to present this legislative program to Congress. So earnestly and valiantly the representatives of this group battled for the farmer's right to a square deal that the bill twice passed the House and Senate and was twice vetoed by an unfriendly president. The second time the McNary-Haugen bill was vetoed, it had passed the house and senate by an overwhelming majority, in fact, it only lacked one vote of the necessary two-thirds to pass the measure over the president's veto.

The Corn Belt committee was called into session on July 6th, 1927, and after serious consideration of the situation and after fully realizing the money lords of the country, controlling the eastern vote, would never willingly grant the farmer an equal opportunity to exist with industry, the following resolution was passed: "If we cannot obtain justice by legislation, the time will have arrived when no other course remains than organized refusal to deliver the products of the farm at less than production costs."

We had hoped in the nomination and election of a president in 1928 the country would concede right of production costs to those who produced the food and raw material for the rest of society, and the splendid representatives of 36 organized farm groups unanimously declared to the world in this resolution that unless we were conceded economic equality we would organize and refuse to deliver the products of our farms for less than production costs.

The absolute failure of the present Congress, whether because of intellectual ability or a lack of patriotic courage, has miserably failed to correct a situation in this republic, unparalleled in history, consequently, we feel the time has arrived for the men and women who live upon the farms, to resort to drastic measures to protect their homes from confiscation.

A meeting was called for May 3rd, 1932, in the city of Des Moines, Iowa, to which all groups were invited, both agriculture, business, professional, and labor, to discuss the action necessary to save the farmers of this nation from complete destruction. It was a monster meeting of earnest men and women, and in this meeting the Farmers' Holiday Association was born, and I wish to assure you that it is the last stand of American agriculture in defense of their rights and their homes.

Farm groups, both great and small, meet the challenge of their exploiters in the establishing of the Corn Belt committee. Farm groups, individual farmers, are now called upon to again meet the challenge and redeem the resolution of July 6th, 1927.

Congress has just ended a long and arduous session, but, seemingly, the objective aimed at by both the major political parties was to prepare for the campaign of 1932, instead of relieving the situation of despair and desolation of the present time. Not a single measure of relief was passed that did not carry with it an increased burden of debt and usury. The one thing that would restore prosperity again to this nation was defeated each time it was proposed, that is, an inflation of the currency to that point that would reduce the value of the dollar as measured in other things practically to the same point that it was in 1920.

If we are ever able to obtain the legislation necessary to place agriculture on an economic equality with industry, it will be when we use our economic power, which is the only power left the farmer today.

The Farmers' Holiday Association proposes to fix a fair valuation on farm products, based on production costs, and to refuse to deliver until those prices are conceded. Some may call this a strike. Very well. If it is a strike for the farmer to refuse to deliver his products for less than production costs, it is also a strike when the merchant declines to deliver his goods for less than cost and carriage.

We propose that society, as a whole, shall recognize the farmer's right to be considered the same as other serving groups of society. Railroad corporations, because of the fact that they were performing a public service, were conceded by the federal government the cost of operation, plus a five and one-forth per cent profit on their investment, and I wish to ask my listeners—Is it more of a public service to transport the food products of this nation than it is to produce them?

The utility corporations have, by the federal courts, been conceded the right to fix the price for their services, that, after all operating expenses are paid, they shall have from six to eight per cent return on their capital investment, and this is true of every other business.

Why should the groups of society expect the American farmer to produce the food and raw material that makes existence possible for them, and deliver his product at a price below production costs, which inevitably means bankruptcy and destruction?

In calling a farmers' holiday, we are simply putting into operation a program that has been adopted by many cities in the Middle West, to protect the assets of their banks.

No one should criticize either the banks or the officials of those cities that adopted drastic methods to protect the property of those institutions from depreciation, in fact, destruction, neither should any group criticize the farmers for refusing to see the value of their holdings depreciated to the extent that the labor of a lifetime is destroyed and in their old age, they are left homeless and in poverty.

The governor of our state joined in with a group of Iowa farmers last September in an effort to stabilize the corn prices. This effort was commendable, but its failure was inevitable, because of its lack of militancy and universal support. For a movement of this kind to succeed, it should have the support and encouragement of the commercial and professional groups, as well as agriculture. It should be entirely divorced from any particular organization, because in order to succeed, it must have the same individual and organizational support that prevailed in the old Corn Belt committee. This program means the restoration of the farmer's purchasing power, the power to pay his debts, the ability to purchase the things he so sadly needs, in the operations of his home and his farm. This will mean prosperity to the business institutions and to the professional world. For example, concede to the farmer production costs and he will pay his grocer, the grocer will pay the wholesaler, the wholesaler will pay the manufacturer, and the manufacturer will be able to meet his obligations at the bank. Restore the farmer's purchasing power and you have re-established an endless chain of prosperity and happiness in this country. Continue the present policy and you will not only wreck the farmer's home, but in such wrecking, you will wreck every institution that is dependent upon the prosperity of the farmer.

We are at the parting of the ways. The time is too short to temporize longer. The people of the United States must be saved from the destructive desolation that is due us in the coming winter. Therefore, the national Farmers' Holiday association is appealing to the individual farmers, to the co-operative groups, and to all farm organizations to forget all their differences and join in a united effort to correct the situation before it is everlastingly too late to save the farm home, that has been builded by the sweat, the toil, the sacrifice, of those who occupy them.

To achieve these ends, some legislation will be necessary. There were a few bills introduced in the last session of Congress that if enacted into law would have very materially corrected the present situation. It is not difficult to determine as to the effect of a bill that would provide an increase in the volume of money.

The Frazier bill, which proposed to re-finance the farmer by an issue of government currency. The Patman bill, which proposed to pay a just obligation we owe the soldiers in legal tender government currency.

The direct cause of the present distress was deflation of the currency or monopolization of the economic life blood of this nation. Any measure that would inflate the currency and assure us an honest dollar is the remedy. The legislators serving the money lords of the country very frequently use the term "honest dollar" in their opposition to the government exercising its sovereign prerogative to the nation's currency.

In 1920, it required $3.00 to measure a bushel of wheat. Through the process of deflation or making money scarce, $1.00 would measure the same quantity of wheat. We did not hear this group of many servers talking about a dishonest dollar, but when we proposed to reverse the situation and bring the value of a dollar back to where it was when the great majority of our debts were created, immediately they sent up the cry for an "honest dollar."

Senator [William] Borah, as reported in yesterday's paper (July 19th) says: "We can never pay out under the present program and under present conditions. There is nothing ahead but chaos and disaster, unless we boldly undertake to bring prices back to what they were when a substantial portion of our current debts were obligated, and that only an expansion of the currency would enable us to avoid chaos and disaster." In fact, every thinking man realizes that prices must be brought back by an expansion of the currency.

The farmer has a perfect right to insist that he be permitted to pay his obligation with a dollar of the same purchasing power as the one he borrowed.

How will we go about to accomplish this desired end?

Economists everywhere realize and frankly admit that the present economic system is entirely broken down—that not only the farmer is facing desolation and disaster, but our business and financial institutions are on the verge of universal collapse.

The farmer, by withholding his product, cannot only restore a price that will cover production costs, but will have a powerful influence in shaping desired legislation.

In the perfecting of this Farmers' Holiday plan, we will have a marketing committee starting from the townships to the county, from the county to the state, and from the state to the national, without intervention, and it will be a farmer's marketing program built by himself, owned, controlled, and operated by himself, without the obstruction of cumbersome federal machinery, that invariably degenerates into a political machine.

Farmers of the Middle West, you are standing with your backs to the wall, you have pinned your faith in the past to parties and institutions provided for you by the men higher up. They have failed you in your hour of need—the time has arrived when, if your problems are solved and your right to prosperity and happiness restored, it will be through your own efforts.

Let's take the Farmers' Holiday program into every state, county, and township that produces human food. I thank you.

Milo Reno: Farmers' Union Pioneer, 1866–1936: A Memorial Volume, edited by Roland White (Iowa City: Athens Press, 1941), pp. 148–153

*   *   *

THE FARMERS GO ON STRIKE
Donald R. Murphy

THE BLOCKADE OF SIOUX CITY

On a paved road in northwestern Iowa, a truck loaded with cream cans bowls along. Suddenly a long-chain stretched between two trees bars the road.

From the sides of the highway, where they have been lounging under the trees in the tall grass, a dozen tanned men, the leader waving a red flag, bar the road. There are pitchforks handy for puncturing tires, rocks for cracking windshields, clubs to persuade the truck driver.

"Where you bound?"

"Sioux City."

"What you got?"

"Cream."

"Turn around and get outa here. Don't you know the Farmers' Holiday is on?"

Usually the truck backs up. Sometimes the driver takes a chance and tries to break through. A few of these chance-takers have finally retreated with broken windshields and punctured tires. The cream has been dumped in the road.

This is a picture of the most dramatic phase of the Farmers' Holiday—the attempt of a group of Middle Western farmers to enforce a strike designed to stop the movement of all farm products to market.

In a dozen counties in northwestern Iowa, and to a lesser degree in other counties, farmers are picketing the roads and stopping shipments. In several small towns produce buyers have agreed to shut up shop during the holiday. Elevators are considering refusing to buy grain until the holiday is over. Up in the Sioux City area special deputies have been sworn in and are riding a few trucks daily through the picket line.

In some cases truck drivers and farmers refuse to accept protection by deputies and stay home. "I've got to stay on living here," said one. "I guess I'll leave the truck in the shed for a while." Leaders of the strike, disclaiming any desire to use violence, insist that social ostracism of strike breakers will hold farmers in line. A farmer with hostile neighbors is helpless at threshing and at silo-filling time.

The strike is the culmination of a growing sense of injustice by corn-belt farmers. Specifically it is the response to years of exhortation by Milo Reno, veteran leader of the Iowa Farmers' Union, and his associates. For years, Reno has told farmers that eventually they would have to go on strike and starve city people into giving the farmer a square deal. The farmers that are supporting the holiday have backed the old McNary-Haugen bill, the more recent Frazier bill to refinance farm mortgages at a low rate of interest, and other farm legislation of a so-called "radical" type. They have seen these bills beaten and have watched farm prices go down and down since the big crash in 1920. For them the depression has lasted, not three years, but twelve.

This year farms are being taking over by mortgage holders at an increasing rate. Renters are finding that this year's crop will not pay cash rent. Farm buying power is down to 50 percent of the pre-war average.

To many farmers, it seemed that the time for direct action had come. Early this spring the Iowa Farmers' Union, traditional leader of left-wing movements in farm affairs, began to discuss plans for Farmers' Holiday during which all farmers would be pledged to refuse to sell any farm products. The agitation was continued, mainly in Iowa but also in several other Midwestern states, through the summer. Organizers carried pledge cards for farmers to sign. Finally the Iowa strike was called to start August 8.

In a manifesto adopted by farmers from Iowa, North and South Dakota, Illinois, Minnesota, and Nebraska, at a meeting in Des Moines, August 15, the organizers of the movement said:

> Self-preservation is still the first law of nature and we agree to keep all of our products which can possibly be kept on the farms and hold same until the time shall have arrived when farm products shall bring a market price equal to the cost of production.
>
> We pledge ourselves to protect one another in the actual possession of our necessary homes, livestock and machinery as against all claimants.

What is "cost of production?" The Farmers' Union works it out this way: Allow the farmer 5 percent on his investment in real estate, 7 percent on investments in personal property and equipment, and $100 a month for his own labor. To obtain this return, the union figures that on an average 160-acre Iowa farm with normal production, prices would have to be as follows: ninety-two cents a bushel for corn, forty-nine cents a bushel for oats, $11.25 for hogs, thirty-five cents a dozen for eggs, and sixty-two cents a pound for butter fat. On Monday, August 8, when the Farmers' Holiday was supposed to start, the farm prices on these products were: twenty-two cents for corn, eleven cents for oats, $3.85 for hogs, fifteen cents for eggs, and eighteen cents for butter fat.

The call for the holiday directed farmers to stay off the market for thirty days or until prices reached "cost of production." Iowa was to start the ball rolling. Minnesota, Illinois, and South Dakota were expected to come in the second or third week. North Dakota and Nebraska were also listed as prospects.

The first week of the strike in Iowa showed few results. Receipts of farm products at the different markets dropped off little if at all. In the second week, however, a new factor entered. The milk producers at Sioux City, who are getting only two cents a quart for whole milk, went on strike. These farmers began to hold up milk trucks and dump the milk.

The area around Sioux City has a good many Farmers' Union members and many more supporters of the Farmers' Holiday. These farmers seized the opportunity opened by the milk strike, joined the milk-strike pickets and began to stop, not only milk trucks, but trucks carrying any farm produce to town. The movement spread to an area including many of the counties in northwestern Iowa. Picketing, sometimes accompanied by mass action to turn back trucks, was common on many main highways. Even in northwestern Iowa, however, many towns were unaffected by the movement.

It is not entirely an accident that the area in which the Farmers' Holiday is strongest is roughly the same area of recent Bank Holidays. In this section lately, banks have adopted an extra-legal device to protect themselves against frightened depositors. They have persuaded the mayor in each town to declare a holiday, with all business houses closed, for a week or ten-day period. During this time, crews of business men have made the rounds of the depositors and obtained statements from them permitting the bank to retain the deposits for a period of some months, with the depositor not being allowed to check out any of his money except in specified small amounts.

The campaign to get these statements from depositors has been handled like the old Liberty Loan drives. Farmers reluctant to give up their deposits because they have been accumulated to meet interest or taxes, have been harassed by teams of solicitors until they signed. In cases where farmers have refused to sign, and banks have reopened, the banks have refused to let the non-signers have their money.

The Bank Holiday has furnished a fine argument for the backers of the Farmers' Holiday. They have used it vigorously. Even conservative farmers who take no part in the Farmers' Holiday movement seem pleased to see the bankers squirm when their own trick is turned against them.

Right now, in the third week of the Iowa strike, the usual guess is that the holiday will be confined to northwestern Iowa. The amount of produce going to market in that section is being cut down, but not enough to affect prices. If the balance of the state and other states join in, some real reduction in the flow of produce to market might be obtained. Of course, even if this should happen, the resultant rise in the price of farm products would hardly help the holiday supporter. The better prices would go to the farmers who continue to sell their products. As soon as the holiday backers would throw their products on the market again, any scarcity-induced rise in prices would collapse and the holiday backers would get the resulting low prices. The backers of the holiday claim that once higher prices are obtained they will be maintained by a system of feeding farm products into the market gradually.

In the long run the pledge of these farmers to protect each other against foreclosure may turn out to be more important than the strike. Certainly, even if the holiday ends with no real results, the irritation of farm people against low prices will not cease. There will be another outbreak. It may logically take the form of neighborhood defense against foreclosures. Such a program would have considerably more backing than the present strike. Even now, conservative farmers who see no success in the holiday movement express considerable sympathy for the project or for any project aimed at raising farm prices and keeping farmers on their own farms.

Farmers have submitted with surprising meekness to a long period of deflation. Orthodox and conservative, they have followed the conventional methods of trying to obtain reform by petitioning Congress for action. Instead of getting help, they have seen Coolidge veto two McNary-Haugen bills, and have seen Hoover block farm bills at the last session. Meanwhile farm prices have slipped lower and lower; farmer after farmer has met foreclosure, and no serious attempt—or so it seems to farmers—has been made by those in power to improve conditions. After twelve years of this it relieves a farmer's feelings a good deal to throw a rock through a windshield or to take any positive step, no matter how futile it may ultimately prove to be, that seems to lead toward better prices.

The Farmers' Holiday will probably fail in obtaining any substantial reduction of the flow of farm products to market; it will undoubtedly fail in an attempt to affect prices to any extent. It remains, however, a significant symptom of the state of mind of a great conservative class which has borne depression for twelve years and which is finally ready to employ radical measures that seem to have it a chance to save itself from general bankruptcy. Unless farm prices go up this will not be the last outbreak in the corn belt.

New Republic 72 (August 31, 1932):66–67, from Des Moines, Iowa

*   *   *

Nebraska Farmers in Action
Lief Dahl

The open warfare which is sweeping rapidly across the agrarian front throughout the country has had its most interesting development during recent months in the state of Nebraska. Here the more insurgent farmers have broken away from the official Farmers' Holiday Association, and are now carrying out a program of direct action. The rebel group now numbers six thousand members in the state as against the two thousand adherents of the parent organization. Through a hundred Committees of Action, or district nuclei, the group is making open and highly organized resistance to all attempts at foreclosures, repossessions, and farm confiscations.

The first display of mass action by the insurgent group occurred as a protest against the seizure of two trucks whose owners, badly hit by the low farm prices, had been unable to meet their payments. Without bothering about the formality of a sheriff, the sales company had driven off the trucks and parked them in the company's sheds at Newman Grove. The loss of the trucks was naturally a serious matter for the farmers, who would be unable to support themselves without machines to do their trucking.

The farmers in the district talked the incident over and decided that it was a "double-geared crime." The Nebraska Holiday Association (the rebel group) got busy, and the following day seventy-five determined farmers assembled, organized themselves into a body which they called "The Red Army," and marched over to the company offices where they wheeled the two trucks out of the sheds and turned them over to the farmers. The commander of the "Army" turned to his men and, as a parting insult to the law, asked whether there was anything else they wanted in the shed. The next day, law-abiding citizens of the town sent a committee to the sheriff protesting against his inactivity in the matter. "I am absolutely powerless," he replied, "in the face of such organized outlawry."

Another incident was the Avery sale near Petersburg. For the last fifty years, old Avery had worked as a hired hand and tenant farmer for a local banker. Last year he died, and the banker, realizing that he might have difficulty in collecting the four-hundred-dollar chattel mortgage which apparently represented the fruits of old Avery's half-century of toil, induced Avery's two sons to sign a new mortgage. He then foreclosed. This means taking away all the boys' livestock and farm machinery. The Holiday Association heard about the sale, marched to it three-thousand strong, and presented its demands: the costs of the sale, amounting to fifty dollars, were to be at the expense of the banker and the note was to be reduced considerably. The banker made a suave speech to the effect that he had had no intention "of setting these boys and their dependents on the road," but had "ordered the sale merely for the purpose of probating the property of the late Mr. Avery." This was too much for the crowd and the Committee determined to hold the sale then and there. It was decided that nobody wanted the goods except the two Avery boys and that "any other bidders will have to deal with the crowd." The sale was held at bargain price, cows bringing twenty-five cents and three pieces of farm machinery going for a nickel each. The banker obtained $7.10 for his note.

Later there was a foreclosure against the old Williamson couple near Platte Center. The banker had heard of the Holiday Association and took precautions. He drove all the chattels into town, and announced the sale for ten in the morning in the belief that the Committee of Action could not mobilize the farmers in sufficient strength at that hour. The Committee went to the Williamson farm. They found the old couple completely despondent and destitute; not only their cattle and machinery, but their entire crop of grain had been taken away. They then called on the banker, and told him he was "an unconscionable barbarian." The latter asked the Committee leader what he "suggested." "Mr. Banker, we do not suggest, we *demand*." The Committee of Action thus voiced the maturity and strength of the organized farming class. It presented two alternatives. Either the renewal of the note for at least a year, the immediate return of all the chattels to the Williamsons, plus the payment of all the costs of the sale and the repair or replacement of any property lost or damaged, or a forced sale, four thousand farmers coming into town on a Wednesday and seeing that the $400 note was wiped out for $1.98.

As Mid-Western farmers generally mean what they say, the banker agreed to every demand. The sequel is interesting. While the cattle were in town, seven pigs died of cholera. The banker had to replace these and vaccinate the rest of the herd. He had to send a carpenter to repair the Williamsons' crib. The result of this attempted chattel sale was a bill of costs and damages which almost equaled his note.

The $1.98 sale is the last recourse of the farmers. It is applied when the banker remains obdurate and refuses to accept the Committee's terms.

There is also the story of a farmer in Holt County by the name of Clasey. His goods were advertised for sale to cover a paltry one-hundred-and-thirty-five-dollar note. Neighbors told him to go to the Holiday Association, but he was slow to make up his mind. The day before the sale Clasey became frantic, realized that nothing would stop his being put on the road and, cranking up his Ford, drove south a hundred miles to find some members of "this here Holiday bunch." The Antelope County Holiday Association sent one of its officers back to Clasey's precinct. That night he gathered enough farmers for a meeting, and told them they couldn't let a neighbor be sold out. The morning of the sale, the newly formed Committee of Action got into cars and drove over the countryside, calling farmers from their cornfields, getting them to unhitch their teams and move on to the Clasey farm. They arrived, reenforced by others who had driven the hundred miles from the Antelope County Holiday Association, and forced the bank officials to renew the note.

These Committees of Action have spread like wildfire. There are about a hundred of them in east-central Nebraska, and on the average two or three are being formed each night. They are elected by the farmers in a precinct, and directed usually by the poorer farmers, who face the threat of foreclosure and repossession more immediately and hence will struggle more actively against it. The Committee of Action becomes a trouble center. Farmers drive up from the neighboring town to show their Committee a threatening letter from a banker or insurance company. The Committee sees what can be done about it. The farmers are learning to stand together. Some years ago they would have regarded foreclosure as an index of bad farming and felt little sympathy. Today they are seeing these things as caused by the working of a system outside their individual control, and are realizing the need for acting collectively. They have built in these Committees of Action a form of organizations closely resembling the Soviets of the 1905 and 1917 revolutions.

As the rebel Farmers' Holiday movement grows in strength— and it now embraces all but eight Nebraska counties—the business class and the Catholic Church are joining in a concerted move against it. Lecturers of Russia are covering Nebraska with bloody tales about the liquidation of the *kulak*. In Keya Paha County, three organizers of the Holiday Association were driven out by a mob of business men and county officials. The situation has not yet reached the point of open terror. As the militancy and strength of the Holiday Association grows, it may.

As for ideologies—in Nebraska actions are preceding words. But the farmers are beginning to think. On the march down to Washington, they saw bread lines, and thin gruel passed out to children when wheat was rotting on their farms. "What's wrong," one of them said to me, "is those peoples that are standing between the farmer and the workers. We'll have to jerk them out. Then the important people will get closer together."

"But that's Communism," I replied.

"Communism hell, that's necessity."

New Republic 73 (January 18, 1933):265–266, from Newman Grove, Nebraska

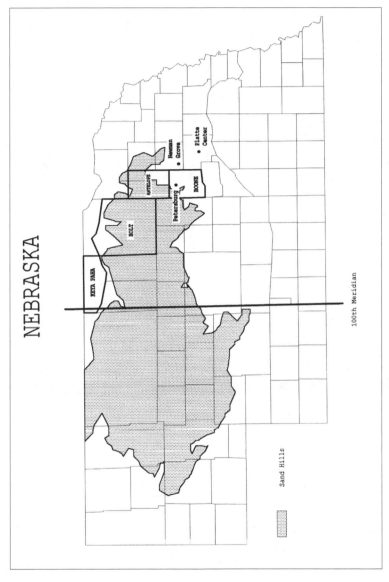

NEBRASKA

Sand Hills

KEYA PAHA

HOLT

WHEELER

BOONE

Newman
Grove

Petersburg

Platte
Center

100th Meridian

Farm fervor spreads as Nebraska farmers break away from the Farmers' Holiday Association and take more direct action through their Nebraska Holiday Association. Map by Michael Shambaugh-Miller.

FARMERS MARCH ON WASHINGTON, 1932

Farmers "marched" to state capitals to protest during 1931 and 1932, and they organized a march to Washington, D.C., in late 1932. Although the farmers' march on Washington was overshadowed by the Bonus Army, which had been ejected from Washington in July 1932, and by a hunger march organized by the Communist Party, the farmers' movement was viewed with some alarm.

CAPITAL POLICE TO PERMIT FARMERS' MARCH
SO LONG AS PROTEST MEETING IS PEACEABLE

WASHINGTON, Nov. 10—Police will not interfere with the entrance of delegates into Washington for the farmers' national relief conference Dec. 7, farm representatives were told today by Police Superintendent Brown. He gave this assurance on being told that the farm delegates were coming for a peaceable conference and would stage no public demonstration other than a parade. For this, he said, they would have to obtain a permit.

The first caravan of farmers will start next week from Seattle on its journey across the continent. Madison County, in eastern Nebraska, is the point where delegates from the Far West and Northern tier of states will stop over for two days of rest. Here meetings are planned to welcome the incoming farmers and then, with increased numbers, they will start east.

They will come in six columns, which will thread their way through all but four states. Farmer delegations are ready to join these columns in more than thirty states. They are timed to arrive in Washington on Dec. 6.

Farmers' letters to the executive secretary indicate one of the points to be discussed will be demands for the protection of farmers from immediate disaster. This would include no evictions, a moratorium on the debts which farmers cannot pay, and cash relief to relieve hunger. A national program of action for carrying out these demands will be formulated.

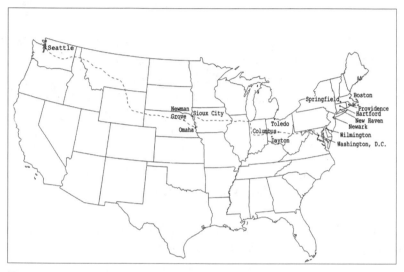

Farmers march on Washington, D.C., 1932. Map by Michael Shambaugh-Miller.

The letters are said to indicate that the average farmer is not hoping that some scheme like the export debenture or allotment plan will bring about a rapid rise in prices. Instead they indicate a belief that farm prices will stay low as long as 12,000,000 city people remained unemployed.

The conference will emphasize the common interest between destitute farmers and partly or wholly unemployed city workers.

These demands will be presented to Congress, the President, and other Federal authorities, with recommendations that they take action. Then, upon returning home, farmer delegations will present the same demands to local, county, and state governments.

However, according to its organizers, the conference will not deal with governmental action alone. The delegates in Washington will make plans to be followed in case their demands are not complied with. Discussions will cover a possible farm strike and work out how the city consumer can be protected during the strike; they will also cover the resistance of communities of farmers to evictions and a general attack on middlemen's profits.

New York Times, November 1, 1932

* * *

CORN BELT FARMERS
TO MOVE ON CAPITAL

MOTOR CARAVAN BEING PLANNED
FOR TRIP TO WASHINGTON TO
PETITION CONGRESS

"MARCH" WILL BE ORDERLY

BUT JUST WHAT WILL BE DEMANDED
OF CONGRESS SEEMS TO BE
SOMEWHAT OF MYSTERY

OUTCOME OF FARM STRIKE

FAILURE OF THAT MOVEMENT HAS LED
TO SERIES OF RADICAL PLANS
AMONG DISCONTENTED

Roland M. Jones

OMAHA, Nov. 24—The farmers' strike may be dead, but its restless soul goes marching on in projects conceived in the spirit of that queen of Kansas populism [Mary Ellen Lease] who once urged her followers to raise less corn and more hell.

The Farmers' Holiday Association still functions under the leadership of Milo Reno, its organizer and generalissimo, although cold weather and the interference of the law took all the glamour out of roadside picketing and broke the back of the strike. Its members may still be withholding their produce from the markets, but if so the markets have not noticed it. Chiefly it appears to be functioning as a kind of focus for discontent and the nucleus for movements calculated to make trouble for somebody else and therefore to result eventually in everlasting benefit to the American farmer.

Given an agitator with an assertive ego, a persuasive tongue, a flair for leadership, and a few credulous followers with nothing else to do and a willingness to try anything once, it becomes a simple matter to start a "movement." The most promising for the time being is the plan for a farmers' "march" on Washington. The prospectus of that movement is still somewhat vague and its scope quite undefined although the date for its start is but a few days away.

The "march" will be conducted by motor truck caravan. This caravan, Nebraska promoters assert, will be mobilized in Madison County of this state. There it will be joined by several truckloads of farmers from the Far West. A second concentration will be made at Sioux City, and other trucks are expected to join on the way through Iowa. Participants to qualify must be either farmers or recently dispossessed farmers. Although some help is expected from friendly farmers along the way, the purpose is to get along with a minimum of panhandling. Marchers have therefore been advised to take along plenty of blankets and not less than $10 in money; more if possible.

DEMANDS ARE UNCERTAIN

Just what the marchers will demand of Congress, when and if they get to Washington, is not entirely clear. Broadly speaking, it is farm relief. Specifically it probably will be some form of direct price fixing for agricultural products, a moratorium on farm mortgage indebtedness, and the taking over of the entire farm debt by the Federal Government at a low rate of interest and a period of sixty years or so within which to amortize the principal. Leaders talk about something analogous to the terms offered Italy in the funding of its war debt.

This march is quite distinct from bonus, hunger, or unemployment marches, some struggling elements of which are already under way in the Middle West. Sympathy has been expressed for these, but the present effort, it is said, is to be by, of, and for farmers solely, although there is some suspicion that its personnel, if any, may be recruited from the same sources that furnished some of the nondescript membership of the roadside picket camps during the height of the farm strike.

Behind the movement is the belief that the government can be persuaded by a show of numbers to do something that it would not otherwise do in spite of the catastrophic failure of this theory when tested by the bonus-seeking veterans. The leaders promise good order and decorum. But then the leaders of the Farmers' Holiday movement never expected, when they promoted that affair, the use of force and disorder which the farm strike developed.

FARM KLAN PROPOSED

Another "movement" mysteriously hinted at is the organization of an agricultural secret society, a sort of farm Ku Klux Klan. There was much whispering about it at the recent Farmers' Union convention in this city, but what its purposes are and even whether there is or will be such an organization have been kept a closely guarded secret.

The Union, which is operative in fourteen States and sponsors many cooperative enterprises, some of them doing an impressive volume of business, gave its convention over almost entirely to politics. The Nebraska publication of the organization, in its report of the convention, rather slyly and dryly commented that not more than twenty-five minutes of two days' meetings were devoted to cooperative affairs. It concluded by incorporating in its resolutions most of the important agriculturalisms of the past and present, including greenback inflation, the free coinage of silver, the assumption of the farm debt by the Federal Government with a long term of years at low interest for repayment, a mortgage moratorium pending this arrangement, and direct price fixing.

In the meantime, while the Corn Belt seethes with movements and the rumors of movements, the most effective form of direct farm relief has been going on quietly in numerous isolated localities to enforce their own moratorium on debt and delinquent tax collections. The sale of delinquent taxes has been almost a flat failure where it has been conducted, partly due to pressure from the farmers and partly to the inability of tax title buyers to borrow money at the banks. In more than sixty Iowa counties the annual sale has been postponed to give farmers a chance to pay up without being put to the trouble and expense of redeeming their property.

The same sort of pressure is being brought to discourage sales under farm mortgage foreclosure. In one judicial district in Nebraska the judges have announced that they will give farm debtors every possible chance to delay proceedings and will refuse to issue default decrees of foreclosure or confirm sales under foreclosure where there is no defense.

New York Times, November 27, 1932

*   *   *

POLICE PLAN TO BAR MARCH ON CAPITOL

ALSO MAY MAKE "HUNGER" GROUP SHOW FUNDS FOR UPKEEP BEFORE ENTERING CITY

OVER 600 REPORTED ON WAY

BANDS CONVERGING ON WASHINGTON FROM MID-WEST AND NEW ENGLAND POINTS

Farmers Also on Move

———

Foreclosure Victims Will Arrive in Capital at Week-End for Farm Relief Conference

———

WASHINGTON, Nov. 28—Police today planned three additional obstacles to the threatened communistic hunger march upon the capital next Monday when Congress convenes. At the same time it was reported from authoritative sources that police and Department of Justice officials would probably call upon President Hoover for troops if their strength was more than 1,500 and they became unruly.

Scattering reports today gave hope to police that the size of the "army" would be considerably less than the 3,000 expected, but the possibility of picking up recruits en route was not overlooked.

All three "obstacles" considered today, if carried out, probably will precipitate trouble. One is that the group will not be permitted to enter the city en masse; the second is to determine that every individual has sufficient funds to care for himself while in the city, and the third would be for the police to refuse permission for a parade to the Capitol.

Senate and House officials charged with policing the Capitol grounds have announced that no permit will be granted for a parade before the Capitol, and police say it would be more than foolish to grant a permit for a parade to the Capitol.

Eight "columns" in all, according to the Unemployed Council of America, are scheduled to converge just outside Washington late Saturday or Sunday afternoon. One of these is to leave New York later in the week.

To complicate the police problem, between 350 and 500 farmers will arrive here Sunday afternoon to attend the Farmers' National Relief Conference. These farmers are bona fide farm owners or farmers who have been dispossessed. Each was elected by twenty-five of his neighbors.

The conference is the outgrowth of the Farmers' Holiday movement which originated in Iowa last summer. They plan to hold a four-day conference to adopt a petition to be presented to Congress.

Both groups are using the same methods of transportation—trucks and private automobiles—and police expect trouble in distinguishing between the farmers and the radicals as they enter the city. Arrangements have already been made to house and feed the farmers.

TRUCKLOAD AT ALBANY
ALBANY, Nov. 28—EIGHTEEN MARCHERS WHO LEFT SCHENECTADY IN THE MOTOR TRUCK FOR WASHINGTON TODAY ARRIVED HERE THIS AFTERNOON.

HUNDRED PASS THROUGH HARTFORD
HARTFORD, CONN., NOV. 28—ABOUT 100 HUNGER MARCHERS FROM BOSTON, SPRINGFIELD, PROVIDENCE, AND OTHER NEW ENGLAND CITIES PASSED THROUGH HARTFORD THIS AFTERNOON ON THEIR WAY TO WASHINGTON, D.C.

TWO GROUPS ENTER OHIO

COLUMBUS, Ohio, Nov. 28—Two groups of hunger marchers entered Ohio today and stopped at Toledo and Dayton en route to Washington. Meanwhile, at Cincinnati, a group of avowed Communists demanded aid for another contingent expected there Wednesday.

About 500 of the "marchers," traveling in twenty touring cars and seven trucks, entered Toledo after an escort of Michigan State police had brought them to the state line from Detroit. They were taken to the Community Welfare House by Toledo police and fed there.

Fifty Toledo men are expected to join the group when it leaves there.

About fifty "marchers" evaded Sheriff's deputies near Dayton and entered the city to make speeches at a park. The Sheriff had hoped to swing them away from Dayton.

They were fed and housed tonight at Salvation Army Headquarters. There was no disorder.

Cincinnati police estimated at 200 the delegation of avowed Communists that called at the office of City Manager C. A. Dykstra to demand help for "marchers." Police arrested two men and a woman and broke up the group.

150 Reach New Haven

NEW HAVEN, Conn., Nov. 28—New England's hunger marchers, en route to Washington, reached here from Boston today after having picked up recruits in Providence, Hartford, and other cities.

Carl Reeve of Boston, captain of the column, said 150 marchers would continue their trek tomorrow. The arrivals were greeted here by a mass meeting sponsored by the New Haven Unemployed Council.

The marchers were quartered in a lodge hall tonight. They expected to reach New York tomorrow night.

Patman Opposes Marches

WASHINGTON, Nov. 28—Representative Patman of Texas, who sponsored the bonus bill passed by the House last session, announced to newspaper men upon his return to the capital today that he was prepared "to carry on the fight for payment this session."

"I am opposed to any marches on Washington this winter," he said. "While these people have a perfect right to come, they should understand that it only hurts their cause. This is just as true of hunger marchers as bonus marchers."

Farmers Off for Capital

Nebraska Caravan Starts out With Oregon and Idaho Groups

NEWMAN GROVE, Neb., Nov. 28—Twenty-eight northeastern Nebraska farmers, in two motor trucks, left here today on their long trek to the Farmers' Relief Conference in Washington, D.C.

Delegations from Oregon and Idaho joined the Cornhusker State delegation here, just before the caravan moved eastward. Other state groups are expected to merge with the motor-truck line as it chugs "on to Washington."

Leaders of the "march" said their first stop will be in Omaha and that the members will be the guests of a farm implement company for a meal in the Nebraska metropolis.

The farmers expect similar caravans from other sections of the country, and representatives of the various national farm organizations, to join them in Washington to draw up a program for agriculture to be presented to Congress.

The caravan is not sponsored by any farm organization. The Nebraska group, which sought participants under the name of "Farmers' Holiday Association (Madison County)," elected officers before departing and made Anton Rosenburg of Newman Grove president.

BONUS MARCH TOMORROW

GROUP WILL LEAVE HERE AT SAME TIME AS HUNGER DELEGATION

About sixty veterans who have banded themselves together in the movement known as the Veterans' Rank and File attended a meeting last night at 154 West Twentieth Street, sponsored by the Committee of Fifty, to make plans for the bonus march on Washington. This march, although it will coincide with the national "hunger march," will be separate. Some of the members of the Khaki Shirts, one of the numerous offsprings of W. W. Waters's Bonus Expeditionary Force, are cooperating in plans for the second bonus march, and representatives of the Khaki Shirts of New Jersey attended the meeting last night.

The first contingent of the bonus army—about forty-five strong— will gather at the New York headquarters of the Rank and File tomorrow morning about 7 o'clock and from there will go to Union Square, where the "hunger marchers" will gather at the same time. After a brief meeting, distinct from the farewell meeting of the "hunger marchers," the truck will go to Newark, where about 150 veterans are expected to join the New York delegation. During the week other contingents will be sent off as fast as transportation, clothing, and food can be provided.

The men expect to govern themselves en route and while in Washington by committees instead of by the leadership of a single man, and they are determined to camp at the same point in the District of Columbia as the B.E.F. used. National headquarters for the new movement has been established at 105 I Street, Northwest, Washington. Louis Walker presided at the meeting.

New York Times, November 29, 1932

*   *   *

Hunger on the March
Edward Dahlberg

The Washington hunger march, though it produced no sensational results, was nevertheless significant as another example of the growing use in America of the hunger march as a vehicle for mass protest. It was no sporadic spectacle. To be understood it must be viewed in relation to two other demonstrations—the march on Washington last spring of the bonus army, composed of the homeless and uprooted, and the recent Farmers' National Relief Conference, which was the culmination of riots, evictions, mortgages, and starvation. Both were essentially hunger marches.

Of the three groups the bonus army was the largest, numbering 45,000 at its peak. It was also the least organized and politically the least aware. Perhaps one of the major reasons for this is that most of the veterans were caught up in the amorphous, floating population of declassé workers. Economically unconnected and having no impetus toward collective protest except recurrent joblessness and social spleen, their understanding of the forces that had deracinated them was very befuddled.

The farmers, on the other hand, despite hunger and taxes which have reduced many of them to serfdom, still have their roots in the soil. As producers they are fully conscious of their position in relation to non-producers—the bankers and the middlemen. As a result, they have come to realize the interdependence of the farmer and the city worker. At the farmers' conference in Washington the repeated slogan was that if the farmer and the city worker do not stand and fight together, they will starve together.

Taken as a whole, these organized units of unemployed, including steel workers, miners, farmers, war veterans, and city proletarians, are rapidly developing the political art of permanent and cyclical mass protest. Following close in the wake of the three thousand hunger marchers who descended on Washington in the first week of December and who promised to return in greatly increased numbers this spring came the farmers. The leaders of the farmers' conference demanded a half-billion dollars for immediate relief. If they gain this objective, which, in the words of one farmer, "to the United States isn't equal to a raindrop off a waterspout," they will come back with other demands. And now a new bonus army, which has risen out of the dust of the militia that evicted them with gas and bayonets last July, is straggling back to the capital.

No realistic appraisal of the Washington hunger march is possible without some picture of its organization and at least a brief mention of strategy and police tactics. Each of the three thousand men and women was directly delegated to represent from one to two hundred jobless, underfed Americans who could not come themselves, either because of their families or because they no longer had the physical stamina for a cross-country truck-march. With dimes, nickels, and quarters, those who stayed at home had created an authorized delegation to go to Washington to demand unemployment insurance, a cash payment of $50 for winter relief, and $10 for each dependent.

Cumulative evidence from the very outset seems to point to official sanction of provocative acts by the police. The Wilmington episode was the inevitable result of what appeared to be a tacit agreement between the authorities and the police. In Wilmington, Delaware, men and women were indiscriminately clubbed and beaten because they had attempted to assemble and speak; they were, besides, tear-gased inside the church which they had rented. Moreover, all along the line repeated attempts were made to discourage and dispirit the marchers. Difficulties were raised so that they could not obtain sleeping quarters, hold demonstrations, or even communicate with hundreds of thousands of other hungry Americans.

Having failed to split up the marchers and to turn them back, the authorities then proceeded to terrorize them. Accordingly, on Sunday, December 4, the hunger marchers were met in Washington by a large police escort and shunted into an isolated street, which was immediately sealed by heavy cordons of police at both ends. Twelve hundred policemen, seven hundred deputized firemen equipped with tear gas, sawed-off rifles, and sub-machine-guns, in addition to the militia which was held in readiness in the barracks, were prepared to meet three thousand unarmed, wary, worn, and undernourished men and women.

The street in which the marchers were imprisoned for nearly three days lies between a railroad yard and a treeless hill on the outskirts of town. The yard, glutted with empty Pullman cars that could have housed from ten to fifteen thousand homeless people, was covered by plain-clothes men to cut off any escape that way. On top of the hill were machine-guns, which at first, and to an unprepared observer, looked like a battery of cameras. The tear-gas squad was stationed on the bluff. The photographer from the *Washington Herald*, who was standing on the roof of a truck, was carrying a gas-mask. One of the officers of the tear-gas squad said to a reporter: "The trouble with the Ford job was that they only had $1,000 worth of gas." He went on to explain that $10,000 had been spent on gas for the present "hunger marchers' job." Four trucks were filled with it. In each policeman's kit there were two lots of tear gas to one of sickening or D.N. gas.

On Sunday the marchers were held virtually incommunicado. Besides, there was no water, no hydrant on the street. Not until evening was a truck permitted to leave to bring back cans of water. Many of the men and women went to bed without it. On December 5, while

Congress on the floor of the House was arguing for and against beer, there was not enough water to drink and none to wash with in the hunger camp. There were no sanitary arrangements either, and men and women were harassed and chased from one place to another by jeering policemen. The second day the marchers were given permission to build a toilet. Four different times the men had gone ahead with this, in each instance having received the approval of the police inspector, and each time the police doctor had informed them that they would have to construct it elsewhere in order to comply with sanitary regulations! In the face of this, and notwithstanding the fact that the police had violated the most fundamental health rules provided by law and medicine, the marchers maintained unbroken discipline and order. They carefully refrained from offering the police the slightest provocation.

There were no cots or beds in the camp. Although "sympathizers," among whom were Quakers, radicals, workingmen, and humanitarian citizens of Washington, had offered accommodations sufficient to house a thousand hunger delegates, the police would not release them for the night. Some slept in trucks. Others, ill with fever and exposure, old and young, men and women, fatigued and with nothing in their stomachs but a cup of coffee and a sandwich, lay down on the cold asphalt. For pillows they used ragged bundles or shoes.

Sick men and women could not get hospital attention without the approval of the police doctor. When a feverish marcher was taken out, it was feet first. As one was being carried out to the ambulance, a policeman said: "Well, I guess it would be inhuman to let him die!" At the same time it was apparent that the police were dominated by a determination which one officer expressed when he said: "Let him die here. We don't want him to die in Washington." It would not do to allow a hungry American to die of starvation on the streets of the capital. The hunger marchers were political prisoners and were accorded the treatment meted out to criminals, with the difference that even in the most backward jails convicts are at least provided with food and water.

The next day the hunger camp hummed with cameramen, detectives, reporters, and stool pigeons. The citizens of Washington were still sanctimoniously isolated from the marchers. In accordance with this policy, Major Brown, the Police Commissioner, who wanted to perform his duties with more competence than General Glassford, his predecessor, who had been "too easy" with the B.E.F., issued a Foch-like pronouncement: "They will not parade."

Congress had opened its session. Members of the League of Professional Groups and the National Committee for the Defense of Political Prisoners were knocking at the door of every Senator and Representative who, they thought, might evince some interest in the constitutional rights of American citizens. Legal machinery was set in operation by liberals in an attempt to obtain an injunction restraining the police from holding the marchers.

The police, having failed to incite the hunger marchers to riot, started a campaign of more pernicious provocations and red-baiting. The tear-gas squad on the hill began to "test" the bombs by throwing them into a bonfire. As the bombs exploded, the wind, which was blowing in the direction of the delegates below, carried the sickening fumes into the trucks where men and women were sitting and standing, causing them much discomfort. Committees of citizens passing back and forth were spat upon and jeered at. Whenever a marcher came near, one policeman would leer at another with "Hello, Comrade."

Doubtless the press played a large role in all this. In order to give their stories a sexy and gamy flavor some papers stated that men and women were sleeping standing up locked in each other's arms. The newspapers had previously run column articles declaring that each hunger marcher was receiving five dollars a day from Moscow. Sensation rather than fact was the dominant feature, and the following kind of reporting was typical. A headline ran: "Rumor, Dynamite in Communists' Trucks." Below, in small letters, was "Rumor Unfounded." This must have helped to inflame the police force. As a matter of fact, one police officer said that he knew there was a nest of machine-guns in one of the marcher's trucks. However, no investigation was ever made. And even when articles, representing the opinions of individual reporters who had actually witnessed the scene, were sympathetic to the hunger marchers, the headlines, expressing the editorial policies of the paper, were more often than not at complete variance with the stories.

Toward five that afternoon the marchers fell into ranks. Two columns, each four abreast, extended down the street for more than half a mile. It was a dress rehearsal for the parade the following day. Since no permit had been granted, the police inspector took the demonstration for a threat and put in a riot call. A siren rang out over the hill. Motorcycle cops bounded over the bluff, buses of policemen were unloaded. The police with clubs in their hands dared the marchers to cross the line where the rope was stretched across the width of the street.

Banners were hoisted by the marchers: "We Demand Shelter for the Homeless," "We Demand Unemployment Insurance," "Fight Against Starvation." The red-front band started to play the "Internationale" as the ranks came nearer and nearer the rope. As the tear-gas squad stood in readiness, bombs poised in their hands, one yelled: "The yellow rats, why don't they do something? I'm rarin' to go!" Then, when it seemed as if the bombs were about to descend, a plain-clothes man turned his head the other way saying, "I'm not going to look at this." At that moment the writer, who was also standing on the bluff next to the tear-gas squad, felt as if he had been turned over in an automobile accident and had lost consciousness for several seconds. In geometric formation and with the clicking precision of typewriter keys the marchers made a left-squad turn. The police jeered hysterically and hunger marchers booed.

Later, Senator [Edward P.] Costigan [D-Colorado] came out and was indignant at what he saw. [Representative Fiorello] La Guardia [R-New York] was there and equally aroused. Congressmen [Philip D.] Swing [R-California] and [Thomas R.] Amlie [R-Wisconsin] visited the camp, among others. Howard Williams of the L.I.P.A. said that if there were not police, there would be no trouble. That night about four hundred men and women were allowed to leave the camp and sleep in lodgings in Washington. The police, many of whom were drunk, broke loose and slashed the tires of seventeen trucks.

The permit to parade the next day was granted, but the guard surrounding the marchers was so thick that some of the unsuspecting spectators in the throngs must have thought it was a police and firemen's parade on the way to a ball and that the hunger marchers were a crowd of curious civilians following it. The crowds neither booed nor cheered. There was in Washington that morning all the semblance and surcharged atmosphere of martial law. The citizens were explosively timorous. Perhaps something of the tense and electric silence with which they watched the hunger marchers may be explained in terms of Mark Twain's "The Mysterious Stranger," in which but one man of all those who threw stones at a beautiful witch really had a grudge against her. The others threw stones because each one was afraid that the man standing next to him was antagonistic.

It seems that the significance of the hunger march, which must include the bonus army and the farmers' conference, and its place in the political history of the United States will depend not so much upon the present, tentative reactions of public opinion as upon the kind of organizing and mass maneuvering it may release in the near future. Prognostications will be much more in order by the end of 1933, the year of our lord Franklin Delano Roosevelt.

The Nation 135 (December 28, 1932):642–644

NEW VIOLENCE IN THE MIDWEST, 1933

*While Congress, in special session, wrestled with bills to provide re-
lief for farmers and other Americans, warnings from the Midwest
indicated that even the most normally peaceful people, farmers and
schoolteachers, were becoming desperate. The Senate approved the
first major farm bill the day after a judge was dragged from his courtroom in Le Mars, Iowa.*

TEACHERS STAGE
NEW CHICAGO RIOT

OVER 3,000 DEFY POLICE AND
GUARDS TO DEMAND TAX
PAYMENTS BY BANK

BANK ACCOUNTING ORDERED

TRUST COMPANY MUST REPORT
FUNDS HELD IN ESCROW FOR
PROPERTY TAXES

TAX STRIKE BILL APPROVED

MEASURE FOR RELIEF OF COOK COUNTY
IS VOTED BY HOUSE; GOES TO
STATE SENATE

CHICAGO, April 26—Minor casualties, caused by fists and clubs, marked the second invasion this morning of the financial centre by about 3,000 school teachers, to force payment of $30,000,000 [in] back salaries. The district was turned into an armed camp, and some of the banks were forced to bar their doors to all except pass-book holders.

This afternoon police reserves were called to the City Hall when the teachers attempted to storm the Council meeting. The police stood three deep to hold the "invaders" back, the latter shouting at the top of their voices for their "rights as voters" to attend the meeting. They were finally admitted and remained to applaud Mayor Kelly when he described his efforts to assist the School Board.

Another group of teachers jammed the galleries of the Board of Education, which deferred until its meeting two weeks from today a vote to close the schools from May 12 until October.

The teachers, at liberty during this week's Spring vacation, gathered at Congress Street and Michigan Avenue. Heavy police guards had been posted outside and inside the five banks where they created disorderly scenes Monday, but they made a surprise move and descended upon the Chicago Title and Trust Company on West Washington Street.

DEFY MOUNTED POLICE

The company, which does a large receivership business, holds about $10,000,000 in escrow for the payment of taxes of property owners, according to State's Attorney Courtney.

Fists and clubs were swung vigorously as teachers, policemen, and bystanders clashed in hand-to-hand scuffling. Two teachers were reported slugged, several others were slightly injured, five women fainted, policemen and bank guards were scratched by the women, newspaper reporters were slapped and pedestrians jostled.

The teachers defied mounted policemen who tried to break through the massed crowd, and fought with all who sought to enter or leave the building. The doors of the building were locked while many teachers were inside.

While a committee of nineteen teachers conferred with Holman D. Pettibone, president of the company, others stood in the street singing "The Star-Spangled Banner" and "America" and shouting: "Give us this day our daily bread" and "Pay your taxes!"

BANKER PACIFIES CROWD

When the first advance was made upon the building a plate glass window was broken. The clash occurred between teachers and police and private guards of the Title and Trust Company. When the male teachers roughly handled persons who were attempting to get through the crowd, the latter replied in kind. A score of fights were going on at one time.

Mr. Pettibone was prevailed upon to address the demonstrators from a second story window.

"So far as this company is concerned," he said, "the taxes have been paid on any property we own. Don't crucify the wrong people. Go to the Legislature. That is where your remedy is, and we are glad to help you in obtaining relief.

"We have more than 300 properties in receivership at present that cannot pay their taxes. The receiver has been paid just like a janitor or any other employee. We feel that is no more than right."

About the same time, on the petition of State's Attorney Courtney, County Judge Jarecki was issuing an order upon the trust company officials to appear before him May 9 with an accounting of all the funds placed in escrow with the company by other property owners for payment of their taxes.

The teachers then made for the First National Bank in small groups, hoping thus to gain entrance and stage a demonstration there. They were frustrated when word of their intention reached the bank. At one entrance fifteen mounted policemen lined up, ready to disperse the crowd. The teachers shifted to the Clark Street side. There all doors were closed and guarded.

At Springfield the bill aimed at the Cook County tax strike was passed in the House by a vote of 112 to 25 and was speeded to the Senate, where Mayor Kelly is expected to plead for its passage tomorrow.

New York Times, April 27, 1933

*   *   *

IOWA FARMERS ABDUCT JUDGE FROM COURT,
BEAT HIM, AND PUT ROPE AROUND HIS NECK

LE MARS, Iowa, April 27—District Judge Charles C. Bradley was dragged from his court room this afternoon by a crowd of more than 600 farmers. They slapped him, blindfolded him, and carried him in a truck a mile from the city, where they put a rope around his neck and choked him until he was nearly unconscious. His face was smeared with grease and his trousers were stolen.

The abduction followed Judge Bradley's refusal to swear he would sign no more mortgage foreclosures.

The farmers had entered his court room to discuss with him hearings which are to determine the constitutionality of two new laws relating to mortgage foreclosures.

The judge requested them to take off their hats, and to stop smoking cigarettes.

"'This is my court," he said.

At his words the farmers, wearing bandanna handkerchiefs over their faces, arose, hauled him off the bench, slapped him and shook him, and finally carried him bodily out of the court house onto the lawn.

There they made their demand that he swear that he would not sign any more foreclosure actions. Judge Bradley, who is about 60 years old, defied the crowd and was jeered and again slapped.

Next they put him on a truck and drove to a crossroad, where they reiterated their demands, but the judge continued to refuse.

A rope was then put about his neck, and when someone gave it a pull Judge Bradley fell, only partly conscious, but still refusing to comply with the request.

The farmers then dragged him to his feet, carried him to the side of the road, and threw the loose end of the rope over a sign, but Judge Bradley defied them to "go on."

"Make him get down on his knees and pray," one of the farmers shouted.

The judge was pushed to his knees.

"I will do the fair thing to all, to the best of my knowledge," he said.

One of the farmers removed a hub-cap from a truck and placed it on the judge's head.

Oil and grease from the cap ran down his face and the farmers threw dirt on him, which stuck to the oil.

After the "prayer" the farmers removed Judge Bradley's trousers and filled them with dirt from the roadside. Then they drove off, leaving the begrimed jurist standing in the middle of the road.

He was taken back to town in a car by Wilber DePree, son of the Rev. J. J. DePree.

"I'd rather not say," he replied in answer to queries as to whether he would seek prosecution of his abductors.

Earlier in the day farmers reported to be the same who participated in the judge's abduction were held off by twenty-two deputies at Primghar, Iowa, while Sheriff Ed Loemkuil directed the sale of John Shaffer's farm.

O. R. Montzheimer, attorney for mortgage holders, was seized as he left the court house, forced to kiss the American flag and to promise not to bring further foreclosure actions.

New York Times, April 28, 1933

*   *   *

IOWA TROOPS RULE
FARM RIOT AREAS;
MOB BLOCKS A SALE

————

MARTIAL LAW IS DECLARED IN
PLYMOUTH COUNTY, WHERE JUDGE
WAS ABDUCTED AND BEATEN

————

CROWD ROUTS DEPUTIES

————

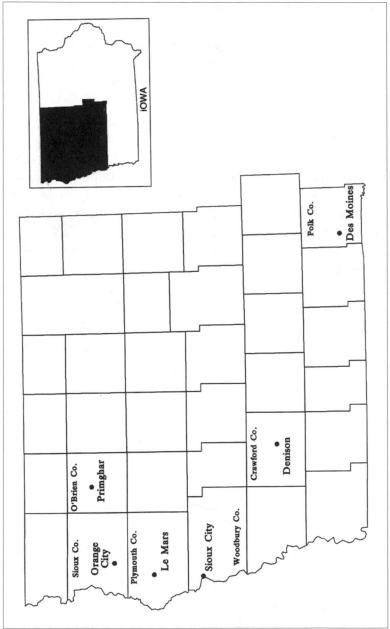

Iowa farm riots break out in Le Mars, Primghar, and Denison. Mobs block foreclosure sales. Map by Robert Watrel.

OFFICERS ARE FORCED TO STOP
DENISON FORECLOSURE AND
GOVERNOR SENDS MILITIA THERE

COURTS SPLIT ON NEW LAW

STATE ACT AIMED TO HELP DEBTORS
IS UPHELD AND HELD
UNCONSTITUTIONAL IN DECISIONS

LE MARS, Iowa, April 28—Martial law was established here to-day under a proclamation by Governor Clyde Herring and the arrival of 250 National Guardsmen as a result of the attack yesterday on District Court Judge C. C. Bradley by farmers who demanded that he refuse to sign foreclosure papers.

Other state troopers were ordered to Denison, Iowa, sixty miles from Sioux City, after 800 farmers had attacked six state agents, a sheriff, and forty special deputies when they attempted to conduct a foreclosure sale on J. F. Field's farm.

The crowd stopped the sale after a fight in which many were slightly injured.

Governor Herring's martial-law order covered all Plymouth County.

Terming the attack on Judge Bradley "a vicious and criminal conspiracy and assault upon a judge while in discharge of his official duties, endangering his life and threatening a complete breakdown of all law and order," he authorized the troops to work beyond the borders of the county if necessary.

"The public peace and good order will be preserved upon all occasions and throughout the county, and no interference will be permitted with officers and men in the discharge of the duties under this order," the proclamation read.

DOUBTS CROWD ALL FARMERS

The Governor declared he believed Sioux City hoodlums were in the crowd that attacked the judge. He urged the newspapers not to be too quick in describing the assailants as all farmers. Talk of "Red" agitators was also heard.

In Le Mars rumors of outside help for the farmers was not taken seriously. Persons who saw a hundred or more men sweep into the court room of Judge Bradley while court was in session, who saw the jurist slapped and choked and otherwise maltreated before a noose was placed around his neck, asserted that many in the crowd were recognized as farmers from O'Brien, Plymouth, and Sioux Counties.

"It seemed to be a crowd without direction," said one observer, "moving under the impulses of mob psychology. The members had gone into the court to demand that Judge Bradley refuse to sign any more foreclosure actions. When he declined to promise that on oath, the mob seemed to move mechanically about seizing him."

This observer said that the plague of drought and grasshoppers had well nigh ruined farmers in this section before the low prices of farm products in the last year or two added to their troubles.

Meanwhile Judge Bradley, suffering only slight effects of the manhandling by the mob, presided over a routine court session. He said he had not recognized any of those who seized him, although he had been on the district bench for many years.

The troops are under command of Colonel Golden C. Hollar. The men carried full field equipment and are quartered for the time being in the armory.

New York Times, April 29, 1933

DROUGHT, HEAT WAVES, AND DUST STORMS
FROM THE GREAT PLAINS, 1934–1936

In late April 1931, a combination of unusual factors resulted in a great dust storm that enveloped much of Oregon and Washington and even carried dust out over the Pacific Ocean so thick that one ship's captain reported "visibility so low it necessitated navigation as in fog." Local newspapers reported on the vast damage done by the storm, and the Monthly Weather Review *(May 1931), published by the U.S. Weather Bureau, gave a full report with pictures. Still, the rest of the nation paid scant attention. Weather charts would later show that a dry cycle began in the Great Plains and the Midwest in 1930, but farmers, politicians, and newspapers seemed far too preoccupied with other serious matters to give much sustained attention to the weather in 1932 and 1933. But the great dust storm in early May 1934 that spread from the Plains to Washington, D.C., and New York and then far out over the Atlantic Ocean changed that thinking.*

The years 1934, 1935, and 1936 were marked by drought, intense heat, and dust storms in both summer and winter. From 1934, when it published an article on the great dust storm of that May, to 1937, the Monthly Weather Review *reported fairly extensively on heat, drought, and dust storms with an occasional piece on brown snow storms. In February 1935, the publication carried an article that summed up, with clinical detachment, the data on the dust storms that had occurred between November 1933 and May 1934. "Dust storms," the report stated, "cause much discomfort to human beings and animals through inhalation of the drifting particles, and also deposit much dirt generally. Their major damage, however, is the removal of productive topsoil from agricultural regions, however much the removed soil may benefit another region where it may be deposited." A June 1936 article dealing with the dust storms in the southwestern Plains showed that the Weather Bureau had discovered that dust storms had killed people: "In Colorado . . . the suffocating dust storms occurred frequently from March 12 to 25, 1935, bringing death to 6 persons and serious illness to more than a hundred others. Sickness continued in this section, where lung congestion was reported to have been aggravated by the dust laden air. In the more seriously affected areas, the dust lay from a few inches to more than 6 feet deep, and considerable livestock perished from starvation and suffocation."*

During the period 1934–1936, newspapers carried many grim stories of the extensive human suffering incurred by heat, drought, and dust storms. In 1940 Lawrence Svobida, a Kansas farmer who had seen his farm and all his work blown away by the storms and had nearly died from dust inhalation, published a book called An Empire of Dust *recounting his 10 desperate years trying to raise wheat in western Kansas. Svobida concluded that with a few exceptions, the Great Plains was a desert that could not be reclaimed. Many thoughtful observers in the 1930s shared Svobida's views, as no doubt did some of those who saw the film* The Plow That Broke the Plains, *but the end of the dry cycle between 1936 and 1939, along with the vast efforts sponsored by the Soil Conservation Service, contributed to a recovery on the Great Plains.*

*   *   *

Huge Dust Cloud, Blown 1,500 Miles, Dims City 5 Hours

White Particles Treble Density of City's Normal Atmosphere, Veiling the Sun

-----

Weigh 300,000,000 Tons

Soil, Loosened by Drought in West, Hovers High in Air — Belt 1,800 Miles Wide

Eyes, Throats Affected

Hospitals Ease Discomfort of Many—Cloud Will Pass to the South Today

A cloud of dust thousands of feet high, which came from drought-ridden states as far west as Montana 1,500 miles away, filtered the rays of the sun for five hours yesterday, and New York was obscured to a half-light similar to the light cast by the sun in partial eclipse.

A count of the dust particles in the air showed that there were 2.7 times the usual number, and much of the excess seemed to have lodged itself in the eyes and throats of weeping and coughing New Yorkers.

Chicago investigators, who had a head start because the dust cloud reached them the day before, estimated for the Associated Press that 300,000,000 tons of dust, which used to be topsoil in the valleys of the Missouri and Mississippi Rivers, had been swept aloft by a strong northwest wind and sprinkled over half the nation.

In many parts of the country the dust added to the losses of farmers, already suffering heavily from the lack of rain. Crop estimators began revising their yield figures throughout the grain states.

EXPECTED TO BLOW ON TODAY

The local Weather Bureau held out hope last night that today the city would look up at a more nearly normal sky, although it was feared that some of the effects of the dust cloud probably would be apparent for another twenty-four hours. Winds promised to blow the bulk of the cloud to the south.

New York presented an odd appearance at the height of the phenomenon. At 3 P.M. attendants in the tower of the Empire State Building looked north into a gray haze in which not even Central Park was visible. An observer at Newark Airport reported visibility there to be only two miles. The Statue of Liberty, seen from the twenty-ninth floor of the Whitehall Building, where the Weather Bureau has its offices, was a smudge of gray. Its outlines [were] barely distinguishable.

The period of "greatest opacity"—so described by Dr. James H. Kimball, Weather Bureau meteorologist, was from 11:45 A.M. until about 5 o'clock. Reports received at the bureau showed that aviators had been forced in some places to ascend 15,000 feet to find clear air. It was not possible to tell whether the cloud, which afflicted almost the entire northeastern section of the country, was that thick in all places.

NO MENACE TO HEALTH

Despite the many inconveniences suffered by persons forced to go about their usual business in the dust laden air, the Department of Health was convinced that there was no danger that disease would be spread.

This view was based in part on the fact that the dust came from the clean open spaces. One official remarked that no normal person would be adversely affected by swallowing a bit of "sterile dirt."

A little greater density, it was explained, would have resulted in difficulties for such persons as sufferers from sinus infections. Dusty air irritates the mucous membrane of the nasal passages, health officials said, and so it was fortunate that the air did not get thicker.

The Manhattan Eye, Ear and Throat Hospital, 210 East Sixty-fourth Street, reported that many more patients than usual came to have foreign substances removed from their eyes.

Officials of the Weather Bureau agreed that had it not been for that cloud of dust New York would have enjoyed brilliant sunshine all yesterday.

WIND PICKED UP LOOSE SOIL

"The explanation of the dust cloud is simple," said Dr. Kimball. "The surface soil in the upper Missouri and Mississippi Valleys was fine and loose as a result of the drought. All that was needed was a persistent and direct wind. This wind, from the northwest, came down on Wednesday and picked up much of that surface and carried it across the Mississippi. Last night the cloud was reported in Illinois, Kentucky, and western Tennessee.

"This morning by 9 o'clock the advance guard got to Scranton, and it was observed in New York between 9 and 10 o'clock. Above the dust the clouds were broken, and all this obscurity was caused by the dust."

He pointed out the window, where the outline of Governor's Island was discernible but the section of Brooklyn just across Buttermilk Channel was only a smudge, with an occasional black stack or tall building showing.

Although the dim form of Liberty could be seen at Bedloe's Island, the buildings at the base of the monument were hidden. Staten Island could not be seen, and the Jersey shore was only a streak of gray. The sun remained strong enough to cast somewhat indefinite shadows of the pedestrians in Battery Park, twenty-nine stories below.

The water of the harbor was slate-colored, and the sun tipped occasional ripples with dirty silver. No harbor craft were visible beyond the tip of Governor's Island.

"The rear edge of the cloud," continued Dr. Kimball, "is now along a line from Harrisburg to Albany. Our records show that Nashville is the most southerly point reporting the cloud since it was formed, and St. Paul the furthest north."

On the basis of those figures the dust cloud was held to be about 1,800 miles wide, but the official figures were not complete enough to show whether it was unbroken across that great stretch.

HUMIDITY BELOW NORMAL

One effect of the dust was to dry the air. At noon the humidity was 34 per cent, against a normal 57 per cent for this time of year.

There was a similar dust cloud last November, but that one did not reach New York City, and officials at the Weather Bureau were unable to say when there had been a phenomenon of the kind in this region. The November disturbance resulted in a great triangle of dust with its base along a line from Huron, S.D., to Amarillo, Texas, and its apex at Milwaukee. Visibility got as low as 300 feet in Omaha on that occasion, and in many places lights were turned on in the daytime.

Dr. James H. Scarr, Weather Bureau meteorologist, advanced the theory that yesterday's dust cloud had persisted because it was far above the ordinary cloud layers and hence was not affected by rainstorms over which it had passed.

"I'm not certain whether that's true," he said, "but the showers have not washed it down. It seems to be settling by gravity. This dust was carried up several thousand feet. I spent my youth in the South, where such occurrences are more common, but I don't remember one in which the dust was carried so high.

"I can't say I like the taste of this air. It reminds me of working at the tail-end of a straw-stacker in the loft of a barn. It cuts off my free breathing."

FILTERS MEASURE DUST

The measurement of 2.7 times the usual number of dust particles in the air came from the National Broadcasting Company's studios. The air conditioning apparatus there brings air in from the outside and sends it through filters of finely spun glass. The dust made it necessary to change the filters frequently.

Normally the company's microscope shows that the incoming air contains 227 dust particles per square millimeter. Yesterday the figure was 619. Radio engineers scoffed at the theory that the dust had been the cause of the static in the air the last few days.

Dr. E. E. Free of New York University made some tests of the air on the seventeenth floor of the Flatiron Building, Twenty-third Street and Fifth Avenue, and announced that it contained forty tons of dust per cubic mile.

At the New York Meteorological Observatory in Central Park the apparatus for fixing the amount of dust in the air was of no use because it is equipped to deal with city dust, which ordinarily is black. The dust cloud was white.

The recording disks of the automatic air filter at the Central Park station are white. Black ones would have been required to show what happened yesterday.

The observatory did establish, however, that the rays of the sun were only about 50 per cent of the normal for a clear day. James Decker, assistant observer, said most of this loss could be blamed on the dust, which began to affect the pyrheliometer—the instrument which measures sunshine—about 9 A.M. From that time on, the fall from normal was pronounced.

The dust cloud was noted early in the afternoon off Nantucket Island. Captain Heinrich Dau, master of the Hamburg-American liner *Deutschland*, said last night when his ship reached quarantine several hours late that he had been delayed by a peculiar atmospheric cloudiness during most of the day.

"It wasn't really like dust, and there was no dust on the decks under foot," he said. "But the air was gray and reminded me of the times I have passed Cape Verde Islands where the sand of the Sahara Desert was blowing for miles out to sea."

Pilots of air liners serving New York reported that the dust was very noticeable in the air, but it did not interfere with schedules. United Air Line fliers, in from Cleveland, said they had flown at normal altitudes of 8,000 to 10,000 feet to get the benefit of tail winds. The dust appeared as a dull haze, they said, but did not interfere seriously with visibility.

On the planes of TWA between Newark and Pittsburgh, planes made their usual schedules, flying under a ceiling of about 1,800 feet. Line pilots reported that in midafternoon the dust seemed to be passing out to sea.

HOUSEWIVES KEPT BUSY

New York housewives, inured to the usual trouble of keeping their homes dusted despite the particles that constantly drift through windows, had their tasks multiplied by 2.7 yesterday. The problem was epitomized atop the Empire State Building, where the stone ledges on which sight-seers lean, ordinarily a darkish gray, were covered with a film of white. In midafternoon, however, the breeze got strong, and soon the entire tower was well dusted.

From suburban communities came numerous complaints about the added drudgery of housekeeping. In Westchester First Sergeant H. A. Gay of the New York State Police was vexed because the hardwood floor of the lounge in the Hawthorne Barracks, freshly waxed in the morning, was under a thick coating. He kept men wiping the desks all day long, but they could not keep up with their work.

New York Times, May 12, 1934

*   *   *

DROUGHT, DUST, DISASTER

Last week AAA [Agricultural Adjustment Act] reported it had spent $67,600,000 to reduce the U.S. wheat crop for 1934. At the same time the Department of Agriculture gave out its May estimate for the winter wheat crop: 461,000,000 bu. [bushels], which was 31,000,000 bu. less than the April estimate and 171,000,000 bu. less than the five-year average. There was little connection between the expenditure and the shrinkage, for a crop reduction agent more potent than AAA was at work. From Saskatchewan to Texas, from Montana to Ohio, hardly any rain had fallen for a month. As dry day followed dry day, crop estimators lopped 2,000,000 bu. from their wheat prediction every morning. Before the week was out the winter wheat estimate had fallen to 442,000,000 bu.

In Washington these were dry statistics, but in the Midwest, disastrous facts. In North Dakota, which had barely an inch of rain in four months, there was no grass for cattle. Farmers tramped their dusty fields watching their dwarfed stand of grain shrivel and perish. A baking sun raised temperatures to 90°, to 100°. And still no rain fell. Water was carted for miles for livestock. Towns rationed their water supplies. In Nebraska the State University agronomist gloomily predicted that many fields would not yield over 5 bu. of wheat per acre (normal average: 15 to 20 bu.). In Minnesota they mocked Washington's crop predictions as gross overestimates. Farmers planting corn raised clouds of dust like columns of marching troops.

Then came the wind, great gusty blasts out of the Northwest. It lifted the dust from the parched fields and swirled it across the land. It tore the powdery soil from the roots of the wheat and deposited it like snowdrifts miles away. Concrete highways were buried under six inches of dust. The rich fertility of a million farms took to the air: 300,000,000 tons of soil billowing through the sky. Housewives in Des Moines could write their names in grime upon their table tops. Aviators had to climb 15,000 ft. to get above the pall. A dust storm 900 mi. wide, 1,500 mi. long swept out of the drought-stricken West.

In dust-darkened Chicago excited Board of Trade brokers bid up wheat prices 55¢ [cents] in one day (the maximum), raised the price to 93¢ a bu.—up 17¢ in two weeks. That day 6,000 tons of finely divided wheat fields fell on Chicago's roofs and sidewalks. And the dust swept on, until its thick haze could be seen from the windows of the Department of Agriculture in Washington. It hung for five hours like a fog over Manhattan—the greatest dust storm in U.S. history, proof to the East of an unbelievably successful crop reduction in the Midwest.

But the Administration was not grateful for this help from the Hand of God. No fear did it have of a real wheat shortage, for the U.S. consumes only 600,000,000 bu. of wheat a year, has 250,000,000 bu. left over from last year. With a winter wheat crop of 442,000,000 bu., in addition to a spring wheat crop of probably half as much, the U.S. will not starve. But how farmers will make out is another matter. They would have so little wheat to sell that, in spite of a high price, they would lose severely. Moreover the drought had dried up pastures and ruined the hay crop.

God's crop reduction may cost the U.S. far more for relief than man's crop reduction cost in processing taxes. The Cabinet devoted an entire session to considering the problem. Relief administrator Harry L. Hopkins promised $450,000 cash to Wisconsin, North Dakota, South Dakota. The Government also promised to buy a "substantial number" of cattle in drought areas, to ask railroads to reduce freight charges on cattle going out and feed coming into desolated states.

Finally soft drizzles began throughout the Midwest, enough to lay the dust. But soaking rains were needed to save what was left of the crops, and soaking rains had not yet come.

Time 23 (May 21, 1934):16

*   *   *

Dust Changes America
Margaret Bourke-White

Vitamin K they call it—the dust which sifts under the door sills, and stings in the eyes, and seasons every spoonful of food. The dust storms have distinct personalities, rising in formation like rolling clouds, creeping silently like formless fog, approaching violently like a tornado. Where had it come from? It provides topics of endless speculation. Red, it is the topsoil from Oklahoma; brown, it is the fertile earth of western Kansas; the good grazing land of Texas and New Mexico sweeps by as a murky yellow haze. Or, tracing it locally, "My uncle will be along pretty soon," they say; "I just saw his farm go by."

The town dwellers stack their linen in trunks, stuff wet cloths along the window sills, estimate the tons of sand in the darkened air above them, paste cloth masks on their faces with adhesive tape, and try to joke about Vitamin K. But on the farms and ranches there is an attitude of despair.

By coincidence I was in the same parts of the country where last year I photographed the drought. As short a time as eight months ago there was an attitude of false optimism. "Things will get better," the farmers would say. "We're not as hard hit as other states. The government will help out. This can't go on." But this year there is an atmosphere of utter hopelessness. Nothing to do. No use digging out your chicken coops and pigpens after the last "duster" because the next one will be coming along soon. No use trying to keep the house clean. No use fighting off that foreclosure any longer. No use even hoping to give your cattle anything to chew on when their food crops have liter-ally been blown out of the ground.

It was my job to avoid dust storms, since I was commissioned by an airplane company to take photographs of its course from the air, but frequently the dust storms caught up with us, and as we were grounded anyway, I started to photograph them. Thus I saw five dust-storm states from the air and from the ground.

In the last several years there have been droughts and sand storms and dusters, but they have been localized, and always one state could borrow from another. But this year the scourge assumes tremendous proportions. Dust storms are bringing distress and death to 300,000 square miles; they are blowing over all of Kansas, all of Nebraska and Wyoming, strips of the Dakotas, and half of Colorado, sections of Iowa and Missouri, the greater part of Oklahoma, and the northern pan-handle of Texas, extending into the eastern parts of New Mexico.

Last year I saw farmers harvesting the Russian thistle. Never before had they thought of feeding thistle to cattle. But this prickly fodder became precious for food. This year even the Russian thistles are dying out, and the still humbler soap weed becomes as vital to the farmer as the fields of golden grain he tended in the past. Last year's thistle-fed cattle dwindled to skin and bone. This year's herds on their diet of soap weed develop roughened hides, ugly growths around the mouth, and lusterless eyes.

Years of the farmers' and ranchers' lives have gone into the build-ing up of their herds. Their herds were like their families to them. When AAA officials spotted cows and steers for shooting during the cattle-killing days of last summer, the farmers felt as though their own children were facing the bullets. Kansas, a Republican state, has no love for the AAA. This year winds whistled over land made barren by the drought and the crop-conservation program. When [Secretary of Agriculture Henry] Wallace removed the ban on the planting of spring wheat he was greeted by cheers. But the wheat has been blown completely out of the ground. Nothing is left but soapweed, or the expensive cotton-seed cake, and after that—bankruptcy.

The storm comes up in a terrifying way. Yellow clouds roll. The wind blows such a gale that it is all my helper can do to hold my camera to the ground. The sand whips into my lens. I repeatedly wipe it away, trying to snatch an exposure before it becomes completely coated again. The light becomes yellower, the wind colder. Soon there is no photographic light, and we hurry for shelter to the nearest farmhouse.

Three men and a woman are seated around a dustcaked lamp, on their faces are grotesque masks of wet cloth. The children have been put to bed with towels tucked over their heads. My host greets us: "It takes grit to live in this country." They are telling stories: A bachelor harnessed the sandblast which ripped through the keyhole by holding his pots and pans in it until they were spick and span. A pilot flying over Amarillo got caught in a sand storm. His motor clogged; he took to his parachute. It took him six hours to shovel his way back to earth. And when a man from the next county was struck by a drop of water, he fainted, and it took two buckets of sand to revive him.

The migrations of the farmer have begun. In many of the worst-hit counties 80 percent of the families are on relief. In the open farm country one crop failure follows another. After perhaps three successive crop failures the farmer can't stand it any longer. He moves in with relatives and hopes for a job in Arizona or Illinois or some neighboring state where he knows he is not needed. Perhaps he gets a job as a cotton picker, and off he goes with his family, to be turned adrift again after a brief working period.

We passed them on the road, all their household goods piled on wagons, one lucky family on a truck. Lucky, because they had been able to keep their truck when the mortgage was foreclosed. All they owned in the world was packed on it; the children sat on a pile of bureaus topped with mattresses, and the sides of the truck were strapped up with bed springs. The entire family looked like a Ku Klux Klan meeting, their faces done up in masks to protect them from the whirling sand.

Near Hays, Kansas, a little boy started home from school and never arrived there. The neighbors looked for him till ten at night, and all next day a band of two hundred people searched. At twilight they found him, only a quarter of a mile from home, his body nearly covered with silt. He had strangled to death. The man who got lost in his own ten-acre truck garden and wandered around choking and stifling for eight hours before he found his house considered himself lucky to escape with his life. The police and sheriffs are kept constantly busy with calls from anxious parents whose children are lost, and the toll is mounting of people who become marooned and die in the storms.

But the real tragedy is the plight of the cattle. In a rising sand storm cattle quickly become blinded. They run around in circles until they fall and breath so much dust that they die. Autopsies show their lungs caked with dust and mud. Farmers dread the birth of calves during a storm. The newborn animals will die within twenty-four hours.

And this same dust that coats the lungs and threatens death to cattle and men alike, that ruins the stock of the storekeeper lying unsold on his shelves, that creeps into the gear shifts of automobiles, that sifts through the refrigerator into the butter, that makes housekeeping, and gradually life itself, unbearable, this swirling drifting dust is changing the agricultural map of the United States. It piles ever higher on the floors and beds of a steadily increasing number of deserted farmhouses. A half-buried plowshare, a wheat binder ruffled over with sand, the skeleton of a horse near a dirt-filled water hole are stark evidence of the meager life, the wasted savings, the year of toil that the farmer is leaving behind him.

The Nation 140 (May 22, 1935):597–598

* * *

LETTERS FROM THE DUST BOWL
Caroline A. Henderson

For twenty-eight years Caroline A. Henderson and her husband have been farming in Oklahoma. For the past five years her household has been one of many that have fought as best they might the devastating effects, first of the unprecedented drought, and then of the resulting dust storms. Her letters, written to a friend in Maryland, open a vivid and pathetic chapter of American agriculture.

Eva, Oklahoma

June 30, 1935

MY DEAR EVELYN: —

Your continued interest in our effort to "tie a knot in the end of the rope and hang on" is most stimulating. Our recent transition from rain-soaked eastern Kansas with its green pastures, luxuriant foliage, abundance of flowers, and promise of a generous harvest, to the dust-covered desolation of No Man's Land was a difficult change to crowd into one short day's travel. Eleanor has laid aside the medical books for a time. Wearing our shade hats, with handkerchiefs tied over our faces and vaseline in our nostrils, we have been trying to rescue our home from the accumulations of wind-blown dust which penetrates wherever air can go. It is an almost hopeless task, for there is rarely a day when at some time the dust clouds do not roll over. "Visibility" approaches zero and everything is covered again with a silt-like deposit which may vary in depth from a film to actual ripples on the kitchen floor. I keep oiled cloths on the window sills and between the upper and lower sashes. They help just a little to retard or collect the dust. Some seal the windows with the gummed-paper strips used in wrapping parcels, but no method is fully effective. We buy what appears to be red cedar sawdust with oil added to use in sweeping our floors, and do our best to avoid inhaling the irritating dust.

In telling you of these conditions I realize that I expose myself to charges of disloyalty to this western region. A good Kansas friend suggests that we should imitate the Californian attitude toward earthquakes and keep to ourselves what we know about dust storms. Since the very limited rains of May in this section gave some slight ground for renewed hope, optimism has been the approved policy. Printed articles or statements by journalists, railroad officials, and secretaries of small-town Chambers of Commerce have heralded too enthusiastically the return of prosperity to the drouth region. And in our part of the country that is the one durable basis for any prosperity whatever. There is nothing else to build upon. But you wished to know the truth, so I am telling you the actual situation, though I freely admit that the facts are themselves often contradictory and confusing.

Early in May, with no more grass or even weeds on our 640 acres than on your kitchen floor, and even the scanty remnants of dried grasses from last year cut off and blown away, we decided, like most of our neighbors, to ship our cattle to grass in the central part of the state. We sent 27 head, retaining here the heifers coming fresh this spring. The shipping charge on our part of the carload was $46. Pasture costs us $7.00 for a cow and calf for the season and $5.00 for a yearling. Whether this venture brings profit or loss depends on whether the cattle make satisfactory gains during the summer and whether prices remain reasonable or fall back to the level that most people would desire. We farmers here in the United States might as well recognize that we are a minority group, and that the prevailing interest of the nation as a whole is no longer agricultural. Hay for the horses and the heifers remaining here cost us $23 per ton, brought by truck from eastern Oklahoma.

The day after we shipped the cattle, the long drought was temporarily broken by the first effective moisture in many months—about one and one-quarter inches in two or three gentle rains. All hope of a wheat crop had been abandoned by March or April.

Contrary to many published reports, a good many people had left this country either temporarily or permanently before any rains came. And they were not merely "drifters," as is frequently alleged. In May a friend in the southwestern county of Kansas voluntarily sent me a list of the people who had already left their immediate neighborhood or were packed up and ready to go. The list included 109 persons in 26 families, substantial people, most of whom had been in that locality over ten years, and some as long as forty years. In these families there had been two deaths from dust pneumonia. Others in the neighborhood were ill at that time. Fewer actual residents have left our neighborhood, but on a sixty-mile trip yesterday to procure tractor repairs we saw many pitiful reminders of broken hopes and apparently wasted effort. Little abandoned homes where people had drilled deep wells for the precious water, had set trees and vines, built reservoirs, and fenced in gardens—with everything now walled in or half buried by banks of drifted soil—told a painful story of loss and disappointment. I grieved especially over one lonely plum thicket buried to the tips of the twigs, and a garden with a fence closely built of boards for wind protection, now enclosing only a hillock of dust covered with the blue-flowered bull nettles which no winds or sands discourage.

It might give you some notion of our great "open spaces" if I tell you that on the sixty-mile trip, going by a state road over which our mail comes from the railroad, and coming back by a Federal highway, we encountered only one car, and no other vehicles of any sort. And this was on Saturday, the farmers' marketing day!

The coming of the long-desired rain gave impetus to the Federal projects for erosion control. Plans were quickly made, submitted to groups of farmers in district gatherings, and put into operation without delay.

The proposition was that, in order to encourage the immediate listing of abandoned wheat ground and other acreage so as to cut down wind erosion, the Federal Government would contribute ten cents per acre toward the expense of fuel and oil for tractors or feed for horses, if the farmers would agree to list not less than one fourth of the acreage on contour lines. Surveys were made promptly for all farmers signing contracts for either contour listing or terracing. The latest report states that within the few weeks since the program was begun in our county, 299,986 acres have been ploughed or listed on these contour lines—that is, according to the lay of the land instead of on straight lines with right-angled turns as has been the usual custom.

The plan has been proposed and carried through here as a matter of public policy for the welfare of all without reproach or humiliation to anyone. It should be remembered that 1935 is the fourth successive year of drought and crop failure through a great part of the high plains region, and the hopelessly low prices for the crop of 1931 gave no chance to build up reserves for future needs. If the severe critics of all who in any way join in government plans for the saving of homes and the restoration of farms to a productive basis could only understand how vital a human problem is here considered, possibly their censures might be less bitter and scornful.

At any rate the contour listing has been done over extensive areas. If rains come to carry forward the feed crops now just struggling up in the furrows, the value of the work can be appraised. The primary intention of the plan for contour listing is to distribute rainfall evenly over the fields and prevent its running off to one end of the field or down the road to some creek or drainage basin. It is hoped that the plan will indirectly tend to lessen wind erosion by promoting the growth of feed crops, restoration of humus to denuded surfaces, and some protection through standing stubbles and the natural coverage of weeds and unavoidable wastes. One great contributing cause of the terrible dust storms of the last two years has been the pitiful bareness of the fields resulting from the long drought.

I am not wise enough to forecast the result. We have had two most welcome rains in June—three quarters of an inch and one-half inch. Normally these should have been of the utmost benefit, though they by no means guarantee an abundant feed crop from our now sprouting seeds as many editorial writers have decreed and they do nothing toward restoring subsoil moisture. Actually the helpful effects of the rains have been for us and for other people largely destroyed by the drifting soil from abandoned, unworked lands around us. It fills the air and our eyes and noses and throats and, worst of all, our furrows, where tender shoots are coming to the surface only to be buried by the smothering silt from the fields of rugged individualists who persist in their right to do nothing.

A fairly promising piece of barley has been destroyed for us by the merciless drift from the same field whose sands have practically buried the little mulberry hedge which has long sheltered our buildings from the northwest winds. Large spaces in our pastures are entirely bare in spite of the rains. Most of the green color, where there is any grazing, is due to the pestilent Russian thistles rather than a grass. Our little locust grove which we cherished for so many years has become a small pile of fence posts. With trees and vines and flowers all around you, you can't imagine how I miss that little green shaded spot in the midst of the desert glare.

Naturally you will wonder why we stay where conditions are so extremely disheartening. Why not pick up and leave as so many others have done? It is a fair question but a hard one to answer.

Recently I talked with a young university graduate of very superior attainments. He took the ground that in such a case sentiment could and should be disregarded. He may be right. Yet I cannot act or feel or think as if the experiences of our twenty-seven years of life together had never been. And they are all bound up with the little corner to which we have given our continued and united efforts. To leave voluntarily—to break all these closely knit ties for the sake of a possibly greater comfort elsewhere—seems like defaulting on our task. We may have to leave. We can't hold out indefinitely without some return from the land, some source of income, however small. But I think I can never go willingly or without pain that as yet seems unendurable.

There are also practical considerations that serve to hold us here, for the present. Our soil is excellent. We need only a little rain—less than in most places—to make it productive. No one who remembers the wheat crops of 1926, 1929, 1931, can possibly regard this as permanently submarginal land. The newer methods of farming suggest possibilities of better control of moisture in the future. Our entire equipment is adapted to the type of farming suitable for this country and would have to be replaced at great expense with the tools needed in some other locality. We have spent so much in trying to keep our land from blowing away that it looks foolish to walk off and leave it, when somewhat more favorable conditions seem now to "cast their shadows before." I scarcely need to tell you that there is no use in thinking of either renting or selling farm property here at present. It is just a place to stand on—if we can keep the taxes paid—and work and hope for a better day. We could realize nothing whatever from all our years of struggle with which to make a fresh start.

We long for the garden and little chickens, the trees and birds and wild flowers of the years gone by. Perhaps if we do our part these good things may return some day, for others if not for ourselves.

Will joins me in earnest hopes for your recovery. The dust has been particularly aggravating to his bronchial trouble, but he keeps working on. A great reddish-brown dust cloud is rising now from the southeast, so we must get out and do our night work before it arrives. Our thoughts go with you.

August 11, 1935

MY DEAR EVELYN: —

On this blistering Sunday afternoon, I am, like Alexander Selkirk,

Monarch of all I survey;
My right there is none to dispute.

There is no one within a mile and a half, and all day I've seen just one person pass by in an old stripped-down Ford.

Will and Eleanor went early this morning with a family of neighbors to visit the dinosaur pit in the next county [Cimarron County] to the westward—about seventy miles from here—where the State University is engaged in excavating the bones of some of these ancient monsters, reminded of a time when there was plenty of water even in the Panhandle.

It seemed impossible for us all to leave home at once, so I stayed here to care for a new Shorthorn brother, to keep the chickens' pails filled with fresh water, to turn the cattle and horses in to water at noon, and to keep them from straying to the extremely poisonous drought-stricken cane. We spent the better part of a night during the week trying to save two of the best young cows from the effects of the prussic acid which develops in the stunted sorghum. We thought they would die, and I am not sure yet whether they recovered because of the liberal doses of melted lard and molasses or whether the poison was not quite strong enough to be fatal. It produces a paralysis of the respiratory system, and when death occurs, as it frequently does, it is due to suffocation from lack of oxygen.

Ever since your letter came, I have been thinking how different are the causes of our personal difficulties. It is hard for us prodigals in this far country, in our scarcity of all things, not to feel envious of the Del Mar Va pigs luxuriating in potatoes, peaches (and cream?), and the delicious Youngerberries. But, as I started to say, our own problems are of a quite different sort. We cannot complain of laziness on the part of our citizens. Oklahoma is one of the first states to get away from direct relief. Official reports of the administrators here emphasize the eagerness with which people accept any sort of work to help themselves and to make unnecessary the acceptance of public aid. In our county the FERA [Federal Emergency Relief Administration] force is being cut down. Three case workers and two from the office force have been dismissed during the past week.

This progress toward more nearly normal conditions of employment occurs in the face of the most critical farm situation that we have ever encountered. For over a month we have had no rain, and the two light local showers early in July had only a slight and temporary effect. All hope of an adequate forage crop has now followed into oblivion the earlier hopes of wheat and maize production. We have no native or cultivated hay crops. The cattle stay alive thus far on weeds, but the pastures are destitute of grass. Many think it can never be restored. The heat is intense and the drying winds are practically continuous, with a real "duster" occurring every few days to keep us humble. After the government erosion control project was carried through there was, for a time, a partial cessation of the dust blowing. But as the freshly upturned earth is pulverizing under the influence of continued heat and wind and entire lack of moisture, it too is ready to blow. A recently established Oklahoma law permits the County Commissioners to require the working of land that is being allowed to blow to the detriment of other farms stopped, and I note that one such order has recently been issued in our county.

You asked about the soil erosion control program and what could be done with an allowance of ten cents per acre. That amount just about covers actual expenses of fuel and oil for listing with a large tractor. Possibly it leaves a slight margin if listing is done with a lighter outfit. In no case was any allowance made for a man's labor or the use of his farming equipment. The plan was proposed to encourage widespread and practically simultaneous working of the blowing fields, with a reasonable proportion on contour lines. Undoubtedly it has been of great benefit, and had rains followed, as everyone hoped, we should feel that we were approaching the turn in the long road. As a matter of fact, the complete absence of rain has given us no chance to test the effectiveness of the contour listing. A few people signed up for terracing as a more permanent method of conserving and distributing the longed-for moisture—if it ever comes! Will has been working early and late with one of the county terracing machines, laying up ridges on contour lines for every foot of fall. He hopes to be ready tomorrow to turn the machine over to a neighbor who will also make the experiment. Later on he would like to run the terrace lines across the pasture lands, but the future for us is most uncertain.

Everything now depends on whether a definite change of moisture conditions occurs in time for people to sow wheat for 1936. The "suitcase farmers"—that is, insurance agents, preachers, real-estate men, and so forth, from cities near or far—have bet thousands of dollars upon rain, or, in other words, have hired the preparation of large areas of land all around us which no longer represent the idea of homes at all, but just parts of a potential factory for the low-cost production of wheat—if it rains.

A short time ago a big tractor, working for one of these absentee farmers across the road from our home, accidentally hooked on to the cornerstone of the original survey and dragged it off up the road. All these many years that stone has marked the corner of our homestead. I have walked past it hundreds of times as I have taken the cows to their pasture or brought them home again. Always it has suggested the beauty of the untouched prairie as it was when the surveyors set the stone, the luxuriant thick turf of native grasses—grama grass, buffalo, and curly mesquite—the pincushion cactuses, straw-color and rose, the other wild flowers which in their season fulfilled the thought of Shakespeare:

The summer's flower is to the summer sweet,
Though to itself is only live and die.

The cornerstone has also suggested the preparation for human occupation—the little homes that were so hopefully established here, of which so very few remain. After twenty-nine years, eight places in our township, out of the possible 136 (excluding the two school sections), are still occupied by those who made the original homestead entry. And now the stone is gone and the manner of its removal seemed almost symbolic of the changes that appear inevitable.

We can't see why your wheat prices should be so hopelessly low. You may judge now a little of how we felt in 1931, with wheat at less than "two bits" per bushel! The price here has recently been about a dollar a bushel, several cents above the Kansas City price. I suppose the idea is to discourage shipment, as there is not enough wheat in this area now to provide for fall sowing—if it rains—and seed wheat must be shipped in.

One morning at the store, being in a reckless mood, I invested a dime in five small tomatoes and wished you might be getting something like that price for your surplus. Potatoes cost us around thirty cents a peck. I hope the protest of the Maryland growers has been successful in giving them some return for their work. Peaches are priced at four pounds for a quarter, but are not for us. So count your mercies, lady. It may surprise you to see how numerous they are.

The last sack of flour cost $1.69, and twelve-ounce loaves of good bread are still to be had for a nickel, considerably less than the price we paid during the dear old days of reputed prosperity—before processing taxes were a subject for political debate and court consideration. We feel rather proud that the proprietor of the Elkhart flour mill which we have patronized for many years has withdrawn from the group of Kansas millers suing the government for recovery of the processing tax. He explained his position by stating that, as the benefits derived from these taxes had been an actual lifesaver for farming and general business interests in this section, he would not seek to embarrass the government in its attempt to collect the tax. His independent action in refusing to join in the raid seems worth mentioning in these days when individualism is supposed to be dead.

It's time to do the evening work, put the guinea pig to bed, and begin to watch for the return of our explorers. I do hope weather conditions are favoring the growth of your crops.

January 28, 1936

DEAR EVELYN: —

As I have said before, our own problems seem of slight moment as compared with yours. Yet more than ever of late "the day's journey" has indeed seemed to "fill the whole long day." As yet there are no decisive changes, no clear light on our way. Late in the summer, before Eleanor returned to her work in the medical school, she drove the tractor for her father, and with the help of the old header they worried down the scattering, scanty crop of sorghum cane and Sudan grass which had made all the growth it could through the hot, dry summer. That there was anything at all to harvest we attribute to the new planting methods encouraged by the Soil Erosion Control Service, of listing on contour lines and laying up terraces to check the run-off in whatever rains might come. A shower the night they finished cutting and another about ten days later, conserved in the same way, gave us most fortunately a second cutting over the same fields, and a few loads of maize fodder from spots here and there on another part of the farm. These crops of roughage have little or no market value, but are indispensable if one plans to winter any cattle. The old, nutritious native grasses which used to provide winter pasturage are forever gone. Killing frosts happily came later than usual. In October, I drove the tractor myself and we two cut and hauled and put into the barn loft (including the earlier cutting) some twenty tons of fodder from two hundred acres, expensive feed when regarded as the entire outcome of a year's work and investment, yet essential to our attempt at carrying on.

As you know, however, wisely or otherwisely, this region has permitted wheat growing to become its main concern. The wheat situation around us is so varied and precarious as to be most difficult of appraisal. Our own acreage is fairly typical of the general condition. We have a little wheat that came up in September, made a fair start, and for a time furnished pasturage for the small calves. A part of it was early smothered out by the drift from near-by fields. Part of it would yet respond to abundant moisture if that were to come. Much of the early-sown wheat did not come up. Some of the seed sprouted and died before reaching the surface. Other portions remained dry until sprouted by a light rain in December. Most of that still lies dormant waiting for warmth to promote its growth. Large areas were drilled after the December rain, with varying results as to germination.

After the four- to-six-inch snow of early January, the editor of our county paper was asked by the United Press for a candid report of actual conditions. His estimate allowed the county as a whole a 25 per cent chance; not, if I understood him, a fair chance for a 25 per cent crop, but about one chance in four for anything at all. His statement showed that fall and winter precipitation so far had been a trifle over half the normal amount for that time of year. And you must try to remember that a failure this year would mean five in succession for a large part of the high plains region. So our great problem here is production, after all. You can readily see that the conditions I have so hastily outlined promise no protection against the ravages of dust storms if the spring winds rage as in previous years.

On the whole it is not surprising that here and there some bitterness should have been felt and expressed, perhaps immoderately, over the recent AAA decision in the Supreme Court. People here, businessmen as well as the farmers themselves, realize that the benefit payments under the AAA and the wage payments from Federal work projects are all that have saved a large territory here from abandonment. A December statement by the Soil Conservation Service reports an area in five states, including part or all of sixty-eight counties and 87,900 square miles of territory, as in need of active measures for protection and control of the dust storm menace. Mr. Bennett, director of the Service, regards this as the greatest "physical problem facing the country to-day." I was astonished to find by a little primary arithmetic that the area involved is equal to that of all the New England states, with New Jersey and Maryland and about half of Delaware added for good measure.

The desolation of the countryside would admittedly have meant the ruin of the small towns, entirely dependent as they are upon country patronage. It will also mean—if it must ever be abandoned through utter exhaustion of resources and sheer inability to hang on any longer—a creeping eastward into more settled and productive territory of the danger and losses originating in the arid wastelands. It is a problem now that no merely individual action can handle successfully.

But to return briefly to the Supreme Court decision. It has naturally been the cause of much regrettable confusion. It would probably have caused even more disturbance had there not been a background of hope that something may yet be done to compensate for the disappointments necessarily involved.

Farmers are not asking for special favors. They ask only an even chance as compared with other workers. But people don't understand.

Perhaps the many books on pioneer life with the usual successful and happy outcome have helped to give a wrong impression and perpetuate the idea that country people live on wild game and fish and fruits and in general on the free bounty of heaven. Many people have no idea of the cash expense of operating a farm today, or the work and planning required to keep the wheels going round, to say nothing of a decent living or suitable education for the children. This year we are keeping a separate account of expenses for car, truck, and tractor, all of which are old and frequently in need of repair. I fear we shall be horrified and discouraged by the close of the year. Not that I should willingly return to the long, slow trips of fifteen miles to town in a jolting wagon. Not that I want to take it out of the flesh and blood of horses in the hot heavy work of seed time and harvest—if they come again. But we can't combine the modern methods of work with the income of our early pioneering, when $200 used to cover all of a year's expense.

I think I told you of shipping our cattle to pasture. It proved to be a disastrous mistake. To keep in tune, I suppose we should blame Secretary Wallace or the broad-shouldered Mr. Tugwell, who likewise had nothing to do with it. Really the source of trouble was our own erroneous impression that grass is grass, and that our cattle would gain if they could have ample pasturage. Evidently other factors of acclimatization must be considered. Our experience was duplicated in that of many of our neighbors, most of whom, on finding their cattle in far worse condition in the fall than in the spring, decided to sell for whatever their stock would bring. Perhaps they were wise to do so. We shipped ours back, availing ourselves of the drought rates for such shipments. In the spring we had paid 85 per cent of the regular rate. In the fall, to encourage reshipment and the restocking of the country if possible, the government rate was 15 per cent of the regular charge.

I was quite alone here for a week while Will went after our little bunch. He had to unload them late at night ten miles from home.

That was November first, and most of our efforts and resources ever since have been devoted to trying to bring our cattle back to a normal condition. They are gaining slowly, but our homegrown feed is disappearing rapidly, and the grain feed of threshed maize which we must purchase, while about right in price for the seller at $1.10 per hundred, is piling up expenses. We have sold one mixed bunch of older cows and summer calves. That will help a little toward caring for the others, but there couldn't be much direct gain, as you will agree, in selling eleven head for $225. Still this is better than we could have done a year or two ago, when cattle were practically without value. In general, there has been an improvement in farm prices, both absolutely and relatively, which has given us courage to keep on working, and has kept alive our hope for some definite change in weather conditions that may once more make our acres fruitful and restore to us some sense of accomplishment.

At present this great southwestern plains region, most of which has been perseveringly tilled during the fall and winter so as to cut down the loss by wind erosion even if the wheat proves a disappointment, seems to be lying asleep like the princess in the fairy tale. Perhaps you can share with us the painful longing that soon the enchantment may be broken, that the deliverer may come with the soft footfalls of gentle rain and waken our homeland once more into gracious, generous life.

Perhaps it is a sin to parody anything as beautiful as Ulysses. Yet as we gay, lonely old people sit here by the fire tonight, planning for the year's work, my thoughts seem bound to fall into that pattern.

> *It may be that the dust will choke us down;*
> *It may be we shall wake some happy morn*
> *And look again on fields of waving grain.*
> *So good night, dear friend, and a happier tomorrow.*

March 8, 1936

DEAR EVELYN: —

Since I wrote to you, we have had several bad days of wind and dust. On the worst one recently, old sheets stretched over door and window openings, and sprayed with kerosene, quickly became black and helped a little to keep down the irritating dust in our living rooms. Nothing that you see or hear or read will be likely to exaggerate the physical discomfort or material losses due to these storms. Less emphasis is usually given to the mental effect, the confusion of mind resulting from the overthrow of all plans for improvement or normal farm work, and the difficulty of making other plans, even in a tentative way. To give just one specific example: the paint has been literally scoured from our buildings by the storms of this and previous years; we should by all means try to "save the surface"; but who knows when we might safely undertake such a project? The pleasantest morning may be a prelude to an afternoon when the "dust devils" all unite in one hideous onslaught. The combination of fresh paint with a real dust storm is not pleasing to contemplate.

The prospects for a wheat crop in 1936 still remain extremely doubtful. There has been no moisture of any kind since the light snow of early January. On a seventy-mile drive yesterday to arrange for hatchery chicks and to sell our week's cream and eggs, we saw more wheat that would still respond to immediate rainfall than I, with my stay-at-home habits, had expected to see. A few fields were refreshingly green and beautiful to look upon. There seems no doubt that improved methods of tillage and protection are already yielding some results in reducing wind erosion. But rain must come soon to encourage growth even on the best fields if there is to be any wheat harvest. Interspersed with the more hopeful areas are other tracts apparently abandoned to their fate. A field dotted thickly with shoulder-high hummocks of sand and soil bound together by the inevitable Russian thistles presents little encouragement to the most ardent conservationist. My own verdict in regard to plans for the reclaiming of such land would be, "Too late." Yet such fields are a menace to all the cultivated land or pasture ground around them and present a most difficult problem.

The two extremes I have just suggested—that is, the slight hope even yet for some production on carefully tilled fields, and the practically hopeless conditions on abandoned land—are indicative of the two conflicting tendencies now evident through an extensive section of the high plains. On the one hand we note a disposition to recognize a mistake, to turn aside from the undertaking with the least possible loss and direct one's time and energy to some new purpose. On the other hand we observe that many seem determined to use even the hard experiences of the past, their own mistakes and other people's, as warning signals, pointing the way to changes of method and more persistent and effective effort right where they stand.

The first attitude may be illustrated by an incident of the past week, the attempt of former neighbors to sell the pipe from the well on their now deserted homestead. This may not seem significant to you. But to old-timers in this deep-water country, so nearly destitute of flowing streams, the virtual destruction of a well of our excellent, life-nourishing water comes close to being the unpardonable sin against future generations.

The same disintegrating tendency is shown in a larger and more alarming way by the extent to which land once owned and occupied by farm families is now passing into ownership of banks, mortgage companies, assurance societies, and investment partnerships or corporations. The legal notices published in our county paper for the past week include two notices of foreclosure proceedings and nine notices of sheriff's sales to satisfy judgments previously rendered. These eleven legal actions involve the ownership of 3,520 acres of land, the equivalent of twenty-two quarter sections, the original homestead allotment in this territory. In only two cases apparently had the loan been made from one person to another. Four life insurance companies, one investment company, and one joint-stock land bank are included among the plaintiffs.

These forced sales take place just outside of the window of the assessor's office, and we were told that they have now become merely a matter of routine. No one tries to redeem the property in question;

no one even makes a bid on it; in fact, no one appears but the sheriff and the lawyer representing the plaintiff.

I am not questioning the legal right of these companies to take over the title of the farms for their own security or that of the people whose money they have invested. In a sense their action in pressing their claims may hold some encouragement for the rest of us, since it suggests that they look in time for a return of value to the acres which at present no one seeks to rescue. In addition to the large amount of land now owned by these corporate interests, very many farms belong to nonresident individuals. The "quarters" north and south of our own place are so held, while the one on the west has recently been taken over by an investment company. Unquestionably this remote control stands in the way of constructive efforts toward recovery.

Yet there are numerous evidences of the persevering restoration of which I have written. The big road maintainers keep the highways in excellent condition. New license tags are appearing on cars and trucks. Churches, schools, and basketball tournaments continue much as usual. One village church reported forty people in attendance on one of the darkest and most dangerous of the recent dusty Sundays. The state agricultural college for this section has an increased enrollment this year. More people are managing in some way—we hardly see how—to keep in touch with the world of news and markets, politics and entertainment, through radio service. A local implement agency recently sent out invitations to a tractor entertainment with free moving pictures of factory operation and the like. The five hundred free lunches prepared for the occasion proved insufficient for the assembled crowd. Within a few succeeding days the company took orders for three tractors ranging in price from around $1200 to $1500. Some people must still have faith in the future!

More impressive to me was the Saturday rush of activity at the small produce house where we did our marketing. Cars kept driving up and people coming in with pails or crates or cases of eggs. Cream was delivered in containers of all sorts and sizes, including one heavy aluminum cooker! Eggs were bringing fifteen cents per dozen and cream thirty cents a pound of tested butterfat. No large sums of money were involved. In many cases the payments were pitifully small, but every such sale represents hard work and economy and the struggle to keep going.

At the hatchery they spoke of slow business through the extremely cold weather. The young man in charge also referred to the changes or postponements in people's plans because of their failure to receive the expected payments under the now extinct allotment plan. With spring in the dusty air, however, and renewed hope that the government contracts will later be fulfilled, orders were coming in encouragingly.

We plan ourselves for four hundred baby Leghorns about the middle of April. That will be an increase for us, but is about the safest small investment we can make to yield an all-the-year-round return. We shall have to put quite a bit of work and expense into the brooder house to keep out the dust, and the rain—if it ever comes. But we are happier to keep on trying.

This impressionistic account of conditions here and of our hope for the future would scarcely be complete without some mention of government assistance. We have had only slight contact with the Rehabilitation Service. We know that the man in charge here is taking his work seriously, trying to give definite aid and encouragement to those who have reached the end of their small resources and have lost hope and courage. He stopped here the other morning to see whether we really meant it when we promised the use of our tractor and other equipment to a young man in the neighborhood who is trying to make a new start for himself and wife and small daughter through a rehabilitation loan. In spite of seriously adverse conditions, this agent, who meets many people, spoke of a rather surprising general spirit of optimism. I suppose there is something of the gambler in all of us. We instinctively feel that the longer we travel on a straight road, the nearer we must be coming to a turn. People here can't quite believe yet in a hopeless climatic change which would deprive them permanently of the gracious gift of rain.

To me the most interesting and forward-looking government undertaking in the dust bowl centers about the group of erosion control experiments scattered over a wide area. The Pony Creek project, fifteen miles east of our home, includes all of one congressional township and parts of three others, seventy square miles altogether, or something over 42,000 acres. This is a pretty seriously damaged area, principally devoted to wheat growing, and even now blowing badly. If the methods employed succeed in checking the drift and in restoring productivity, much will have been accomplished, both of intrinsic value and of use as a simulating object lesson. We hope some day to drive over and see how they are progressing.

We talked about this work with the young man who helped us last summer to run our terrace lines. At present they are employing 140 men from WPA [Works Progress Administration] rolls who would otherwise be idle and in need of relief. The work is frankly experimental. It includes such activities as surveying contour lines, laying up terraces, cleaning out fence rows piled high with drifted soil, filling gullies to prevent washing in that longed-for time of heavy rainfall, cutting down dead trees and brush, digging holes for the resetting of trees in favorable locations, testing the adaptability of different types of grass to the difficult task of reseeding wind-blown spaces, and so on. Altogether it is just such work as a provident farmer would like to get done if he had the time and means. It is done without expense to the farmers who agree to cooperate in the plan. Our young friend smiled when I asked about "regimentation." The farmers do promise to maintain for five years, I believe, the terraces built for them and to follow a system of crop rotation. But plans for planting and cultivation are worked out for each place in individual conferences, to suit the farm and the farmer. Don't worry about the stifling of individuality. "It can't be did," as one of our preachers used to say. Of course no one can predict yet the result of these experiments, but they seem to me abundantly worthwhile.

Our personal plans—like those of all the rest—are entirely dependent on whether or not rain comes to save a little of our wheat, to give grass or even weeds for pasturage, to permit the growing of roughage for the winter, and provide some cover on the surface and promote the intertwining of rootlets in the soil to reduce wind damage. Our terraces are in good condition to distribute whatever moisture may come. We hope we have learned a little about protecting the soil which is the basis of our physical life. In the house the poinsettia and

Christmas cactus are blooming a second time and the geraniums blossom in spite of the dust. Eleanor has just sent us budded hyacinth and daffodil bulbs in little moss-filled nests. They will help us to look forward for a time at least.

March 13, 1936

We must try to get this mailed tomorrow. It has been a terrible week, with one day of almost complete obscurity, and others when only a part of the sun's rays struggled through the gloom with a strange bluish luminance. On such days each little wave of the troubled water in the stock tank glitters with a blue phosphorescent light. When I dip out a pail of water to carry to the henhouse, it looks almost as if it were covered with a film of oil. On days like this, when William Vaughn Moody's expression "dust to eat" suggests a literal danger, we can't help questioning whether the traits we would rather think of as courage and perseverance are not actually recklessness and inertia. Who shall say?

Atlantic Monthly 157 (May 1936):540–551

RAINMAKING AND RAINMAKERS

Since the beginning, humans, in their innocent faith or their lim-itless arrogance, have claimed to be able to bring or stop rain or find water under the earth through magic, prayer, machinery, explosions, vapors, or other devices. Many of these old devices were used in the Great Plains in attempts to break the great drought of the 1880s and 1890s. Some reappeared at places of local drought on the Plains there-after or were used to try to bring rains to arid areas. For example, from 1907 to 1913, C. W. Post attempted to force rain from the skies over west Texas by firing off cannons.

Just as the first settlement in the Great Plains brought rainmak-ers, the recent past continues the tradition. In the 1950s some news-papers noted that rain accompanied President Dwight D. Eisenhower when he visited drought-stricken south Texas. In summer 1971 drought in west Texas and in the Florida Everglades brought into view one Indian rainmaker, many rainmakers of the old kind, cloud seeders in airplanes with silver iodide, and prayers from the Texas Legisla-ture. Both Texas and Florida got rain. The cloud seeders claimed it was their work that brought rain to Florida.

The few news stories printed here must stand for the many ac-counts of similar attempts made in the 1930s to entice rain. The short account about President Franklin D. Roosevelt as rainmaker is not entirely free from some doubt that it was merely a happy coincidence that rain followed the president from Devils Lake, North Dakota, to Rochester, Minnesota.

RAIN MACHINES FAIL,
KANSAS TRIES PRAYER

WICHITA, Kan., June 27— Prayer bands have been organized throughout Kansas to end the drought. The Catholic as well as the Protestant churches in Wichita, Kinsley, Dodge City, Garden City, Liberal, and Hutchinson hold prayer services in behalf of rain.

Several salesmen with apparatus for making rain have tried to sell their services, but thirty years ago Kansas invested in rain-making machines which failed and they are skittish of the new apparatus.

New York Times, July 1, 1934

*   *   *

Praying for the rain that machines failed to make. Map by Robert Watrel.

The President's Devils Lake Speech

DEVILS LAKE, N.D., Aug. 7—Following is a stenographic report of the informal remarks of President [Franklin D.] Roosevelt
here after he returned from a fifty-mile automobile tour of the
district:

> I cannot honestly say that my heart is happy today, because I
> have seen with my own eyes some of the things that I have been
> reading and hearing about for a year and more. The reason I came
> here was that I wanted to see something at first hand of a problem
> that has perplexed me and perplexed many other people ever since
> I have been in office.
>
> It is a problem. I would not try to fool you by saying we know
> the solution of it. We don't. I believe in being frank, and what I can
> tell you from the bottom of my heart, truthfully, is this: If it is pos-
> sible for us to solve the problem, we are going to do it. I saw some
> signs along the road that said: "You gave us beer, now give us wa-
> ter."
>
> Well, that beer part was easy.
>
> That was something that could be controlled very definitely by
> human agency. It was a question of what the people of this country
> wanted, and when they made it clear they wanted beer back again
> they got it. But when you come to this water problem through here
> you are up against two things. In the first place you are up against
> the forces of nature, and, secondly, you are up against the fact that
> man in his present stage of development cannot definitely control
> those forces.
>
> I think it was more than a year ago that the delegation of this
> state in the Senate and the House first talked to me about the prob-
> lem of this watershed in northern North Dakota. I have been study-
> ing it ever since.
>
> It is all very well to say "let us have a dam across the Missouri
> River." I would love to do it, but when a great many engineers tell
> me they haven't found a safe place for that dam, there isn't a man or
> woman in the Devils Lake area that would ask me to build a dam
> that might go out and drown many thousands of people.
>
> In other words, I have a responsibility. I cannot build a dam
> unless I have the best engineering assurance that it is not only the
> right thing to do but the safe thing to do. And the result is, my

friends, that today there is more of what you might call government talent—experts from different departments in the government service—fine people with good knowledge and training—and they are getting the views of civilians and state employees and trying to find a solution of this problem.

Soon after I get back to Washington, many of the studies being made this summer by engineering and agricultural officials will be completed. I will give an opportunity to people who don't agree with their conclusions to come and be heard. You know, I believe in action.

On the 4th of March, 1933, we had a parallel. It was not just one section of one state or a few sections in a few states. It was the whole of the United States. The United States was up against it. I asked the people of the United States at that time to have courage and faith. They did. Today, out here, I do not ask you to have courage and faith. You have it.

You have demonstrated that through a good many years. I am asking, however, that you keep up that courage and, especially, keep up the faith.

If it is possible for government to improve conditions in this State, the government will do it. I assure you the interests of these communities are very close to my heart. I am not going to forget the day I have spent with you. We hope that nature is going to open the heavens. When I came out on the platform this morning and saw a rather dark cloud I said to myself, "Maybe it is going to rain." Well, it didn't. All I can say is, I hope to goodness it is going to rain, good and plenty.

My friends, I want to tell you that I am glad I came here. I want to tell you that I am not going to let up until I can give my best service to solving the problems of North Dakota.

New York Times, August 8, 1934

*   *   *

ROOSEVELT, "RAIN-MAKER," IS HAILED IN NORTHWEST

ST. PAUL, Aug. 8—President Roosevelt was receiving the plaudits of Minnesota and North Dakota citizens today as a rain-maker.

While the Chief Executive did not claim this power, a check showed that last night's rainfall in the two states, in some cases the first in a long period, by coincidence, followed the route of the Presidential party.

In North Dakota the rain was described by P. J. Olson, experiment station agronomist, as of the greatest benefit to corn, which he predicted would be revived in all except extreme cases.

Rain follows President Roosevelt's tour in North Dakota. South Dakotans continue to pray for rain. Map by Robert Watrel.

The rain cut a path about 100 miles wide across North Dakota and Minnesota, with the heaviest fall in the cities the Presidential train visited. In each case the showers came about seven hours after the Presidential special had departed. In talks in the drought area the President expressed a hope for early rain.

New York Times, August 9, 1934

*   *   *

South Dakota City Prays

MITCHELL, S.D., July 10—Business halted, merchants bent their heads, and housewives knelt in supplication today as Mitchell's population prayed for rain.

The prayers rose from a drought-seared land to a cloudless sky and a blazing sun that had scorched the area relentlessly for days.

Bells in the city's thirteen church towers tolled the signal to the people, 11,000 in number, to fall to their knees, and nearly all responded. The temperature stood at 104 degrees.

No rain had fallen here for more than a week. For seven days the mercury had risen above 100, and once to 114. Fields were burned brown. Farmers had turned to WPA [Works Progress Administration] labor. Mayor George Frederick then decided to proclaim a day of prayer and issued a proclamation in cooperation with the churches, the joint announcement reading:

"Because of the dire need for rain in our community and in cooperation with the Mayor's proclamation, resting on God's promise 'to heal the land if his people will humble themselves and pray' (II Chronicles, vii, 14), the Christian organizations are sponsoring a day of prayer for rain, Friday, July 10."

The first prayer was at 11 A.M. In mid-afternoon a mass prayer meeting was held in the Presbyterian Church and another was held tonight. Other churches were open all day so members might offer individual prayers.

Mitchell is on the fringe of the most seriously affected drought area of South Dakota, which stretches west, north, and south from here. Some early grain can still be harvested in this region if rain comes immediately.

There was a trace of rain here on June 26, .06 of an inch on June 27, and .02 on July 2, but none since then, and there is a five and a half inch deficiency.

New York Times, July 11, 1936

III

Historians View the Dust Bowl Years

MEN, WOMEN, AND CHILDREN
THE PERSONAL RESPONSE

The personal response by farmers to the Dust Bowl and the farming crisis in the 1930s was influenced by gender. Farm families sought every possible way to survive. Women usually acted individually, seeking innovations in farm management and sales. Farm women cut their budgets and produced more food; they tried raising new plants and animals, particularly poultry; and they took additional jobs, frequently teaching, to supplement the family's income. As Mabel Hickey McManus of Lyman County, South Dakota, found, the Great Depression forced an alteration of traditional female farm roles.

Men tended to band together. Farm activism has a strong institutional tradition, and many male and some female farmers joined existing organizations or formed new ones. Of the latter group, the Farmers' Holiday Association was the most instantaneous, and it provided an institutional umbrella under which farmers with a variety of ideologies could pursue the cause of agrarian survival. In the rush to prevent foreclosures and to push farm prices up, farmers took

Dust storm in Franklin, Nebraska, 26 March 1935. (Courtesy Nebraska State Historical Society.)

precipitous, albeit justifiable, action. As Morris Cope of Plymouth County, Iowa, concluded, this meant participating in blockades, leading marches, organizing groups of farmers to stop foreclosures, and even attacking a judge.

Many Plains residents also turned to religion for explanations of the catastrophe. Women from Alva, Oklahoma, sewed a Job's comforter inscribed with an admonition that the drought was punishment for their sins. Others concluded that dust storms were God's will and so one needed to accept them. Perhaps the recollection of young Ida Mae Norman, from the Oklahoma Panhandle, to Black Sunday was the obvious one for most children and many adults; she thought the world had come to an end and that Armageddon was at hand.

The personal responses of the men, women, and children of the Dust Bowl took a variety of forms, each individual searching to find a compelling explanation for the environmental debacle.

PLAINS WOMEN: RURAL LIFE IN THE 1930S
Dorothy Schwieder and Deborah Fink

During the Great Depression, farm families throughout the nation experienced severe economic difficulties. Since then, historians and other scholars have analyzed and reanalyzed the basic problems of American agriculture and the solutions offered to those problems. Only recently, however, have the scholars begun to take a wide view of rural society during the 1930s and begun to look at the dynamics of the farm family: the roles, influences, and contributions of farm women and the work roles and treatment of farm children.[1]

In keeping with this broadened understanding, we will examine the work roles of plains women during the Great Depression by studying rural society without assuming that agriculture, as represented by crop and livestock production, subsumed the entirety of farm life. Although farm women performed similar tasks regardless of their location within the so-called breadbasket of the central United States, we believe that a close examination of farm women's roles in Nebraska and South Dakota, with particular emphasis on Boone and Lyman counties, will indicate a distinctive plains pattern. Work roles were often the same as those of farm women in other parts of the Middle West, but the results of that work and the difficulties women encountered were strongly influenced by the plains environment, particularly during the Great Depression.[2]

BOONE AND LYMAN COUNTIES

Nebraska and South Dakota each contain areas designated as prairie as well as plains. The eastern one-third of each state provides a natural transition between the prairie to the east and the Great Plains, sharing geographic features with both environments. The features of the prairie disappear by the center of these states, and the environment is the true Great Plains. Except for the Black Hills, Badlands, and Nebraska Sand Hills, western South Dakota and Nebraska are semiarid, flat, and generally lacking trees. In South Dakota, the two environments are demarcated as East River and West River, with the Missouri River serving as the dividing line. Nebraska is similarly divided environmentally but lacks a visible boundary.[3]

Both Boone County, Nebraska, and Lyman County, South Dakota, are technically in the Great Plains, but the two regions differ somewhat in physical and climatic features. Boone County is located in the eastern one-third of Nebraska and is divided by the 98th meridian, commonly accepted as the dividing line between the prairie and the Plains. Roughly one-third of the county lies to the east of that line. The yearly precipitation averages 25.48 inches. Farmers in eastern Boone County, like producers in the prairie region to the east, have mostly concentrated on raising corn, while the western part of the county is hilly range land.[4] Lyman County, some 120 miles further into the Great Plains and along the 100th meridian, can be described as lying within the Great Plains proper. Rainfall averages 18 inches per year. Lyman County's population peaked in 1910 (10,848), reflecting an increase of 312 percent from the previous census report. By 1930, Lyman County's population had decreased considerably to 6,335 residents while Boone County's population had stabilized at 14,738.[5]

The 1930s did not bring the first hint of depression to these counties. While South Dakota and Nebraska farm families did well during World War I, realizing profits from both farming and livestock production, the 1920s brought a drastic deflation of farm prices, which forced many farms and rural banks into insolvency. In Nebraska between 1921 and 1923, one-quarter of the state's farms failed, and by the end of the decade, 650 banks had closed. South Dakotans experienced a similar situation. Only one state bank failed in 1921, but by 1925 the number had risen to more than 175. By the 1930s, farmers in Nebraska and South Dakota were already in the midst of a severe economic dislocation.[6]

FARM WOMEN'S LIVES

By the eve of the Great Depression, farm women in both Boone and Lyman counties had come to terms with a harsh and uneven environment and had established fairly set work routines. Farm women's labor and economic roles were varied, with women not only handling all household tasks but also raising poultry and eggs, which provided considerable income for the family. Women often helped with the milking and almost always handled the processing of the product, including separating the milk and cream and churning butter. Often cream and butter were sold. Mabel Hickey McManus remembered that, as a young girl growing up on a Lyman County, South Dakota, farm, churning was mostly her work. Because her mother, Margaret Hickey, was particular about the working, salting, and final preparation of the butter, Mrs. Hickey did that herself. Mabel McManus described the sale and delivery process:

> Butter for sale was molded in a pound mold, and wrapped in wet sterilized white cloths. Delivery to customers was made early in the morning before the heat of the day and because of this careful process our butter was sold for four or more cents a pound more than other butter. The top price we ever received for butter was twenty cents a pound.

The butter used by the Hickey family "was packed in stone jars with a white cloth on top and light layer of salt on the cloth." The family also made cottage cheese from their milk.[7]

Like most farm women, Margaret Hickey made the clothing for her family. Before her marriage she had been a seamstress, which undoubtedly made the sewing easier. Even with twelve children, however, she made all their coats, pants, shirts, dresses, and even petticoats. Because she could not find patterns available in the local stores, Mrs. Hickey "cut her own, using the measurements of each person." She also knit stockings and mittens for the daughters and stockings for her husband and sons.[8]

In addition to heavy work routines, farm women had to contend with extreme weather conditions. Charles and Clara Hayes arrived in central Lyman County in March 1919. They started building a barn the following fall, but a blizzard struck in late October, before the barn was completed, and killed most of their chickens. Because the roads were impassable, the family sometimes went to church in a bobsled. Weather also made it more difficult for them to receive proper medical service. The county's only physician, Dr. F. M. Newman, lived in the center of the county and frequently traveled by horse and buggy to deliver babies and to treat the sick. Often simply contacting the doctor was difficult.[9]

A major consideration for rural women in both counties was isolation, although the residents of the more populous Boone County did not experience quite the same degree of isolation as did those of Lyman County. In 1930, Lyman County had 3.9 persons per square mile while Boone County had 21.3 persons per square mile. Regardless of population variations, however, farm people in both counties found themselves unable to travel in bad weather. By 1930, a high percentage of farm people in both counties owned automobiles, but neither county had any hard surfaced roads and just over 5 percent of the roads were graveled. Thus the automobiles sat unused for long periods each year. In Lyman County during the winter months, farm families found themselves cut off from the outside for weeks at a time.[10]

THE DEPRESSION COMES

Drought hit South Dakota in the early 1930s and Nebraska a few years later. Both states were particularly hard hit in 1934 and 1936. Between 1930 and 1935, Lyman County received 13 percent less rainfall than normal while Boone County received 16 percent less. In Lyman County, drought-stunted crops were 51 percent of normal and pasture conditions were 57 percent of normal. In Boone County, the percentages were 62 and 58, respectively. Distress can also be measured by the amount of per capita federal relief dispensed in these counties. As Francis Cronin and Howard Beers have pointed out, federal aid is the "end result of all contributing conditions [moisture deficiency, crop failure, pasture damage, and depletion of livestock] expressed in terms of human want." Using the Cronin and

Beers data, Lyman County's per capita federal aid between 1933 and 1936 was $198 while Boone County's share was $84. By 1936, Boone County faced even greater drought than before, with rainfall declining to 12.63 inches. The following year, Boone County pastures and crops were reduced to 5 percent of normal production. In 1938, the local newspaper, *The Albion News*, carried notices of thirty-eight sheriff's sales while dozens of other families voluntarily liquidated their assets.[11]

Along with drought, both South Dakota and Nebraska experienced infestations of grasshoppers in the 1930s. In a few counties in South Dakota, farm people experienced grasshopper epidemics every year from 1930 to 1935. During one of the most extreme infestations, farm wife Ella Boschma, who resided in eastern South Dakota, remembered that grasshoppers consumed everything around the farm. They ate all the garden produce, even eating the cork out of the water jug left in the field. At one point, checking the potato patch, she looked down: "The ground was just weaving. And I said 'what is that?' And it was just, they were just hatching by the millions, little tiny things. And it just made the ground kind of weave."[12]

In Boone County, Nebraska, a woman who married in 1930 and started farming on rented land in 1936 remembered a similar incident. Her five-year-old daughter frequently carried lunch to her father when he worked in the field. The farm wife remembered: "Her [daughter's] doll always went along. One time she left it out in the field and when we found it the next day the hordes of grasshoppers had eaten all of its clothes off."[13]

The drought of the thirties almost halted traditional agriculture production in Lyman County. In 1936, conditions were so bad that the Charles and Clara Hayes family "never pulled out a piece of machinery to harvest anything." Even though rainfall was limited during the spring, summer, and fall, heavy snows continued during the winter. Harry and Edith Mills had to dig tunnels between the house, the barn, and the chicken coop, a backbreaking job. The family burned coal and wood and cowchips, but by early spring the cook stove and heater had to be fed with corn as well.[14]

WOMEN FIGHT BACK

With the advent of the Depression, farm women in both states found themselves with a double burden. Even during somewhat prosperous times, given the heavy responsibilities of domestic and farm chores and the absence of social interaction, farm women found themselves faced with heavy work. By the 1930s, they needed to produce even more and stretch their meager resources even further. Farm women's letters appearing in *Nebraska Farmer* in the early 1930s tell about their lives and describe how their work was bringing their families through the hard spell.[15] The first line of defense against the Depression was increased subsistence production. One woman told of how, when the rain failed, her mother put a barrel of water on runners and dragged it out to water the garden.[16] Women planted large potato patches and made clothing from flour sacks. A woman wrote to *Nebraska Farmer* detailing the following strategy for managing: In addition to grinding their own grains for flour, breakfast cereal, and cornmeal, she had raised 100 pounds of pinto beans; canned 22 quarts of stringbeans, 40 quarts of tomatoes, 200 quarts of cherries, 50 quarts of apples, and 40 quarts of beef and pork; and cured six hams and rendered 70 pounds of lard. By going without tea and coffee and substituting her labor for money, she had cut her grocery bill from $700 in 1929 to $249 in 1932.[17]

Nebraska farm women also wrote *Nebraska Farmer* about the new and creative ways that they earned extra money during the thirties. They reported selling garden plants, baby ducks, salads, canned goods, cottage cheese, and yeast cakes as well as churning butter, raising canaries, and hooking rugs for sale. As before the 1930s, some farm women made approximately $20 a month by providing room and board for a country school teacher. During the extreme deflation of the 1930s, $20 was a substantial supplementary income.[18]

A major response of farm women to the Depression was to produce more food. An important woman's chore was raising large vegetable gardens and even in years of normal precipitation, this constituted considerable work, as women had to rig up means of watering the gardens between rains. During the 1930s, as income from crops and livestock production was curtailed, farm women often thought first of expanding their gardens. Many women, in writing to both *Nebraska Farmer* and *Dakota Farmer*, made it clear that the food raised in their gardens went a long way toward supplying the families' food supply. Raising larger gardens, canning the produce, and relying more on butchered meat meant the difference between survival and failure for many farm families. Even in the midst of great suffering, farm women not only managed to be extremely thrifty, but many also managed to feel considerable satisfaction from this work.

> We do our own butchering, raise as much food as the grasshoppers will allow, make our own soap, can all we can and utilize everything possible to add to our means and fill that gap science calls the stomach. We always bought bread but now I bake and oh, what satisfaction it is to turn flour, lard, salt and yeast into crusty, brown loaves or to magically mix eggs, sugar, flour, etc. into a cake or pie. . . !
>
>   There is so much pleasure for us if we but open our eyes and see it.[19]

During the Depression, Dakota Farmer carried the column "Help One Another" as a regular part of the "Home Page." Week after week, the column carried hints from women readers as to how they had reduced expenditures for their families. Some women wrote that they had stopped buying most household supplies and made them at home. A number of women wrote that rather than using commercial cleanser, they used fine ashes for scouring and cleaning. Many women wrote about making their own soap. Moreover, women sent in recipes for toothpaste, furniture polish, fly paper, fly spray, hand lotion, and stove cleaner.[20]

As these examples show, it was the small enterprises carried on in the margins that provided cash for the household when major crops and livestock enterprises failed. A 1935 article in Nebraska Farmer indicates that at least some people at the time recognized the significance of these activities:

> Sidelines have saved many a trying situation during the last few years. Often it is the wife and mother who finds pleasure in doing

something profitable to help her family. Some women have turned to chicken raising, others to baking, needle work, painting or various other lines of endeavor.[21]

Not only were women working hard to save money but they were also working to make money.

DOLLAR VALUES OF WOMEN'S WORK

While it is impossible to put a precise dollar figure on all work done by farm women, it is possible to establish a general value. In a study done in the mid–1930s, Day Monroe, a home economist with the Department of Agriculture's Bureau of Home Economies, gathered information on living expenses of low, moderate, and high income farm families around the nation. Moderate income families, Monroe found, had a median income of $965. Of the amount, the family paid out 55 percent in cash and provided 45 percent in-kind in the form of housing, fuel, ice, and other products furnished the household by the farm.[22]

Farm women's contributions in the 1930s are further documented by studies in both South Dakota and Nebraska. In 1935, the South Dakota Agricultural Experiment Station conducted a study similar to Monroe's. They discovered that in Jones County, located in central South Dakota just west of Lyman County, the total value of farm living was $1,068.93, 29.5 percent in-kind and 70.5 percent in cash. Jones County farm families valued their food, the area most reflective of farm women's work, at $568.01, with 50.9 percent produced on the farm while 49.1 percent was purchased. A 1936 Nebraska Extension Service study of 356 Nebraska farm women revealed that the farm families consumed an average of $1,227.66 worth of living expenses. That included women's production of $183.00 worth of food and purchase of $206.61 worth of food.[23]

Poultry was a major contribution of farm women to the farm economy. Plains farmers were well aware of the significance of poultry production in relation to other farm enterprises. In the February 1932 issue of Nebraska Farmer, the business and markets editor wrote: "While eggs and poultry have been selling at considerably lower prices than prior to the 1930s, they have held up much better than feed prices, so that the hen in recent months has been affording one of the most profitable methods of disposing of farm grains." The editor added that in December 1931, farm women were selling eggs at 55 percent and chickens at 75 percent of "the average of that month from 1923 to 1928, while grains were only about 40 percent of their average for the corresponding time."[24]

While women in both Boone and Lyman counties probably worked harder at raising chickens during the 1930s than before, federal census data indicate that at least their efforts to produce hens (chickens over either three or four months, depending upon census classification) were less successful than before the 1930s. In the 1930 census, 85 percent of Lyman County farms listed hens. That number had risen to 86 percent by 1940, but the actual number of hens had declined from 85,554 in 1930 to 58,336 in 1940. The dozens of eggs produced had also declined, dropping from 585,831 in 1930 to 296,413 in 1940. Boone County farm women experienced a fairly similar situation. In 1930, 95 percent of the county's farms had hens, while that number decreased to 90 percent in 1940. The number of hens decreased more radically than in Lyman County, dropping from 190,497 to 123,439, but the number of dozens of eggs produced dropped only from 1,017,893 to 708,185.[25] Boone County women apparently were more successful in their hen and egg production, probably because of a greater availability of feed and more local markets.

Some farm women, including farm daughters, took jobs outside the home to bring in badly needed money. One young woman in Boone County related the way her teaching contributed to the family budget:

> During the time I taught . . . I didn't make big wages, but teachers did get paid. . . . I loaned my dad money to buy a tractor to continue farming, bought my brother-in-law a car that he thought he had to have, and then, of course, I had to save enough to go to summer school to renew my certificates, too. . . . On top of that, I saved up enough to furnish my house when I got married. All the furniture and dishes and linens. That much in seven years.[26]

POPULATION DECLINE

The deepening stress of the 1930s is reflected in the restricted number of children born in Lyman and Boone counties as the decade wore on. Women's child care constituted a major contribution to the rural economy, as women had almost complete responsibility for the small children who were the future rural workers. Before they reached the age of five, children made no economic contribution to the household, yet they made continual demands on the resources of their mothers. Even so, children were a source of pleasure and pride and most women desired to have at least some.

Rural women's fertility has tended to be higher than that of urban women, and this continued in Boone and Lyman counties, even though they also showed a declining rate of fertility. The fertility rate in Boone County dropped from 93.1 in 1930 to 90.6 in 1940 (Table 1). Because South Dakota's vital statistics were unreported until 1932 and appear to have been irregularly reported for the remainder of the decade, a comparable computation for Lyman County is impossible. Census reports do, however, provide the number and age of children, and this provides a rough indication of fertility. The percentage of the population under the age of five decreased by 8 percent in Boone County and 16 percent in Lyman County. Even though the women of Lyman County appear to have restricted their fertility to a greater degree than did Boone County women, the fertility rate seems to have remained somewhat higher in Lyman than in Boone County through the Depression years (Table 2).[27]

Other evidence of deepening stress is net out-migration. The population of Lyman County declined by 20 percent and the population of Boone County by 18 percent during the 1930s. When the figures are corrected by including the natural increase as measured in the cumulative excess of births over deaths, the Boone County net out-migration was 29 percent. While a comparable figure cannot be tabulated for Lyman County, its apparently higher rate of natural increase suggests its net out-migration was probably over 30 percent. It was young adults who left Boone County, while there was actually a slight increase in the number of persons over the age of forty-five. Likewise in Lyman County, the heaviest out-migration occurred among those who were between the ages of 10 and 24 in 1930. This selective depopulation intensified the responsibility of those working-age women who remained in the area and continued to serve as principal caretakers for the increasing proportion of dependent children and elderly persons.[28]

CONCLUSION

A brief look at farm women in the prairie state of Iowa helps provide a comparison to life in South Dakota and Nebraska. While plains women faced almost insurmountable difficulties in raising additional poultry and eggs, Iowa farm women were more successful: although their egg production dropped from 188,385,897 in 1930 to 168,204,052 in 1940, that drop was far less severe than in South Dakota and Nebraska. Iowa farm women also had many more opportunities to socialize than did plains women. A higher percentage of Iowa farms (84 percent) had telephones in 1930 than did either Lyman County (41 percent) or Boone County (77 percent), and the number of Iowa farms (67 percent) that retained telephones by 1940 remained higher than in Lyman County (37 percent) or Boone County (37 percent). Iowa also had more miles of hard surfaced and graveled roads during the 1930s, making it possible for farm people there to travel more easily and more often. Finally, out-migration in Iowa was considerably less than in the plains states, indicating less disruption of kinship ties and less emotional distress in dealing with family members leaving the area. The heavier density of population alone meant the Iowa farm women were physically closer to one another, in many cases close enough to walk from one farm to another.[29]

As the Depression dragged on through most of the 1930s, farm women in both South Dakota and Nebraska appeared less optimistic about farm life, and letters to farm journals increasingly indicated that some were losing heart. In 1938 a farm woman wrote to *Nebraska Farmer* of her deep disappointment that her daughter, who had graduated from high school and was working in town, was now preparing to marry a farmer:

They will start farming with a load of debt. When I think of the struggle ahead for her, I actually ache. I didn't plan this kind of life for her, but what can I do? Has some mother had a similar experience?[30]

Still, the majority of letters to *Nebraska Farmer* appeared optimistic. From 1938 to 1940, Blanche Pease, the wife of a tenant farmer in central Nebraska, wrote a series of features called "Daughter of Nebraska," in which she examined farm life. In one of her first features she wrote: "Prairie Haven is a rented house, and ours is a happiness made up of the singing drums of nature, good neighbors and good books." Later she wrote: "Like a mother I may recognize [Nebraska's] shortcomings but her good points overcome them. Nebraska, how your charms enchant me! You are the song that sings within my heart!" South Dakotans expressed much the same sentiments. Frequently they were cast in the following vein: "I think South Dakota is a pretty good place. If you stick with it when its dry, it'll sure stick with you when it's wet." Their letters to Dakota Farmer certainly expressed unhappiness with the Depression, but they continued to be at least cautiously optimistic. They believed the situation would soon get better and their faith in South Dakota's future remained intact.[31]

Almost every action taken by plains women in South Dakota and Nebraska was tempered by the exigencies of their localities. Given their roles of wife, mother, homemaker, and farm producer, they found themselves with the full range of work responsibilities of farm women elsewhere, but the Great Plains environment provided them with far fewer options for dealing with hard times. As settlement on the Plains underwent several major in- and out-migrations, federal officials and agricultural experts began to temper their expectations of what the region might produce and what would be necessary to cope with the environment. Consequently, farming practices changed and people adjusted their crop and livestock operations to fit with the environment. The same changes, modifications, or adjustments did not seem to take place, however, within the female sphere. In fact, in many families, women were expected to increase their output of foodstuffs or of products for sale to compensate for the lack of income from crops and livestock. At the same time, women were responsible for keeping up their family's spirits and determination.

Throughout the 1930s, even though women worked harder to raise larger gardens and more chickens and eggs, the droughts, grasshoppers, and other environmental hazards partially negated their extra work. Working longer, scrimping on purchases, and producing unusual commodities such as canaries helped farm women reduce expenses and raise income, but such adaptations could not completely compensate for the drought, the dust, and the Depression. The decline in birthrate indicates that women were shepherding their time and energy carefully as they struggled to pull their families through the hard times. Given the limitations of climate and terrain, farm women on the Great Plains faced a limit to their ability to endure and survive. The plains environment taught its own lessons and made its own demands on those who lived there. For plains farm women in Nebraska and South Dakota, partial amelioration of hardships and a great deal of toleration became a way of life.

NOTES

1. For rural children see Elizabeth Hampsten, "Child Care on the Homestead Frontier," paper presented at the second National American Farm Women in Historical Perspective Conference, Madison, Wisconsin, October 1986. For the new rural history see Robert Swierenga, "Agricultural and Rural Life: The New Rural History," in James B. Gardner and George Rollie Adams, eds., *Ordinary People and Everyday Life: Perspectives on the New Social History* (Nashville: American Association for State and Local History, 1983).
2. See Walter Webb, *The Great Plains* (Boston: Ginn and Company, 1931) for a complete discussion of the Great Plains environment; see Deborah Fink, *Open Country, Iowa: Rural Women, Tradition, and Change* (Albany: State University of New York Press, 1986) for a full discussion of farm women's lives in northwest Iowa; and see Deborah Fink and Dorothy Schwieder, "Iowa Farm Women in the 1930s: A Reassessment," paper presented at the Women in Agriculture Conference, New Mexico State University, February 1983.
3. See James C. Olson, *History of Nebraska* (Lincoln: University of Nebraska

Press, 1966), and Herbert S. Schell, *History of South Dakota*, 3rd ed., rev. (Lincoln: University of Nebraska Press, 1975) for a full discussion of geographical and climatic conditions, especially chapters 13, 14, 18, and 23 in Olson and chapters 12, 13, and 19 in Schell.

4. Rainfall in Boone County for the 1930s computed from U.S. Department of Agriculture, Weather Bureau 1930-1941, Climatological Data for the United States by Sections, Nebraska Section, Lincoln, Nebraska; and Olson, *History of Nebraska*, pp. 154-155.

5. U.S. Department of Commerce, Bureau of the Census, Sixteenth Census of the United States, 1940; Population (Washington, D.C.: Government Printing Office, 1943) 2: 472; and Schell, *History of South Dakota*, p. 11.

6. Dorothy Weyer Creigh, *Nebraska: A Bicentennial History* (New York: Norton, 1977), p. 185; and Schell, *History of South Dakota*, p. 277.

7. Leona King, ed., *Early Settlers in Lyman County* (Pierre: State Publishing Company, 1974), p. 180.

8. Ibid.

9. Ibid.

10. Population density computed from data in Sixteenth Census of the United States, *1940: Population*, Vol. 2: 472 and 615; U.S. Department of Commerce, Bureau of the Census, *Fifteenth Census of the United States, 1930: Agriculture*, Vol. 2, Part 1: The Northern United States (Washington, D.C.: Government Printing Office, 1932): 1202, 1155; and *Sixteenth Census of the United States, 1940: Agriculture*, Vol. 1, 1st and 2nd series, State Report, Part 2: Statistics for Counties: 493, 611.

11. Francis D. Cronin and Howard W. Beers, *Areas of Intense Drought Distress, 1930-1936* (Washington, D.C.: Works Progress Administration, Division of Social Research, 1937), Series 5, No. 1, pp. 25, 44-45; *Albion News*, 2 September 1937 and 24 February 1938; and Weather Bureau, 1930-1941.

12. Interview with Ella Boschma, Bon Homme County, 21 July 1972, No. 390, South Dakota Oral History Project. The names of the informants and general description of the contents can be found in *The South Dakota Experience: An Oral History Collection Of Its People*, Vols. 1-5. Copies of all interviews are located at the South Dakota State Historical Department, Pierre, and at South Dakota State University, Vermillion. The drought also produced dust storms which not only aggravated erosion and farming problems but also greatly complicated housekeeping chores.

13. Deborah Fink interview, Boone County, Nebraska, 24 February 1987. Following accepted anthropological practice, the names of those interviewed by Fink are not published but are on file with the interviewer.

14. King, ed., *Early Settlers in Lyman County*, pp. 178-245.

15. *Nebraska Farmer*, 17 March 1934, p. 12.

16. Fink interview, Boone County, Nebraska, 26 March 1986.

17. *Nebraska Farmer*, 17 March 1934, p. 12.

18. *Nebraska Farmer*, 30 April 1932, p. 8.

19. *Nebraska Farmer*, 23 July 1932, p. 10; see Deborah Fink, "Sidelines and Moral Capital: Women and Nebraska Farms in the 1930s," paper delivered at the Conference on American Farm Women in Historical Perspective, Madison, Wisconsin, October 1986.

20. *Dakota Farmer*, 14 January 1933, pp. 16–17; 18 March 1933, p. 95; 13 May 1933, p. 153; 16 September 1933, p. 261; 3 March 1934, p. 113; 14 March 1936, pp. 146–147; and 4 December 1937, p. 648.

21. *Nebraska Farmer*, 27 April 1935, p. 6.

22. Day Monroe, "Patterns of Living of Farm Families," *Farmers in a Changing World: The Yearbook of Agriculture, 1940* (Washington, D.C.: Government Printing Office, 1940), p. 850.

23. W. P. Kumlien et al., *The Standard of Living of Farm and Village Families in Six South Dakota Counties, 1935*, Bulletin No. 320 (Brookings: South Dakota Agricultural Experiment Station, 1938), p. 59; and *Nebraska Farmer*, 28 August 1937, p. 8.

24. *Nebraska Farmer*, 20 February 1932, p. 24.

25. *Fifteenth Census of the United States, 1930: Agriculture*, Vol. 2, Part 1: The Northern States: 1202, 1155, and *Sixteenth Census of the United States, 1940: Agriculture*, Vol. 1, 1st and 2nd Series, State Reports, Part 2, Statistics for Counties, p. 520.

26. Fink interview, Boone County, Nebraska, March 1986.

27. Computed from census data on Boone County, 1934–1943, and *Vital Statistics of the United Data for United States* (1931–1940), Part 2, Natality and Mortality Data for the United States (labeled by place of residence); and also age cohort stability as seen in Lyman County in *Sixteenth Census of the United States, 1940: Population*, Vol. 2, Part 6, and for Boone County, *Sixteenth Census of the United States, 1940: Population*, Part 5: 615.

28. Ibid.

29. Department of Commerce, Bureau of the Census, *Sixteenth Census of the United States 1940: Agriculture*, Vol. 1, 1st and 2nd Series, State Reports, Part 2: Statistics for Counties (Washington, D.C.: Government Printing Office, 1942): 119.

30. *Nebraska Farmer*, 26 March 1938, p. 6.

31. *Nebraska Farmer*, 24 September 1938, p. 11; King, ed., *Early Settlers in Lyman County*, p. 193. By 1938, conditions had greatly improved in South Dakota in regard to agricultural production.

TABLE 1

Fertility Rates (Number of Births per 1,000 Women, Ages 15–44) for Boone County

	Boone County	National Average, White Women
1930	93.1	87.1
1940	90.6	77.1

Computed from 1930 and 1940 Censuses and from 1930 and 1940 Vital Statistics.

TABLE 2

Children Under Age Five in Lyman County, South Dakota, and Boone County, Nebraska

	Women Ages 15–44	Children Under Age 5	Children Under 5 per 100 Women, 14–44
BOONE COUNTY			
1930	3,222	1,549	48
1940	2,483	1,095	44
LYMAN COUNTY			
1930	1,252	698	56
1940	990	464	47

Computed from Fifteenth and Sixteenth Censuses of the United States.

Farmer Rebels in Plymouth County, Iowa, 1932–1933

Rodney D. Karr

The Farmers' Holiday movement flared into rebellion at a time when agricultural prices plummeted to discouraging levels and farmers were threatened with the loss of their land. From August 1932 until April 1933, the Holiday movement achieved its greatest attention in the vicinity of Sioux City, Iowa. Immediately north of Sioux City, in Plymouth County, militant farmers brought recognition to agriculture's depression plight by boldly picketing highways and halting foreclosure sales. In April 1933, these rebellious farmers destroyed what had been a hopeful movement when they hauled a judge from his courtroom in Le Mars and nearly lynched him on the outskirts of town.[1]

A description of Iowa Holiday movement activists can provide important information about participants in direct-action rural protest movements. On occasion 1,000 to 1,500 Plymouth County farmers picketed highways. One hundred to three hundred local farmers attended events of the most serious violence. Although their movement lacked extensive formal leadership, Plymouth County farmer rebels received national attention and provoked a countywide declaration of martial law in May 1933. These farmers, mostly concentrated in a restricted area of the county, resorted to bold measures in the face of financial ruin. They displayed special local characteristics while continuing a rich tradition of American agrarian activism.

PHASES OF REBELLION

Rebellious farmer activity in Plymouth County developed in two phases. In August and September 1932, farmers began a strike by withholding agricultural products from market. During the strike, picketers blocked highways, and in some instances strikers besieged legal officials and non-cooperating farmers. From January to April 1933, the rural protest entered an anti-foreclosure phase in which farmers moved to save one another from forced sales and evictions. During this second phase the rebellion's most serious violence erupted. The most extreme activism occurred in Le Mars, Iowa, on April 27, 1933, when 250 angry farmers rushed the courtroom of District Judge Charles C. Bradley. Bradley was scheduled to hold hearings on an Iowa mortgage moratorium law, and the farmers sought his support of the moratorium. When the judge refused to promise his coopera-tion, the farmers roughly escorted him from the bench and nearly lynched him at a country crossroads.[2]

Immediately after this violence, speculation mounted about par-ticipants in the rural uprising. Iowa Governor Clyde Herring pro-claimed martial law in the county, declaring "Sioux City hoodlums were in the crowd that attacked the judge."[3] Within a week of the courtroom incident, Park A. Findley, who as head of the Iowa Bureau of Investigation investigated the protest, claimed "red backing" ex-isted in the local upheaval. Charges of Communist involvement had surfaced as early as the farm strike of the previous autumn. Despite the concerns about outside influences, however, available evidence suggests that the farm revolt in Plymouth County was a movement of and by local farmers.[4]

Arrests made during the farm strike of 1932 failed to turn up any outsiders. The first arrests for blockading highways in the Sioux City area occurred on September 13. The *Sioux City Journal* announced the arrest of five men on that date; all were farmers from the terri-tory surrounding Sioux City. When officials attempted to clear the highways around Sioux City and made the first mass arrest of pick-ets, they detained ninety protesters in the Woodbury County jail in Sioux City. Of these ninety, a reporter discovered that "five were farm owners; twenty had owned farms and were now renters; twenty-five had always been renters; fifteen were farm boys living with their par-ents; seventeen were laborers long living in the community; and there were eight packing house employees."[5]

In Plymouth County as in Woodbury, officials arrested no "out-side agitators." The first arrests followed the near-lynching of Judge

Bradley, and local press coverage reported all thirty-eight arrested as county residents.[6] Unfortunately, Plymouth County court records are missing for pertinent cases: the criminal court files of Morris Cope, Ed Casper, Martin Rosburg, and Dick Popken, all significant figures in the incident, are missing. Most of the arrests occurred while Plymouth County was under martial law; therefore, the Iowa National Guard was in charge of all arrests during a two-week period. Two previous scholars of the farm rebellion, John Shover and Lowell Dyson, were unable to locate National Guard records of this incident. Newspaper reports provide the best available arrest evidence. Of the thirty-eight persons arrested in Plymouth County, all were farm owners, farm renters, or farm hands.[7]

A BIOGRAPHICAL PROFILE

As well as individuals arrested in Woodbury and Plymouth counties, the majority of participants in the local Farm Holiday movement from August 1932 to May 1933 were local farmers. An interesting pattern emerges from local newspaper coverage of the farm strike, the anti-foreclosure campaign, and the assault on Judge Bradley. Newspaper reports of organizational meetings, leaders, committee members, incidents of farm activism, and arrests reveal sixty different names in some way associated with the Plymouth County farmers' rebellion. Fifty-six of the sixty were Plymouth County farmers or farm workers and three were farmers from neighboring counties.[8] Only one person actively involved or associated with the rebellion appeared to be an outsider: "Mother" Ella Reeve Bloor, reportedly from Sioux City and formerly from North Dakota. Ironically, Bloor's position as a prominent figure in the Communist party escaped the attention of local newspapers.[9]

The farm revolt in Plymouth County was distinctly a minority movement. On most occasions only 10 to 12 percent of the area farmers could be counted at meetings or at protest activities. Newspapers specifically named only 2 to 3 percent. Rarely does an activist movement attract large numbers of participants, so the mere physical assembly of large groups of from 200 to 1,500 farmers to strike, to protest, and to stop sales indicates the strength of the Farm Holiday movement in the county. Moreover, the number of Plymouth County participants is significant in comparison to other areas of farmer activism. John Shover found that Plymouth County was unsurpassed in numbers of farmers actively involved in rebellion incidents. Shover has also noted that Plymouth ranked second in frequency of incidents of farmer activism.[10] Even though a minority of the county's farmers participated in the agrarian movement, they did so with notoriety and an effectiveness that place Plymouth County in the center of the 1930s farm rebellion.

The 1934 *Plymouth County Atlas and Farm Directory* provides a reasonably accurate geographic distribution of farmer activists. Of the fifty-six Plymouth County names in press reports during the rebellion, fifty-two can be located. The majority of rebellious farmers lived in the southeastern section of the county, thirty-two in the six southeastern townships of the county, with Stanton and Henry townships accounting for eighteen. Of the thirty-eight farmers arrested in Plymouth County, thirty-five can be located in the *1934 Atlas*. Seventeen arrested farmers resided in the southeastern townships of the county, eleven in Stanton and Henry townships. Such heavy concentration in one area suggests special circumstances in that portion of the county.[11]

Twelve convictions resulted from the investigation and trials of those involved in Bradley's assault. Three protesters were given minor contempt citations and nine were convicted on various assault charges. Once again this extremely activist element resided in the southeastern section of the county. Five of the convicted men lived in Stanton, Lincoln, or Union townships.

Perhaps the key to the Plymouth County rebellion, centered as it was in the southeastern portion of the county, can be found in the landholding status of participating farmers. Shover found, through thirty-five personal interviews, that survivors of the farm uprising were almost unanimous in their belief that the movement was one of property holders.[12] Plymouth County land-ownership records, however, call for some revision of Shover's interpretation. The majority of the farmers involved in the movement were not owners. Only thirteen of these fifty-six farmers owned land in 1933, among them the official leaders of the local Holiday association. C. J. Schultz, president of the Plymouth County Farmers' Association, held the largest amount of land, claiming 266 acres. The thirteen property-holding farm activists averaged 230 acres at a time when a typical farm in the county was only 190 acres. Nine of the thirteen property holders resided in the southeastern townships of the county; seven maintained their land in Stanton and Henry townships. Shover's contention of a property-holder's rebellion does not fit the evidence from Plymouth County. The small element of property-owning farmers may have provided important leadership in the local revolt, however.[13]

Of the forty-three non-property holders involved in some way in the rebellion, thirty-nine can be located in the 1934 *Atlas*. These farmers again concentrated in the southeastern part of the county. Non-propertied farmers were certainly affected by the depression but were not threatened with loss of land. Sixteen of the non-propertied class farmed with or for their parents. These farmers normally could have expected to inherit their parents' property at some future date. In Plymouth County in the 1930s, this situation presented special circumstances that contributed to some of the most serious violence of the agrarian rebellion.[14]

Two previous studies of the farm revolt concluded that the average age of participating farmers exceeded forty. Frank Dileva found that the farmers in many scattered incidents of the Iowa rebellion averaged 42.5 years of age. Shover determined, through a questionnaire distributed in the early 1960s to former Holiday participants, that their average age during the rebellion was 43.5 years.[15] But a somewhat younger average age emerges from the list of fifty-six Plymouth County activists. Newspapers reported ages for sixteen of the identified men and the average of these ages was 34. With the ages of less than one-third of the actively involved farmers available, conclusions must obviously be tentative. Nevertheless, the fact that the average age for Plymouth County farmers seemingly differs by as much as eight to nine years from earlier studies may be meaningful. With parents twenty-five to thirty years older, farmers in line for parental land may have inherited the land or assumed general management of a farm by age forty-two or forty-three. A farmer at age thirty-four, working with his parents on a farm, however, was liable to find his parents still actively involved in the operation. Thus, the relatively young rebellious farmers in Plymouth County found themselves propertyless and threatened, not by the loss of their own land, but by the loss of a family farm which might someday be theirs. For more than one-fourth of the identified farmer activists in Plymouth County, this potential loss posed real danger.[16]

CONCLUSION

Farmers endangered by potential loss of family land in a small section of the county established an interesting combination of circumstances. In a restricted area of the county, important elements of the farm rebellion merged. Influential propertied farmers such as C. J. Schultz possessed leadership talents. In the same area, an element of relatively young, unpropertied farmers, who stood to inherit family farms, were concentrated. Set against these human features, the southeastern part of the county experienced the most severe impact from the depressed agricultural conditions of 1930 to 1933. In this environment, propertied leaders, would-be land holders, and unpropertied farmers, all threatened with the loss of their livelihood, combined to mold the 1932–33 agricultural rebellion in Plymouth County.

The individual biography of one Plymouth County farmer may be illustrative of the nature of those who rose in rebellion. Morris Cope was a successful, thirty-five-year-old farmer, seriously threatened by the depression. He was a member of the Farmers' Holiday Association, but he operated independently and left an indelible mark on the rebellion. Throughout the unrest, Cope appeared at significant events although he held no official position among the farmers. He apparently was the chief organizer in an attempt to blockade Plymouth County roads during the 1932 strike. Later, at a crossroads meeting on August 30, 1932, Cope and others were shot at for their organizing efforts. In January 1933, during the anti-foreclosure movement, Cope agitated for a march on the state capitol. On April 27, 1933, prior to the assault on Judge Bradley, Cope led a group of Plymouth County farmers to nearby Primghar, Iowa, and attempted to stop a foreclosure sale. In a fight with local sheriff's deputies at that location Cope suffered head injuries which later required medical attention. On the same day, he also reportedly led the attack on Judge Bradley in Le Mars. After the assault on the judge, he avoided arrest for over two months. A local doctor later revealed that he had treated Cope's head injury, after which Cope fled to South Dakota with another suspect. He eventually surrendered and was convicted on assault charges based on testimony that he had indeed led the attack on Bradley. His sentence of one year in the state penitentiary, paroled to the county jail, was the harshest sentence awarded for illegal protest actions in Plymouth County.[17]

Cope had been successful as a farmer. He lived and farmed in Union Township in southeastern Plymouth County, near the town of Kingsley. He owned only eighty acres of land but farmed across the road from his father and younger brother. Cope was primarily a hog producer and apparently an ingenious operator: he invented a hog house door which received a patent in July 1933. Following the Bradley assault, a reporter from the Omaha *World-Herald* visited Cope's father. The reporter found that Jacob Cope had farmed in the same location for twenty-five years as one of northwest Iowa's most prosperous farmers. The Cope farmstead featured a large eighteen-room house. Until just prior to the local uprising, Jacob Cope had held 550 acres of excellent farm land. On January 9, 1932, however, he had 510 acres of mortgaged land foreclosed. By the planting season of 1932, he owned only forty acres of farmland because he could not meet mortgage and tax payments. Moreover, Cope was embittered because he had acquired his land immediately after World War I and felt the debts he had incurred were honest debts. By 1933, those debts had rendered him a poor and downcast man. The father hoped to leave his 550 acres unencumbered to his sons, but by 1932 and 1933 there was little left for inheritance. The father had seen much of a life's work lost in a few months; the son had seen his hopes for the future wiped out by depression conditions.[18]

With this background, Morris Cope embarked on desperate actions in 1933. Wallace Short, a one-time mayor of Sioux City, a former

Iowa legislator, a minister, and publisher of the local labor newspaper, the *Unionist and Public Forum*, sympathized and worked with the farm activists. Commenting on the agricultural rebellion and hard times, Short argued that "at such times men turn their backs on the question of what is legal, and act with energy and conviction on their sense of what is right."[19] Certainly Morris Cope was one of the most energetic of the rural insurgents of the 1930s. His case was, if not representative, surely indicative of the desperation of activist farmer rebels in Plymouth County.

NOTES

1. Midwestern farmer activism of the early 1930s claims a rich historiography. Frank D. Dileva, "Farmers Revolts in Iowa" (M.A. thesis, Drake University, 1952) and Howard Wallace Lawrence, "The Farmers' Holiday Association in Iowa, 1932–33" (M.A. thesis, University of Iowa, 1952) initiated historical scholarship of Iowa's Farm Holiday movement. Julius Korgan expanded this scholarly work in "Farmers Picket the Depression" (PhD dissertation, American University, 1961). The best known work focusing on the Farmer's Holiday is John Shover's *Cornbelt Rebellion: The Farmers' Holiday Association* (Urbana, Illinois, 1965). A native Iowan, Lowell K. Dyson, provided further study with "The Farm Holiday Movement" (PhD dissertation, Columbia University, 1968) and expanded his work on the subject in *Red Harvest: The Communist Party and American Farmers* (Lincoln, Nebraska, 1982). More recently, on the fiftieth anniversary of the Iowa farmers' rebellion, a discussion unfolded in the fall 1983 issue of the *Annals of Iowa* concerning the level of organization and the presence of even informal leadership in that farm movement. See especially Joseph F. Wall, "The Iowa Farmer in Crisis, 1920–1936," pages 116–127, and the comment following by George Mills.
2. *Le Mars Globe-Post*, 1 May 1933.
3. *New York Times*, 29 April 1933, 1.
4. *Le Mars Semi-Weekly Sentinel*, 2 May, 16 September 1933.
5. *Sioux City Journal*, 14 September 1932; Mary Heaton Vorse, "Rebellion in the Corn Belt," Harper's, December 1932, 4.
6. *Le Mars Globe-Post*, 1, 4, 29 May; 13, 20 July 1933; *Le Mars Semi-Weekly Sentinel*, 12 May and 1 June 1933; Sioux City Journal, 1, 3, 11 May 1933.
7. Plymouth County Criminal Court Records, Cases 782 A, 789 A, 791 A, and 792 A, Court House, Le Mars, Iowa; Shover, *Cornbelt Rebellion*, 121; *Le Mars Semi-Weekly Sentinel*, 12 May and 1 June 1933; and *Sioux City Journal*, 1, 3, 11 May 1933.

8. *Le Mars Globe-Post*, August and September 1932 and January, February, April, and May 1933; and *Le Mars Semi-Weekly Sentinel*, August and September 1932 and January and May 1933.

9. *Le Mars Globe-Post*, 9 January 1933; John L. Shover, "The Communist Party and the Midwest Farm Crisis of 1933," *Journal of American History* 51 (September 1964), 255; Dyson, *Red Harvest*, 107–109. Bloor, along with Harold Ware and Lement Harris, provided the nucleus of a Communist effort to lead the farm revolt.

10. Shover, *Cornbelt Rebellion*, 3–46.

11. *Le Mars Globe-Post*, August and September 1932, January and May 1933, 13, 20 July 1933; and *1934 Plymouth County Atlas and Farm Directory* (Sioux City, 1934), 1–25. The *Atlas and Farm Directory* provides data for the year 1933. *Le Mars Semi-Weekly Sentinel*, 12 May, 1 June 1933; and *Sioux City Journal*, 1, 3, 11 May 1933.

12. Shover, "Communist Party and Farm Crisis," 248–249. Shover traveled the area of the farm rebellion in 1961 and located and interviewed the survivors.

13. *Atlas and Farm Directory*, 1–25; Iowa State Department of Agriculture, *Iowa Yearbook of Agriculture, 1933*, 222.

14. Ibid.; *Le Mars Globe-Post*, August and September 1932 and January, February, April, and May 1933; *Le Mars Semi-Weekly Sentinel*, August and September 1932 and January and May 1933.

15. Dileva, "Farm Revolts in Iowa," 108; Shover, *Cornbelt Rebellion*, 17. Thirty-four former Holiday members responded to Shover's questionnaire.

16. *Le Mars Globe-Post*, August and September 1932 and January, February, April, and May 1933; and *Le Mars Semi-Weekly Sentinel*, August and September 1932 and January and May 1933; *Atlas and Farm Directory*, 1–25.

17. *Sioux City Journal*, 31 August 1932, 4, 11 May 1933; *Le Mars Globe-Post*, 2 January 1933, 20 July 1933; *Le Mars Semi-Weekly Sentinel*, 9 June 1933, 21 July 1933. A search of Plymouth County Sheriff's Department records revealed two pieces of information of interest in the Cope case. First, on June 12, 1934, Sheriff Ralph Rippey requested a reduction to time served in Cope's sentence which was to run until August 1934. Second, a letter written on May 8, 1933, from C. W. McNaughton, state agent in charge of Plymouth County investigations, to Park A. Findley, head of the Iowa Bureau of Criminal Investigations, suggests a protective attitude about local tenant farmers, and some informal leadership on Cope's behalf. Cope wrote a letter threatening a Colorado tenant planning to move to Plymouth County. In later trial testimony, five witnesses acknowledged that the letter, signed by the Farmers' Holiday Association was the work of Cope. Plymouth County Sheriff Department Criminal Files, File Number 105 and 106, Le Mars, Iowa.

18. *Atlas and Farm Directory*, 18–19; *Le Mars Semi-Weekly Sentinel*, 4 July 1933; *Omaha World-Herald*, 1 May 1933, 2; "Plymouth County Transfer of Lands," Book Number 5, Court House, Le Mars, Iowa, 6; James R. Parker,

"The Farm Holiday Movement in Northwest Iowa," unpublished manuscript, Iowa State Historical Department, Des Moines, 38.
19. Mrs. Wallace Short, *Just One American* (Sioux City, 1943), 153.

"A God-Forsaken Place"
Folk Eschatology and the Dust Bowl
Brad Lookingbill

On an idyllic Sunday in April 1935, people from Lubbock, Texas, to
Topeka, Kansas, went on picnics, planted gardens, visited neighbors,
and attended church. Communities had been punished with depression and drought, yet on that spring day Plains men and women felt
assured that peace and safety had returned. Suddenly in midafternoon
the air turned cold, and people noticed then that the sky had become
filled with birds, fleeing from some unseen force. Fifteen-year-old Ida
Mae Norman, driving home from a Palm Sunday church service with
her family, saw a thin strip of black on the horizon north of Guymon,
Oklahoma. Seconds later, they were enveloped in a wall of dust. She
later recalled: "I was so frightened. I thought the world had come to
an end." She feared that the foreboding dust storm might be a "signal
for Armageddon."[1]

The teenage girl's fear reflected a common response to dramatic
ecologic and economic shifts. From the Puritan's "Day of Doom" in
colonial history to Hal Lindsey's *Late Great Planet Earth* in recent
years, apocalyptic strains have echoed throughout American culture
and remained malleable to particular historical circumstances.
Premillennial dispensationalism, the eschatological form popular in
the twentieth century, regards events not as harbingers of a progressive evolution into the Kingdom, as postmillennialism contended. Instead, individuals saw omens of disaster as increasing trials which
would precede the imminent return of Christ in judgment and salvation.[2] This paradoxical faith, constructed within the social experience
and from the religious traditions of grassroots Christian piety, per-

sisted in the folklore articulated throughout southwestern Kansas, northwestern Oklahoma, southeastern Colorado, and the Texas Panhandle. The folk eschatology of the Dust Bowl signified the continuing connection between lay religious belief and a fundamentalistic Christian subculture.

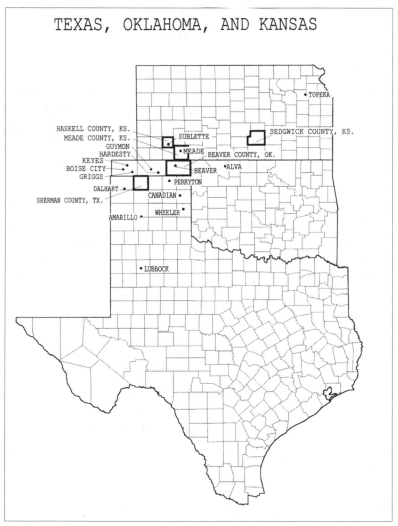

Texas, Oklahoma, and Kansas communities whose organized religious reactions to the severe dust storms have been documented. Map by Michael Shambaugh-Miller.

"Black blizzards": a dirt storm in Dalhart, Texas. (Courtesy Southwest Collection, Texas Tech University.)

"Popular and inexpensive recreation": the First Methodist Church of Merkel, Texas. (Courtesy Southwest Collection, Texas Tech University.)

Panhandle dust storm, Perryton, Texas. (Courtesy Southwest Collection, Texas Tech University.)

"A prelude to the apocalypse": a dust storm in downtown Dalhart, Texas. (Courtesy Southwest Collection, Texas Tech University.)

"A man could get religion in a God-forsaken place like this." Methodist Church, Plainview, Texas. (Courtesy Southwest Collection, Texas Tech University.)

DEPRESSION CHALLENGES, AND INITIAL CHURCH REACTIONS

Communities throughout the short-grass Plains in the 1930s faced a series of challenges. Economic depression reduced the price of wheat, a critical commodity for regional agriculture, from $1.16 per bushel in 1926 to $0.68 by 1930. In addition, climatological records from 1932–36 recorded the most extreme drought in the history of the southern Great Plains. Soil erosion and high winds took a severe toll and produced over 352 dirt storms, large and small, usually in the early spring. The U.S. Soil Conservation Service reported storms in which visibility was reduced to less than a mile and listed 72 in 1937, the top figure for the period.

Though most of the sandstorms were short and light, the rare but destructive black blizzards created greater awe in residents' minds than in other dusty times. Scrambling for a piece of stable land, individuals often linked together the economic downturn and environmental hazards and recognized the dirty thirties as the greatest tribulation of their lives.[3] Religious folklore, in addition to other variables within the cultural equation, contributed to this perception of the hard times.

While communities struggled for survival, religious institutions remained important sources of social continuity. Although total population in both Kansas and Oklahoma declined, church membership increased in the Southwest region from 1926 to 1936, growing slightly from 4,457,592 to 4,525,679. Methodist, Baptist, Church of Christ, Lutheran, and Mennonite Brethren groups all experienced marginal growth in membership, with a greater increase during these years than during the preceding ten years. For example, in forty-seven rural Protestant denominations in Sedgwick County, Kansas, the total membership increased only slightly during the twenties, but they increased by 14 percent between 1930 and 1935. Members under the age of twenty-one increased by 64 percent in the early years of the Depression, and attendance at Sunday morning services increased 25 percent from 1930 to 1935 in the county. Drought and economic depression presented obstacles for some established churches in the southern Plains. Several of them declined, consolidated, or even closed, continuing a trend that had already begun earlier in the 1920s.[4]

Although mainline Protestant activities continued in static conditions in most rural Plains locales, a few new Christian churches experienced dramatic surges in membership and participation. The Assemblies of God reached 148,043 members in the entire Southwest by 1936, a 208 percent increase from 1926. In Texas and Oklahoma, this particular Protestant denomination multiplied its membership five times during the ten-year period, and membership quadrupled in Kansas. The Church of the Nazarene also doubled its membership in all three states. One resident, referring to the Nazarene Church of Sublette, Kansas, commented: "They are very religious and quite emotional. They take their religion very seriously and are very hard in their condemnation of other people's conduct."

Another denomination, the Pentecostal Holiness Church, also increased significantly. Total membership in Oklahoma reached 2,315 in 1936, increasing from the 1926 mark of 1,573. During the quadrennium of 1913 to 1937, the Oklahoma conference of the Pentecostals raised the second highest amount of finances in the entire national denomination, and only three conferences exceeded it in assets. They also increased their world missions activities during the Depression decade, when it might have been expected that economic difficulties would inhibit such activities.[5]

Each of these "religions of rigor" offered a comforting spiritualism to the laity. They assured believers of happiness in the world to come while easing the burdens of this life with the claim that money, status, and power were unimportant for salvation.[6]

FUNDAMENTALISM ON THE SOUTHERN PLAINS

Evidence from the hardest hit regions of the southern Plains reveals the importance of religious institutions to particular communities. For example, in Hardesty, Oklahoma, the Apostolic Faith Church organized in 1933 after a revival where "eighty souls were saved." In nearby Wilburton and Morning Star, church membership increased over 100 percent in 1933 and 1934, and a new Church of Christ was built in Keyes, Oklahoma. The United Methodists of Meade, Kansas, recorded that the drought "tried the souls of the people," but the church thrived during the decade. The Church of God in Beaver, Oklahoma, held a mortgage burning service on 17 September 1938, following the completion of a new building.[7] Some churches reported that donations declined due to the economic downturn, but Reverend L. R. Scarborough reported in the *Baptist Standard* that the church in Lubbock, Texas, led the way in the "tithing movement." Reverend Mark A. Dawber, reporting for the Home Missions Council of the Methodist Episcopal Church, concluded that the people of the drought region maintained their levels of contributions because "this was a real test of Christian faith."[8]

Countless residents reported religious activities as popular and inexpensive recreation, and insisted that the hard times might end if people would simply go to church more often. Though some laity reported shame in being unable to attend church due to their lack of proper clothing, one pious schoolteacher from Wheeler, Texas, responded: "In my own case I have always gone to church regardless of the kind of clothing I had. I feel that my prime motive was to worship God. I believe that people who give lack of proper clothing as an excuse for not going to church just want an excuse or they are not truly Christian." Another woman agreed and faithfully declared: "I am optimistic because of the drought because my Lord has promised that all things work together to good to them that love God. . . . We have always attended church regularly, but we have received more spiritual blessings and a closer bond to Christians since the drought." Members suffered from the burdens of adverse weather and a bad economy, but they were ones which many faithful were willing to bear.[9]

Fundamentalist religion left an indelible mark upon the membership of local churches. By 1936, over one-third of the total population of the southern Great Plains maintained church membership, and low church Protestant denominations dominated religious life there. For example, 91 percent of Oklahoma's church members claimed a Protestant faith, while a majority of these emphasized Biblical literalism, individual morality, and a premillennial eschatology. The last of these provided a major impetus for evangelical growth in American culture and served as a building block for conservative traditions regardless of denomination. A similar pattern homogenized churches in Haskell

County, Kansas, where people expressed similar fundamentalist beliefs, even those who did not regularly attend church.[10]

Essentially, the Old Time religion that marked frontier life in the region had survived over the years, and the pattern of revivals and camp meetings continued throughout the Dust Bowl decade. Over 109 tents were assembled for a camp meeting near Beaver, Oklahoma, in August 1934, with people flocking to the meeting from the drought states. A Kansas newspaper reported that the experience benefitted numerous communities, for the meeting closed with "souls at the altar earnestly seeking God and pressing their cases before Him." The Nazarene Church in Sublette, Kansas, ran newspaper advertisements for a revival, reminding people of the relationship between the drought and deliverance: "Get the dust out of your eyes and make the closing services a time of soul saving."[11] Revivalists determined that the spiritual fields remained ripe for harvest, though much of the farmland appeared barren.

Local pastors and districts, often independent from major denominations either formally or simply in practice, spoke little of relief during the 1930s but emphasized instead depravity and grace. A popular Sunday morning radio program in Kansas compared the problems of the people with the persecutions of the Savior. A survey of Sunday sermons listed in one newspaper of a southern Plains community reveals such titles as "Is There Any Hope for the Hopeless Today?" "Jesus and the Problems of Life," "Holy Suffering," "The Future Life," "Dust Storms and God," and, most appropriate, "I Thirst." In February 1935, clergy from the Perryton, Texas, District of the Methodist Episcopal Church–South cited the need to return to "the fundamentals of religion" in order to resolve the crises of the depression years. Echoing the view espoused by a strong religious minority in the 1920s, West Texas Methodists maintained that the greatest threat to Plains communities remained whiskey and immorality rather than economic deprivation, as they proclaimed that the "hour of destiny" had arrived in the fight against the forces of spiritual decay. Regardless of their numbers, a vocal assortment of conservatives and evangelicals, working from their own definition of righteousness, dominated political debate in population centers as large as Amarillo.[12] According to the messages proclaimed throughout the southern Plains, an essential part of any relief for those who suffered included repentance and faithfulness to the Almighty.

As the economic and environmental decline continued, conservative religious voices persisted in their emphasis upon the spiritual crisis of the day. Rev. M. E. Markwell of the Methodist Church in Boise City, Oklahoma, questioned the community: "Who have we been serving, who are you serving today? . . . If ye were God's servants, ye would receive better pay. God has been kind and merciful, we have been selfish and unappreciative." These clergy believed that the hope for the region remained in a return to the traditions which united the communities in the past, and so messages about resilient faith and inevitable punishment resounded throughout. One minister, writing in a Baptist newspaper in Texas, ordered people to seek relief from adversity through the Lord: "If you are a failure it is because you have no faith." Those who suffered deserved their fate because "there is no such thing as Chance. Everything is test, or punishment, or reward, or prevision." A minister from the Methodist Episcopal Church in Meade, Kansas, praised the God-sent punishment of the day: "We are reminded very forcibly of the greatness of our sin, and at the same time, of the greatness of God's love and kindness toward us. . . . We also realize that we have deserved nothing but damnation on account of our sin."[13] These strident voices suggested that an angry God unleashed the hard times to chastise a prodigal people, and only an appeased God would lift the yoke.

THE GREAT TRIBULATION

While the years of dust, drought, and depression persisted in the High Plains, a number of ministers and churches began to sense that the adversity experienced by the laity represented a part of the Providential plan for revival in the last days. A few religious sects held meetings on street corners and began to warn people to be ready, for the portentous events "were fulfillment of the signs of the times and heralded the approach of the end of the world." One prayer group in Kansas appealed to the citizens of the Plains to reconsecrate their lives and prepare themselves for "God's own way and judgment to deliver us from this dust peril lest . . . a worse calamity come upon Us."[14] The Baptist Standard of Texas declared that the sinners of the world should prepare themselves for tribulation:

> Eminent leaders agree that the world, after a cycle of disturbance that has shaken the foundations of every phase of life, political, social and economic, is ready. . . . Then indeed would mankind intelligently be able to face this world crisis, judgment that has come upon us and our boasted civilization and work itself through to peace and normalcy.[15]

For those who viewed the crises of the depression years as a part of the divine plan, the future would reveal more hardship if humans failed to repent and labor for the Lord.

For a vocal and prophetic minority, the crisis presented a sign of God's vindictive punishment on an apostate people as well as hope for His imminent return. "The nations that forget God," declared a Southern Baptist convention resolution in 1932, "shall not prosper." Reverend Gerald B. Winrod, a popular Kansas crusader who organized the Defenders of the Christian Faith, observed that the signs of the times in the 1930s confirmed that the great tribulation was approaching. Commenting specifically on the Depression, he advised that "more religion—rather than more legislation—is the need of the hour."[16]

Though the precise expectations of every person remain difficult to measure, anecdotal evidence suggests that apocalyptic dread became a common belief among the grassroots population. Frequent statements by farmers included: "We're in the last days before Christ returns, [problems] will get worse," and "Sin is to blame for the whole thing. God uses it for his purposes." In Boise City, Oklahoma, the local newspaper opened one article with a quote from Scripture, identifying the economic crisis in the community with Ezekiel 22:12–13 in which the Lord declared: "Behold, therefore, I have smitten my hand at thy dishonest gain which thou hast made, and at thy blood which has been in the midst of thee."[17] One Oklahoman reported that a foreboding mood prevailed throughout the drought region, and that "always in the back of hearts and minds stood the question: Are we being punished by an angry God? If so, what is next?" Warned a letter to the *Amarillo Globe-News,* "Only a complete turning to God can prevent the complete collapse of this portion of Texas in which we live." The signs of God's impending judgment and wrath abounded, according to its author, with riots, strife, grief, rumors of war, and floods all signaling the end of time; but there was still time to "turn your paper over to God."[18] Certainly not everyone flocked to these explanations, although their appearance in a variety of local newspapers and personal recollections suggests that such dismaying thoughts tempted residents.

Secular voices across the dry prairies articulated the fear that the dust storms represented another divine visitation. One Russell County, Kansas, newspaper, in the midst of a front page full of bulletins about raging dust storms, printed a stern warning: "A Curse for Disobedience? The Lord shall make the rain of thy land powder and dust; from heaven shall it come down on thee, until thou be destroyed. Deut. 28:24." In Amarillo, Texas, a local columnist discussed the frequent calls that he received concerning the incessant sandstorms. Folks expressed to him a conviction that the days of dust were "a visitation from the Lord" and fulfilled the curses of disobedience declared by the Scripture. Nevertheless, the columnist doubted the concerns, because "I can't believe He would select the very best people for punishment when there are others so much more deserving of His wrath."[19] Even the toughest souls felt the frustration and rationalized reasons for the dirt barrage.

The drama of the noisome black blizzards of the 1930s brought a sense of utter helplessness to individuals in the midst of a hostile environment, and terror clutched the hearts of some as dust stifled communities. The *Lubbock* (Texas) *Avalanche-Journal* reported that two people became "hysterical because of the expressed fear that the world was coming to an end." The *Topeka Daily State Journal* received phone calls throughout one dramatic dust storm, with one startling voice declaring: "Watch for the second coming of Jesus Christ. God is wrathful."[20] Delores Marie Wilmot, a resident of the Oklahoma Panhandle during the Dust Bowl years, recalled an early duster and the frightening and perplexing image of the darkened sky:

> We thought the end of the world was surely coming, you know because, well, we went to church all of the time and they had these traveling evangelists, and they preached the old fire and everything else was going to fall on you anytime; and I used to sit there bug-eyed and so scared of what the Lord was doing or going to do to us. And so I thought, boy, here it's come! And I wasn't the only one because, well, I was just a kid but there was a lot of adults that thought this was it. They had never seen anything like it before![21]

Wilmot as well as other residents survived countless dust storms over the years. She expressed the apocalyptic mood which prevailed when the foreboding rollers appeared upon the horizon of the High Plains in the 1930s.

When the awesome dirt storms rolled over the southern Plains with turbulent black clouds that showered dust instead of rain, some concluded that the apocalypse had arrived. The black blizzard of 14 April 1935 stands as the worst one in the memories of most residents. It arrived on a Sunday that had been marked by clear skies and calm weather. Witnesses who viewed the ominous cloud on the horizon felt "the Wrath of God descending at one time" to punish everything in its path. The black roller engulfed the northeastern sky and advanced across the southern Plains, with hundreds of birds flying before the storm seeking shelter.[22] In Liberal, Kansas, the local newspaper reported that during the storm's climax, "some people thought the end of the world was at hand when every trace of daylight was obliterated at 4:00 P.M." Alarmed people fell to their knees and prayed for forgiveness as the wall of dirt approached, and railroad workers at Dalhart, Texas, reportedly feared that "the world had come to an end."[23] The cataclysmic images of Black Sunday dominated the recollections of those who witnessed the incredible vision of the duster.

Reports of Judgment Day abounded and fueled the image of terrorizing dust storms. Few storms reached the magnitude of that particular day, but fifty years later Dessie M. Hanburry of Amarillo, Texas, vividly recalled the foreboding image of doom: "We thought the world

was coming to an end. It was so dark, you couldn't see the light in the
room. I've never witnessed a darkness so dark." In future decades,
this remained the archetypical storm against which survivors measured all others. In another instance, a woman in Griggs, Oklahoma,
reported that the mighty roller clouds frightened her into believing
that "the Lord was returning to gather His flock." A family trapped
in a car near Beaver, Oklahoma, during Black Sunday "thought the
world was coming to an end." In Sherman County, Texas, Mrs. Joe
Billington remarked that not one ray of light appeared for twenty-five
minutes, which some thought a prelude to the apocalypse.[24] The black
blizzard raged for hours, submerging everyone in its path of darkness
and in an unforgettable experience.

Countless people across the High Plains voiced their fears in
eschatological language. This common pattern of individual reaction
underscored the influence of popular religious myths. Wanita Brown,
while living near Amarillo, Texas, noticed the dramatic weather and
described her haunting reaction: "And the dust was just rolling in,
just like a fog coming in, and in no time it was as dark as night. Yes, I
remember that day. You know, we couldn't imagine whether the world
was coming to an end or what." Larue Young of Canadian, Texas,
thought "perhaps the world was coming to an end. This sand storm
was a terrible thing, and it was one of the experiences in my life
that I will never forget." The Urban family of Perryton, Texas,
also recalled that the dusty apocalypse seemed to climax the years
of tribulation, and that "a lot of people were just frightened to
death—they thought it was the end of the world. It was real grue-
some." "Almost universal," according to another survivor, was the
anxiety that this violent Sunday afternoon might be the end of the
world.[25]

SEEKING ANSWERS IN FOLK BELIEFS

Some local preachers from evangelical sects declared that the
drought revealed part of the Almighty's plan. A "Job's Comforter"
near Alva, Oklahoma, proclaimed that "the drought is a direct punishment for our sins. . . . Days of grace and mercy and rain for this great

prairieland are forever past." After all, some fearfully suggested, the Scriptures prophesied: "And thy heaven that is over thy head shall be brass, and the earth that is under thee shall be iron." Life seemed as scriptural as Revelations, since "one woe has passed and behold, there came two woes more hereafter." The Nazarene Church in Meade, Kansas, reported that the seating capacity had been filled for every service "because people are awakening to the warnings of God's word, that financial conditions and crop shortages are dependent upon some- one greater than man."[26] Hence, individuals were urged by pious com- munity spokesmen to attend church in order to save their bank ac- counts and crops as well as their souls.

As the value of farm property dropped by forty percent during the 1930s, people throughout the troubled southern Great Plains found that their folklore provided answers concerning the cause of the diffi- cult days. One resident of Wheeler, Texas, observed: "I think the drought was sent to us from God because of the wicked and perverse ways of the people existing today. Deut. 28:15 and 24." Another Texan concurred when responding about the impact of the Depression: "I go to church more for spiritual guidance and strength. My belief is that God is punishing us for the way we live."[27] Evelyn Harris, while writ- ing to a friend in Oklahoma concerning the hardships of the farm, felt that farmers should accept their present adversity without complaint: "They forget that the Lord giveth and the Lord taketh away, and that we, as farmers, are powerless to do anything about it either way [when] some other act of God destroys our crops."[28]

Others, however, were not so certain of the favor of Providence. One native expressed the universal cry of Job in the *Boise City News* of Oklahoma: "Why is it when we ask so little of life sometimes and conduct ourselves to the best of our ability, we should be punished so severely?" Buren Sparks of Texas believed that he had the answer. During the late twenties, people had turned their back on God and pursued the pleasures of life; but then came "the Depression, the drought, falling prices, and you are broke like all the other big ranchmen." Now, God released the winds of dust upon the region. After recounting a parable of a family searching for their lost son in a dust storm, he concluded that "to be lost in hell is a million times worse than being lost in a sand storm. Sandstorms can touch your body but not your soul."[29]

Some individuals found strength to cope with the blowing dirt in a vicarious vision which transformed the physical struggle into a supernatural one. One pious woman commented: "When I see a dust storm coming, I feel that it is God's will—so I try to like it." Another resident trapped in the dirt claimed that the dark blizzards were sent to force people to "think of the beautiful day after the storm"; the punishing climate helped her "look forward to the resurrection." Les Dodson of Sherman County, Texas, believed "a situation like this brings the inhabitants' hearts and thoughts closer to God. A dry season certainly is a time to get a little dust on your knees from kneeling in prayer." Stoical statements resounded in the dusty assault, and a philosophical Kansas farmer scrawled the spiritual battle cry on a dust-encrusted window: "Take it and like it, In God we trust!"[30]

The fearsome sight of the increasing dust storms in the midst of other trials conjured up numerous scriptural analogies and metaphors. A resident of Beaver County, Oklahoma, recalled being trapped in an unexpected duster: "When I saw the wall of dirt, I just wondered if like Tyre and Sidon we were to be buried here." The blizzards descended "like an Old Testament plague," a floating "pestilence . . . like the dust-laden scourge visited upon the Egyptians." Overwhelmed by a week-old dust storm, one Kansas farmer reacting to New Deal agricultural programs speculated to Senator Arthur Capper that the blowing conditions reflected the "wrath of Almighty God" for the "unpardonable sins of destroying crops and livestock when millions were on the verge of starvation."[31] Nature itself revolted against humanity with assaulting dust storms, and many people relied upon common folk beliefs to comprehend the destruction of their way of life by a force beyond their control.

The drama of the black blizzard of 14 April 1935 left an indelible mark on the folklore of the Dust Bowl region. In Pampa, Texas, noted folk balladeer Woody Guthrie watched the dust storm roll in like "the Red Sea closing in on the Israel children." In the ballad of the "Dust Storm Disaster," he sang that "the worst of the dust storms that ever filled the sky" appeared and "they thought the world had ended, and they thought it was their doom."[32] In light of the environmental crisis of the 1930s, Wilma Elizabeth McDaniel, an Oklahoma poet, concluded: "A man could get religion in a God-forsaken place like this." Perhaps the most famous piece of literature about the Dust Bowl experience, John Steinbeck's *The Grapes of Wrath*, suggested the popular apocalyptic mood in its title.[33]

Rather than social commentary, most indigenous poets and writers in the 1930s filled their work with lamentations about the cruel climatic conditions.[34] For example, Elmyr Doran Warren of southwest Texas penned a poem entitled "The Dust Storm" in which he describes the supernatural origin behind the dirty thirties:

> *How long, Oh God, we pray Thee,*
> *Must we pay this terrible price*
> *For wheat thrown into an Ocean*
> *Or burned—what a sacrifice!*
> *We know that Thou art ruling,*
> *We can not read Thy plan;*
> *In darkness, like children we pray Thee—*
> *It is hard to understand.*
>
> . . . .
>
> *We ask Thee, Heavenly Father,*
> *To be with us through this hour*
> *That all might know Thy wisdom,*
> *That all might feel Thy power;*
> *Give us hope on through this pall of dust,*
> *And strength to say "Thy will be done."*[35]

The folk culture accepted the dust, drought, and depression as part of a divine plan; they had been caused by God, and only faith in His will could deliver the region from the trials.

Meanwhile, the boosters of the region, employing this common religious rhetoric, opined that even a divine disaster represented a blessing in disguise. John L. McCarthy, a local writer, editor, and businessman from Dalhart, Texas, praised the wondrous workings of Providence for the storms. In "A Tribute to Our Sand Storms," McCarthy wrote: "Let us in stentorian tones boast of our terrific and mighty sandstorms and of a people, a city, and a country that can meet the test . . . and the God capable of such gigantic destructive demonstrations of nature can be just as calm and tender as the hushed quiet before the storm or the bright day which follows."[36] William Baker, a county agent from Oklahoma, wrote in a poem that folks on the land told him the dusters were "a punishment to man so dumb to plow the land for more income." Nevertheless, Baker told them that the "acts of God" were unlikely to strike the same place twice, and the sensible response was to go right back and rebuild and replant. In fact, newspapers and insurance companies across the region argued that the drought was an "act of God," something beyond human control and wholly unexpected. Individuals were able to absolve themselves of any environmental responsibility by attributing the Dust Bowl crisis to a punitive and protective Providence.[37]

CONCLUSION

Historian Walter Prescott Webb wrote that the vicissitudes of Great Plains life created an "illusion of unreality" in the minds of residents. People did not intentionally exaggerate their descriptions of the dust storms, the effects of the drought, or the adversity of the Depression. Instead, they resorted to metaphors or analogies ingrained in folkways for lack of a better means to convey the impression left by hard times. Although much of the blowing dirt and drought lacked the extreme drama of Black Sunday, the religious symbolism provided an available and convenient method to explain the sense of foreboding and calamity ushered in by the decade. Furthermore, such statements as "black as when Jesus was hanging on the cross" were concepts related to the fact that the most vicious dust storms struck during the Easter season.[38] Men and women reacted to two different phenomena when they responded to both the Depression and the environmental problems; the former could be labeled human-made, the latter ascribed to natural forces. The responses of locals rarely separated the two events. Rather, according to their statements of popular faith, the cataclysmic events together represented a visitation by an angry God to bring about the end of the world or at least the end of sin. Perhaps this *mentalité* emerged syncretic with the fact that the competitive agricultural system, fundamental to socioeconomic stability in southern Great Plains communities, remained greatly dependent upon the unpredictable rhythms of a harsh environment.

Fundamentalistic religious beliefs functioned as both an escape and a creative force by pointing to the economic and environmental calamity as evidence of Heaven's mysterious ways. These notions became rooted in the regional culture by the 1930s and complemented the disastrous conditions.[39] The cataclysmic vocabulary employed by clergy, and especially laity, tended more to an expression of a conservative cultural mood rather than an intrinsic part of a theological system. Hence, individuals may not have been able to explain the theological nuances of either premillennial dispensationalism or denominational orthodoxy, but in rural communities across the region, residents found a vivid illustration of the wrath of God. They only needed to step into their fields where crops had withered under the blazing sun, or to speak with a neighbor who had lost a farm through a bank foreclosure.

The history of popular religion in America is in some sense the history of the changing ways in which individuals have explained their relationship to an encompassing world and to a God who has been assumed to be active in human history in general and their personal history in particular. In the Dust Bowl of the 1930s, people drew upon their cultural background to explain calamitous events and ecological warnings. In this case, men and women steeped in the symbol and myth of a rugged folk eschatology found a paradoxical assurance in the climatic and climactic movements of the invisible hand of Providence.

Note: The author would like to express his appreciation to Dr. Gerald Thompson of the University of Toledo for his insight and advice with the manuscript.

NOTES

1. Ida M. Norman, in Anne Reifenberg, "Black Sunday: The Day the Dust
   Bowl Got Its Name," *Dallas Morning News* (Dallas, Tex.), 14 April 1985,
   p. 28A; Donald Worster, *Dust Bowl: The Southern Plains in the 1930s*
   (New York: Oxford University Press, 1979), p. 18.
2. For detailed discussions of millennialism and popular religion, see Paul S.
   Boyer, *When Time Shall Be No More: Prophecy Belief in Modern Ameri-
   can Culture* (Cambridge: Harvard University Press, 1992); David D. Hall,
   *Worlds of Wonder, Days of Judgment: Popular Religious Belief in Early
   New England* (New York: Knopf, 1989); Lois P. Zamora, ed., *The Apoca-
   lyptic Vision in America* (Bowling Green, OH: Bowling Green University
   Popular Press, 1982).
3. See Pamela Riney-Kehrberg, "In God We Trusted, In Kansas We Busted . . .
   Again: A Social History of Dust Bowl Kansas" (Ph.D. diss., University of
   Wisconsin–Madison, 1991); Guy Logsdon, "The Dust Bowl and the Mi-
   grant," *American Scene* 12 (1971): 4–5; Paul H. Carlson, "Black Sunday:
   The South Plains Dust Blizzard of April 14, 1935," *West Texas Historical
   Association Yearbook* 67 (1991): 6; James C. Malin, "Dust Storms," *Kansas Historical Quarterly* 14 (May–November 1946): 129–44, 265–96, 391–
   413; R. Douglas Hurt, *The Dust Bowl: An Agricultural and Social History* (Chicago: Nelson-Hall, 1981); Paul Bonnifield, *The Dust Bowl: Men,
   Dirt, and Depression* (Albuquerque: University of New Mexico Press,
   1979); William E. Riebsame, "The Dust Bowl: Historical Image, Psychological Anchor, and Ecological Taboo," *Great Plains Quarterly* 6 (Spring
   1986): 127–36.
4. U.S. Bureau of the Census, *Census of Religious Bodies: 1936*, vol. 1 (Washington, D.C., 1941), pp. 60–61, table 7; Bonnifield, *The Dust Bowl* (note 3
   above), pp. 185–202; Dwight Sanderson, *Research Memorandum on Rural Life in the Great Depression* (New York: Social Science Research Council, 1937), pp. 93–94.
5. U.S., *Census of Religious Bodies* (note 4 above), p. 346, table 25; pp. 375–
   85, 412, table 29; George H. Paul, "The Religious Frontier in Oklahoma:
   Dan T. Muse and the Pentecostal Holiness Church" (Ph.D. diss., University of Oklahoma, 1965), pp. 125–27, 140; Robert T. Handy, *The American
   Religious Depression, 1925–1935* (Philadelphia: Fortress Press, 1968), pp.
   14–15; Martin E. Marry, *The Noise of Conflict, 1919–1941*, vol. 2 of *Modern American Religion* (Chicago: University of Chicago Press, 1991).
6. Robert M. Anderson, *Vision of the Disinherited: The Making of American
   Pentecostalism* (New York: Oxford University Press, 1979); James D.

Hunter, *American Evangelicalism: Conservative Religion and the Quandary of Modernity* (New Brunswick, N.J.: Rutgers University Press, 1983), pp. 23–72.

7. *Guymon Daily Herald* (Okla.), 24–25 April, 24 September, 1 October, 12 November 1976; Pauline Grey, *Pioneer Stories of Meade County Kansas*, 4th ed. (Meade, Kans.: Meade County Historical Society, 1985), pp. 39–40; Marylou McDaniel, ed., *God, Grass, and Grit: A History of the Sherman County Trade Area* (Hereford, Tex.: Pioneer Book Publishers, 1971), p. 56; Robert R. Wilson and Ethel M. Sears, *History of Grant County Kansas* (Wichita: Wichita Eagle Press, 1950), p. 184; Bonnifield, *The Dust Bowl* (note 3 above), p. 190.

8. L. R. Scarborough, "A Great Peril in Our Progress," *Baptist Standard*, 4 July 1935; Mark A. Dawber, "The Churches in the Dust Bowl," *Missionary Review of the World* 62 (September 1979): 194–95.

9. Ruby Winona Adams, "Social Behavior in a Drought Stricken Texas Panhandle Community" (Master's thesis, University of Texas, 1939), pp. 66, 78.

10. Not only is the term *fundamentalist* problematical for scholars of lay religion, but its meaning is also disputed among theologians themselves. In the 1930s, fundamentalism represented a Biblicist, Calvinistic orthodoxy, an evangelical spirit, individualistic morality, and a millenarian eschatology. For useful discussions, see George M. Marsden, *Fundamentalism and American Culture: The Shaping of Twentieth Century Evangelicalism, 1870–1925* (New York: Oxford University Press, 1980); Ernest R. Sandeen, *The Roots of Fundamentalism: British and American Millenarianism, 1800–1930* (Chicago: University of Chicago Press, 1970); Kenneth K. Bailey, *Southern White Protestantism in the Twentieth Century* (New York: Harper and Row, 1964). For church membership, see U.S., *Census of Religious Bodies* (note 3 above), pp. 270–72, table 22; Earl H. Bell, *Culture of a Contemporary Rural Community: Sublette, Kansas*, Rural Life Studies: Vol. 2, Bureau of Agricultural Economics, U.S. Department of Agriculture (Washington, D.C.: Government Printing Office, 1942): 86–90. For an interesting account of Dust Bowl migrant religion in California, see James N. Gregory, *American Exodus: The Dust Bowl Migration and Okie Culture in California* (New York: Oxford University Press, 1989).

11. *Meade County Press* (Meade, Kansas), 30 August 1974; *Sublette Monitor* (Kans.), 18 April 1935; Worster, *Dust Bowl* (note 1 above), p. 170.

12. *Amarillo Daily-News* (Texas), 2 February 1935, 14 April 1935, 17 July 1935; Clifford R. Hope, "Kansas in the 1930s," *Kansas Historical Quarterly* 36 (Spring 1970): 11; David Nail, *One Short Sleep Past: A Profile of Amarillo in the Thirties* (Canyon, Tex.: Staked Plains Press, 1973), pp. 35,

97; Joel A. Carpenter, "Fundamentalist Institutions and the Rise of Evangelical Protestantism, 1929–1942," *Church History* 49 (March 1980): 63–75.

13. Anderson M. Baten, "Faith in Yourself," *Baptist Standard*, 21 March 1935; *Meade County Press*, 28 February 1935; *Boise City News* (Okla.), 18 April 1935.

14. Dust Bowl Manuscripts, W. S. Campbell Collection, Western History Collections, University of Oklahoma, hereafter cited as Dust Bowl Manuscripts; *Dodge City Daily Globe* (Dodge City, Kans.), 29 March 1935; *Topeka Daily State Journal*, 23 March 1935; Walter Davenport, "Land Where Our Children Die," *Collier's* 100 (18 September 1937): 73; Hurt, *The Dust Bowl* (note 3 above), p. 56.

15. Ernest O. Sellers, "A Spiritual Awakening," *Baptist Standard*, 21 February 1935.

16. Robert Moats Miller, *American Protestantism and Social Issues, 1919–1939* (Chapel Hill: University of North Carolina, 1958), p. 116; Bailey, *Southern White Protestantism* (note 9 above), p. 112; Leo P. Ribuffo, *The Old Christian Right: The Protestant Far Right From the Great Depression to the Cold War* (Philadelphia: Temple University Press, 1983), pp. 101–24.

17. *Boise City News*, 21 March 1935; Thomas F. Saarinen, *The Perception of Drought Hazard on the Great Plains*, Department of Geography Research Paper No. 106 (Chicago: University of Chicago Press, 1966), p. 107.

18. Dust Bowl Manuscripts, (note 14 above); *Amarillo Globe-News*, 12 April 1935; Nail, *One Short Sleep* (note 12 above), p. 114.

19. "Southwest Breezes," *Hutchinson Herald* (Hutchinson, Kans.), 24 March 1935; *Amarillo Globe-News*, 10 June 1935, pp. 55–56; Nail, *One Short Sleep* (note 12 above), pp. 113–14.

20. *Avalanche-Journal* (Lubbock, Tex.), 31 May 1938; *Topeka Daily State Journal* (Kans.), 20 March 1935; Avis D. Carlson, "Dust," *New Republic* 82 (1 May 1935): 333; Worster, *Dust Bowl* (note 1 above), p. 17.

21. Delores Marie Wilmot, interview by Joan Kachel, 22 May 1979, Oral Interview Collection, No Man's Land Historical Museum, Goodwell, Oklahoma.

22. *Meade Globe News*, 18 April 1935; Bonnifield, *The Dust Bowl* (note 3 above), pp. 1–3, 75–76; Carlson, "Black Sunday" (note 3 above), pp. 5–17; James Wesley Ware, "Black Blizzard: The Dust Bowl of the 1930s" (Ph.D. diss., Oklahoma State University, 1977), pp. 57–58.

23. *Liberal News* (Kans.), 15 April 1935; Vance Johnson, *Heaven's Tableland: The Dust Bowl Story* (New York: Da Capo Press, 1974), p. 156; Michael Parfit, "The Dust Bowl," *Smithsonian* 20 (June 1989): 46.

24. Terin Miller, "Panhandle's Black Sunday Remembered," *Amarillo News-Globe* (Tex.), 14 April 1985, p. 18A; Bonnifield, *The Dust Bowl* (note

3 above), p. 2; *Herald-Democrat* (Beaver, Okla.), 18 April 1935; Mrs. Joe Billington, in McDaniel, ed., *God, Grass, and Grit* (note 7 above), p. 56.

25. Wanita Brown, interview by Ronnie Rittenberg, 2 April 1989, transcript, Panhandle-Plains Historical Museum, Canyon, Texas; Mr. and Mrs. H. B. Urban, interview by Diane Urban, 15 June 1974, ibid.; Larue Young, interview by Bob W. Young, 30 June 1974, ibid.; Dust Bowl Manuscripts (note 14 above).

26. Caroline Henderson, "Dust to Eat," ed. Virginia C. Purdy, in *Chronicles of Oklahoma* 58 (Winter 1980): 440–54; Haran Miller, "When Searing Drought Smites the Farm," *New York Times Magazine*, 27 May 1934, p. 7; *Meade County Press*, 21 March 1935; Pauline Grey, *Pioneer Stories* (note 7 above), p. 38; Stanley Vestal, *Short Grass Country* (New York: Duell, Sloan, and Pearce, 1941), p. 193; Dawber, "The Churches in the Dust Bowl" (note 7 above), p. 394; Marilyn Coffey, "The Dust Storms of the 1930s," *Natural History* 87 (February 1978): 81.

27. A. D. Edwards, *Influence of Drought and Depression on a Rural Community*, Case Study in Haskell County Kansas, Social Research Report No. 7, Farm Security Administration and Bureau of Agricultural Economics, U.S. Department of Agriculture (Washington, D.C.: Government Printing Office, 1939); Adams, "Social Behavior" (note 9 above), pp. 80, 73.

28. Evelyn Harris, "Letters of Two Women Farmers," *Atlantic Monthly* 152 (August 1933): 241.

29. *Boise City News*, 18 April 1935; Parfit, "The Dust Bowl" (note 22 above), pp. 52–53; Buren Sparks, "Dust Storms and Providence," *Baptist Standard*, 9 May 1935.

30. Adams, "Social Behavior" (note 9 above), pp. 66, 82; "Agriculture: 500,000 Tons of Dust Cover Kansas and Points East," *Newsweek* 5 (30 March 1935): 6; Les Dodson in McDaniel, ed., *God, Grass, and Grit* (note 7 above), p. 54.

31. "Dust: More Storms Wreak Destruction in the Southwest," *Newsweek* 5 (20 April 1935): 11; *Amarillo Daily-News*, 3 March 1935, 5 March 1935; *Herald-Democrat*, 18 April 1935; James B. Beddow, "Depression and New Deal: Letters From the Plains," *Kansas Historical Quarterly* 43 (Summer 1977): 141–42; Miller, "When Searing Drought Smites" (note 25 above), p. 7; Coffey, "The Dust Storms of the 1930s" (note 26 above), pp. 73–82.

32. Joe Klein, *Woody Guthrie: A Life* (New York: Knopf, 1980); Woody Guthrie, *Library of Congress Recordings*, Elektra Recordings (no recording number); Woody Guthrie, *Dust Bowl Ballads*, Folkways FH 5212.

33. Wilma Elizabeth McDaniel, in William Howarth, "Beyond the Dust Bowl," *National Geographic* 166 (September 1984): 337; John Steinbeck, *The Grapes of Wrath* (1939; rpt. New York: Viking Press, 1986); David E. Smith, "Millenarian Scholarship in America," *American Quarterly* 17 (1965): 548–549.

34. Kenneth Porter, "Anthology of Kansas Verse," *Kansas Magazine* (1937): 35–37; Robert Smith Bader, *Hayseeds, Moralizers, and Methodists: The Twentieth Century Image of Kansas* (Lawrence: University of Kansas Press, 1988), pp. 72–93.

35. Elmyr Doran Warren, "The Dust Storm," in *The Wind in the Cotton-woods*, ed. John L. McCarthy (Dalhart, Tex.: Dalhart Publishing Co., 1916), p. 211.

36. John L. McCarthy, "A Tribute to Our Sand Storms," John L. McCarthy Papers, Amarillo Public Library, Amarillo, Tex.

37. William Baker, "Dust Bowl Blues," unpublished poem, No Man's Land Historical Museum, Goodwell, Okla.; Miller, "When Searing Drought Smites" (note 26 above), p. 7; J. Russell Smith, "Drought—Act of God and Freedom," *Survey Graphic* 23 (September 1934): 412; Dwight Sanderson, *Research Memorandum on Rural Life in the Great Depression* (New York: Social Science Research Council, 1937), p. 92; *Liberal News*, 15 April 1935; *Amarillo Daily News*, 15 April 1915; Worster, *Dust Bowl* (note 1 above), pp. 113, 138, 170; Bonnifield, *The Dust Bowl* (note 3 above), pp. 185–202; R. Douglas Hurt, "The Dust Bowl," *The American West* 14 (March/April 1977): 23.

38. Walter Prescott Webb, *The Great Plains* (1931; reprint Lincoln: University of Nebraska Press, 1981), pp. 453, 481; George Williams, *Wilderness and Paradise in Christian Thought* (New York: Harper and Brothers, 1962), pp. 4–7, 130; Silvia Grider, "Black Easter: April 14, 1935," in *Diamond Bessie and the Shepherds*, ed. William M. Hudson (Austin, Texas: Encino Press, 1972), pp. 61–71.

39. Harry G. Lefever, "Religion of the Poor: Escape or Creative Force?" *Journal for the Scientific Study of Religion* 16 (September 1977): 225–36; for a full analysis of the regional approach to culture, see Patricia Nelson Limerick, Clyde A. Milner II, and Charles E. Rankin, eds., *Trails: Toward a New Western History* (Lawrence: University Press of Kansas, 1991).

VEHICLES FOR EXPRESSING THE FARMERS' RAGE—INSTITUTIONAL ACTIVISM

During the 1930s, farmers throughout the upper Midwest and the Great Plains joined a grassroots uprising to stop the attack on their way of life. Farm organizations that advocated dynamic solutions, such as the Farmers' Union, grew, and their leaders helped direct and mold the growing rage on farms and ranches.

The nascent Farmers' Holiday Association (FHA) was popular in 1932, and the organization spread throughout the northern Plains. The FHA actively encouraged a farm strike to try to elevate the extremely low farm prices. The Farm Holiday movement was particularly attractive to farmers in Nebraska and North Dakota, where it aggressively pursued a lengthy legislative agenda. In South Dakota the FHA seemed less responsive, in part because of geography, conservative traditions, and local political parties.

Radical agrarianism also emerged. Ella Reeve Bloor and other Communists actively sought to recruit farmers in a projected workers-farmers alliance, which was accomplished through the United Farmers League (UFL). In South Dakota the UFL organized direct action to oppose foreclosures and met with some success until South Dakota's attorney general led a legal assault on the organization. Radical agrarian organizations, as well as other, more conventional grassroots responses, were generally short-lived in the 1930s, but they were very popular with many farmers of the Dust Bowl.

The Farm Holiday Movement in Nebraska
John L. Shover

In the late summer of 1932 while a defeated Bonus Army retreated from the nation's capital and a depression-plagued administration contended for its political existence, a rebellious spirit stirred in the Missouri Valley of Nebraska and Iowa. To the old rhetoric of Populism was added a militant direct action reminiscent of long-dead Daniel Shays. Farmers threw picket lines across highways to blockade markets or forcibly intervened to prevent foreclosure of farm mortgages. With corn marketing at ten cents a bushel and hogs at three dollars a hundred-weight, their purchasing power barely a third that of 1914, the farmers demanded a price equal to "cost of production plus a reasonable profit." They endeavored to halt all foreclosure sales at a time when fifty-seven percent of Nebraska farms were mortgaged, and the number of foreclosures and bankruptcies per one thousand farms was rising from twenty-two in 1931 to fifty-eight in 1933.[1]

The Farm Holiday movement was a grassroots uprising in a time of frustration and rapid social change. The price and mortgage emergency underscored the fact that the midwestern farmer was losing his traditional independence and was ensnared in economic forces he could not control. As such accepted values of free enterprise economics as a just reward for labor and the automatic working of a benevolent economic system were shattered by desperate depression conditions, some few farmers momentarily embraced extremist remedies, but the rank and file of participants in the Farm Holiday were concerned only with immediate goals such as raising prices in thirty days or stopping a forced sale today. The Farmers' Holiday was a spontaneous movement lacking effective organized leadership. Once the crop reduction program of the Agricultural Adjustment Act [AAA] presented a viable alternative to radical action, even though that alternative was anathema to the leaders and accepted with misgivings by most farmers, neither the persuasion of the leaders nor the ideology they professed could rouse the intensity of the earlier movement.

A parallel exists between the Farm Holiday of the thirties and the Populist movement of the nineties. The economic emergencies that prompted the two movements were similar. In ideology, both portrayed the farmer as humble and down-trodden, oppressed by conspiring external forces symbolized by the satanic middleman or the Wall Street financier. Both embraced remedies which ostensibly would free the farmer from these external bonds and restore his traditional economic sovereignty, and both floundered when returning prosperity undercut their grassroots support.

THE FARM STRIKES

The farm strike, the initial phase of the Farm Holiday, began in Iowa and its center of activity was in the western counties of that state. However, it crossed the boundaries to affect Nebraska farmers whose circumstances were similar to their Iowa neighbors and who shipped products to the same markets. In Nebraska the Farm Holiday was for the most part concentrated in Douglas, Washington, Dakota, Thurston, and Dixon counties, all in the northeast corner of the state. It was basically a movement of corn-hog and cattle raising farmers; incidence of rebellious activity drops in counties with a cash-grain economy, and there is only negligible activity in wheat areas of Nebraska or adjoining states. In the Missouri River Valley counties of Iowa and Nebraska, farm incomes were among the highest in the nation; family farming was the traditional pattern; plumbing, radios, and automobiles were more common than in other farm regions. The Iowa counties where the farm strike centered had the highest gross income per acre in the state. The average land value per acre in the Nebraska counties with principal Farm Holiday activity was $126.25 per acre, compared with the state average of $50.58. Hogs, the principal product of the area, were considered a relatively stable commodity price-wise, yet the purchasing power of hogs (computed on the 1910–1914 index) had been 102.6 in 1926, it was 62.1 in 1931, and hit a low of 41.4 in 1932. Never in the history of American agriculture had hog prices declined so precipitately. In short, these were farmers who had a high level of expectation; in an unprecedented time of crisis they rebelled quickly.[2]

When the farmer surmised that his economic predicament was the result of impersonal market forces beyond his control, he was in part correct, but the crisis of the thirties was also partly the result of the farmer's own land speculation a decade earlier. In the halcyon days of the World War the American farmer supplied a world market and prices climbed accordingly. Encouraged by abundant demand and high prices, land, equipment, and buildings were mortgaged to buy more and more farmland. The Iowa counties where the Farm Holiday had its strongest support were centers of a feverish land boom in the early twenties. At Le Mars, Plymouth County land had been auctioned from the courthouse steps and banks had loaned as much as one thousand dollars on unsecured notes. Here in 1933, at the height of the anti-foreclosure fury, a judge pressing foreclosure actions narrowly escaped lynching.

As farm prices crept downward through the twenties, unpaid debts increasingly troubled these farmers. The economic collapse in 1929 subjected banks and lending institutions to irresistible pressures and foreclosures multiplied. There were fewer forced sales in Nebraska than in adjacent states, but even so the number per 1,000 farms increased from 21.8 in 1931 to 34.4 in 1932 and 58.2 in 1933.[3]

The idea of a farmers' marketing holiday was borrowed both from organized labor and from the bank holidays frequent in the Midwest after 1929. The Farmers' Holiday Association itself was created at Des Moines in May 1932, when an assembly of thirteen hundred, drawn largely from the Farmers' Union, pledged to initiate on July 4 a strike to terminate only when prices reached ninety-two cents per bushel of corn and $11.25 per hundred weight for hogs.[4]

Milo Reno, chosen to head the association, was a longtime evangelist of farmer causes. He had served for nine years as president of the Iowa Farmers' Union and in 1932 headed the Union's life insurance company. Along with his executive duties, he often preached in rural pulpits and fiddled for country barn dances. He had supported the McNary-Haugen plan, but in the twenties he had several times suggested that if farm prices failed to improve, produce should be withheld from market until a fair return was obtained.[5]

A farmers' strike was declared in Polk County (Des Moines) on August 8, but the focal point quickly shifted to Sioux City, where pickets appeared on the highways north of town three days later. The Holiday merged with a local battle of milk producers demanding a price higher than the present two cents a quart. By August 15, fifteen hundred pickets had virtually sealed the northern route to the Sioux City market. Maintaining a road blockade at the Woodbury-Plymouth County line, pickets leaped on running boards as farm trucks crept uphill in low gear or threw logs and threshing machine belts in the path of approaching vehicles. Save for occasional fisticuffs and a few broken windshields, there was little violence; most truckers simply turned back. One hundred special deputies were recruited to keep open the roads, but the Woodbury County sheriff did not prevent the stopping of vehicles or the using of persuasive techniques. On Thursday, August 18, hog receipts at Sioux City were half those of the preceding Thursday.[6]

As the selling holiday fanned out from Sioux City, the bridge linking Woodbury County with Dakota County, Nebraska, constituted the major gap in an increasingly solid barricade. To close the breach a Holiday Association was formed in Nebraska August 18. Vowing that "no farm produce of any nature whatsoever" would pass their lines, five hundred farmers marched from the courthouse at Dakota City to take position on highways 20 and 77 leading toward Sioux City.[7]

The moving spirit in the Nebraska movement was J. Fred Kriege of South Sioux City, who claimed that he, "personally and alone, started the Farmers' Holiday movement actively in Nebraska."[8] A graduate of the University of North Dakota law school, he had turned to farming for the love of it after practicing one year in Sioux City. His farm, located in Dakota County overlooking the Missouri River, carried a twelve thousand dollar mortgage. In August 1932, Kriege told Bruce Catton, an N.E.A. staff writer: "You can go in debt $2,000 in one year to pay for the privilege of farming these days—and you work your head off besides."[9] Kriege was a perennial crusader. He was active in Democratic party politics; he had led a campaign to reduce bridge tolls; and he had presented to Governor Bryan a plan to monetize farm commodities. Like Reno, he had lost faith in all established political methods, and sounding a note of desperation, he said to the gathering at Dakota City: "It is up to the farmers themselves . . . to go thru with this program, nobody else will help us. The zero hour has arrived lets get into action [sic]." He held sanguine hopes for the success of the Holiday and believed that farmers to achieve their ends would guard the roads all winter.[10]

PROBLEMS IN THE HOLIDAY MOVEMENT

Despite the optimism of Kriege or Reno there was little chance that the farm strike could long continue or materially affect farm prices. Two major handicaps militated against its success. First, there was a lack of discipline and second, the economic program of the Holiday was unsound.

The first problem was the lack of discipline and control. Although the leaders emphatically counselled against violence, there was no authority to govern thousands of pickets scattered over highways for over a hundred miles. When an agreement was reached in the Sioux City milk dispute some pickets still refused to allow dairy trucks to pass. Around Council Bluffs, where Pottowattomie and Harrison county farmers blockaded Omaha from the Iowa side of the river, county officials, less compliant than those in Woodbury County, informed Clinton Savery, organizer of the blockade, that he would be personally responsible for any violence or property damage. When Savery attempted to dissuade the pickets he was taunted with shouts of "sell-out!" "I have washed my hands of the entire mess. The strikers are beyond my control," he protested. On August 24, deputies in an automobile with tear gas cans mounted on the running boards ran a gauntlet of farmers armed with clubs and rocks. When forty-three were arrested, a sullen mob of five hundred, undaunted by machine guns in the hands of amateur deputies, swarmed over the courthouse lawn at Council Bluffs and threatened to storm the jail if the prisoners were not released by dusk. An eleventh-hour parley and arranging of bail averted imminent bloodshed and tragedy.[11]

With the disorder at Council Bluffs, Nebraska authorities grew fearful of an expanding blockade around Omaha. Outside the city about a thousand men—tenants, farm boys, and city unemployed lacking shelter, food, or money—set up an impromptu camp. Not only were they without leaders but one informed a reporter they were there because they had "too much leadership already." As at Sioux City, the farm produce blockade coalesced with an attempt of milk producers to gain recognition from the city's dairies for a producers' cooperative marketing association and win higher prices for raw milk. Although the milk producers claimed to operate independently of the Farm Holiday, pickets halted dairy trucks and dumped milk at the city's outskirts. Governor Charles Bryan on August 24 commissioned additional deputies in all counties north of Omaha and insisting that "the whole thing has been stirred up by agitators from Iowa" ordered that all pickets from Iowa should be arrested for inciting to riot. On the nights of August 30, August 31, and September 1 there were pitched battles of deputies and pickets at the Omaha city limits. On September 1 a thousand spectators watched as forty deputies were pelted by logs and rocks while they conducted farm trucks through a line of one hundred fifty pickets on Dodge Street.[12]

In the last days of August, strikers and deputies clashed in Woodbury County, Iowa; fourteen pickets at Cherokee were injured by a shotgun blast; at Clinton, across the state, farmers again threatened to storm the county jail. As peaceful picketing rapidly turned to riot, an unsympathetic *New York Times* correspondent in Omaha asserted, "[The] national leadership blew up, frightened at the appearance of the ugly monster into which its innocent child had so unexpectedly grown."[13]

The second problem was the unsound economic foundation of the farm strike idea. There was no conceivable possibility that blockading a single market could reduce the over-all supply of agricultural produce sufficiently to increase the farmers' price. When receipts of grain and livestock dwindled to zero at the Sioux City market, there was an increase at neighboring markets. Indeed, prices for farm products dropped to a year's low while the farm strike was in progress. Even had the farm strike been temporarily successful, the withheld produce released like an opened floodgate on the market at its conclusion would have broken the bottom out of the farm price structure.

From a practical standpoint, a farmer could not long participate in an embargo that deprived him of all income. There was livestock to be fed; there were families to be maintained. To keep marketable hogs and cattle on the farm meant added costs. Eventually the farmer had to sell at any price. Pressure of this sort led Farm Holiday leaders to announce on August 30 that the barricades would be relaxed sufficiently to allow hard-pressed farmers to market products. It was clear that an embargo of long duration could not be maintained.[14]

Nevertheless, the farm strike served one important purpose—it gave unrivaled publicity to the plight of the depression-plagued farmer. Governors and legislators of the farm states, quite aware on which side their political bread was buttered, could not fail to heed. Governor Warren Green of South Dakota supported the farmers' plea for cost of production and hinted that he might invoke legal sanction for an orderly farm embargo. The Farmer-Labor governor of Minnesota, Floyd B. Olson, would have gone so far as to proclaim martial law to support the strikers. On the other hand, while Governor Dan Turner of Iowa ventured no active support, neither did he attempt to deter the strikers. He spurned requests that the national guard be dispatched to the troubled areas. At Green's suggestion the governors agreed to meet in Sioux City on September 9 to hear appeals of the Holiday leaders and perhaps agree on a program of common action. As a corollary, the summoning of the conference provided the leaders of the farm strike a rationale for the abandonment of a movement that was already crumbling.[15]

The most outspoken dissident among farm belt governors was Charles W. Bryan of Nebraska. Despite his long associations with farmer causes, the brother of the "Great Commoner" could see nothing but "hard feelings and some bloodshed" resulting from the Farm Holiday. Governor Bryan insisted that the farm problem was national in scope and could not be assuaged by local picketing and farmers' strikes. The real enemy, he argued, was "the powers in Washington" and the remedy was "the repeal of legislation which caused this condition and not temporizing with the effects." "For one set of farmers to attack and assault another class of farmers on the public highway can only cause loss to all concerned and can only lead to anarchy and rebellion," he stated on September 1. As for the governors' conference, he declared that "the people of this nation have suffered more as a result of surveys and conferences than any other alibis they have been afflicted with." He did not attend the Sioux City meeting.[16]

Milo Reno, Fred Kriege, and other Holiday spokesmen proposed to the four governors and five representatives attending the conference[17] a four point program: (1) State mortgage moratoriums putting a temporary stop to all foreclosure proceedings. (2) A special session of Congress to enact the Frazier Bill (providing for federal refinancing of farm mortgages through issuing of fiat money). (3) Voluntary action by farmers to withhold goods from market. (4) Most important and most controversial, a demand for state enforced embargoes against the sale of farm products at less than cost of production. The governors expressed little sympathy for the far-reaching requests of the Holiday leaders. There was no legal precedent to allow a state to ban completely a creditor's proceedings against his debtor. The embargo proposal would have compelled by force of law all farmers, regardless of their sympathy for the withholding movement, to keep produce at home. "When you insist on an embargo on farm products and picketing of roads, you ask the impossible," Governor Turner declared.[18]

The upshot of the governors' conference, therefore, was a series of tame recommendations to President Hoover including such time-worn panaceas as tariff protection for farmers, currency expansion, and a request that federal and private agencies desist from foreclosures. Although there was little in the governors' memorial which bore resemblance to Farm Holiday Association demands, Reno stated that he was "on the whole" satisfied with the conference, but was disappointed by the lack of an embargo. This satisfaction was not shared by all Holiday members. A week later a convention of the Nebraska Farm Holiday Association resolved: "we consider the governors' conference at Sioux City a dismal failure, and we call upon the farmers, farm workers, and those dependent on Nebraska farming to join in the struggle for immediate action."[19]

The days following the governors' conference were a time of confusion and ambiguity for the Farm Holiday movement. Some pickets, defying the truce order, remained on the highways. At South Sioux City they refused to abandon their posts and informed Kriege that victory for the strike was near. These strikers incited the ire of law enforcement officials. One hundred of them brawled with deputies north of Sioux City on September 8 and again on September 15. Meanwhile, the leaders hastily evolved a plan less dangerous than blockading highways to maintain the momentum of the movement. An embargo "beginning at the farm gate" was to be inaugurated September 20—no grain or livestock would be marketed for thirty days. The agitation, however, had passed high tide. There were crops to be harvested. Cold weather drove wildcat pickets from the roads. By November all was quiet on Iowa and Nebraska highways.[20]

At the height of the farm strike in Nebraska, two major markets, Sioux City and Omaha, had been subjected to blockade. Farm holiday activity had been reported in eleven northeastern counties: Douglas, Washington, Dakota, Thurston, Dixon, Cass, Cedar, Colfax, Sarpy, Saunders, and Wayne. In addition meetings had been held in Cumings, Dodge, Madison, Pierce, and Burt counties.[21] This grassroots protest, the most forceful demonstration of agrarian discontent in the twentieth century, had for a brief moment focused national attention upon the desperate condition of the midwestern farmer, but it had not contributed to an amelioration of that condition. The withholding action had not reduced the number of hogs marketed at Iowa stockyards and a declining price trend beginning in July 1932 was not offset.[22]

NEBRASKA FARMERS ORGANIZE

In an attempt to capture this vagrant impulse of farm protest for more clearly defined purposes, sixteen hundred Nebraska farmers convened at Fremont on September 16 to formally organize a state Holiday Association. The platform adopted there summarizes the major demands of the movement:

We demand cost of production for farm products, plus an amount which will insure us a decent standard of living.

We demand a moratorium on mortgages and interest for poor farmers until the prices they receive are adequate to insure them their share of the good things of life.

We demand the cancellation of feed and seed loans made by the government.

We demand that the heavily mortgaged land of the poor farmers be exempt from taxes, this exemption to take effect before December 1.

We demand a moratorium on rents until prices of farm products equal the cost of production plus an amount for decent living.

We demand there be no eviction.

We demand increased prices to farmers come not from higher prices to city consumers but from profits of the middleman and the money interests.

We support a call for a national emergency farm relief conference at Washington when Congress convenes December 1.

Harry C. Parmenter of Yutan, vice-president of the Nebraska Farmers' Union, was elected president, A. O. Rosenberg of Newman Grove, vice-president; F. C. Crocker of Lincoln, secretary, and J. Fred Kriege, who had organized the first blockade at Dakota City, was named one of the state's representatives to the national board of directors.[23]

Despite the failure of the marketing strike, there remained one area where direct action by the newly formed organization could achieve concrete results—preventing the sale of foreclosed farm property. Masses of milling farmers or a noose dangling threateningly from the haymow silenced prospective bidders when mortgaged property was sold at auction.

Nebraska was a principal center of activity in this "penny auction" movement which began late in August 1932 when three hundred farmers, called together by Andrew Dahlsten, former chairman of the Non-Partisan League of Nebraska, and Harry Lux, of Lincoln, met in Madison County. Learning of a scheduled foreclosure sale at Elgin, Antelope County, a committee was chosen to contact the owner, who was a young widow, and the auctioneer. The latter agreed to accept a single bid. On October 6 farmers from forty counties were present at the sale. All offered items, chickens, cattle, or horses, sold for five cents each, and there were no opposing bids. The total proceeds of the sale were $5.35; the mortgagor, the receiver for the Elgin State Bank, reluctantly accepted the settlement. A few days later at Petersburg fifteen hundred farmers limited a chattel foreclosure sale to $7.10. At Newman Grove, seventy-five men, identifying themselves as the "red army" of the Nebraska Farm Holiday Association, dragged from a garage two trucks a sales company had reclaimed from a delinquent farmer and returned them to the purchaser.[24]

ENTER COMMUNISM

The agrarian crisis of the thirties was so acute and the foreclosure resistance was so little guided by the state Holiday organization that the situation was ideal for exploitation by opportunistic political groups. Shortly after the Petersburg sale Lux and Dahlsten were approached at the latter's Madison County farm by Robert Hall and Harold Ware of the Communist Party. Out of this meeting emerged a branch of the Farm Holiday Association known as the "Madison County Plan" that was closely linked with a determined Communist offensive in American agriculture.

Although Harry Lux twenty-five years later recalled that the Communist contact with the anti-foreclosure resistance came only after the Petersburg sale in October, the resolutions adopted and the officers elected at the convention in Fremont in September indicate that the radical influence, that would rend the Nebraska Farm Holiday throughout its entire existence, was already present. The first two planks of the Fremont platform were demands Milo Reno had been making, but the reference to "poor farmers" as a distinct class, the blanket declaration against all eviction, and the final plank endorsing the forthcoming Washington farm relief conference bore the earmarks of the radical group. Parmenter and Crocker, the president and secretary, respectively, were strong Reno supporters, but Vice-President Anton Rosenberg was one of the leaders of the Madison County faction.[25]

The Communist Party had only recently developed an interest in the protests of the property-owning farmers of the Midwest. The first reports of the farm strike in the Daily Worker were coupled with attacks upon Milo Reno and other Farm Holiday leaders and admonitions to the striking farmers to elect their own governing committees and continue their struggles over the heads of the "misleaders."[26] When farmers assembled in Sioux City at the time of the governors' conference, Mother Ella Reeve Bloor, a veteran party agitator, presided at a small gathering which issued a call for a National Farm Emergency Relief Conference to meet in Washington on December 1. It was toward this forthcoming conference that the Communists directed their principal efforts among farmers in the autumn of 1932.[27]

The two hundred-fifty delegates at the Washington conference adopted a series of militant demands which included outright cash relief to poor farmers, direct government sale of farm products to consumers, a demand for easier farm credit, and a complete moratorium on taxes, rents, and mortgage payments for all farmers. Harry Lux and Jess Green of Nebraska played a prominent part in the proceedings, and Rosenberg was elected president of the Farmers' National Committee for Action founded at the convention.[28] The Daily Worker gave extensive and laudatory coverage to the conference, and such Communist stalwarts as Mother Bloor and her son Harold Ware were active participants.

Returning from Washington, the Madison County leaders swung into vigorous action to organize the growing anti-foreclosure sentiment in Nebraska. By January they estimated that two to three farmer "committees of action" were being formed nightly and that six thousand members had been recruited from central and eastern Nebraska.[29] All the opposition to foreclosures was not under the domination of this group; for example in Dakota County Fred Kriege was organizer of a county arbitration board which acted as an unofficial court of equity in settling rent and mortgage disputes.[30]

The major energy of the radical group, however, was directed to a dramatic march on the state capital scheduled for February 15. The marchers would demand of the legislature adoption of a stringent anti-foreclosure law and the program of the Farmers' National Committee for Action. One particularly belligerent leader estimated that the demonstrators would number two hundred and fifty thousand and if the state legislature failed to take action they would tear down the state capitol. As the plans of the radicals neared fruition, leaders of the National Farm Holiday organization in Nebraska grew fearful of the untoward direction the movement was taking. Early in February, F. C. Crocker, the secretary, wrote Milo Reno: "This will be the battle of my lifetime this week. It is and has been Communism pitted against Reno in Nebraska."[31] The *Daily Worker* of February 11 declared: "Harry Parmenter, state president of the Association and F. C. Crocker, secretary, have been doing everything within their power (with the aid of the capitalistic newspapers) to break up this march and thus make it possible for the bankers and their politicos to go ahead, unhampered, in making laws that will enable them to have an excuse to continue their campaign of robbing the farmers." Shortly before the day of the demonstration, Crocker circulated a mimeographed flyer to the Holiday membership:

> Communism works in mysterious ways. In the Nebraska Farm Holiday Association, COMMUNISTIC agitators advocate no membership dues for State and National Org. work. . . . Communism has built up a prejudice against state and National Holiday Officers. . . . Communists have circulated their literature. . . . Communists have shown their moving pictures. . . . Their Agents are with us. . . . They deny their idenity [sic]. . . . They are now publishing a paper for the Nebraska Farmers. . . . Communistic money from the Five Year Plan of Russia is being used to Communize the World. . . . Is Russian money being used in Nebraska at this time?[32]

To checkmate further the extremists' demands, Crocker met on February 14 with Tom Allen, acting as governor in the absence of Charles Bryan, and together they made arrangements to have introduced in the legislature a moratorium law based on that of Iowa.[33]

The highly vaunted march of February 15 fell short of the sanguine hopes of the radical leaders. Some three thousand farmers marched in the streets of Lincoln bearing signs "Wives and Children

Have the First Mortgage" and listened to speeches by Lux and other leaders from the steps of the capitol building.

Even without the drama of the demonstration at Lincoln the opposition to foreclosures was already having results. On January 30, Governor Bryan appointed a conciliation commission which would attempt to mediate between debtors and lending institutions. Harry Parmenter was one of the original members. The court of the ninth district, whose jurisdiction extended over most of northeastern Nebraska, announced a mortgage moratorium of indefinite duration.[34] Many eastern insurance companies suspended foreclosure actions and on March 2 the Nebraska legislature provided for a two year moratorium on mortgage foreclosures. By April, particularly in eastern Nebraska, farm foreclosures had ceased.[35]

The militant phase of this successful anti-foreclosure drive was almost entirely the work of the radical group. Most of the "penny auctions" in Nebraska centered in Madison and neighboring counties: Antelope, Platte, Boone, Stanton, and Cedar. Harry Lux was the organizer of the protest at a sale in Wilber, Saline County, in which he and seventeen others were arrested. Other sales were halted by farmer action in Washington, Hamilton, and Knox counties.

The split between the two factions left a permanent scar on the Nebraska Farm Holiday Association. The national never succeeded in organizing within the state a consolidated movement such as functioned in Iowa, Minnesota, Wisconsin, or the Dakotas. The Madison County unit lingered for several years with meager numbers, sending representatives to the various conferences sponsored by the Farmers' National Committee for Action. In January 1934, Milo Reno was asked by a reporter to comment on the claim of the Communists that they had organized the Nebraska Farm Holiday Association of 25,000 members. He replied, "Those communists formed a rump association in Madison County, Nebraska, but it didn't amount to a damn. And it didn't have anything to do with us."[36]

THE NEW DEAL IMPACT

Meanwhile, the advent of a new national administration with a vigorous legislative program that seemed to offer hope to Iowa and

Nebraska farmers redirected the attention of the agrarian protestants of the Midwest. The two states had reversed their traditional Republican political allegiance to return resounding majorities for Roosevelt. Farm Holiday members had good reason to support the new administration. The agricultural plank of the Democratic Party platform had concluded with the intriguing promise: "Enactment of every constitutional measure that will aid the farmer to receive for basic farm commodities prices in excess of cost." An Iowan, Henry A. Wallace, who had been associated with Milo Reno in support of the McNary-Haugen plan, was named Secretary of Agriculture.[37]

But the legislative mills grind slowly for the anxious agitator. There was in Washington distressing talk of "domestic allotment," a plan—anathema to cost of production zealots—which would limit the farmer's output in place of guaranteeing his price. The Frazier-Lemke Bill, providing for federal refinancing of farm mortgages at one and one-half percent plus an annual one and one-half percent payment on principal, had long been slumbering in Congressional processes. The earlier farm strike had won the attention of state governments; perhaps a revival of direct action would stimulate a national administration. The fifteen hundred delegates attending the National Farm Holiday convention in March believed so, for they made bold threats of a nationwide strike to begin May 13 if "legislative justice" had not been accorded by that time. In a radical mood that harked back to Populism, they demanded not only the Frazier-Lemke Bill and a federal guarantee of cost of production, but complete state and federal mortgage moratoriums, federal operation of the banking and credit system, currency inflation, and an income tax graduated to confiscate all great wealth accumulations.[38] Reno, less impatient than the membership, counseled delay; farm prices were creeping upward; passage of a new federal farm bill was imminent. In March, Congress had created a Farm Credit Administration and granted it power to refinance farm mortgages, float "rescue loans" to underpin second mortgages, and develop techniques to persuade creditors to make reasonable adjustment. On May 12, one day before the scheduled strike, the Agricultural Adjustment Act passed Congress. Reno, in St. Paul, hastily conferred with Governor Floyd B. Olson, the warmest political friend of the Holiday, and persuaded him to make public his conviction that the Roosevelt administration was doing something for the farmer and that the strike should be delayed to await results. Reno conveyed the advice to his followers by radio and the May strike was postponed.[39]

After a short-lived recovery, farm prices sagged, but most important it became clear that the new administration was unsympathetic to cost of production price guarantees. The parity formula pegged farm prices to relative purchasing power during the base years 1910–1914, and in sharp contrast to the panaceas of the Farm Holiday leaders, attacked the farm surplus through curtailing production rather than attempting to provide a market for all the farmer could produce. The irate leaders quickly surmised that their principal enemy within the administration, the chief advocate of domestic allotment, was Secretary of Agriculture Wallace. Studies of the New Deal make clear that Roosevelt and most of his advisors were as devoted as the most avid farm rebel to achieving farm recovery and maintaining in the process the integrity of the small family farm. The Holiday leaders demanded more—any recovery plan should in no way limit the farmer's right to determine what he produced and how much. Government should require that processors pay a price for farm produce that squared with the farmer's own idea of equity.

ENTER FASCISM

By autumn, the Holiday leadership was in full-blown rebellion against the New Deal agricultural program and they were vainly attempting to whip up the grassroots sentiment that had sustained the movement the preceding year. When Secretary Wallace announced on October 8 the details of his corn-hog program,[40] Milo Reno condemned it as a "brazen attempt to bribe the farmer to surrender the little independence he has left." But Reno's call for a renewed strike brought only seventy-five pickets to their old stations north of Sioux City and only a few northeastern Nebraska farmers responded. Law enforcement officials quickly quashed rash acts of violence.[41]

A delegation of midwestern governors, responding to Farm Holiday pressures, carried demands for cost of production guarantees directly to Washington. They were sharply rebuffed by the President and the Secretary of Agriculture. Back in the corn-belt, Reno called for a "major offensive" in the farm strike and declared that "the responsibility for whatever happens in the future will rest squarely on the shoulders of the administration and Secretary Wallace in particular."[42] Reno's pleas that farmers should refuse payment proffered them under the A.A.A. corn loan program[43] were ignored or defied. The local paper at Le Mars, Iowa, which once had supported the Holiday, expressed what seemed to be the attitude of most Iowa and Nebraska farmers: "We don't care if Milo Reno does say you shouldn't touch any of that money. When you get a chance to get Uncle Sam's check for anywhere from $300 to $1,000, and even more, there's something wrong with you if you don't take it."[44] A growing conviction that the administration had concern for the farmers' welfare and the slow improvement in farm prices had driven pickets from the highways—they would never return.

In the weeks and months to come, Milo Reno's disillusion expanded to encompass not only the A.A.A., but the entire New Deal. Henry Wallace he described as "the worst enemy the farmer has ever had in an official position," the A.A.A. was the child of "brain-busters" allied with the United States Chamber of Commerce; the New Deal was an attempt to "Russianize" America.[45] A supporter of Father Coughlin and the Townsend old age pension plan, Reno before his death was vainly trying to forge anti–New Deal groups into a third party coalition and he looked with favor on Huey Long as a potential standard-bearer.[46]

In Nebraska, Fred Kriege's thinking paralleled that of Reno. Like Reno, he had been an ardent Roosevelt supporter in 1932; he outlined to the president-elect on November 14, 1932, a complex and disjointed plan for establishing a new monetary system using stored farm crops as security. Minimum farm prices paid in the new currency would be fixed by law. His proposal was reminiscent of the sub-treasury system of the Farmers' Alliance fifty years before. Although lacking official encouragement, throughout 1933, Kriege bombarded the President with lengthy defenses of his plan. With words suggestive of the Populist crusaders of the nineties he condemned "ruthless, unscrupulous, unchristian middlemen," reproached all bankers as "present day money-lenders . . . desecrating the economic temple," and damned the Hoover administration: "under the Golden Calf banner of this foreign conceived plutocratic vessel, its Unholy Diabolic Crew has laid waste to our bountiful, fair, and once prosperous country." The only acknowledgments were curt official notes stating that the suggestions had been received. Nonetheless, Kriege became convinced that parts of his plan had been bodily incorporated in the new Commodity Credit Corporation, for which he had been given no recognition. As it became apparent that the New Deal fell short of cost of production guarantees or the total fiscal overhaul he demanded, he became disillusioned. In one of his proposals to the President he had concluded: "The National Administration has made a good start. . . ." In his own hand he later appended the words: "for the bankers."[47]

Kriege had remained outside the bitter factional strife in the disjointed Nebraska Holiday movement. Although both he and Milo Reno were voluminous letter-writers they did not correspond. However, Kriege was in contact with the national movement through Emil Loriks, the president of the South Dakota Farmers' Holiday. He was in no way tempted by the Madison County radicals. Neither was he persuaded in May 1933 to cast his lot with the Modern 76ers, another extremist group of quite different vintage, which sought also to seize upon the same well-spring of discontent. Lester Barlow of Stamford, Connecticut, the founder of this group, was an almost legendary figure who had fought with Pancho Villa, invented a depth bomb used by the navy in the World War, and later enjoyed a considerable reputation as a munitions expert. Barlow, a crusader who sought to liberate capitalism from the dictatorship of "high finance," had met Kriege when he campaigned for Roosevelt in Sioux City in 1932.[48] In a letter of May 1, 1933, Barlow wrote Kriege that after correspondence and conversations with the new President,[49] he had concluded that Roosevelt was an "irresponsible lightweight, a political adventurer and opportunist." The Modern 76ers were already organizing in northwest Iowa, and now Barlow urged Kriege to lend his efforts to a fantastic plan: Unless within a year the productive citizens would organize themselves into a powerful military structure, the nation would

"go down" to rioting and bloodshed. As a military expert, Barlow offered to place himself at the head of a citizens' army with headquarters at Sioux City. Once 25,000 were so organized, Barlow would submit a program to the President: eliminate all millionaires; institute
government ownership of all public services including insurance companies; operate all industries through the citizens' army until "a new
order may be established"; reorganize completely the structure of
representative government; eliminate the stock market; and arrange
for international disarmament. Should the President fail to acquiesce
in such a program, which to Barlow's way of thinking he had promised
in the 1932 campaign, the citizens' army would carry out his promises
for him.[50]

Kriege was not persuaded to carry discontent to the extremes
advocated by Barlow, but in a social environment ripe for panaceas,
there were other havens for the disappointed. By the end of 1933,
Fred Kriege had cast his lot with the opponents of the New Deal; he
joined the picket lines in November and a year later resigned from
the Democratic party. He was among the host attracted to a compelling Sunday afternoon radio voice from Royal Oak, Michigan, plead-
ing for inflation and scorning the heavy-handed control of international financiers. Kriege complimented Fr. Charles Coughlin for his
"flaying of isms and personalities . . . even the President for straying
from true democratic principles" and added: "Your views and methods not only clicked with my beliefs but also with my ideas of fighting
for convictions." Voicing his disappointment and frustrations he wrote:

> The farmers' necessary reserve commodity production [Kriege's
> plan] should be reorganized as a blessing of God and as a basis for
> stabilizing his credits instead of a cure and a destroyer of the credit
> value of all of his commodity production, as held in the past and still
> held by the high finance soviet hybrid school of thought—parroted
> by Henry Wallace, Tugwell, and their strip of Real Red Radicals.
> The president cannot escape responsibility for their policies; he ap-
> pointed them and is upholding their actions.[51]

Yet Kriege, like Reno, was a prophet without a cause. The vast
majority of farmers cooperating in the domestic allotment program

and the meager two percent of Nebraska votes returned for William Lemke,[52] the only candidate in 1936 who in any way approximated Farm Holiday objectives, testified to just how completely the incipient protest had been quelled. The promise of amelioration, by the New Deal, of the economic crisis into which these ordinarily stable farmers had fallen in 1932 had undercut the Farm Holiday movement.

CONCLUSION

The Farmers' Holiday at its peak in the fall and winter of 1932 was a spontaneous uprising against intangible enemies, an impassioned movement of strongly individualistic men oppressed by circumstances they could not understand or control. Coordinated leadership was absent, and once the underlying grassroots sentiment was stilled, all the force of the radical, or the demagogue, could not raise it. When farmers blockaded highways or obstructed legal proceedings they were radicals, but radicals in method alone. "Cost of production" or the program of the Farmers' National Committee for Action as principles were unimportant so long as there was money to meet the next mortgage payment. Men who halted trucks or threatened county courthouses were willing, even enthusiastic, to embrace an economic remedy at total variance with that of their leaders.

In its ideology as proclaimed by Reno or Kriege, the Farm Holiday was deep-rooted in traditional thinking. In an age of commercial agriculture the leaders of the movement conjured up the Jeffersonian dream of the independent, virtuous yeoman beset by powerful and immoral enemies. Like the great prophets of the nineties, their legatees in the thirties saw at the center of the farmer's problem a sinister conspiracy of brokers and middlemen. They too substituted a simple symptomatic remedy for critical analysis of causes. Thus, cost of production was a still-born descendent of free silver. Like the Populists, they overlooked the speculative machinations through which in so large a measure the farmer had woven his own fate. They spurned solutions which in any way compromised the traditional individualism and self-government of those chosen of God who labored in the earth. And like the Populists they misgauged the sentiment of their followers in fail-

ing to perceive that those temporarily fallen from economic grace
sought not a panacea to solve all their problems but only an immediate amelioration of their condition.

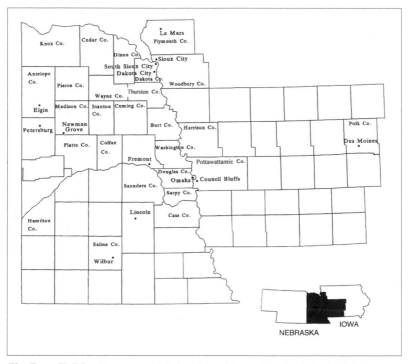

The Farm Holiday Movement in Nebraska and Iowa. Map by Robert Watrel.

NOTES

1. Addison E. Sheldon, *Land Systems and Land Policies in Nebraska* (Lincoln, 1936), 293–294; United States Department of Agriculture, Bulletin
   #354, "The Farm Real Estate Situation" (Washington, April 1935), 31.
2. Charles P. Loomis and J. Allen Beegle, *Rural Social Systems* (New York,
   1950), 165–267; Lauren P. Soth, *Agricultural Economic Facts Basebook
   of Iowa* (Ames, 1936), 120; United States Department of Agriculture, *Yearbook of Agriculture*, 1932 (Washington, 1933), 784; William Allen White,
   "Farmer Takes His Holiday," *Saturday Evening Post* CCV (November
   26, 1932), 6–7; United States Department of Commerce, Bureau of Census, *United States Census of Agriculture*, 1925, *The Northern States*, I
   (Washington, 1927), 1134–1147.

3. United States Department of Agriculture, Bulletin #354, loc. cit., 31; *New York Times*, November 16, 1933.
4. Howard W. Lawrence, "The Farmers Holiday Association in Iowa, 1932–1933." Unpublished thesis, M.A., The University of Iowa, 1952, 24–26.
5. Ibid., 18–19.
6. Frank D. Dileva, "Iowa Farm Price Revolt," *Annals of Iowa* XXXII (January 1954), 175–176; *Sioux City Journal*, August 19, 1932.
7. *Des Moines Register*, August 18, 1932; *Omaha World-Herald*, August 18, 1932.
8. J. Fred Kriege to Governor Franklin D. Roosevelt, November 14, 1932, Kriege papers, private collection held by Kriege family, Hayward, California.
9. J. Fred Kriege to Hon. A. S. Goss, December 19, 1933, Kriege papers; *Indianapolis* (Indiana) *Times*, August 31, 1932.
10. MSS Speech to Farmers' Holiday Association of Dakota County, August 18, 1932, Kriege papers.
11. *Sioux City Journal*, August 23, August 26, 1932; *Des Moines Register*, August 20, August 25, 1932; *Omaha World-Herald*, August 25, 1932.
12. *Omaha World-Herald*, August 24, August 30, August 31, September 1, 1932; *New York Times*, August 24, 1932.
13. September 4, 1932.
14. *Sioux City Journal*, August 31, 1932.
15. Ibid., August 28, September 1, 1932.
16. Ibid., August 28, September 2, 1932. The legislation to which Governor Bryan referred was the Agricultural Marketing Act of 1929.
17. Present at the conference were Governors Turner of Iowa, Green of South Dakota, Olson of Minnesota, and Shafer of North Dakota. Also in attendance were representatives of the governors of Nebraska, Ohio, Wisconsin, Wyoming, and Oklahoma.
18. *Sioux City Journal*, September 10, September 11, 1932.
19. Ibid., September 16, September 24, 1932.
20. Dileva, loc. cit., 199–200; *Sioux City Journal*, September 3, 1932.
21. *Sioux City Journal*, August 25, 1932; *Omaha World-Herald*, August 15–September 8, 1932, passim.
22. The number of hogs marketed in Iowa was 750,525 in July, 1932; 804,335 in August, 787,352 in September, 806,035 in October. Computed on the 1910–1914 base the index numbers for Iowa hog prices were July, 58; August, 53; September, 49; October, 41; November, 38; December, 33. Soth, *Agricultural Economics Facts Basebook of Iowa*, 16.
23. *Sioux City Journal*, September 16, 1932.
24. Sheldon, *Land Systems and Land Policies in Nebraska*, 294–295; Leif Dahl, "Nebraska Farmers in Action," *New Republic* LXXIII (January 18, 1933), 165–166; Harry Lux, "The Farm Holiday Story," *U.S. Farm News* (Des Moines, Iowa) XXXVII (May–June 1959), 2–4.
25. Harry Lux, loc. cit.; the *Daily Worker* (New York), September 21, 1932 claimed that the radical group completely captured the Fremont convention.

26. *Daily Worker,* September 3, 1932.

27. Ella Reeve Bloor, *We Are Many* (New York, 1940), 235–236.

28. *Daily Worker,* February 24, 1933.

29. Dahl, loc. cit.; Lement Harris, "The Spirit of Revolt," *Current History* XXXVIII (July 1933), 426. The Madison County Plan had a good press. Leif Dahl, organizer of the farmers' march on Lincoln. claimed Madison County as his residence and served later as assistant executive secretary of the Farmers' National Committee for Action [FNCA}. Lement "Lem" Harris was the executive secretary of the F.N.C.A.

30. J. Fred Kriege to Hon. A. S. Goss, December 19, 1933. Kriege papers.

31. F. C. Crocker to Milo Reno, February 1933. Milo Reno papers, private collection held by U.S. Farmers Organization, Des Moines, Iowa.

32. Copy in Reno papers.

33. Crocker to Reno, February 19, 1933. Reno papers.

34. Knox, Antelope, Pierce, Madison, Wayne, Stanton, and Cumings counties.

35. Sheldon, *Land Systems and Land Policies in Nebraska,* 195–296; *New York Times,* January 15, 1933; Dahl, "Class War in the Corn Belt," *New Republic* LXXV (May 17, 1933), 12–13.

36. *New York Sun,* January 3, 1934, clipping in Reno collection, University of Iowa Library, Iowa City.

37. Roland A. White, *Milo Reno* (Iowa City, 1941), 86.

38. Lawrence, "The Farmers Holiday Association in Iowa," 70–71; *New York Times,* May 4, 1933.

39. Arthur M. Schlesinger, Jr., *The Coming of the New Deal* (Boston, 1959), 45; George H. Mayer, *The Political Career of Floyd B. Olson* (Minneapolis, 1951), 153.

40. Farmers who reduced swine production to seventy-five percent of their last two years average would be paid five dollars per hog on the remaining twenty-five percent balance and thirty cents per bushel would be paid on the twenty percent of corn acreage kept out of production.

41. *New York Times,* October 22, October 29, 1933.

42. Mayer, *Floyd B. Olson,* 153–154; Russell Lord, *The Wallaces of Iowa* (Boston, 1947), 360–361; *New York Times,* November 5, November 11, 1933.

43. A farmer was loaned 45¢ per bushel for corn sealed on his premises. The loan could be repaid at 4% interest, but if the market price at the time of sale was less than 45¢ the corn could be forfeited. If the market price was higher the farmer could repay the loan, retaining the profit.

44. Quoted in *New York Times,* November 17, 1933.

45. Dale Kramer, *The Wild Jackasses: The American Farmer in Revolt* (New York, 1956), 244; Milo Reno, speeches of May 13, 1934, December 30, 1934, February 10, 1935, quoted in Roland White, *Milo Reno,* 27, 162, 186; *New York Times,* May 4, 1934.

46. Reno, speech of February 10, 1935, quoted in White, *Milo Reno,* 138; *New York Times,* April 9, 1935.

47. J. Fred Kriege to Franklin D. Roosevelt, November 14, 1932; Kriege,

unpublished MSS, "An Indictment of the Money Changers and the Middle-west Commodity Orderly Marketing System for Permanent Farm and National Prosperity," August 4, 1933, Kriege papers.

48. *New York Times*, May 6, August 13, 1932; August 28, 1940; March 26, 1955. Lester Barlow, *What Would Lincoln Do?* (Stamford, Connecticut), 1931, passim.

49. Barlow had talked at least once with Roosevelt between election and inauguration day. M. A. LeHand to Lester Barlow, December 2, 1932, Roosevelt collection, Franklin D. Roosevelt Library, Hyde Park, New York.

50. Barlow's movement eventually coalesced—and faded—with the Huey Long movement. Lester Barlow to the writer, October 19, 1961. In an interview with the writer on January 4, 1962, Mr. Lester Barlow pointed out that the letter to Fred Kriege of May 1, 1933, was written at a time when he believed there was serious danger of a military dictatorship in the United States. His plan was designed to provide a strong, organized defense against such an eventuality. Any reforms he advocated were to be carried out by ballot, not by force. Mr. Barlow remains basically in sympathy with the program he advocated in 1933, except in place of government ownership of public services he would now favor a cooperative system and rather than eliminate the stock market he would forbid all marginal buying.

51. Kriege to Thomas Ashford, October 7, 1935; Kriege to Rev. Charles E. Coughlin, February 10, 1935, Kriege papers.

52. *The World Almanac and Book of Facts for 1958* (New York, 1958), 598.

THE NORTH DAKOTA FARM STRIKE OF 1932
Larry Remele

The farm strike of 1932 swept North Dakota with the suddenness of a prairie thunderstorm. From the indication of militant unrest during July to the appearance of pickets at marketing points in late September, the gravitation of the state's hard-hit farmers into organizations which aimed to force price increases through crop and livestock withholding and to resist farm foreclosures by mass action occurred so rapidly that success seemed assured. Yet, the apparent unity created by desperate economic circumstances could not overcome the deep divisions among the farms, and the strike fell apart almost as quickly as it had begun.

Agitation against the economic conditions created by the Depression flourished in North Dakota during the summer of 1932. A combination of commodity prices which dipped to record-setting lows during a bumper crop year[1] and a rising wave of mortgage foreclosures[2] put many farmers into untenable situations and led to a cry for new leadership and new ideas. Emblematic of the discontent, the revitalized Nonpartisan League won a smashing victory in the June Primary election over Republican opposition linked to the policies of President Herbert Hoover, and William L. Langer, who based his bid for the gubernatorial nomination on a platform of cleaning house in Bismarck, rode with a protest vote that brought the League back to dominance in the nation's most rural state. Outside the partisan arena, the North Dakota Farmers' Union worked to win a state-instituted moratorium on foreclosures and to focus rural attention on the need for tight farmer organization. Its activities procreated the Farmers' Holiday Association [FHA], the unit that put the call for change into militant action.

Although a North Dakota Holiday Association did not actually form until July 31, the development capitalized on a variety of agitation that ranged from the creation of the "$1 Wheat" organization to mass protest meetings chaired by Farmers' Union officials. In the former instance, an idea first promoted by Dell Willis of Tolna at a July 4 picnic in the Nelson County town of Hamar spread with dramatic speed throughout the state and into surrounding grain-growing areas;[3] Willis' plan called for voluntary withholding of wheat from the market until prices reached one dollar per bushel, a figure deemed sufficient to repay the cost of raising the grain and to provide a small profit. Once the price goal had been achieved, the crop would be gradually filtered onto the market in order to keep the price up.[4] Willis' idea proved extremely attractive. The voluntary aspect, the descriptive name, the originator's image as an "ordinary North Dakota farmer,"[5] and a fast-paced speaking campaign resulted in "$1 Wheat" winning wide endorsement from businessmen, government officials, and townspeople, as well as farmers.[6] Its drawbacks, however, caused it to decline in popularity as quickly as it had grown; for example, the voluntarism permitted no control over selling, and the one-crop focus neglected the other commodities which provided farm income. Moreover, the group systematically canvassed for members mainly in the Devils Lake region near Willis' home and there the "$1 Wheat" strike, called on August 15, proved the most effective. Other regions, less organized and more distant, proved less able to sustain the unenforced strike.

THE FARMERS' UNION IN NORTH DAKOTA

For its part, the Farmers' Union pushed its anti-Depression remedies at protest meetings[7] which petitioned for the foreclosure proposal, demanded larger harvest loans, and supported the Frazier Debt Refinancing Bill at that time pending before Congress.[8] Speakers at these meetings generally included state Farmers' Union President Charles C. Talbott, Nonpartisan League [NPL] Senators Gerald P. Nye and Lynn J. Frazier, Representative James Sinclair, congressional candidate William Lemke, other NPL officials, and sympathetic business and professional people. Invariably, resolutions calling for "cost of production" for farm products passed unanimously.[9]

The leadership assumed by the Farmers' Union well fitted the progressive image that the comparatively youthful state organization had gained.[10] Chartered in 1927, the North Dakota arm of the Farmers' Educational and Cooperative Union of America had attracted many farmers to its program of co-operative purchasing and marketing, educational activities, and other associated benefits. To a large degree responsible for its growth was Charles C. Talbott, a Forbes (Dickey County) farmer and NPL leader who had been an early convert to the cause and who had been elected President of the North Dakota unit at the first state convention.[11] Talbott's leadership of the Farmers' Union aimed primarily at building the organization into a recognizable economic and political force, and he therefore ceaselessly hammered away at the themes of interdependence and cooperation. From these ideas developed the emphasis on the local unit as the source of strength, a fact which lent credence to Talbott's frequent claim that the Farmers' Union was truly a "grassroots" movement.

THE JAMESTOWN STRIKE CONVENTION

Talbott chaired the meeting of Farmers' Union leaders that created the temporary Holiday Association.[12] Although he had earlier denied that such a move was planned, his remarks to the assembled delegates in Jamestown expounded the need for a new and militant organization. The discussions accordingly took on decidedly frank overtones. In the words of one participant, I. A. Kampen of Hannaford, "Phrases like 'direct action,' 'armed resistance,' 'night ride,' etc., were freely bandied back and forth, showing the temper of the farmers present."[13]

Those feelings found their way into the resolutions adopted by the delegates. Along with expressing the desire to form a Holiday Association, the recommendations demanded that the "courts and governments of our state . . . invoke special police powers . . . to prevent the forced sale of farm commodities for the satisfaction of liens and indebtedness thereon until the price level for such commodities shall have reached the cost of production." Moreover, the writers agreed "to assist and protect each other in the sale of enough mortgaged property and commodities to furnish funds for harvest, threshing and living expenses," to hold the balance of their produce on the farms "by joint action against the claims of all creditors," to "protect one another in the actual possession of necessary home, livestock and machinery as against all other claimants," and to appoint committees "in the various cities, villages and townships, who shall, in case of emergency, call out the entire membership." To justify these potentially extra-legal actions, the delegates asserted that men should be guided by "the natural law of human rights as opposed to property rights" and that "society has no moral or just right to expect or force any group . . . to perform services for less than the cost of performing such services." The concluding resolutions declared firm opposition to any restrictions on the constitutional rights of free speech and assembly and called for governmental limitations on income, inheritances, and excess wealth as a means of more equitably distributing the benefits of mass production technology.[14] In establishing the militancy of the new farmer's group as well as setting up a temporary organizational structure, the resolutions clearly reflected that the rural situation was drastic and required strong, decisive action that would have radical implications. Yet, the resolutions contained an overwhelming aura of preparation for expected attacks from opponents, and this aggressive defensiveness in large part explains the North Dakota strike. In a more positive light, the resolutions emphasize equality under the law, cooperation among equals, and a strong strain of self-help; all are basic components of any American creed.[15]

The Farmers' Union meeting selected interim officers for the farm strike group. Vice presidents Oliver Rosenberg of New Rockford, Harry Peterson of Plaza, and Edwin Cooper of Buxton and Secretary-Treasurer Mrs. Chris Linnertz of Minot filled a slate designated to assist temporary President Usher L. Burdick of Fargo with getting the organizational work underway. Burdick,[16] a veteran politician and farm leader, brought a wealth of personal and political prestige to the new Holiday Association. A Dakota resident since 1882 and a former Republican legislator, Lieutenant Governor, and unsuc-

cessful gubernatorial candidate, he ranched near Williston and operated an influential law practice in Fargo. He had helped form the Farm
Bureau in North Dakota in 1921 and led it until 1924. Like Talbott, he
had joined the Farmers' Union early in its state career, and at the
time of his election he was Assistant United States District Attorney.
Burdick had run unsuccessfully for a Republican congressional nomination in 1932, and was well-known in North Dakota for his outspoken
progressivism.

Burdick supported the "$1 Wheat" idea and had addressed a large
gathering at Spiritwood Lake one day before the Jamestown meeting, expressing the opinion that, "if this is to be a war of ballots or
bullets, we must settle it."[17] In that the other speaker at that meeting, Fred Cuthbert of Devils Lake, represented the Willis organization at the Farmer Union gathering, his nomination may well have
been preplanned. Burdick undoubtedly helped unify the two movements, but his selection to be temporary president apparently had
some opposition.[18]

AFTER JAMESTOWN

When the delegates disbanded to take the organizational task back
to their homes, they left Jamestown with a real sense of urgency. The
speedy formation of county units in three cases reflects their hurry.
The first permanent county organizations of the Farmers' Holiday
Association came into being on August 7, 1932, at Bowman and Finley.
Both organized at meetings called by individuals who had been delegates at Jamestown, and in each instance the person responsible was
elected to head the county FHA.

Bowman County farmers responded to a call issued by Otto
Schade, President of the Bowman Farmers' Union Oil Company. When
more than 300 showed up at the meeting, the planners shelved preliminary preparations and nominated a permanent county FHA executive committee to handle the membership solicitation. Schade became the county president, an initial example of locally-active Farmers' Union leaders who headed Holiday units. Too, the resolutions
adopted by the Bowman County group parallelled those of the

Jamestown meeting, an occurrence followed almost without exception by subsequent organizational meetings.[19] In Steele County, farmers assembled at the request of Thomas Devlin, county Farmers' Union President and a member of the Resolutions Committee at the Jamestown convention. Their meeting, described as "jammed to the doors" by the *Steele County Press*, agreed to similar resolutions, elected Devlin to be county leader and made County Agent A. D. Collette their Secretary, another first of many such instances in North Dakota.[20]

The Bowman and Steele Farmers' Holiday Associations, together with a Griggs County group organized on August 10,[21] preceded other counties by several weeks. Importantly, the leadership roles given county Farmers' Union officials and county agents established precedents that subsequent organizations elaborated upon by including elected county officials[22] and in many cases local newspaper editors.[23]

Other counties took more time with their organizational process but evidenced no less enthusiasm. Typical of this was Williams County. Here, the initial push came largely from county Farmers' Union Secretary Harvey Solberg. Active in farm organizational work and president of his county's "$1 Wheat" group,[24] Solberg arranged the first FHA meeting in Williams County for August 7,[25] at which it was decided to drop further "$1 Wheat" connections and to solicit the entire county before establishing a permanent FHA executive board. Solberg set the tone for the effort; he declared, "We have for months made a great commotion regarding conditions and what we should do and could do—if—. Here is the medium for action. We can soon know whether we can act as well as talk." In his view,

> You farmers have nothing to lose. It is a case of fight or take the peasant's yoke. The time for talk is past. Strike and strike hard and make it as uncomfortable for the scab farmer who won't join with you as you can. By refusing to join, he shows utter selfishness and is throwing down his fellow farmers for what he hopes will benefit him personally.[26]

Such fervor accelerated the canvassing work, and the local press added its encouragement. Editorial comment in Williston newspapers

asserted that "the farmer has everything to gain and little, if anything, to lose" and backed the strike as a device that "will bring industry to its knees before the farmer whose supplications have gone un-
heeded for years."[27] By August 18, reports circulated that over 1,500
county farmers had joined the Holiday Association,[28] and estimates of
membership ran between 75 and 95 percent of those eligible. Some
pockets of resistance did appear.[29] Dairy farmers, in particular, feared
that their perishable commodities would rot if held on the farm, and
at least one individual challenged the strike idea as a device to enable
the flour millers to dispose of their backlogs of stored grain.[30]

The Williams County FHA reached the final stage on August 19
with the election of Joseph Wegley as permanent chairman and the
selection of an executive committee reflecting all segments of opinion
about strike tactics. Wegley, a rural Williston farmer, firmly opposed
picketing as a means of enforcing the strike but said that he would
accede to the wishes of the majority of the members in the question.[31]
In view of the dissention that shook the Williams County FHA during
September and October, his election statement proved significant.

Like Williams County, six other counties took a less precipitant
path to organization during August. FHA units formed in Slope,
Mountrail, McKenzie, McLean, Foster, and Ward counties.[32] The latter unit, created on August 23 with the familiar use of Farmers' Union
expertise and manpower, brought into the state Holiday Association
the county that would lead the strike.

As swiftly as the North Dakota Farmers' Holiday Association
grew during August, the state still lagged far behind the national organization. The national commodities strike officially began on August 15,[33] and events around Sioux City, Council Bluffs, Des Moines,
and Omaha soon attracted headlines throughout the nation. Tightly-knit
picketing led to confrontations between FHA members and law enforcement officers, and the resulting violence, injuries, property damage, and mass demonstrations elicited much unfavorable publicity for
the national association and its president, Milo Reno of Iowa.[34] On the
other hand, the visible evidence of militancy stimulated the unorga-
nized agricultural states, and North Dakota leaders took advantage
of the publicity to push the local efforts.[35]

These accelerated efforts brought some success as Stutsman, Morton, Ransom, and Grant counties finished their preparations during the first week in September.[36] However, enthusiasm waned when Reno announced a cooling-off period before the special Midwestern Governor's conference scheduled for September 9–11 in Sioux City, and hopes soared for official help with rural problems.[37] However, the conference failed to produce executive endorsement of strike-related actions or any promises of official cessation of mortgage foreclosure sales; picketing at once reignited in Iowa, and the organization drives in other states revived with new intensity.

THE FARMERS' HOLIDAY ASSOCIATION ORIGIN IN NORTH DAKOTA

Formation of the permanent North Dakota Farmers' Holiday Association occupied a two-day conference in Bismarck immediately after the Governor's conference closed. The delegates, 200 individuals, representing 30 of the state's 53 counties, confirmed Burdick as state President and chose an executive board composed of Vice-President Oliver Rosenberg of New Rockford, Secretary-Treasurer Mrs. Chris Linnertz of Minot, and National Representative Bert M. Salisbury of Minnewauken.[38]

The main speakers at the September sessions, Talbott and Burdick, sounded the necessity of complete organization and of unity among the strikers, and emphasized the dire straits in which the farmer now operated. Talbott warned that a civil war might well develop from the strike but reaffirmed his conviction that a "spontaneous . . . and voluntary action . . . will accomplish a complete embargo of surplus food commodities in this area."[39] Burdick's presidential statement placed the future of the North Dakota strike on thorough organization. Picketing would not be necessary, he said, and the goals could be reached within 60 days if the work was done well. Stressing the importance of the action, Burdick put the solution to the Depression squarely on restoring the buying power of the "40,000,000 people" in agriculture, the "basic industry." "Many people," he continued, "are afraid that the situation will lead to war. That time is past. We are engaged in a war now—a war to save our homes." The strike, in his view, would awaken the nation to the farmer's circumstances.[40]

With such relatively moderate comments, North Dakota Holiday Association officials served notice that the strike, called for September 20, was intended to be much less spectacular than that in Iowa. Press reports reminded state residents that Burdick wanted no picketing or violence of any kind. Here, however, the organizational structure of the state FHA caused problems for the state leaders. Local township units that formed the basis of the Holiday Association, rejected the minimal dues, and made the decisions concerning activities within their environs were two levels removed from the executives,[41] and this situation in large part accounts for the disparity between Burdick's pronouncements and the sight of North Dakota farmers blockading marketing centers, a eventuality which happened almost immediately after the start of the state's strike.

AFTER BISMARCK

Creation of the permanent body pumped new life into the FHA's membership drive. Between September 15 and the beginning of the North Dakota action, Burke, Dunn, Cass, and Traill counties finalized FHA units,[42] and eight more finished before the month's end.[43] Nine counties would enter the ranks during October,[44] and Burleigh and Divide would follow before the end of the year.[45] Thus, by the beginning of the North Dakota Holiday strike, 17 counties had FHA units ready. Of the remaining 36 counties, only one had failed to organize by mid-1933.[46]

State-wide uncertainty multiplied following Burdick's strike call.[47] In Cass County, the newly-formed Holiday Association called on Governor [George] Shafer to decree an embargo on commodity shipments and to enforce compliance with the state militia.[48] The idea, tried unsuccessfully in early September by "$1 Wheat" leader Dell Willis and endorsed by NPL gubernatorial candidate William Langer,[49] received unfavorable publicity out of fear violent confrontations would ensue. As he had done earlier, however, Shafer refused to implement what he called an "absurd" idea; the state, he said, had no powers to stop individuals from exercising their right to sell whenever they wanted and to whom they pleased.[50] This failure to attract official endorsement of the strike notwithstanding, the North Dakota Holiday Association continued to rally its members. Press releases claiming that 36 counties and 50,000 North Dakotans had joined surfaced in many state newspapers,[51] and endorsements by Chambers of Commerce and governmental figures showed up throughout the state. Local newspapers printed comments by county FHA officers that underscored the concept of "peaceful persuasion." Simultaneously, the beginning of the Minnesota strike with picketing at Worthington on September 19 and the apparently related picketing near Bemidji caused increased speculation about the course that the North Dakota strike would take.

THE STRIKE

On September 20, 1932, the North Dakota farm strike began. In keeping with Burdick's wishes, no pickets interfered with traffic. However, Adams County FHA members set an apt introductory note when they paraded through Hettinger.[52] Their 20-vehicle caravan carried banners proclaiming "No More Forced Collections, No More Foreclosures, No More Evictions," "No One Ever Broke Through Our Picket Lines, No One Ever Will," and "We Are Broke But They Have Not Got Our Goat." A manure spreader labeled "Hoover's Platform" graphically punctuated the demonstration. Halting at the Adams County courthouse, the paraders interrupted a district meeting of Lions Clubs, and a verbal confrontation ensued between T. E. Hagen, an FHA organizer, and W. Murray Allen of Grand Forks, district governor of the Lions. As Allen pointed out that the service club wanted to promote good will between the farm and business communities, Hagen charged the talk really aimed to divert attention from the farm holiday. The shouting match continued until Hagen's followers silenced him, and the meeting eventually closed by creating a joint committee to discuss "mutual problems." Worthy of note is that resolutions opposing violence and picketing had been passed by the Adams County FHA.

Reports on the beginning of the North Dakota strike noted that marketing had not markedly decreased,[53] and this led directly to full scale picketing at northwestern North Dakota towns. Ward County FHA leaders monitored the movement of grain and cattle into Minot on September 20 and 21, found the strike order violated freely, and thereupon called an emergency meeting of the county executive board. There, a picketing resolution passed without opposition.

An established center of both farmer and labor agitation,[54] Minot and Ward County had presented a fertile ground to FHA organizers. The first FHA meeting, chaired by county Farmers' Union President A. G. Burgeson of Douglas on August 7, heard a variety of viewpoints on the subject of the proposed farm strike, the moratorium, and the participation of businessmen in the movement and decided to have township Farmers' Union secretaries handle the initial contact work. The 500 in attendance enthusiastically cheered comments from businessmen and a representative of the Minot Unemployed Citizens' League who offered to exchange labor for wheat, as well as the Farmers' Union spokesmen. However, a "harangue" by a Ward County communist received little serious consideration.[55] During succeeding days, Ward County organizers cemented the backing of the business community; a conclave of FHA leaders and Minot businessmen resolved in favor of the strike efforts without there being "a word of discord during the entire meeting."[56] One speaker estimated that "98%" of Minot businessmen sympathized with the movement. On August 21, the county set up its permanent Holiday unit and elected "prominent south Prairie farmer" W. A. Schaefer as President. Schaefer, an advocate of peaceful persuasion who said that the FHA should "endeavor to avoid ill will," intensified the organizational work and sought to restrain the more action-oriented members who were "tired of all this dilly-dallying about the strike."[57]

Although the Ward County FHA anticipated complete participation by area farmers in the strike, continued grain and livestock hauling on September 20 and 21 brought out the pickets.[58] On September 22, several hundred farmers massed at the Farmers' Union Co-op Elevator in Minot at 6:00 A.M., organized into teams, and dispersed to guard the entrances to the city. Despite a "wrangle" over the shipment of two carloads of livestock and the confusion inherent in such a hastily-organized action, the picketing transpired almost without incident; the strikers turned back many loads of grain and stock without violence.[59]

Reaction to the decision came immediately. Farmers' Union Vice-President Walter Maddock asserted that Burdick's strike order expressly forbade such action and declared, "I would have counseled against picketing."[60] Press comment across that state remarked on the local nature of the Minot blockade and publicly worried about the potential for violence. According to the *Williston Herald*, "The situation is made to order for agents provocateur." Most newspapers agreed, but the *Valley City Times-Record* credited the "change from peacefulness to aggressiveness" to the persistence of some farmers in rushing their produce to market.[61] The *Minot Daily News* portrayed the local state of mind when it surveyed four city hospitals and 20 physicians in search of strike-related injuries; none were reported.[62]

As the first days of picketing passed, Ward County strike leaders refined their techniques and extended the coverage. Incidents of blockade running and verbal eruptions between strikers and produce-hauling farmers elicited an order prohibiting the use of railroad ties and telephone poles for blocking the road; thereafter, pickets stretched a rope bearing a red flag across the road to announce the checkpoints. All vehicles were inspected by the 10–20 men on duty at each station, and occasional loads of produce and grain passed through the lines when the owner could prove that he needed the cash, that the foodstuffs were to be processed for home use, or that his township chairman had approved the shipment. Holiday leaders deliberately kept the local food supply well-stocked.[63] Expressions of sympathy and support, ranging from resolutions adopted by the Minot Trades and Labor Assembly to delivery of food and cigars by businessmen to the pickets, heightened a feeling of goodwill that characterized the Minot action.[64]

The Minot example rapidly fanned out to other Ward County communities. Strikers picketed at Berthold on September 22, at Makoti, Donnybrook, and Carpio on September 23, and at Des Lacs and Sawyer on September 24.[65] Adjacent counties joined the movement, and within days towns in McLean, Mountrail, Bottineau, and Burke counties found themselves under similar pressure from local Holiday Associations.[66] Pickets would later appear at scattered shipping points in Williams and McKenzie counties as well.[67] However, picketing in the North Dakota strike was confined to the state's northwestern counties. Other sections argued the question thoroughly but voted not to enforce the strike order with force. The general feeling among the members was that such action would create more problems than it would solve.[68]

Although the Minot area provided the initiative, the center of activity soon shifted to southern Ward, western McLean, and Mountrail counties. Picketing shut off the flow of grain and livestock into the smaller towns in these areas and in some cases erupted into violence. As feelings became aroused, the charge that radicals or communists had incited the aggressiveness of the strikers reverberated through the local and regional press. Shortlived picketing in Burke County, at Williston, and at Watford City exposed even further the deep divisions within the local Holiday Associations. In each of these areas, the tactic generated a power struggle within the FHA or the community.

As an example, McLean County farmers opened their strike with nearly complete local support. Enthusiastically endorsed by local businessmen, assisted by county political figures, quickly organized at massive meetings chaired by Farmers' Union leaders, and strongly encouraged by the local press,[69] the county Holiday Association took to the picket lines on September 28; the movement did not develop systematically, however, and not until October 4 did it become at all effective.[70] Then, the success was shortlived; immediate objections to the tactic caused internal friction, and various township units withdrew their participation. By October 6, only the Ward County line had regular checkpoints established, and the attempt to blockade in that part of the county faded without fanfare by the end of the month.[71]

Events in Mountrail County produced more obvious evidence of local divisions. Led by Harry Hardy of Ross,[72] the Association had mushroomed after the first organizational efforts. Initial sentiment for using the "$1 Wheat" group as the vehicle for protest gave way to favor for the "Iowa plan,"[73] and by August 29 the Farmers' Holiday Association emerged with many townships already "100%" organized and with many farmers already holding their wheat off the market.[74] Local newspapers proclaimed wholehearted support, and the

Nonpartisan League organ, the *Stanley Sun*, went so far as to criticize national FHA President Milo Reno for declaring the early September cooling-off period in the strike.[75]

When the North Dakota farm strike opened on September 20, Mountrail County entered without reservations. Picketing began very soon after that in Ward County; in fact, Chairman Hardy travelled to Minot to "learn how the picketing was being done,"[76] and the mechanics of the strike in Mountrail County mirrored the Ward techniques.[77] Pickets first appeared at Parshall on September 27 and then at Plaza, Wabek, Van Hook, Sanish, and Stanley. Newspaper reports emphasized the peaceful nature of the action and discounted rumors that the pickets were armed.[78] Local businesses and citizens provided lunch, and editor "Old Man" Rogers of the *Parshall Plainsman* reflected the depth of sympathy in that community when he editorialized, "Don't look for the *Plainsman* next week; there is no business, our exchequer is empty, and we'd rather be out on the picket lines anyway."[79]

DISUNITY

All the outward signs of goodwill, however, could not completely smooth over the local divisions exacerbated by the action, and soon opposition mostly from townspeople broke the strike in the county's northern half. When picketing ended at Stanley on October 2, the *Stanley Sun* summarized with one sentence that spoke volumes: "Maybe the farmers who served on the picket lines could not stand to be called 'communists,' maybe they could not stand the ridicule cast their way by the few who were being affected by the strike, maybe they discovered that the sentiment of business in general in Stanley was against them, and so they quit."[80] The continuation of strike-related militancy in the southern part of the county into mid-October steadily raised tempers toward the boiling point. An elevator operator at Parshall reported that he had been threatened with a beating if he failed to comply with strike orders,[81] an assault case rose from an attempt by an individual to run the picket lines,[82] and a planned try to crash the lines by 20 farmers from south of Parshall was averted only after arbitration by the Mountrail County State's Attorney and the

Sheriff.[83] In the latter instance, the chance of massive confrontation brought 100 extra pickets to duty, including reinforcements from Ward County, but an agreement which lowered the number of pickets and permitted limited movement of traffic into Parshall forestalled any violence. Some of the problems in the Parshall area reportedly resulted from the activities of bill collectors who were threatening seizures of mortgaged property unless cash payments were made, thus forcing some farmers to sell in order to obtain the funds.

Picketing in southern Mountrail County ended on October 17. Business interests in the affected area had become outwardly hostile, but Farmers' Union backing continued.[84] Although some farmers wanted to reinstitute the picketing, the devastating sleet and snow storm which swept through North Dakota on October 19–20 stopped the Mountrail County strike's militant phase.

The Ward, McLean, and Mountrail strikes had parallels in Williams County, even though the picketing of Williston markets lasted only two days. County FHA leader Joseph Wegley, denying that he had issued the picketing directive, charged that "communists"[85] had formulated the order on September 27, and Williston newspapers branded the move an "attempt to steal the show from the Holiday Association." Despite implications to the contrary, the pickets were FHA members and had mustered at an ad hoc emergency session which had passed a picketing resolution. Although 200 people attended the meeting, only 40 turned out to picket Williston highways on the next morning. Their blockade stopped no one, and Wegley's emphatic discourse killed the disheartened attempt. The charge of communist leadership in the move drew substance from the visible participation of Ole Aronson, a Communist Party legislative candidate. Williston newspapers also identified many pickets as Communist Party members but printed a disclaimer regarding the political significance.[86] The tactical debate went on, however; the *Williston Herald* judged a passive strike to be sufficiently effective, but the *Williams County Farmers Press* stated that the "considerable leakage" made it clear that only picketing could stop the strike-breaking.[87]

The pro-picketing faction in the Williams County FHA finally assumed the upper hand on October 13 after a speech by national

Farmers' Union President John Simpson in Williston. Simpson called the Farmers' Union the "class union" of the farmers, likened picketing to the "rough stuff" that Jesus Christ had used against the money changers, and challenged FHA members to be a "courageous minority to make a cowardly majority be good." At the subsequent FHA meeting militant Holiday members advised their supporters about stopping traffic with "warning flags and signs . . . warning of obstacles in the path of cars and trucks . . . boards with nails stretched across the road to puncture tires, and logs and telephone poles" and about ways to get cooperation from businessmen and elevator operators.[88] Even with cautious backing from the county press, picketing occurred only at Zahl and Appam, two small towns in the northern part of the county.[89] The responsibility for the second debacle allegedly lay with the township FHA chairmen who had simply not responded to the picketing order.[90] As in Mountrail County, the storm terminated all attempts to make the strike effective.

The other militant strike action in North Dakota at Watford City in McKenzie County and in Burke County saw both picketing and, in the former case, the first mortgage sale disruption in the state by FHA members. Burke County had entered the state Association in early September, and the leadership of editor L. C. Miller of the *Bowbells Tribune* and several other Farmers' Union members proved crucial to its growth.[91] As a result, it became involved in a controversy that revolved around the alleged communist affiliations of the dominant personalities and served as a pawn in the race between the incumbent *Bowbells Tribune* and the *Columbus Reporter* for official county newspaper. Editor Leo Eugene Mahoney of the latter paper, while endorsing the idea behind the FHA, consistently attacked it as a creature of editor Miller's political beliefs.[92] Miller, of course, denied the allegations.

The Burke County Holiday Association originally chose leaders that the *Columbus Reporter* thought "staunch and able" men; although communists and radicals were later said to be trying to "capitalize" on the movement, the *Reporter* asked that it be given a fair trial, an opinion shared by every other newspaper in the county.[93] Picketing began on September 29 at Powers Lake, but not until October 6 did anything "of any consequence" happen. Then, strikers at Coteau and Woburn turned back several loads of stock and opened holding pens. This action, applauded by the *Tribune*, proved to the *Reporter* that "a few communists have taken over the association body and soul, and are taking the matter of enforcing the rules into their own hands." In addition, continued editor Mahoney, "it is regrettable that a few radicals in the county spoil the whole thing for the rest of the members."[94] Whatever the charges and countercharges,[95] picketing and strike actions in Burke County did not last long and never involved the majority of the individuals who were members of the FHA.

In McKenzie County, on the other hand, the presence of radicals influenced the strike's beginning in an obvious way. Created on August 23 and headed by County Auditor Arne Tollefson,[96] the McKenzie County FHA exercised its strength at Sanish on September 26 when a crowd estimated at 300 stopped the marketing of wheat. The following day, Communist Party Senate candidate Ella Reeve ("Mother") Bloor of Minot addressed a meeting in Watford City and set events in motion that ended with pickets taking stations on the town's edges.[97] Dissention halted the picketing on October 1; a second discussion about the tactic debated its viability thoroughly and "with considerable bitterness being manifested at times." Local businessmen successfully objected on the grounds that other county towns were getting the trade that ordinarily would have come to Watford City.[98]

Picketing gave way to another kind of direct action. On October 17, an FHA meeting resolved to take "drastic action if necessary to stop sheriff sales or other foreclosure proceedings by receivers of closed banks in the area" and planned to begin with the October 21 chattel mortgage sale scheduled for the Nils J. Peterson farm near Watford City.[99] Of the 1,000 farmers expected, only several hundred showed up, but they constituted an impressive plurality. The *McKenzie County Farmer* described the incident succinctly: "A large crowd of farmers surrounded the receiver and the sheriff and some plain talking was indulged in by both sides with the result that the meeting adjourned to the office of States Attorney J. S. Taylor where an agreement was finally reached." The agreement, that Peterson could keep his chattels and have his mortgage renewed for one year,[100] marked the first foreclosure sale stoppage by a Holiday Association in North Dakota, an event followed by many more during its long career.[101]

CONCLUSION

Events in the state's northwestern counties offered the most spectacular evidence of the discontent created by the Depression in North Dakota. Although the picketing was an extreme measure, so was the situation, and the Holiday Association used the one in its attempt to counteract the other. The disunity evident in the various county strikes pointed out the differences of opinion on tactical questions, and the inability to make the strikes effective made their continuation impossible. This, moreover, also proved true in the counties wherein no picketing occurred. For an action that initially caused so much fanfare, the picketing ended almost without notice in late October, a casualty of the storm. The Ward County FHA held out the longest, achieved the least notoriety, and displayed the greatest unity.[102] It alone, however, could not achieve the goals.

Despite the failure of the picketing, the Farmers' Holiday Association continued to organize for a long battle. The state executive committee divided North Dakota into regions, assigned organizational chairmen to each, and reached for complete organization during 1933.[103] It made its influence felt in state politics. Burdick's endorsements of William Lemke, Franklin Delano Roosevelt, and William Langer emphasized the FHA's desire for different and "progressive" state and national leadership;[104] in addition, Farmers' Union and Farmers' Holiday Association members ran successfully for offices in the November 1932 election. Their presence contributed materially to the turmoil that rocked North Dakota during the terms of Governor Langer and his successors. The FHA enforced the mortgage foreclosure moratorium that Langer proclaimed in April 1933, supported the embargo on grain shipments that he implemented in October 1933, and provided him with many other features of policy.[105] The ties between Langer's Nonpartisan League, Talbott's Farmers' Union, and Burdick's Farmers' Holiday Association grew constantly closer. Burdick linked all three groups and won election to Congress in 1934 with their backing.

The 1932 farm strike in North Dakota did not accomplish its goals; viewed in that light, it failed. As a symbol of discontent and a medium for change, it assisted the elevation of men avowing so-called farmer's causes to high political office, and it gave evidence of the arrival of the Farmers' Union as a major political and organizational force in North Dakota life. The speed with which the Farmers' Holiday Association grew demonstrated the usefulness of the Farmers' Union local as a medium for disseminating ideas, and the assimilation of Holiday/Union members and goals into Nonpartisan League politics created an alliance that would dominate state political life at least during the term of William Langer. In this sense, the 1932 North Dakota farm strike did not occur in vain.

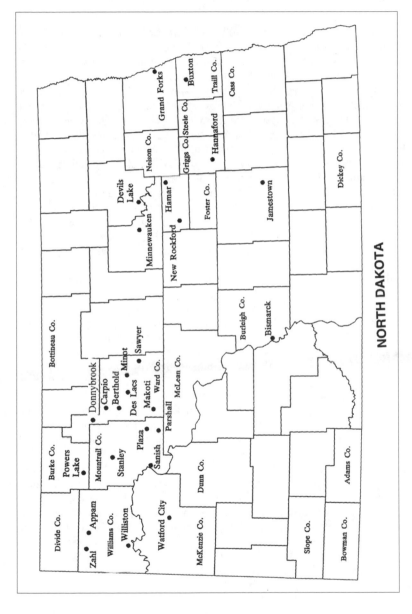

NORTH DAKOTA

North Dakota farm strikes, 1932. Map by Robert Watrel.

NOTES

1. For a description of economic conditions in North Dakota during 1932, see
   Elwyn B. Robinson, *History of North Dakota* (Lincoln: University of
   Nebraska Press, 1966), 396–406. D. Jerome Tweton offers a general sum-
   mary in "The Economic Crisis," in D. Jerome Tweton and Daniel F. Rylance,
   Years of Despair: North Dakota in the Depression (Grand Forks: Oxcart
   Press, 1973). The highest quotation on wheat during the July–December
   period of 1932 was 43 cents a bushel. Average wheat yields by county are
   found in H. L. Walster and P. A. Nystuen, *North Dakota Wheat Yields*
   (Fargo: North Dakota Agricultural College, Agricultural Experiment
   Station, 1948), 28. Per acre average yields during 1932 were significantly
   higher than for any other year of the decade.
2. According to the Greater North Dakota Association, over 11,000 state farmers lost their lands between 1929 and 1932 to mortgage foreclosures. The
   number amounted to somewhat less than one-fourth of the state's total
   farms. See *Farmers Union Herald*, August 1932, 1; the tabulation received wide circulation in the daily and weekly press during August and
   September 1932.
3. Mr. T. S. Kopseng of Bismarck vividly recalls the "button-holing" organizational tactics used by Willis at the picnic. Kopseng, presently a member
   of the State Historical Society of North Dakota Board, at that time managed an elevator in the Nelson County community.
4. For a more complete explanation of the "$1 Wheat" plan, see "Farmers
   Organize to Demand 'Dollar Wheat'," *Devils Lake Daily Journal*, July
   19, 1932, 1. The Devils Lake paper, named by Willis as the "$1 Wheat"
   official publication, is by far the best source of data on the group, but even
   it is incomplete and lacking in depth.
5. Editorial, ibid., September 1, 1932, 4. The editorial develops the Willis
   image as a simple, grass-roots "Man with an idea." His lack of training or
   experience in organizational work and his middle-of-the-road political
   beliefs are emphasized in the article.
6. Prominent individuals and organizations who endorsed the plan included
   former Senator Porter J. McCumber (*Devils Lake Daily Journal*, August
   3, 1932, 1), Devils Lake Chamber of Commerce (ibid., July 23, 1932, 1),
   North Dakota Grain Storage Bureau, Greater North Dakota Association,
   Fargo Chamber of Commerce (*Fargo Forum*, July 28, 1932, 1), Governor
   George Shafer, Bismarck Chamber of Commerce (*Grand Forks Herald*,
   July 31, 1932, 1), William L. Langer (*Selfridge Sioux County Pioneer-
   Arrow*, July 28, 1932, 1), and a host of other political and business leaders
   and organizations.
7. *Minot Daily News*, July 23, 1932, 1, is a news report of one such meeting.
   Reportedly, 1,200 people attended, and the paper reprints the resolutions
   adopted.

8. The moratorium proposal simply would have placed on the state books a law temporarily suspending debt collection via foreclosures on land. It was an attempt to legalize extending the time available for the mortgagee to repay his debt until economic times improved. See John L. Shover, *Cornbelt Rebellion: The Farmers' Holiday Association* (Urbana: University of Illinois Press, 1965), 86–88. The Frazier Debt Refinancing Bill, written by William Lemke and introduced into Congress by Senator Lynn J. Frazier in 1931, provided for refinance of farm mortgages by the federal government at three percent annual interest; its intent was to enable rural debtors to discharge their obligations, and it contained a provision to inflate the currency if that became necessary. See Edward C. Blackorby, *Prairie Rebel: The Public Life of William Lemke* (Lincoln: University of Nebraska Press, 1963),180–181.

9. "Cost of production" meant generally that prices for farm products would be determined on a basis of the farmer's expenses in producing a commodity (seed, gasoline, etc.), adding an allowance for wages for the farm operator, and thereon computing a market price that repaid the farmer his investment and gave him a small profit. Cost of Production prices were to be used only on the portion of the crop consumed domestically; disposal of the surplus was the farmer's responsibility and risk. See Shover, *Cornbelt Rebellion*, 22, 38–39.

10. The only available study of the North Dakota Farmers' Union is Harold V. Knight, *Grass Roots: The Story of the North Dakota Farmers' Union* (Jamestown: North Dakota Farmers' Union, 1947). The book is undocumented.

11. No biography of Talbott exists. General information about this important farm leader is drawn from the obituary published in the *Fargo Forum*, April 9, 1937, 1, and from Knight, *Grass Roots.*

12. *Jamestown Sun*, August 1, 1932, 1. Every daily paper in North Dakota carried the Associated Press story about the creation of the temporary Farmers' Holiday Association on that day, and many printed synopses of Talbott's speech.

13. *Hannaford Enterprise*, August 2, 1932, 1. Kampen edited the Hannaford paper and also served on the executive committee of the Griggs County Farmers' Union.

14. The resolutions are reprinted in most daily North Dakota newspapers for August 1, 1932.

15. See lengthy explanations of Holiday philosophy as interpreted by FHA state President Usher L. Burdick in a letter published in many state newspapers entitled, "Is the Holiday Association of North Dakota Patriotic or Just a Bunch of Hoodlums?" An example appears in the *New Rockford Transcript*, March 3, 1934, 1. Another Burdick explanation is printed in his congressional newsletter of March 25, 1954 (Burdick Papers, Libby Manuscript Collection, University of North Dakota at Grand Forks).

16. No biography of Burdick exists, but general information can be found in the obituary published in the *Fargo Forum*, August 20, 1960, 1, and in parts of other works such as Robinson, *History of North Dakota.*

17. *Jamestown Sun*, August 1, 1932, 1.
18. See the separate article concerning the organization of the FHA in ibid., and the accounts published in other state newspapers. Willis later asserted that the "$1 Wheat" and the FHA had been in contact with each other since July 28 when national FHA President Milo Reno "came to him to explain their 'farm holiday' proposal and unite the two movements." The two men, according to Willis, decided "to organize each along his own line, although there is keen sympathy between them." *Devils Lake Daily Journal*, September 16, 1932, 1.
19. Bowman *Bowman County Pioneer*, August 11, 1932, 1.
20. Finley *Steele County Press*, August 11, 1932, 1.
21. *Hannaford Enterprise*, August 16, 1932, 1; Cooperstown *Griggs County Sentinel-Courier*, August 18, 1932, 1.
22. Some examples include state Senator E. C. Stucke and State's Attorney G. A. Lindell of Garrison in McLean County, state Senator J. H. Burkhart of Minot and Ward County Commissioner August Krantz of Kenmare in Ward County, Dunn County Auditor J. R. Cuskelly and County Agent C. A. Fiske in Mountrail County, Steele County State's Attorney E. T. Meldahl, and Ransom County Auditor John A. Gray. Many other examples of this could be cited. Generally, these individuals did not attempt to get permanent county FHA offices, but many were elected anyway.
23. Although local editors proved surprisingly good propagandizers for the FHA, the individuals connected with co-operative newspapers stood out in their outspoken advocacy. Their newspapers, holdovers from the Non-partisan League's first heyday, generally supported the Langer-led NPL ticket in 1932, emphasized their "progressive" political ideas, and gave much coverage to the Farmers' Union. Examples: Lars J. Siljan of the Garrison *McLean County Independent*, L. C. Miller of the *Bowbells Tribune*, James P. Curran of the Watford City *McKenzie County Farmer*, C. R. Knickerbocker of the *Stanley Sun*, and David Larin of the Williston *Williams County Farmers Press*. Independently-owned papers, however, also "boosted" the FHA. Extremely sympathetic were editors F. ("Old Man") Rogers of the *Parshall Plainsman*, E. D. Lum of the Wahpeton *Richland County Farmer-Globe*, G. D. Colcord of the Minot *Ward County Independent*, and I. J. Moe of the *Valley City People's Opinion*.
24. *Williston Herald*, August 4, 1932, 1.
25. Williston *Williams County Farmers Press*, August 11, 1932, 1.
26. *Williston Herald*, August 11, 1932, 1; Williston *Williams County Farmers Press*, August 11, 1932, 1.
27. Ibid.
28. *Williston Herald*, August 18, 1932, 1.
29. Ibid.; Williston *Williams County Farmers Press*, August 18, 1932, 1.
30. Williston *Williams County Farmers Press*, August 11, 1932, 1.
31. Ibid., August 25, 1932, 1.
32. See the following newspaper accounts: Amidon *Slope County Post*, August 18, 1932, 1; Stanley *Mountrail County Promoter*, September 2, 1932,

1; Watford City *McKenzie County Farmer*, August 25, 1932, 1; Carrington *Foster County Independent*, August 11, 1932, 1; Minot *Ward Independent*, August 25, 1932, 1; *Minot Daily News*, August 23, 1932, 1.

33. The daily press in North Dakota followed the fast-breaking events of the Iowa strike closely; the most extensive coverage appears in the *Fargo Forum* and *Grand Forks Herald* for August 16–29, 1932.

34. Reno, an explosive leader of the national FHA, opposed violence and attempted to stop the Iowa and Nebraska picketing. He strongly advocated the concept of cost of production. For biographical information, see Shover, *Cornbelt Rebellion*; Roland A. White, *Milo Reno: Farmers' Union Pioneer* (Ames: Athens Press, 1941); or Dale Kramer, *The Wild Jackasses: The American Farmer in Revolt* (New York: Hastings House, 1956).

35. As an example of the scheduling of the organizing tours, on September 2, 1932, Talbott, Nye, and Maddock appeared at meetings in St. Anthony and Flasher (Morton County) and Carson (Grant County) during the evening following political conferences in Bismarck. Poor roads often delayed the arrival of the speakers, but the crowd waited; the Carson gathering stayed until 11:00 P.M., and the meeting lasted until well after 2:00 A.M.

36. See the following newspaper accounts: *Jamestown Sun* (Stutsman), September 2, 1932, 1; *Montpelier Magnet* (Stutsman), September 2, 1932, 1; *New Salem Journal* (Morton), September 9, 1932, 1; Lisbon *Ransom County Gazette*, September 8, 1932, 1; Elgin *Grant County News*, September 8, 1932, 1.

37. Attended by Governors George Shafer of North Dakota, Warren Green of South Dakota, Dan Turner of Iowa, Floyd B. Olson of Minnesota, and representatives of the chief executives of Wisconsin, Ohio, Wyoming, Nebraska, and Oklahoma, the conference heard two days of proposals from individuals, organizations, corporations, and banks for alleviating the rural economic situation. The FHA proposed a four-point plan that included an embargo on farm commodities, moratoriums on farm and chattel mortgages, and a special session of Congress to enact the Frazier Debt Refinancing Bill. The governors, with the exception of Minnesota's Olson, refused to support such a plan and instead called for congressional action to ameliorate farmer grievances. See the *Grand Forks Herald*, September 9, 10, 11, 12, 1932, 1, for the Associated Press accounts of the meetings.

38. *Minot Daily News*, September 12, 1932, 1; *Grand Forks Herald*, September 13, 1932, 1; *Fargo Forum*, September 13, 1932, 1.

39. Ibid.

40. *Minot Daily News*, September 14, 1932, 1; *Valley City Times-Record*, September 14, 1932, 1; *Mandan Pioneer*, September 13, 1932, 1; *Fargo Forum*, September 14, 1932, 1.

41. See James William Dodd, "The Farmer Takes a Holiday" (Unpublished M.S. thesis: North Dakota State University at Fargo, 1960), for a good discussion of FHA organizational structure.

42. *Bowbells Tribune* (Burke), September 16, 1932, 1; *Killdeer Herald* (Dunn), September 22, 1932, 1; *Casselton Reporter* (Cass), September 23, 1932, 1; Mayville *Traill County Tribune*, September 22, 1932, 1.
43. Fryburg *Billings County Pioneer*, September 29, 1932, 1; Hettinger *Adams County Record*, September 29, 1932, 1: Minnewauken *Denson County Farmers Press*, September 23, 1932, 1; *Marion Sentinel* (LaMoure), September 30, 1932, 1; Ellendale *Dickey County Leader*, September 29, 1932, 1; *Oakes Times* (Dickey), September 29, 1932, 1;, Forman *Sargent County News*, September 29, 1932, 1; *Grand Forks Herald* (Grand Forks), September 30, 1932, 1. A Holiday Association allegedly formed in Oliver County during this period, but no dates or accounts are available.
44. Wahpeton *Richland County Farmer-Globe*, October 7, 1932, 1; *Valley City Times-Record* (Barnes), October 10, 1932, 1; Michigan *Nelson County Arena*, October 7, 1932, 1; *New Rockford Transcript* (Eddy), October 14, 1932, 1; Towner *Mouse River Farmers Press* (McHenry), October 14, 1932, 1; *Bottineau Courant* (Bottineau), October 5, 1932, 1; Mohall *Renville County Farmer*, October 13, 1932, 1; *Mott Pioneer Press* (Hettinger), October 13, 1932, 1; in Stark County, a press environment more hostile than most precluded notice of the FHA's formation in early October at Belfield.
45. *Bismarck Capital* (Burleigh), October 27, 1932, 1; Crosby *Divide County Journal*, December 9, 1932, 1.
46. Letter, Usher L. Burdick to Judge Gudmundar Grimson, May 2, 1933, Grimson Papers, State Historical Society of North Dakota.
47. Among many references, see *Fargo Forum*, September 21, 1932, 1.
48. Ibid., September 22, 1932, 1.
49. *Devils Lake Daily Journal*, September 3, 1932, 1; for Langer's response, see, among others, *New Rockford Transcript*, September 10, 1932, 1.
50. Among many, see *Bismarck Tribune*, September 26, 1932, 1.
51. *Fargo Forum*, September 23, 1932, 1. Burdick exaggerated.
52. See ibid.; *Dickinson Daily Press*, September 21, 1932, 1. The local Hettinger *Adams County Record* made no mention of the incident in either its September 22 or September 29, 1932, editions.
53. *Fargo Forum*, September 24, 1932, 1.
54. Minot served as the home of the North Dakota Socialist Party during the second decade of this century, had a turbulent part in the career of the Industrial Workers of the World, is located quite near Deering, the birthplace of the Nonpartisan League, and has had strong railroad unions throughout its history. See Robinson, *History of North Dakota*, 328–339; Henry R. Martinson, " 'Comes the Revolution . . . ': A Personal Memoir," *North Dakota History* 36-1 (Winter 1969), 40–109; Charles James Haug, "The Industrial Workers of the World in North Dakota, 1913–1917," *North Dakota Quarterly* 39-1 (Winter 1971), 85–102.
55. *Minot Daily News*, August 8, 1932, 1; Minot *Ward County Independent*, August 11, 1932, 1.
56. Minot *Ward County Independent*, August 18, 1932, 1.
57. Ibid., August 25, 1932, 1; *Minot Daily News*, August 23, 1932, 1.

58. *Minot Daily News*, September 22, 1932, 1.
59. Ibid. The "wrangle" involved the shipment of two carloads of stock by a buyer. He was permitted to ship the cattle after promising to make no further sales. Several pickets argued vehemently against the compromise by saying that it was unfair to those who had voluntarily submitted to the strikers, but Sheriff R. W. Kennard mediated the dispute and arranged the settlement. Kennard also joined the FHA and "was roundly applauded for his action." Minot *Ward County Independent*, September 22, 1932, 1.
60. Ibid. Maddock's remark was widely quoted in the state's daily press.
61. *Williston Herald*, September 29, 1932, 8; see editorials in the *Grand Forks Herald*, September 25, 1932, 4; *Fargo Forum*, September 27, 1932, 10; *Valley City Times-Record*, September 20, 1932, 2.
62. *Minot Daily News*, September 23, 1932, 1.
63. Ibid.
64. Ibid.; Minot *Ward County Independent*, September 29, 1932, 1, 4.
65. *Berthold Tribune*, September 29, 1932, 1; *Minot Daily News*, September 24, 1932, 1.
66. Stanley *Mountrail County Promoter*, September 29 1932 1; *Stanley Sun* (Mountrail), September 29, 1932, 1; Garrison *McLean County Independent*, September 29, 1932, 1; *Bottineau Courant* (Bottineau), October 5, 1932, 1; *Bowbells Tribune* (Burke), September 30, 1932, 1.
67. Williston *Williams County Farmers Press*, September 29, 1932, 1; *Williston Herald*, September 29, 1932, 1; Watford City *McKenzie County Farmer*, September 29, 1932, 1.
68. The question caused extensive debate at local FHA meetings. See Cooperstown *Griggs County Sentinel-Courier*, September 22, 1932, 1; Forman *Sargent County News*, September 22, 1932, 1; Hettinger *Adams County Record*, September 22, 1932, 1; *Hillsboro Banner* (Traill), October 7, 1932, 2; Milnor *Sargent County Teller*, October 6, 1932, 1; Michigan *Nelson County Arena*, October 7, 1932, 1; Wahpeton *Richland County Farmer-Globe*, September 30, 1932, 1; *Oakes Times* (Dickey), September 29, 1932, 1, and numerous others.
69. Garrison *McLean County Independent*, August 25, 1932, 1–4; September 1, 8, 15, 1932, 1. The *Independent* was cooperatively owned and advocated the NPL political ticket.
70. Ibid., September 29, October 6, 1932, 1.
71. Ibid., October 6, 13, 1932, 1; *Max Enterprise*, October 6, 13, 1932.
72. Hardy, an active Farmers' Union member and county Republican Party central committeeman, also served on the Board of Directors of the cooperatively-owned newspaper, the *Stanley Sun*. He was also well acquainted with the financial problems created by the low farm prices and had suffered a foreclosure action on his own land early in 1932. See Mountrail County Sheriff's Records, 1932, Archives, State Historical Society of North Dakota. Also on the Mountrial County FHA executive committee were County Agent C. A. Fiske and Harry T. Peterson of Plaza, an early leader of the state's temporary Holiday Association.

73. Stanley *Mountrail County Promoter*, August 12, 1932, 1; *Parshall Plainsman*, August 11, 1932, 1; *Stanley Sun*, August 11, 1932, 1.
74. *Stanley Sun*, September 1, 1932, 1; *Parshall Plainsman*, September 1, 1932, 1; Stanley *Mountrail County Promoter*, September 2, 1932, 1; see the latter paper for commentary about wheat withholding in the county prior to the strike, especially the August 19, 1932, issue.
75. *Stanley Sun*, September 8, 1932, 1.
76. *Minot Daily News*, September 27, 1932, 1.
77. For a description of Mountrail County strike techniques, see the *Stanley Sun*, September 29, 1932, 1.
78. Ibid.; *Parshall Plainsman*, September 29, 1932, 1.
79. Ibid.; Stanley *Mountrail County Promoter*, September 30, 1932, 1.
80. *Stanley Sun*, October 6, 1932, 1.
81. Widely reported in the North Dakota press, the incident was recounted in the *Mandan Pioneer* under the headline "N.D. Communists Threatened to Hang Elevator Man if He Bought Any Grain." See the issue for October 3, 1932, 1. The Mountrail County press virtually ignored the alleged dispute.
82. Stanley *Mountrail County Promoter*, October 7, 1932, 1; *Van Hook Reporter* (Mountrail), October 6, 1932, 1; *Parshall Plainsman*, October 13, 1932, 1. The case was dismissed in county court.
83. *Stanley Sun*, October 13, 1932, 1; *Parshall Plainsman*, October 13, 1932, 1.
84. The Parshall Farmers' Union resolved to continue its support and appropriated money to Harry Lucksinger, the local strike leader, for gasoline and expenses on October 18. See *Parshall Plainsman*, October 20, 1932, 1.
85. See Lowell K. Dyson, "The Red Peasant International in America," *Journal of American History* LVIII, no. 4 (March 1972), 958–973, for the story of communist organizing among farmers during the late 1920s. The leader of the International, Alfred Knutson, farmed in Williams County and the organization was headquartered at Bismarck for several years.
86. The Williston story is contained in the *Williston Herald*, September 29, 1932, 1; Williston *Williams County Farmers Press*, September 29, 1932, 1.
87. Ibid., October 6, 1932, 1.
88. Ibid., October 13, 1932, 1.
89. *Williston Herald*, October 20, 1932, 1.
90. Ibid., October 27, 1932, 1.
91. See the campaign initiated by the *Bowbells Tribune* in the issues for July 29, August 5, 12, 19, 26, September 2, 1932. Each issue devotes significant space to the state and national Holiday movements for a weekly paper.
92. *Columbus Reporter*, September 1, 8, 15, 22, 1932, 1. The *Reporter* won the election. Mahoney served 14 years each as mayor and city auditor of Columbus and was an extremely prominent citizen of the community and county.

93. *Bowbells Tribune*, September 9, 1932, 1; *Columbus Reporter,* September 8, 1932, 1, and September 22, 1932, 2; *Flaxton Times*, September 15, 1932, 1; *Portal International*, September 29, 1932, 1. All are Burke County publications.

94. *Bowbells Tribune*, September 30, October 7, 14, 1932, 1; *Columbus Reporter,* October 6, 1932, 1.

95. Ibid.; subsequent issues for October 1932.

96. Accounts of the organizational drive emphasize the Farmers' Union leadership. Watford City *McKenzie County Farmer,* August 11, 18, 25, 1932, 1; Alexander *McKenzie County Chronicle*, August 25, 1932, 1; Arnegard *McKenzie County Leader*, August 26, 1932, 1, 4.

97. Watford City *McKenzie County Farmer,* September 29, 1932, 1.

98. Ibid., October 6, 13, 1932, 1.

99. Ibid, October 20, 1932, 1.

100. Ibid., October 27, 1932, 1; Alexander *McKenzie County Chronicle*, October 27, 1932, 1.

101. The United Farmers' League had previously been active in stopping foreclosure sales in the Oakes-Forbes area of Dickey County and other adjacent places. See the *Oakes Times* (Dickey), October 13, 1932, 4, for an account of one such incident written by a participant. See also: Allen Matthews, "Agrarian Radicals: The United Farmers' League of South Dakota," *South Dakota History* 3–4 (Fall 1973), 408–421.

102. The *Minot Daily News*, November 18, 1932, 2, announces the official end to the Ward County strike. Picketing around Minot had ceased after the October 19 snowstorm.

103. *Minot Daily News*, October 4, 1932, 1; *Fargo Forum*, October 5, 1932, 1.

104. Burdick's letter of endorsement for Lemke appeared in many newspapers: the *Bisbee Gazette*, October 6, 1932, 1, is one such publication. The Associated Press quoted Burdick as endorsing Roosevelt on October 27, 1932; he called FDR "the champion of the 'progressive' case". See the *Grand Forks Herald*, October 27, 1932, 7, among others. Finally, Burdick wrote Langer on October 25, 1932, that most Holiday Association members favored the NPL candidate's election; the letter is filed in the Langer Papers, Libby Manuscript Collection, University of North Dakota at Grand Forks.

105. See Larry R. Remele, "The Public Reaction to the North Dakota Farmers' Holiday Association" (Unpublished MA thesis, University of North Dakota at Grand Forks, 1969); Daniel F. Rylance, "The Political Crisis," in Tweton and Rylance, *The Years of Despair: North Dakota in the Depression*, 28–29.

RESOLUTIONS, PROGRAMS, AND POLICIES OF THE NORTH
DAKOTA FARMERS' HOLIDAY ASSOCIATION, 1932-1937
James W. Dodd

The American farmers experienced a boom during and immediately after World War I. With Europe embroiled in a deadly conflict, the American farmer had ample markets for his produce. This led him to purchase new machinery enabling him to put more land under cultivation, a nice arrangement until the European farmer began to produce crops again. As the wheat fields replaced battlefields in Europe, the world demand for American farm goods declined, leaving a surplus. Congress dropped the support prices for wheat in 1920, and by the end of the year the boom had turned into a bust. Farm prices took a serious dip, largely due to a glutted market; and the farmer turned to the banks for credit to pay for the new machinery he had bought during the shortlived boom. While the rest of the nation was enjoying "normalcy" and prosperity, the farmer faced depressive conditions. During the later part of the decade a slight improvement was noticeable, but not enough to experience the last moments of prosperity. By the end of the decade farm credit had largely been expended, and conditions were growing steadily worse. The early 1930s showed less promise than the late 1920s. Confronted with such conditions, and like past performances, the farmer broke loose from his traditional conservatism and entered the camps of the radicals.

This sudden outburst of agricultural radicalism was expressed most vociferously after 1932 by the Farmers' Holiday Association (FHA). The FHA emanated from a mass meeting of mostly farmers, though some small businessmen were in attendance, in Des Moines, Iowa, May 3, 1932.[1] The organization derived its name from a contemporary event. These men felt if the bankers could close their doors

and take a "holiday," they (the farmers) could also declare a holiday
by refusing to market their goods until farm prices included producing costs. The original purpose of the FHA was to coordinate the activities involved in a marketing strike. It wasn't long before the new
protest movement adopted other purposes, as the strike venture was
not too successful. Among the other purposes was to work for an orderly marketing system; another was to halt the involuntary forced
sales, foreclosures, and evictions by any necessary means. The veteran Iowa farm leader, Milo Reno, was elected head [of] the new organization.[2]

ORIGIN OF THE NORTH DAKOTA FARMERS' HOLIDAY ASSOCIATION

The North Dakota Farmers' Holiday Association (NDFHA) grew
out of two meetings. The first gathering was held in Jamestown, July–
August 1932. Originally called by the North Dakota Farmers' Union
to discuss farm problems, this assembly passed several resolutions.
One of the most important stated "that the farmers of North Dakota
assembled at this meeting proceed to organize and perfect a state unit
of the National Holiday Association, in accordance with the constitu-
tion and bylaws of such national organization."[3] Officers were elected
at this meeting and Usher L. Burdick was given the task of directing
Holiday affairs in North Dakota. He was to be assisted by three
vice-presidents: Oliver Rosenberg of New Rockford, Harry Peterson
of Plaza, and Edwin Cooper of Buxton. Mrs. Christian Linnertz of
Minot was elected treasurer.

During the interim between August 1932 and the following January, various committee meetings were held to initiate a tentative program and draw up bylaws and resolutions for the members to ap-
prove. Such approval was received at the second meeting (Bismarck,
January 18–20, 1933). The officers were approved again, and a group
of bylaws and resolutions was adopted.[4]

The NDFHA grew quite rapidly according to President Burdick.
"In the first six months we put on the rolls 46,000 members and at the
height of the movement, which was in the fall of 1933, the membership had reached close to 70,000."[5] Since membership was open to any

farmers or to anyone operating a service for farmers, this latter figure could be reliable, though it does seem high. Mr. Burdick writes
that the ratio of farmer to non-farmer members was about eight to
two.[6] Each of North Dakota's fifty-three counties had its own unit,
complete with a Council of Defense. In addition there was the state
unit with its Council of Defense. The Council of Defense was the most
important single organ of the North Dakota Holiday Association. The
State Council was charged with the task of serving as a liaison between the national and the North Dakota group. It also coordinated
the activities of the fifty-three county units. The county Councils of
Defense conducted the activities of the county organization. Since the
power of the Holiday Association was derived from its grassroots,
these councils had very important duties. They made the final decisions on how to enforce a marketing strike. If picketing was necessary, the county Council of Defense determined how much and where.
They were most successful, however, in deciding what method to use
to halt forced sales, foreclosures, and evictions. It is no exaggeration
to say that the future of the holiday movement in North Dakota largely
depended upon the actions taken by these groups. Usually the Councils were composed of five members who were willing to devote most
of their energies to make the Holiday a success.

PRIORITIES OF THE NDFHA

The programs of the NDFHA were consistent in one respect. A
close study reveals that the farmer-members were willing to try practically anything showing the slightest possibility of alleviating their
dilemma. It is impossible to discuss all of the Holiday's desires within
the limits of this study. Since there were certain basic wishes that
appeared over and over again in Holiday sources, these must be included. Others have been incorporated in this paper, not because of
their importance, but rather to show the diversity of their wishes.

One of the constant yearnings of the NDFHA was to see Congress pass the Frazier-Lemke Refinancing Bill.[7] This measure was
perennially placed before Congress, but it never did become a law.
Briefly, it provided for governmental refinancing of existing farm

indebtedness at the rate of 1 ½ percent on the principle per annum on the amortization plan. The national government would have issued Federal Reserve notes secured by first mortgages on farms if the bill had been adopted. The co-author of the bill, Congressman [William] Lemke, estimated that the notes would be issued over a forty-seven year period to take up the $9,500,000,000 worth of farm indebtedness.[8] The Frazier Bill would also have permitted farmers to re-purchase the land they had lost since 1920 by borrowing funds from the federal government. Tenant farmers would have been allowed to purchase farms at the same rates. By April 1933, seventeen state legislatures had petitioned Congress to pass this bill.[9]

Another Frazier-Lemke Bill, the amendment to the Bankruptcy Act, did become a law in 1934 but was declared unconstitutional the following year.[10] It was re-passed in 1935, omitting the illegal provisions, and was upheld by the Supreme Court in a 1937 decision.[11] This act provided for a partial three-year moratorium. Any insolvent farmer could file bankruptcy papers and still keep his farm, personal property, and machinery for a three-year period. In addition his debts would be scaled down to the present value of such mortgaged property. The farmer would have to pay an annual rental fee determined by the court. Upkeep and taxes would be deducted from this rental fee, and the remaining amount would be divided among the creditors. If the farmer could pay his debts within the three years, the proceedings were halted and his farm and other property were free from debt. The sentiment behind the Frazier-Lemke Moratorium Act was not so much to enable the farmer to file bankruptcy, but rather to give him a temporary moratorium until better legislation could be adopted by Congress.[12] To the Holiday Association, better legislation meant the passage of the Frazier-Lemke Refinancing Bill or something similar.

COST OF PRODUCTION LEGISLATION

Perhaps the greatest desire of the FHA was to get Congress to pass a bill encompassing the cost of production (COP) concept for all farm products. Cost of production was not original with the Holiday Association; the Farmers' Union had been campaigning for COP many years before the FHA was conceived. COP cannot be simply defined as it meant different things to different farmers, not only in dissimilar areas, but similar areas as well. Basically, cost of production for the farmer was the same as it was for the industrialist. "Cost of production for farm products means that the farmers must determine at the beginning of the year what price each of the commodities he expects to produce must bring, so that the total income from his farm will equal his total cost."[13] How the farmer was to determine his costs was the problem. Most of them did not keep adequate records, and without good estimates the farmer could not accurately measure his costs. One of the greatest difficulties that would have arisen if Congress had passed a COP plan would be to achieve some uniformity. Production costs differed radically in certain areas. Sub-marginal lands, varying labor costs, and seasonal price fluctuations were some of the factors leading to wide differences in determining COP prices. Because of these variable factors, Congress did not seriously consider such a scheme.

After the marketing strike proved unsuccessful,[14] much of the energy of the NDFHA was devoted to keeping the farmer on his farm. One of the earliest resolutions approved by the North Dakota Holiday Association

> Recommended that the courts and governments of our state be called upon to invoke its special police powers in assisting to prevent the forced sale of farm commodities for the satisfaction of liens and indebtedness thereon until the price level of such commodities shall have reached the cost of production. And we call upon the sheriffs, states attorneys, and all other court officers to cooperate in carrying out such a program as to aid in preventing the forced sale of any and all commodities or foreclosure sale or sale on execution to satisfy any and all liens and indebtedness on such commodities.[15]

While this desire did not deal specifically with farms, but rather agricultural products, it shows the importance of COP to the Holiday Association. At the time this resolution was passed, the NDFHA was about to begin a marketing strike scheduled for the later part of August. Enforcement activities were lax as the movement was just beginning in North Dakota. At the January 1933 meeting in Bismarck, three requests were made concerning foreclosures. One petitioned the Industrial Commission to order the Bank of North Dakota immediately to halt foreclosures except in cases of voluntary release by the mortgagor. The second resolution entered a "protest against any foreclosures on mortgages or liens on any of our farms' farm land, equipment, stock, or grain, and respectfully petition the District Judges of North Dakota to refrain from entering any judgment or decree in foreclosures, until the passing of the present crisis."[16] The third recommendation asked that before a District Judge executed a foreclosure order, he should notify the mortgagor by registered mail at least thirty days in advance.

Many of the district judges in North Dakota were cognizant of the Depression and did their best to keep foreclosure actions at a minimum. As judicial officers of the state they were expected to carry out the letter of the law, and if a mortgagee insisted on foreclosing, the judges could do little. Judge John C. Lowe of Minot aided the Holiday Association in a 1933 opinion. He maintained that a mortgagee should desist from foreclosing "in order that the mortgagor may interpose his equitable rights."[17] The jurist continued by stating that "no one foreclosing a mortgage at this time can hope to do more than bid the property in himself and get the property."[18] Judge Lowe opined that this was inequitable as it did not give the mortgagor the right to retain the equity in his property. Other jurists in North Dakota were concerned with the growing number of foreclosure cases. Judge C. W. Buttz of Devils Lake and Judge G. Grimson of Rugby were two such examples. Both of these magistrates worked closely with the NDFHA in trying to keep the farmer on his farm. Judge Buttz is quoted as writing, "I appreciate very much the attitude your Association (Benson County Holiday Association) is taking all the way along the line and if we had an association like that in every county we just wouldn't have any trouble between debtors and creditors. You people have been very helpful to the Governor and myself in these moratorium matters."[19]

One of the strongest resolutions passed by the NDFHA pertained to foreclosures. This announcement was approved at the Bismarck meeting, January 1933:

We, the members of the North Dakota Farmers Holiday Association, do hereby publish and declare to the world our intention to
band ourselves together to prevent foreclosures, and any attempt
to dispossess those against whom foreclosure proceedings are pending or started; and to retire to our farms, and there barricade ourselves to see the battle through, until we either receive cost of production or relief from the unfair and unjust conditions existing at
present; and we hereby state our intention to pay no existing debts,
except for taxes and the necessities of life, unless satisfactory reduction in accordance with prevailing farm prices are made on such
debts.[20]

By banding together the farmers presented a united front against their
enemies. Several examples of this united front are available for this
period. One commonly used method involved a "penny sale." A sale of
this type took place in McKenzie County, North Dakota, to satisfy a
lien. A cow sold for three cents at this auction.[21] Another example
was the sale in Deshler, Ohio, where some 2,000 farmers observed a
sale of machinery and livestock. The total of the received bids amounted
to $2.17 to satisfy a $400.00 mortgage. The new owners "not only refused to take away their new bargains—25¢ horses and 6¢ implements—but arranged to give the property back on a 99-year lease and
added a $5.00 'pot' to it."[22]

THE GOVERNOR'S SUPPORT

Another method that was successfully used in North Dakota, not
only to prevent the loss of machinery and livestock or grain, but also
to keep a farmer on his farm, was a petition to the governor. The most
obvious reason for the success of the petition was the attitude of Governor William Langer. He favored the Holiday program and aided the
organization whenever possible. In some cases Governor Langer took
direct action either by wiring the sheriff to cease foreclosure proceedings in such and such a case, or by calling out the National Guard to
enforce the provisions of his famous moratorium proclamation of April
17, 1933.[23] To cite illustrations of the Governor's action, the following
examples are offered. On April 19, 1934, several hundred farmers gath-

ered at the E. W. Ford farm near Casselton, where eviction papers were to be served on a tenant farmer, Axel Hanson. The Cass County Holiday Association wired the Governor requesting him to declare martial law throughout the state, as there was need to protect renters from losing their homes during seeding operations. Langer refused to declare martial law but he did send a telegram to Sheriff Peter MacArthur requesting him to refrain from evicting Mr. Hanson.[24] In another case that took place the day after Langer issued his moratorium proclamation, Captain Alvin Feickert of the North Dakota National Guard instructed Stutsman County Sheriff O. J. Nygaard to cease from auctioning off a farm.[25]

The circumstances of the case determined what action would be taken. If it could best be handled by the Holiday Association, the Governor would turn the matter over to them. If, however, the NDFHA could not effectively take charge, a message from the governor would carry more weight with a sheriff. One chronicler of the North Dakota farmers' economic struggle states that at

> times attempted evictions under the authority of law represented by the sheriff were foiled by the gathering of hundreds of neighbors determined to stop it. In one instance, to the writer's knowledge, the sheriff of that county anticipated such a gathering by arriving early. He had the evictee's household goods all out in the road, off the premises involved, when the gathering arrived on the scene. He was peremptorily ordered to put everything back as he had found it or else. It was all replaced and the Association (NDFHA) dispersed.[26]

While the Holiday men were not always triumphant in stopping foreclosures, they did enjoy a rather high standard of success. This successfulness is only noticeable, however, in the field of foreclosures and evictions.

INFLATION STRATEGIES

Holiday plans and programs in other fields were pretty much a series of failures. Several of their hundreds of resolutions that ended in defeat were concerned with finance and credit. Their main objective in financial matters was to restore farm credit, and above all, to restore farm purchasing power to what it had been during and immediately after World War I. The FHA nor the NDFHA did not have any set plan to restore the farmers' economy, with the exception that more currency must be placed into circulation. The Holiday leaders naively felt that it wasn't overproduction that destroyed their purchasing power, but rather a lack of money in circulation:

> In a deliberate frameup in 1920, the directors of the Federal Reserve banks deflated the currency to the extent of two billion dollars and inaugurated a period of wild liquidation just at a time when the American farmer was operating on less credit encouraged by the same board under the pretense of having the farmers raise more grain to win the war. That one deliberate act broke the entire agricultural belt, and should be proof enough to demand that every financial racketeer be kept out of any government business in which the handling of money is connected.[27]

As a result of this concept the Holiday men sponsored almost any idea that would increase the money supply.

In a resolution approved at a Bismarck meeting, December 3–4, 1934, the NDFHA went on record as favoring a 60 percent reduction of the farm mortgage indebtedness, including principal and interest, and advocated that the remaining 40 percent be paid over a 15-year period, with interest at the rate of 1 ½ percent on any unpaid balance.[28] In addition, it was agreed that no payments, either on principal or interest, of any loan with the Federal Land Bank should be required to be made "until the farmers receive the county average in bushels and the cost of production as determined by the United States Government Authority."[29] At this same gathering it was determined that Congress should immediately repeal the National Bank Act and the Federal Reserve Act, and in their place a United States Bank should be established to return the function of issuing money back to Congress. Congress should also call in all U.S. interest-bearing bonds and pay for them by issuing money. Furthermore, no interest-bearing bonds should be issued again by the United States Government.

Many other proposals were made with the intent of inflating the currency. The Frazier-Lemke Refinancing Bill was urged most repeatedly, and a Soldier Bonus Bill was recommended. Veterans' pensions, the North Dakota Holiday Association believed, should be restored to their former standards, and invalid soldiers should be pensioned, regardless if their malady could be traced to service during the war.[30] At the New Rockford meeting another ringing resolution was adopted with the intention of creating an inflated currency:

> We demand that a sufficient amount of liquid money be put into circulation as will raise the amount per capita to $75.00 and that any plan which fails to provide the American people with sufficient media of exchange to do our normal and legitimate business will not restore the business life of the nation. We challenge the administration and Congress to prove the assertion that this restoration of the money of the country is inflation. There can be no inflation until there is a complete restoration. Beyond that point, we do not ask for the issuance of money.[31]

As the reader has probably sensed, the NDFHA was especially critical of financial solutions proposed by Congress.

> We feel that the President [Roosevelt] understands, but we doubt if Congress has a true concept of the seriousness of the present situation. By the defeat of the "cost of production" feature of the farm relief bill, and the defeat of the Frazier bill, warrents [sic] the farmers of America in concluding that Congress is still wholly ignorant of the place occupied by agriculture in the cooperative business structure of the nation.[32]

On one occasion, the Association recommended that Congress pass an act canceling all debts on American homes "to the same extent as the obligations due this government for war debts were canceled, and that the time of payment and rate of interest to be paid be adjusted in accordance with our settlement with foreign countries."[33]

One other important area of Holiday desires, the establishment of a uniform marketing system, has not yet been discussed. In one of the earliest suggestions, the NDFHA petitioned FDR to appoint John A. Simpson, President of the National Farmers' Union, as Secretary of Agriculture, and also recommended that he appoint a man from the Midwest as Secretary of the Treasury. The Association felt "there is a vital need to remove the Treasury and Agricultural Departments of the National Government from the hands of the Monied East, which has for years used these Departments in the interest of the Financial Dictators of Wall Street, in order to place them in a position to render their just service to the people of this country."[34]

The establishment of an orderly marketing system could not be easily accomplished. Earlier organizations, such as the Society of Equity and the Nonpartisan League, achieved some changes, yet there was still much to be done. Among the wishes of the North Dakota Holiday association was a demand

> that all Boards of Trade and Chambers of Commerce dealing in the sale of agricultural products be placed under the jurisdiction of the Department of Justice, and that it be made a felony for any person, firm, or corporation to buy or sell any agricultural commodity where the delivery and receipt of the actual commodity does not follow the transaction, and that no Chamber of Commerce be permitted to register more sales than the amount of the actual delivery.[35]

The endeavors of the Holiday men in seeking an orderly marketing system were not as forceful as their actions in preventing foreclosures. Some headway was made, but little could be done by the farmer himself. The present system was tolerable, especially when the farmer was confronted with his other more pressing problems.

PRESSING THE NORTH DAKOTA LEGISLATURE

Under a category of miscellaneous proposals, there are a number of desires broadcasted by the NDFHA to the North Dakota Legislative Assembly. At the Bismarck meeting in February 1933, eighteen bills were recommended to the legislature by the members of the Legislative Committee of the North Dakota unit.[36] To show the diversity of the wishes of the NDFHA, these eighteen recommended bills are listed below.

1. The passage of a one year moratorium, giving the Governor power to extend said moratorium if the present crisis continues.
2. The passage of an embargo bill permitting the Governor to ban the entry of all foreign agricultural products.
3. The passage of the Farm Strike Legalization Bill.
4. The passage of a scrip bill to provide a medium of exchange.
5. The passage of a safe depository law for all checking accounts up to $500.00; such depositories to be state or national banks which provide security, or the County Treasurer; all such checking account funds to be kept 100% liquid, with service charge to cover operating expenses.
6. The passage of a bill providing that all public funds be deposited in the Bank of North Dakota.
7. The passage of a bill permitting the deposit of funds in state or national banks by the Bank of North Dakota instead of in eastern banks, provided federal, state, or municipal bonds are put up to secure the entire amount of such deposit at market value; the Bank of North Dakota to have power to demand additional security whenever market value decreases, and to sell such securities if additional security is not furnished upon such demand.
8. The passage of a bill abolishing deficiency judgments.
9. The passage of a bill reducing the time for the expiration of judgments from ten years to six years.
10. The passage of a bill providing additional exemptions from judgments and mortgages.
11. The passage of a bill prohibiting evasion of the Crop Mortgage Law approved by the people in the November 1932 election.
12. The passage of a bill providing for a state owned Tannery, Woolen Knitting Mill, and a Leather Product and Shoe Factory.
13. The passage of a bill providing that the title to personal property sold or exchanged passes to the buyer upon delivery of such property by the seller to the buyer, when the amount involved exceeds $200.
14. The passage of a bill limiting the interest rate to 6% and limiting all carrying charges to 7%.
15. The passage of a bill giving the Board of Administration the power to suspend all normal schools, the University and the Agricultural College (NDSU), if sufficient taxes do not come in to maintain them, thus avoiding borrowing money to run them.
16. The passage of a Lignite Coal Tonnage Tax.

17. The passage of a gross earnings tax on public utilities.

18. The passage of a stringent chain store tax.

At the bottom of this sheet of proposals was a statement claiming that "these are the minimum demands which must be met under our constitutional form of government to preserve our homes, to lighten the unbearable tax burden, to fulfill the promises made to the people by the representatives and senators of the Honorable Assembly, when they ran for that high office. We desire a Roll Call on all Economic Measures. We are absolutely OPPOSED to all Clincher Motions."[37] These eighteen recommended measures represent only a very small portion of the hundreds of requests the North Dakota Farmers' Holiday Association made to the legislature. They show the wide diversity of the Holiday desires, and they also show the willingness of the NDFHA to "endeavor to get actions out of 'inaction.' "[38]

CONCLUSION

Since the FHA grew out of the conditions that faced the agricultural belt, it is natural to presume that as these conditions became less depressive the Association would decline. Such a decline took place during the latter part of 1933, and each year thereafter the membership showed a steady decrease. President Burdick, in a long statement entitled "Is the Holiday Association of North Dakota a Patriotic Organization or a Band of Hoodlums," has this to say about its future:

> The Holiday Association is not jealous of its future. When the causes that produced it have been relieved, and the things it stands for have come into being, the Association may disappear as mysteriously as it universally appeared. Actual membership isn't necessary when its aims have been fulfilled, but the memory of what it has done in the face of a great public calamity will not be forgotten by the common people of this generation. Will its aims be fulfilled? Yes, if this great nation is to endure. Homeless men, women, and children by the millions was never the intent of the Constitutional Convention in Philadelphia in 1787.[39]

An improvement in farm conditions was one reason for the decline of the NDFHA. There are others that must be considered also. The threat of an oncoming war helped to bolster the economy, and in turn helped lead to the downfall of the Holiday movement. Other farm organizations, such as the Farm Bureau and the Farmers' Union, bit into the membership of the NDFHA. This is especially true in the case of the latter, as the programs in both cases were somewhat similar. President Burdick's resignation in 1936 served as an impetus to an already rapidly declining organization. This is also true on the national front. When Milo Reno died in May 1936, a main pillar of strength was removed at a time when the Association could not afford to lose such strength. This is, however, not to suggest that the new Presidents were not capable. Both Mr. Rosenberg, who succeeded Usher L. Burdick, and John Bosch, Reno's successor, were well qualified leaders. It appears though that Reno and Burdick were the Holiday's main arteries of energy in the National and North Dakota Associations, and when these arteries were severed, no substitute could be made to work for any length of time. Finally, the frustrating failures which the movement had been forced to endure for awhile took their toll. The demise of the Holiday units was rather sudden. In most cases there was no formal disbandonment. It was a product of the times, and when these times became better, the movement died a simple unobserved death.

NOTES

1. *Farm Holiday News*, St. Paul, February 20, 1933. The place of publication changed from time to time. Originally at St. Paul (February 1933–January 1934) it moved to Marissa, Illinois (February 1934–December 1935) and finally to Ames, Iowa (December 26, 1935–August 1936).
2. An excellent summary of Milo Reno's creative life may be found in Dale Kramer's *The Wild Jackasses* (New York: Hastings House, 1956), pp. 191–251. Kramer is a former editor of the *Farm Holiday News*.
3. *Farmers Union Herald*, Jamestown, August 1932. A complete list of resolutions passed at this meeting may be found in the Senator C. W. Fine, Papers, Fargo: North Dakota Institute For Regional Studies, North Dakota State University (hereinafter cited as Fine, Papers).

4. A general summary of this meeting may be found in the *Bismarck Tribune*, January 19–20, 1933; the complete list of resolutions and bylaws is available in the *Farmers Union Herald*, February 1933.

5. Usher L. Burdick, Washington, D.C., letter, December 23, 1959, to the author. The 70,000 estimate is also given in another Holiday source, North Dakota Farmers' Holiday Association, The 1936 Holiday Association's *Handy Book and Manual of Useful Information*, n. pub., n. p., 1936, p. 3.

6. Burdick, Letter to author.

7. This bill was referred to by several different names. In addition to the one above, other common titles were: The Frazier Bill, the Frazier-Lemke Farm Relief Bill, S-1197 and HR-2855.

8. *Dunn County Journal*, Dunn Center, North Dakota, January 19, 1933.

9. The North Dakota Senate passed a resolution (the House of Representatives concurring) in January 1933, urging all state legislatures to petition Congress to pass this bill. See *Congressional Record*, volume 76, part 2 (Washington, D.C.: United States Government Printing Office, 1933), p. 1716.

10. *Louisville Joint Stock Land Bank v. Radford*, 295 U.S. 555, 28 Am. B. R. (N.S.) 397.

11. *Wright v. Vinton Branch Mountain Trust Bank*, 300 U.S. 400, 33 Am. B. R. (N.S.) 353.

12. This is the opinion of Representative Lemke; cited from the *Holiday Handy Book*, p. 13.

13. This is a statement from a radio address of E. E. Kennedy, National Secretary of the Farmers Union; cited from the *Farm Holiday News*, November 15, 1934, p. 3.

14. The most apparent reason for the failure of the farm strike was because the farmers were not in a position to withhold their goods from market for any length of time. The strike movement is considered a success only in the sense that it did advertise the plight of the farmers.

15. Fine, Papers. This resolution was passed at the farmer meeting in Jamestown, July–August 1932.

16. *Farmers Union Herald*, February 1933.

17. Quoted from the *Farm Holiday News*, March 22, 1933.

18. Ibid.

19. Letter to Bert M. Salisbury, Secretary of the Benson County Holiday Association, from District Court Judge C. W. Buttz of Devils Lake, dated November 26, 1935; Bert M. Salisbury, Papers, Fargo: North Dakota Institute for Regional Studies, North Dakota State University.

20. *Farmers Union Herald*, February 1933.

21. Erling N. Rolfsrud, *Lanterns Over the Prairies, Book II* (Brainerd, Minnesota: Lakeland Press, 1950), p. 125.

22. Ibid., pp. 125–126.
23. A somewhat flowery explanation of the Langer proclamation may be found in John M. Holzworth's *The Fighting Governor: The Story of William Langer and the State of North Dakota* (Chicago: Pointer Press, 1938), pp. 23–26.
24. The Hanson incident was taken from an article in *The Farmer Labor Defender* and the *Dunn County Journal*, Dunn Center, North Dakota, April 25, 1934. This paper was published by the NDFHA from February 13, 1934, to March 13, 1935.
25. *Farm Holiday News*, April 1933, p. 4.
26. Ole E. Johnson, *Trials and Tribulations: A Story of the Farmers Economic Struggle* (n. pub., n.p., 1954), p. 18.
27. *Farm Holiday News*, May 1933.
28. A statement to this effect was issued by the NDFHA Executive Board at a meeting in Rugby, May 13, 1933; cited from the *Farm Holiday News*, May 1933.
29. *Farmer Labor Defender* and the *Dunn County Journal*, December 5, 1934.
30. The resolutions favoring the Soldier Bonus Bill and the veterans pension were passed at the New Rockford convention of the NDFHA, March 17, 1934; cited from the Fine, Papers.
31. Ibid.
32. *Farm Holiday News*, May 1933.
33. Fine, Papers.
34. *Farmers Union Herald*, February 1933.
35. Fine, Papers.
36. This committee consisted of Representative William Godwin, Chairman, Senator C. W. Fine, Representative Ben Fedje, and two farmer-members, O. T. Haakenson and Charles Streich.
37. Fine, Papers.
38. Senator C. W. Fine wrote this at the bottom on one of the pages of resolutions adopted by the NDFHA; quoted from Fine, Papers.
39. *Farm Holiday News*, January 1934, p. 1. The statement was issued by Mr. Burdick on December 2, 1933.

RESTRAINED, RESPECTABLE RADICALS:
THE SOUTH DAKOTA FARM HOLIDAY
John E. Miller

During the summer of 1932, as grain and livestock prices dipped to new lows and mortgage foreclosures threatened the farms of thousands of Midwestern farmers, South Dakotans joined their neighbors from nearby states in promoting a Farm Holiday. Roads outside of Sioux Falls, Yankton, Watertown, and Sioux City, Iowa, were blocked off, and one man was killed near Elk Point while trying to run the blockade. Mass meetings of hundreds and sometimes thousands of people enthusiastically called for "cost of production" for agriculture as they uttered their collective cry for economic justice. Yet, as the Farm Holiday impulse spread across South Dakota's borders from Iowa, Nebraska, Minnesota, and North Dakota, the movement in the state generally proceeded along more moderate or even conservative lines than it did elsewhere.[1]

GEOGRAPHY OF THE MOVEMENT

The explanation for the general restraint and less radical tone of the South Dakota movement can be found in geographic influences, the historical development of farm protest activities in the state, the political context, and the character of its leadership. Not surprisingly, activism and confrontation concentrated in the eastern part of the state near the Iowa and Minnesota borders and especially around Sioux Falls and Sioux City. South Dakotans took inspiration from the Iowa organization and its leader, Milo Reno, who spoke at meetings in Mitchell, Hurley, Beresford, and Sioux Falls during the summer and fall of 1932. Once launched, however, South Dakota's population shaped their own response to the situation. As elsewhere, the leaders never managed to keep full rein on their followers, and spontaneous outbursts and demonstrations played as important a role as did planned actions. Located near hotbeds of Holiday activism in northwestern Iowa and southwestern Minnesota, Sioux Falls, Beresford, Elk Point, and Jefferson became foci of activity in the state. Yankton, fifty miles up the Missouri River, entered the news when picketers from Nebraska blocked traffic across the bridge there. Watertown, the center of northeast regional activity and the site of a brief holding action, was near Canby, Minnesota, where one person was shot to death. Big Stone City briefly got caught up in the conflict across the border in and around Ortonville, Minnesota. Aberdeen, forty miles from the North Dakota border, was another site of occasional activity, and the Communist-influenced United Farmers' League was most active around Frederick and Sisseton, which were also near the North Dakota border.[2]

Holiday directors frequently met in Huron, located on the western edge marking the movement's greatest activity. West of the Missouri River very little organization took place outside of Pennington County (home of Rapid City) despite efforts to stimulate interest there. It was in the most densely populated areas, close to the Iowa and Minnesota borders, that the Farm Holiday was most successful.[3] These locations were also home to the most prosperous farmers working the highest valued land in the state, and, in general, they suffered less from drought and depression than did farmers further west.[4] The sparseness of population in the western two-thirds of the state, especially in the West River region beyond the Missouri River, increased the difficulty of drawing people out for meetings and establishing working units. West River farmers and ranchers who depended upon livestock or who were burnt out by drought in 1931 and 1932 had few products to withhold from market even if they had wanted to.

SOUTH DAKOTA CONSERVATISM

The traditional conservatism of West River residents, which has often been noted, also accounts for their standoffishness.[5] The entire state had a reputation by the 1930s for being more conservative than its neighbors.[6] South Dakotans did experience an intense but relatively brief attraction to the Nonpartisan League (NPL) after its organizers swarmed into the state in early 1917. After peaking at around 25,000 members and attracting 48,426 votes for its gubernatorial candidate in 1920 and 46,033 in 1922, it declined rapidly thereafter, its eclipse setting South Dakota apart from North Dakota and Minnesota, where a strong NPL and Farmer-Labor party emerged as perennial powers in state politics.[7] Nor must it be forgotten that Populism had sunk its roots deep in the state, and progressive leaders from Coe I. Crawford to Peter J. Norbeck exerted a major influence on state politics for a generation.[8] South Dakota possessed a tradition of farm protest activity; it lacked the kind of organizational framework for channeling and reinvigorating that impulse which was present elsewhere. And no Floyd Olson or Bill Langer occupied the governor's chair, ready to lead his troops forth into battle in 1932.

Rather, the political context of South Dakota militated against radical farm protest, which can be counted as the third factor in explaining the moderate course taken by the Farm Holiday movement there. The presence of conservative Republicans, who were identified with failed agricultural policies, in the White House and in the governor's chair provided ready targets for frustrated agrarians and fed the flames of discontent that burst forth in the Farm Holiday in the summer of 1932. But after the Democratic landslide carried Tom Berry, a cattle rancher from Belvidere, into the governorship that November, he sought to deflect agricultural protest toward support for the national Democratic administration's farm program. With Franklin D. Roosevelt in the White House, hopes that federal farm policies would usher in better times had the effect of undercutting support for Holiday activities.

MODERATE LEADERSHIP

Both Berry and his Republican predecessor, Warren Green, helped guide the Farm Holiday along the path of moderation by partially identifying with its goals. Green, a "dirt farmer" from Hamlin County, was a colorless executive who won the applause of the Sioux Falls

Argus-Leader and other conservative papers by emphasizing the need for government frugality and administrative efficiency.[9] Well aware of the growing frustration of farmers, Green noted the emergence of the Farm Holiday movement in the state in July 1932, and expressed sympathy for its goals. But he said he "could see no possibilities for aiding the cause" by imposing martial law to enforce holding actions, as was proposed by Governor Floyd Olson of Minnesota, and he insisted on the right of farmers to be free to market their products and the necessity for maintaining law and order.[10] He did endorse the "dollar wheat" plan started in North Dakota, calling for an end to wheat shipments out of the state until prices rose to a dollar a bushel, but he made no effort to duplicate it in South Dakota.[11]

Green agreed to attend a Holiday board meeting on August 26 in Huron, where that evening he addressed a large rally at the city park and indicated his approval of a holding action which was scheduled to begin on September 5, but he also denied the possibility of peaceful picketing and repeated his intention to use his legal authority to keep the roads open. After he sat down, John Simpson, the Oklahoma-based president of the National Farmers' Union, won over the crowd with a far more radical message. "If Constitutions, laws, and court decisions stand in the way of justice and human progress," he cried, "it is time that they be scrapped." Recalling that moment many years afterwards, Emil Loriks, secretary-treasurer of the state Holiday, observed that his words "just electrified the atmosphere of that meeting. Dr. Betts adjourned the meeting but the crowd did not move. They remained seated and in a mighty voice shouted, 'We want Simpson. We want Simpson.' And he was brought back to speak again."[12]

Governor Green, who was anxious to do something for the farmers while avoiding extreme solutions and incitements to violence, obtained swift approval from the Holiday board the next day for his proposal to hold a meeting of governors and farm leaders from fourteen agricultural states in Sioux City on September 9 for the purpose of formulating an "orderly, practical, legal, and nonviolent" program for raising farm prices.[13] The meeting would provide an opportunity for Green and his fellow governors to take stock of, attempt to influence, and possibly benefit politically from farm discontent. Rather than being the targets of criticism, they could help lead and mold farm sentiment. In the meantime, a two-day milk strike around Sioux Falls obtained a price boost there to $1.75 per hundredweight, farmers in Wisconsin established a statewide Holiday organization, and sporadic violence continued around Sioux City.[14]

South Dakotans figured prominently among the 5,000 or so demonstrators who paraded through Sioux City streets on the day the governors' conference began. Joining Green were Governors Floyd Olson of Minnesota, Dan W. Turner of Iowa, and George Shafer of North Dakota, along with representatives sent by the chief executives of Nebraska, Ohio, Oklahoma, Wyoming, and Wisconsin. They listened to testimony from Farm Holiday spokesmen, who predicted the outbreak of revolution in the countryside unless their demands were heeded for state-enforced embargoes on shipments of food until cost of production was obtained. The governors rejected that idea and others calling for state mortgage moratoriums, a special session of Congress to enact the Frazier farm credit bill, and voluntary withholding of goods from market by farmers. The opinion of South Dakota Attorney General M. Q. Sharpe, who served as the conference's executive secretary and legal adviser, that there was no legal foundation for states to embargo goods leaving their borders guided the governors in rejecting that controversial proposal. Instead, they opted for a tepid set of resolutions for transmittal to President [Herbert] Hoover calling for tariff protection for agricultural products, expansion of the money supply, reorganization of the agricultural credit system, and voluntary restraint by creditors on foreclosures.[15]

SOUTH DAKOTA'S STRIKE

The conference had led South Dakota Farm Holiday leaders to postpone their plans for a strike, originally scheduled for September 5. Meanwhile, on September 1 Milo Reno had also declared a "temporary truce" for the national organization.[16] During the Sioux City meetings, South Dakotans participated prominently in discussions among Farm Holiday leaders, who rescheduled the Midwestern farm strike for September 21. E. N. Hammerquist of Farmingdale, South

Dakota's representative on the national board of directors, had the assignment of reading the announcement, which stressed that the strike would be nonviolent.[17] Doubt surfaced during the following week about whether the holding action would actually occur, but a gathering of state Holiday leaders in Sioux Falls on September 18 reaffirmed the decision to go ahead with a voluntary action "beginning at the farm gate" with no picketing and limited to livestock and grain. If no results were forthcoming within thirty days, eggs, butter, and cream would be added to the list.[18] The moderate tone of the strike announcement was perfectly acceptable to Governor Green, who gave it his "full support" and commended its avoidance of picketing. "This movement respects fully the rights of property and the rights of all citizens freely to travel and move their goods in accordance with their desires and needs," he observed. "This movement recognizes a principle that intelligent economists have long recognized, and that is that the successful plan of farm relief will finally come from the intelligently planned and executed movements of farmers themselves."[19]

The issues of picketing and violence constantly bedeviled the Farm Holiday leaders. Where they occurred, negative publicity and public resentment were the results, but picketing and roadblocks also seemed to bring results. Spontaneous demonstrations by farmers revealed the depth of their discontent and prodded government leaders to respond. Emil Loriks reflected this fact when he expressed his hope that a peaceful strike would bring results but also observed, "If prices don't go up, I suppose we'll have to resort to picketing."[20] Loriks usually cautioned people against picketing and violence, emphasizing instead the need for cooperative and educational programs, but like others he remained ambivalent on the issue.

The effects of the strike, which began on September 21, varied from place to place in South Dakota. During the first couple of days, grain receipts at Rapid City and Huron were off and hog sales at Sioux Falls, pork marketing center for the state, fell about half.[21] But things quickly returned to normal. Attention soon shifted to Minnesota, around Ortonville and Canby, where a twenty-five-year-old striker, Nordahl Peterson, was killed on October 4 by a farmer who wanted to keep demonstrators off his property.[22] In the meantime, Holiday leaders busily organized meetings in South Dakota and signed up members while the holding action fizzled out.[23] Meetings in Salem and Brookings formally adopted "no picketing" resolutions and approved a policy of "cooperation rather than violence."[24] Though a spontaneous blockade emerged around Sioux Falls on October 5 and 6, an action disavowed by the Minnehaha County Holiday president, the situation in South Dakota during late September and early October remained generally quiet.

SOUTH DAKOTA DEPRESSION POLITICS

While the Farm Holiday movement was emerging in the Midwest, the 1932 political campaign was heating up.[25] Three years of depression left many people bewildered, frustrated, and alienated, and their tendency was to blame the "ins" for their woes. The Sioux Falls *Argus-Leader* characterized the primary election that spring as "South Dakota's most interesting political race in a generation." Not in the editor's memory had there been so many candidates seeking nomination. Especially notable was the ferment within the Democratic party, which had elected only one governor since statehood (in addition to Andrew Lee, a fusionist Populist during the 1890s).[26]

Factional feuding between Democratic regulars, led by national committeeman W. W. Howes of Huron, and an antiorganization group, headed by U.S.G. Cherry, a Sioux Falls lawyer who captured the party's Senatorial nomination, and L. E. Corey, an editor from Wagner who unsuccessfully ran for the gubernatorial nomination, did not prevent the party from uniting behind Governor Franklin D. Roosevelt of New York for the presidential nomination. South Dakota Democrats were among the first to join his ranks when they unanimously endorsed a slate of Roosevelt-pledged delegates at a Jackson Day dinner in Huron on January 18.[27] Facing no challengers in the primary, Roosevelt captured all ten of the state's delegates on May 3, as the Democrats' vote total doubled their previous high.[28] By that time he had already garnered delegates in North Dakota, Iowa, Wisconsin, Nebraska, and Michigan, and at the Chicago convention the following month Midwestern farm states played a major role in delivering the nomination to him. Roosevelt skillfully tailored his appeal to rural voters, making agricultural rehabilitation a top priority while avoiding committing himself to specific programs. At the Democratic convention, Herbert Hitchcock, head of the South Dakota delegation, expressed his approval for the Democratic farm plank, which promised control of farm surpluses and preservation of the American market for American farmers, although he had earlier been skeptical about preliminary versions of the document.[29]

The Democrats exploited agricultural discontent, aiming appeals at farmers who desired change and criticizing Hoover's Federal Farm Board, tariff policies, and failure to resuscitate farm prices. For many Farm Holiday enthusiasts, Roosevelt represented hope. Lining up with National Farmers' Union president John Simpson, who enthusiastically called for Roosevelt's election, Emil Loriks and other South Dakota Democrats viewed the New York governor as someone who could better agriculture's position. Both Roosevelt and Hoover ended their campaign tours with special appeals to the farm vote. On the eve of the election, Hoover spoke in Springfield, Illinois, St. Louis, and St. Paul, denouncing his opponents for seeking to "play upon discontent" and resorting "to the oldest trick of politics by stimulating a protest vote" against him.[30]

His concern was well-founded, as the Democrats swept the Midwestern agricultural states, winning electoral votes and capturing state office and legislative seats where the party had seldom won anything before. South Dakota was carried along in the landslide, as Roosevelt captured 63.6 percent of the vote in the state. Tom Berry defeated William Green for the governorship. Democrats ousted both incumbent Congressmen and elected every other constitutional officeholder, after years of Republican domination of those positions.[31] The legislative lineups would give Democrats majorities of 29 to 15 in the state senate and 68 to 34 in the house of representatives, virtually reversing Republican majorities of 31 to 14 and 79 to 24 during the previous session. Depressed agricultural conditions figured importantly in sweeping the Republicans out of control in both Washington and Pierre, and now farm leaders looked expectantly for action from the Democrats.[32] Ironically, however, despite the reversal in party fortunes, the political context continued to exercise a moderating influence upon the Farm Holiday movement in South Dakota.

This became immediately apparent during the last two months of 1932. Holiday spokesmen adopted a wait-and-see attitude as people's attention shifted to the new Congress and the new President and the new state legislature. During late 1932 and early 1933 the Holiday movement remained quiescent in South Dakota. The involvement of several of its top leaders in the legislature and state politics operated as a restraining factor, since they desired to make the political system work for them rather than try to operate outside of it.

Governor Tom Berry's campaign had centered on the need for governmental economy, and upon entering office he pressed hard for the elimination of the state sheriff's office, railway commission, state hail insurance, state bonding department, securities commission, and other allegedly unnecessary branches of government.[33] He proposed a budget of $8,033,000 for the biennium, which came in $2,152,000 below expenditures for the previous one.[34] Widespread desire for tax relief for farmers and town dwellers drove the legislature to cut even deeper, reducing the budget $450,000 below the governor's proposal. Emil Loriks, as chairman of the Senate Appropriations Committee, led the economy drive, insisting on deep reductions for state employees' salaries and higher education.[35] On the need for economy, Farm Holiday leaders were in agreement with the most conservative opinion, but they and other farm leaders clashed with conservatives over the issue of taxation. On this question the farm groups, who were calling for a net income tax to relieve some of the property tax burden, were in disagreement with the governor and other proponents of a gross income tax law, which the legislature in fact proceeded to enact over their objections.[36] Despite their concerted efforts, the farm group leaders failed to organize and maintain a unified agricultural block in the legislature. Although 55 of the 103 members in the lower house were farmers, they never were able to achieve consensus on taxation and other issues.[37]

Early in the session, Farm Holiday president Barney McVeigh, who had been Speaker of the House during the 1931 session when the Republicans had still been in control, and secretary-treasurer Emil

Loriks presided at meetings aimed at uniting legislators who were affiliated with the Farm Bureau, Farmers' Union, and the Grange.[38] Though not successful in establishing support for a single program, the meetings were a moderating influence because of their tone of reasonableness and cooperativeness. McVeigh and Loriks insisted that farmers did not seek "class legislation," although some of the Farmers' Union literature asserted as much. The necessity of promoting cooperation between town and country was emphasized, and conservative concerns about foreclosure proposals and other subjects were acknowledged.[39] The partisan split within the movement, represented by Loriks the Democrat and McVeigh the Republican, lessened the likelihood that any fringe group, radical or otherwise, would be able to dominate it. The tensions within the movement were reflected in the legislative outcomes of the session, which included cutting government functions and reducing state expenditures as well as greater leniency for delinquent taxpayers and people threatened by mortgage foreclosures.[40]

When the legislature finished its business at the end of February, people turned their attention to Washington, where Franklin Roosevelt was in the process of translating vague campaign promises for a New Deal into concrete policy. Farm Holiday leaders agreed that national action was necessary to achieve their major goal—guaranteed cost of production—and for a while it appeared that Congress might respond to their satisfaction. The administration's farm bill was nearing the final round of Congressional debate by the time Farm Holiday leaders gathered in Des Moines for their first national convention on May 3 and 4. Although Milo Reno urged moderation and asked the delegates to grant the National Board, made up of the state presidents, the power to determine whether a strike should be called, militant state leaders such as Walter Singler of the Wisconsin Cooperative Milk Pool stampeded the convention into voting for a strike call on May 13. But South Dakota Holiday leaders, still hopeful that a cost of production provision could be incorporated in the farm bill being considered by Congress, counseled a wait-and-see stance, refusing to support the strike action. Responses from other states were likewise lukewarm for the most part, and on the day set for the strike Reno called it off, saying that farmers would wait for the Agricultural Adjustment Act, signed the previous day by President Roosevelt, to go into operation.[41]

HOLIDAY ACTIVITIES

During the first half of 1933, therefore, as Holiday leaders were stymied by popular desires to let the legislative gears turn, the major activity in Holiday regions was spontaneous actions taken by farmers to prevent foreclosures of their properties. Barney McVeigh's warning that violence might result if the legislature failed to provide mortgage relief paralleled similar predictions from other farm leaders around the nation.[42] "Penny" auctions and other demonstrations were frequent during early 1933 in farm regions, especially in northwestern Iowa, the hotbed of the Holiday movement, where more than 100 arrests were made after a group of men dragged district judge Charles C. Bradley from his courtroom in LeMars, drove him out into the country, strung a rope around his neck, and began choking him in an effort to force him to stop further foreclosure proceedings. Milo Reno said he deplored the actions of the farmers, and Emil Loriks and fellow South Dakotans continued to condemn violence, but veiled threats sometimes punctuated their statements nevertheless.[43] The most serious incident in South Dakota occurred in February 1933, when R. D. Markell, a sixty-eight-year-old farmer from Elk Point, died from wounds received when he and his sons were shot while trying to run a blockade of pickets near Sioux City.[44] The following month, in one of several incidents that occurred in the area, a group of 700 Brown County farmers held a Watertown attorney prisoner in the sheriff's office in an effort to force him to postpone a farm foreclosure.[45]

In South Dakota the threat of penny sales was real enough to most creditors that few of them in fact occurred. Holiday leaders worked strenuously to establish a cooperative spirit with banks and lending agencies and to persuade them to renegotiate the terms of the loans. Conciliation committees were set up in counties where the Holiday was active, and they arranged meetings between farmers with delinquent loans and lending agencies who were seeking repayment. Secretary-treasurer Emil Loriks was especially active in this role, logging thousands of miles on his automobile as he drove from town to town organizing Holiday units and using his persuasive powers to work out acceptable terms for both sides in loan disputes. His delicate position in the organization and his desire to retain credibility with both sides in disputes led him to avoid penny sales, but he was informed about them when they did occur. The most dramatic one, by all accounts, occurred near Milbank after a farmer had been foreclosed on. Four or five hundred farmers showed up, and the sheriff and a number of deputies arrived. One of the deputies got a little trigger-happy and fired a shot. Before anyone knew it, Loriks learned, the farmers assembled there "disarmed those fellows so fast they didn't even unbuckle their belts." They just yanked their guns away and told the deputies to get out. Then they proceeded to buy the items for pennies, nickels, and dimes and returned them to the farmer. The rarity of such activities and the Holiday's continual effort to rely rather upon conciliation committees reflected its generally moderate, cautious approach in the state.[46]

Little time elapsed before farm spokesmen began to criticize the new federal farm bill, but the widespread desire to give Roosevelt a chance militated against any early Holiday action. Secretary of Agriculture Henry Wallace soon became a scapegoat for disgruntled farmers, who accused him of misleading Roosevelt and began calling for his removal.[47] By September 22, when South Dakota leaders journeyed to a Farm Holiday conference in Des Moines, they were already getting ready for another strike. "There comes a time when patience ceases to be a virtue," was the message sent out from the Huron Holiday headquarters. "After a period of apparent inactivity, considerable activity is apparent in the S. Dakota division of the National Farmers' Holiday Ass'n at the present time."[48] Growing discontent in South Dakota and other farm states forced Roosevelt to take a variety of moves to conciliate critics, including inflationary gold buying begun in late October.[49] Despite conflicting economic indicators and uncertainty about the trend of national policy, South Dakota Farm Holiday leaders decided to support Milo Reno's decision to launch another holding action.[50] The sporadic holding actions during October and November constituted the last major burst of Holiday activism,

although efforts to keep the movement alive in South Dakota continued during 1934 and, to a lesser degree, for a couple of years after
that. When national Farmers' Union president John Simpson died,
elevating vice president Ed Everson, who was also president of the
South Dakota branch of the organization, to the presidency, Emil
Loriks took over as state president. In order to devote his energies to
the position, he quit both his state senate seat and his position as
secretary-treasurer of the Farm Holiday. McVeigh's successors as
president of the South Dakota Farmers' Holiday were, like Loriks,
men who were highly involved in Farmers' Union activities—Oscar
Fosheim of Howard and Oscar Brekke from Albee.

SOUTH DAKOTA AND NATIONAL FARM POLICY

Governor Tom Berry, like most other Democrats, wanted people
to give Roosevelt time, but like his Republican predecessor he was
willing to appease the Holiday movement with symbolic gestures. On
October 17, 1933, Berry announced his opposition to North Dakota
governor William Langer's imposition of a wheat embargo.[51] The following week, when Milo Reno called for a nationwide farm strike,
Berry criticized the idea, observing that farmers possessed no right
to tell others when they should market their farm products. He urged
people to support the president, as did Senator William J. Bulow and
the state's two Democratic congressmen, Fred Hildebrandt and
Theodore Werner.[52] Peter Norbeck, the lone South Dakota Republican in Washington, supported Henry Wallace's policies while expressing sympathy for the farmers' problems. Regional Holiday meetings
in Sioux Falls and Watertown debated the question of South Dakota's
role in the strike. Drought and grasshoppers had destroyed so many
crops that most state farmers were already observing an involuntary
holiday, Emil Loriks noted.[53]

At the request of Milo Reno, Governor Clyde Herring of Iowa
called a meeting of Midwestern governors on October 30 to discuss
alternative courses of action.[54] Unlike the previous fall, when Governor Green had organized the conference, this time South Dakota's
governor played an inconspicuous role. After endorsing Farm Holi-

day demands for an NRA-type code for agriculture, guaranteed cost
of production, and revised farm loan policies, Governors Herring,
Berry, Langer of North Dakota, Olson of Minnesota, and Schmedeman
of Wisconsin traveled to Washington to press their demands on the
president and Secretary Wallace. Roosevelt, well aware of the seeth-
ing discontent in the farm belt, proceeded with several actions aimed
at the farm problem but stopped short of acceding to the governors'
major demands. While Olson and Langer were critical of the president's
lukewarm response, Herring and Berry reiterated their support for
his position. "I think he's doing everything he can for us," Berry remarked. "I know he wants to help. He may not have the right program for some things but he's sincere."[55]

After Roosevelt's rebuff, South Dakotans responded to Milo Reno's
call to put the farm strike into "full gear" by voluntarily reducing farm
shipments for several days. Pickets blocked the four roads leading
into Swift & Company in Watertown and stood watch at produce plants
there. At Sioux Falls, livestock arrivals were down by 80 percent as
pickets patrolled the roads.[56] But within a few days time receipts were
back to normal and strike momentum had died. State Holiday leaders,
casting about for another means of exerting pressure, decided to des-
ignate Monday, November 20, as "Justice for Agriculture Day," when
all producers and buyers would be asked to cease business for the day
and all communities would be asked to protest "against the continued
degradation of agriculture." The decision showed clearly the caution
and restraint that usually characterized the South Dakota movement.
At the same time that it scheduled the one-day symbolic demonstration and assured continued support for the national farm strike, the
board of directors called for the reopening of creameries and other
processing plants and "frowned" at continued picketing and forced
closing of plants. And while it urged farmers to continue a peaceful
withholding action, it also stated its understanding of the necessity
for some farmers to send their products to market. The Sioux Falls
Argus-Leader, a consistent critic of picketing and violence, commended
the constructive approach of the state Holiday leaders.[57] "Justice for
Agriculture Day" saw reduced activities in some towns. Markets at
Huron, Redfield, DeSmet, and Miller were among the inactive ones;

creameries in Pierre and Mitchell and other communities shut down. In Madison, farmers and businessmen marched together in a big parade. But most markets in Sioux Falls were going full blast and in Rapid City, with some exceptions, it was business as usual. Nevertheless, state president Barney McVeigh said that he was highly pleased. "It demonstrated in virtually unanimous fashion," he said, "that it demands speedy and adequate measures to be taken to restore agriculture to its rightful place in the economic life of the nation."[58]

Governor Berry's proclamation of the day as "Justice for Agriculture Day" in South Dakota reflected once again the willingness of the state's chief executive to give symbolic support to the movement while withholding substantive backing for it.[59] Berry's inclination, like that of Green before him, was to express sympathy for farm distress while defusing the movement's potential for disruption. The tendency of Holiday leaders to overstate their accomplishments also shone through in McVeigh's statement. And the inclination to engage in moderate and symbolic activities could be seen in the decision to hold the demonstration in the first place. Farmer-business cooperation, epitomized in the Madison march, reflected a desire to avoid class-based appeals.

EMIL LORIKS, HOLIDAY LEADER

Cooperation with Main Street businessmen was a frequent theme of Emil Loriks, and the methods used by him and his colleagues in the Holiday movement to attract resources and support constitute the final explanation for the generally moderate tone of the South Dakota phenomenon. The composition of the board of directors reflected as well as anything the inclination to work in league with rather than in opposition to business interests. The five board members consisted of the leaders of the three major farm organizations—E. H. Everson of the Farmers' Union, H. B. Test of the Farm Bureau, and J. J. Martin of the Grange—along with the chairman of the state Chamber of Commerce, W. C. Lusk, and the president of the State Bankers' Association, T. M. Brisbine.[60] The board met infrequently and conferred virtually free reign on the officers to organize local units and manage day-to-day operations.[61] On major issues, such as whether to participate in holding actions called by the national leadership, they came together to decide what South Dakota's response would be, but most of the time direction was set by state president Barney McVeigh and even more so by secretary-treasurer Emil Loriks. Both were members of the legislature, as was E. N. Hammerquist of Farmingdale, South Dakota's representative on the national board. Their positions of influence and responsibility in the legislature—McVeigh as Speaker in 1931 and Loriks as chairman of the Senate Appropriations Committee in 1933—inclined them toward moderation and circumspection in their actions.

Loriks, who during 1932 and 1933 spent thousands of dollars of his own money traveling around the state to attend meetings and organize local units, was a successful farmer who with hired help operated as many as twenty-four horses at a time on his acreage northeast of Oldham. During his frequent absences in Pierre or on the road with Holiday business, his wife Ruth managed the farm, which had been homesteaded by his father, a Swedish immigrant who had helped lay track for the Chicago and Northwestern Railroad in 1880. Young Emil spoke only Swedish at home until he went off to school. His father was basically conservative in outlook and voted Republican, but when Nonpartisan League organizers entered the state at the time of World War I, he joined up. Emil's inclinations as a youth were liberal; in college he debated the affirmative case for women's suffrage, refusing to debate the other side. He admired Woodrow Wilson and in 1924 was a La Follette supporter. During his early years in the legislature during the late 1920s, he was a member of the Farm Bureau, but as he became acquainted with the methods and goals of the Farmers' Union, he switched allegiance and by 1930 was deeply involved in its activities.[62] State party leaders encouraged him to run for the Democratic gubernatorial nomination in 1932, but he felt unable to afford the personal expense of a campaign and doubted his chances on a ticket that seldom ever won.[63] Thus, by the time he took over as secretary-treasurer of the state Holiday in 1932, Loriks was well-established economically and politically and was well-acquainted with people around the state.

His conviction that cooperation worked better than confrontation was evident in his words and actions. From the very beginning, the Farm Holiday solicited business support. Of the 1,200 people at the Sioux Falls meeting on August 18, 1932, launching the Minnehaha County unit, 200 were businessmen.[64] Besides attending meetings, businessmen and lawyers frequently assumed leadership roles and were active in organizing the movement. George Kephart of Beresford and Charles Weller of Mitchell were two attorneys who played especially active roles.[65] Loriks, Hammerquist, and other Holiday leaders emphasized the necessity for business support.[66] At an organizational meeting in Brookings County, three professors from South Dakota State College expressed their willingness to provide information and statistics to help in setting goals. Several prominent businessmen from Brookings were named as county officers.[67] "Strangely, the residents of towns and cities are backing the movement better than the farmers in many instances," Loriks observed in September 1932. "According to reports received at my office, the businessmen of Howard and DeSmet have signed up 100 percent in the Holiday movement and have all paid their dues of 50 cents. Business people are able to see the possibilities of the movement better than many farmers. They are backing it in wonderful shape." E. H. Everson remarked, "It is surprising the general support that is being given to it by business and professional men of all walks of life."[68] Most businessmen certainly saw nothing incongruous in their joining the Holiday and felt welcome by the leaders of the movement.

Further reflecting the moderate tone of Holiday leadership was their continual disavowal of the use of violence. Emil Loriks frequently cautioned against violent picketing, and picketing of any kind was generally frowned upon. The use of "observers" was sanctioned, but since many saw this as just another term for picketers, the result was to give encouragement to picketers. Loriks also warned at times that picketing might have to be resorted to if peaceful protests were unavailing.[69] Holiday leaders had to choose their words carefully, for if they were not supportive enough of their more militant followers they might find themselves with no followers at all. As John Shover observed in his study of the national movement, the most significant results were achieved as a result of spontaneous outbursts by groups of farmers who took things into their own hands, not of the planned activities of the leaders.[70]

After 1935 the problem of how to deal with the Communists became more insistent for farm and labor organizations. The main expression of Communist activity in South Dakota during the 1930s was the United Farmers' League, which was active in the northeastern part of the state around Frederick and Sisseton.[71] Although by 1938 as Democratic candidates for Congress and governor would be smeared by their opponents as Communists, Emil Loriks as secretary-treasurer and Oscar Fosheim as second president of the South Dakota Holiday steered their organization clear of the United Farmers' League and avoided the kind of cooperative action with the Communists that occurred in Nebraska.[72]

CONCLUSION

The South Dakota Farm Holiday was thus a movement in tension. Threats of violence coexisted with general disapproval of the tactic. Conservative bankers and businessmen joined with distressed farmers to seek better conditions for agriculture. Democrats and Republicans, Communists and anti-Communists, poor and moderately well-to-do, radicals and conservatives were thrown together in an organization based upon the consensus that South Dakota's farmers needed and deserved a better deal. Some were confident that the New Deal would help solve their problems, while others denounced the national administration as going either too far or not far enough.

Several factors worked together to guide the South Dakota Farmers' Holiday Association along more moderate lines than its counterparts in nearby states: geography, historical tradition, political circumstances, and the nature of its leadership. In a basically conservative state, the Farm Holiday followed a moderate course.

South Dakota's Farm Holiday. Map by Robert Watrel.

NOTES

1. Paul A. O'Rourke, "South Dakota Politics During the New Deal Years," *South Dakota History* 1 (Summer 1971): 232–234; Robert S. Thompson, "The History of the South Dakota Farmers' Union, 1914–1952" (Master's Thesis, University of South Dakota, 1953), 55–56,67–68.
2. Allan J. Mathews, "The History of the United Farmers' League of South Dakota 1923–1936: A Study in Farm Radicalism" (Master's Thesis, University of South Dakota, 1972); Mathews, "Agrarian Radicals: The United Farmers' League of South Dakota," *South Dakota History* 3 (Fall 1973): 408–421; Lowell K. Dyson, *Red Harvest: The Communist Party and American Farmers* (Lincoln: University of Nebraska Press, 1982), 31, 69–70, 100, 106, 120, 129.
3. A good indicator of the concentration of Holiday activities in eastern South Dakota is the list of counties that were represented at the third state convention of the South Dakota Farmers' Holiday Association in June 1934.
4. In Nebraska and Iowa also the Farm Holiday was most successful in counties with a high proportion of hog and cattle raising farmers who cultivated relatively high-priced land and earned relatively high incomes. John L. Shover, *Cornbelt Rebellion: The Farmers' Holiday Association* (Urbana: University of Illinois Press, 1965), 4–9; Shover, "The Farm Holiday Movement in Nebraska," *Nebraska History* 43 (March 1962): 55.
5. John Milton, *South Dakota: A Bicentennial History* (New York: W. W. Norton, 1977), 122, 141.
6. Ibid., 123; John Gunther, *Inside U.S.A.* (New York: Harper and Brothers, 1947), 237, 247–249; Alan L. Clem, *Prairie State Politics: Popular Democracy in South Dakota* (Washington, D.C.: Public Affairs Press, 1967), 7.
7. Gilbert C. Fite, "Peter Norbeck and the Defeat of the Nonpartisan League in South Dakota," *Mississippi Valley Historical Review* 33 (1946): 236; Clem, *Prairie State Politics*, 32–34, 46.
8. Clem, *Prairie State Politics*, 6–7, 23–36; Calvin Perry Armin, "Coe I. Crawford and the Progressive Movement in South Dakota," *South Dakota Historical Collections* (Pierre: State Historical Society, 1964), 22–23; Gilbert C. Fite, *Peter Norbeck: Prairie Statesman* (Columbia: University of Missouri, 1948); Fite, "South Dakota: Some Observations by a Native Son," *South Dakota History* 4 (Fall 1974): 462–463.
9. Donald D. Parker, "Warren Everett Green," in *South Dakota's Governors*, ed. Charles J. Dalthorp (Sioux Falls: Midwest-Beach, 1953), 49–54; Sioux Falls *Argus-Leader*, 21 December 1931.

10. Sioux Falls *Argus-Leader*, 22, 25 August 1932.

11. Ibid., 24 August 1932.

12. South Dakota *Union Farmer*, 7 September 1932; Emil Loriks, "The Great Depression: The Early Thirties and the Farm Holiday Movement," in *Selected Papers of the First Nine History Conferences, 1969–1977* (Madison: Dakota State College, 1981), 497–501; Studs Terkel, *Hard Times: An Oral History of the Great Depression* (New York: Pantheon, 1970), 227.

13. States included in the conference call were Minnesota, Iowa, North Dakota, South Dakota, Nebraska, Wisconsin, Illinois, Kansas, Montana, Indiana, Colorado, Idaho, Missouri, and Oklahoma. Sioux Falls *Argus-Leader*, 27 August 1932.

14. Sioux Falls *Argus-Leader*, 30, 31 August; 4, 7 September 1932.

15. Ibid., 9–12 September 1932; South Dakota *Union Farmer*, 21 September 1932; Governor's Conference Report (typewritten), 9–10 September 1932, Emil Loriks Papers (currently stored in the Oldham, S.D., Historic House; soon to be deposited with a yet-to-be-chosen library or archives); Shover, *Cornbelt Rebellion*, 51–53.

16. Shover, *Cornbelt Rebellion*, 51; Sioux Falls *Argus-Leader*, 3 September 1932.

17. Sioux Falls *Argus-Leader*, 11 September 1932.

18. Ibid., 19 September 1932.

19. Ibid., 23 September 1932.

20. Ibid., 21 September 1932.

21. Ibid., 22 September 1932.

22. Ibid., 5, 19 October 1932; Shover, *Cornbelt Rebellion*, 54–55.

23. E. H. Everson to Emil Loriks, 3 October 1932; John Eide to Loriks, 23 September 1932; Oscar Fosheim to Loriks, 23 September 1932; Oscar Brekke to Loriks, 6, 23, 29 September 1932; H. P. Richardson to Loriks, 2 October 1932, Emil Loriks Papers.

24. Sioux Falls *Argus-Leader*, 9 October 1932.

25. Arthur M. Schlesinger Jr., *The Crisis of the Old Order, 1919–1933* (Boston: Houghton Mifflin, 1957), 413–439.

26. Sioux Falls *Argus-Leader*, 5 April 1932.

27. Ibid., 19 January 1932.

28. Ibid., 4, 5 May 1932.

29. Ibid., 28 June, 2 July 1932.

30. Ibid., 14 September, 2, 3, 6 November 1932.

31. Ibid., 9 November 1932.

32. *South Dakota Legislative Manual, 1933* (Pierre: State Publishing Co., 1933), 520–570.

33. Joseph V. Ryan, "Tom Berry," in *South Dakota's Governors*, 57–61; Sioux Falls *Argus-Leader*, 13 February; 13 December 1932; 3 January 1933.

34. Sioux Falls *Argus-Leader*, 13 January 1933.

35. Ibid., 4, 26 January; 23 February; 5, 13 March 1933.

36. Ibid., 18, 23, 27 January; 9 February; 17 April 1933.

37. Ibid., 19 January 1933.

38. Ibid., 6, 9, 17 January 1933.

39. Ibid., 10 January 1933; Farmers' Union leaders frequently did insist on the class basis of their organization. President Everson wrote in 1932, "The only way any class can hope to collect from society their rightful share of the earnings of society is through their class organization. The Farmers' Union is the only strictly class organization for farmers." South Dakota *Union Farmer*, 21 September 1932.

40. Herbert S. Schell, *History of South Dakota* (Lincoln: University of Nebraska Press, 3rd ed., rev. 1975), 285–286.

41. Sioux Falls *Argus-Leader*, 13 May 1933; letter from Emil Loriks to the presidents of local Holiday units, 12 May 1933; telegram, Burton Culver to Loriks, 2 May 1933; and C. S. Betts to Loriks, 4 May 1933, Emil Loriks Papers.

42. Sioux Falls *Argus-Leader*, 10 February 1933.

43. Sioux Falls *Argus-Leader*, 28 April; 2, 3 May 1933.

44. Ibid., 4, 5 February 1933.

45. Ibid., 21 March 1933.

46. Terkel, *Hard Times*, 226; Emil Loriks interviews with author, 18 March 1982, 18 October 1984.

47. Ibid., 8 July, 3 August, 23 September 1933; South Dakota *Union Farmer*, 31 May, 28 June 1933; Milo Reno to Emil Loriks, 12 September 1933; letter from Emil Loriks to local units, 3 October 1933, Emil Loriks Papers.

48. South Dakota Farmers' Holiday Association, mimeographed information sheet, c. September 1933, Emil Loriks Papers.

49. William E. Leuchtenberg, *Franklin D. Roosevelt and the New Deal, 1932–1940* (New York: Harper and Row, 1963), 78, 82–83; Arthur M. Schlesinger Jr., *The Coming of the New Deal* (Boston: Houghton Mifflin, 1958), 233–240.

50. Sioux Falls *Argus-Leader*, 27, 28 October 1933.

51. Ibid., 17 October 1933.

52. Ibid., 20, 21 October; 5, 7 November 1933.

53. Ibid., 7, 24 October 1933.

54. Shover, *Cornbelt Rebellion*, 152–153.

55. Ibid., 152–62; Sioux Falls *Argus-Leader*, 29 October–5 November 1933.

56. Sioux Falls *Argus-Leader*, 6–9 November 1933.

57. Ibid., 14, 15 November 1933.

58. Ibid., 20, 21 November 1933.

59. Ibid., 17 November 1933.

60. Ibid., 28 July 1933.

61. Emil Loriks, interview with the author, 16 October 1982.
62. Ibid.; Elizabeth Evenson Williams, "The Inventional Components of Emil Loriks' Agrarian Farmers' Union Rhetoric, 1934–1938" (Master's Thesis, South Dakota State University, 1983), 71–77; John E. Miller, "McCarthyism Before McCarthy: The 1938 Election in South Dakota," *Heritage of the Great Plains* 15 (Summer 1982): 1–21; Loriks, "The Great Depression: The Early Thirties and the Farm Holiday Movement"; Terkel, *Hard Times*, 226–230.
63. Sioux Falls *Argus-Leader*, 19 January 1932.
64. Ibid., 19 August 1932. Attempting to identify the size and characteristics of Holiday membership in South Dakota is a difficult task. Claims by Holiday leaders during the early months of organization that they had twenty or thirty thousand members lined up were clearly exaggerated. Sioux Falls *Argus-Leader*, 3, 16 September 1932. There is a black three-ring binder in the Emil Loriks Papers which includes lists of officers in each county and some incomplete records of dues paid. The best guess is that at its peak in 1933 and 1934 there were several thousand dues-paying members, most of whom were farmers in the eastern part of the state.
65. Sioux Falls *Argus-Leader*, 18, 19 August; 11 September 1932; Charles Weller to Emil Loriks, 8 August, 3 September 1932; George Kephart to Loriks, 4 September 1932, Emil Loriks Papers. Other lawyers corresponded with Loriks about Holiday matters: Otto Kass (Britton) to Loriks, 6 August 1932; Grant L. Parrish (Miller) to Loriks, 20 September, 5 October, 2 December 1932; H. Van Ruschen (Salem) to Loriks, 21 September 1932; H. W. Hembd (Ipswich) to Loriks, 11 September 1932, Emil Loriks Papers.
66. Sioux Falls *Argus-Leader*, 27 July; 13, 20 August 1932.
67. Emil Loriks to J. J. Martin, 13 August 1932; Loriks to H. M. Norfjor, 15 August 1932, Emil Loriks Papers.
68. Sioux Falls *Argus-Leader*, 22 September 1932; South Dakota *Union Farmer*, 27 July 1932.
69. Telegram from Emil Loriks to E. N. Hammerquist, 1 October 1932, Emil Loriks Papers; Sioux Falls *Argus-Leader*, 18, 20 August; 22 September 1932.
70. Shover, *Cornbelt Rebellion*, 86–88.
71. Sioux Falls *Argus-Leader*, 15 December 1932; 17 March, 14 July, 11 November 1933; Mathews, "Agrarian Radicals: The United Farmers' League of South Dakota" and "History of the United Farmers' League of South Dakota."
72. Dyson, *Red Harvest*, 129; Emil Loriks, interview with author, 16 October 1982.

AGRARIAN RADICALS: THE UNITED FARMERS
LEAGUE OF SOUTH DAKOTA
Allan Mathews

Agricultural recessions have caused distress on several occasions
among farmers in South Dakota and have given rise to protest movements that sounded the call for economic justice. The People's Party,
the Nonpartisan League, and the Farmer-Labor Party were among
these movements. In the 1890s South Dakotans joined the People's
Party and helped elect Populist-Democrat Governor Andrew E. Lee
for two terms.[1] Just prior to World War I farmers joined the
reform-minded Nonpartisan League in the search for relief and supported the candidates of the League. This support diminished when
Progressive Republican Governor Peter Norbeck adopted many of
the programs of the League as his own. In the mid-1920s farmers
formed the Farmer-Labor Party, and soon other reform movements
followed.[2]

The threat of foreclosure was the main reason for unrest in the
1920s. Farmers had earlier plunged into debt to enlarge their farms
as heavy rains produced bumper crops and world markets sustained
high prices. Suddenly, about 1924 rains diminished and prices dropped
because of world-wide overproduction. Soon banks failed and foreclosure threatened.

Governor Warren Green later described the situation as "the most
serious [that] has confronted our state in recent history."[3] Urging responsible actions, the governor called leading citizens together at
Huron to seek solutions to the distress. The Committee of Twenty-two
responded with a plan whereby boards of county commissioners could
issue farmers, living in hard hit areas, warrants to buy feed for their
livestock.[4] However, the governor's action was not enough to appease

the spokesmen from the northern and northeastern counties of the state. They demanded a special session of the legislature to declare a five-year moratorium on all debts, interest, and taxes in the state. They also insisted on removal of all past due and unpaid taxes from the records.[5]

Their demands shaped the platform of a new Liberty Party with its base in Roberts County. The party was short-lived, entering candidates in only one contest before its demise, the state election of 1932. The party captured few votes, suffering defeat, as did the Republican Party, at the hands of gubernatorial candidate Tom Berry and other New Deal Democrats. But the farmers, expecting little from the Roosevelt administration in the way of relief, formed organizations to demand help.

Led in northeastern South Dakota by those who had been active in the Liberty Party and its predecessor, the Nonpartisan League, farm protests reflected discontentment with the continuing economic blight. By the mid-1930s half of the banks in the state had failed, and countless farmers had lost their lands.[6] Federal agencies were slow to act. There was near starvation in some homes. So severe was the distress that rural South Dakotans joined the most militant of organizations—the United Farmers League [U.F.L.]. Taking a stand to the left of the larger and more publicized Farm Holiday Association, the Communist-led U.F.L. sank its roots into northeastern South Dakota and gained power that far exceeded its numerical strength. Always demanding, the league was to its members the only hope; to others, it was a dangerous revolutionary force.

FOUNDING THE UNITED FARMERS LEAGUE IN SOUTH DAKOTA

The United Farmers League was founded in the spring of 1923 with headquarters first at Fargo, North Dakota, then at Bismarck. Initiated by farmers living in northwestern North Dakota, formerly a stronghold of the Nonpartisan League, the U.F.L. attempted to influence the infant Farmer-Labor Party to fight for the interests of poor farmers. Though a small organization, the U.F.L. attracted memberships from militant elements in the Nonpartisan League and

Farmer-Labor Party. Confined primarily to the Dakotas in its early years, leaders eventually formed chapters in Minnesota, northern Michigan, and Wisconsin through the influence of the organization's first paper, the *United Farmer*, written by Alfred Knudsen.[7]

By 1931 the U.F.L. made inroads across northeastern South Dakota and was especially vigorous in the Frederick area north of Aberdeen. The Depression of the thirties caused many farmers to enter the ranks of the League because of its advocacy of direct action to stop farm foreclosures and tax sales. The leaders tried first to stop forced sales by persuasion. If that failed, they held "penny sales" in which members bid a few cents per item, then returned the goods to the owners. Or U.F.L. leaders formed committees to investigate the facts of the proposed sale and prevented the auctions with threats, forced adjustments, or the scaling down of the debt. In either case direct confrontation between masses of farmers and the mortgage holders was the method employed.

During the fall of 1931, Ella Reeve "Mother" Bloor and George Maki, both organizers for the Communist Party, made several trips into the Frederick area and laid the groundwork for a successful drought relief caravan to be led by leaders of the U.F.L. Trucks loaded with coal from a mine located near Van Hook, North Dakota, hauled the cargo to destitute farmers near Frederick, and then loaded grain for sale back in North Dakota. This cooperation between the farmers of the two states gave a new dimension to the U.F.L. and enhanced its popularity. Despite the obvious Communist connections of the league, it attracted more and more supporters and inspired actions by other groups. Shortly after the caravan, the Red Cross, the American Legion, and the Boy Scouts and Girl Scouts all mobilized to gather potatoes, vegetables, and old clothes for farmers of the area.[8]

After the successful caravan, Frederick U.F.L. leaders asked Charles Taylor, editor of the *Producers News* in Plentywood, Montana, to organize members in South Dakota, with the promise that local farmers would finance his campaign. He prepared for the organization of locals at Crooks, Viborg, Roslyn, Pierpont, and Columbia, South Dakota. The most viable organization, however, remained at Frederick.[9]

While the South Dakota U.F.L. dealt with local problems, the national headquarters planned more ambitious undertakings. There was a call for a Farmers National Relief Conference in Washington, D.C., to be held in the fall of 1932. Leaders of the conference planned to coordinate the activities of the agrarian program of the Communist Party with those of activist farm organizations. From 7 through 10 December those present heard report after report concerning grim conditions throughout the nation. President Herbert Hoover, Vice-President Charles Curtis, and members of Congress received delegations of farmers. Resolutions issued at the conference asked for federal cash relief, government price fixing, credit relief, and a moratorium on foreclosures. Those in attendance were urged to call state conferences to bring the message to the localities.[10]

The year 1932 was one of rapid growth in farm radicalism. Droughts in 1930 and 1931 caused a decline in cattle production for lack of feed. Production of hogs dropped to the smallest number in fifty years with a corresponding decline in prices. Lamb prices were the lowest on record. The price of corn was down to an average of thirteen cents a bushel in South Dakota, compared to an average of thirty-one cents a bushel the previous year.[11] Foreclosures mounted, and by the end of 1932, renters outnumbered owners in South Dakota.[12] Needless to say, the U.F.L. stood to gain from the resulting distress.

THE PIERRE CONVENTION AND FARMER RADICALIZATION

In February 1933 U.F.L. leaders called a South Dakota Farmers Relief Conference to be held in Pierre. When it became apparent that left-wing forces would dominate the conference, leaders of the Farm Bureau, Farmers' Union, and Farm Holiday Association denied that they had any part in the activities, though this failed to dissuade members of these organizations from attending.[13] Communist organizers who had ingratiated themselves with the leaders of the conference were the main speakers. They included Mother Bloor; Lewis Benzley, president of the United Farmers Protective Association of Pennsylvania; and Lem Harris, executive secretary of the Farmers National

Committee for Action. Relief, security, and a rise in the standard of living were the main objectives of the convention; however, delegates also passed resolutions condemning imperialist wars and supporting workers' demands for cash relief. They also made it known that they favored retention of the primary election law, endorsed a bill before the legislature providing maximum high school fees of seven dollars and fifty cents per month, and opposed direct buying of livestock by packers.[14]

Following the meeting, the rank and file of the delegates marched through the main streets of Pierre carrying banners demanding that the state government stop all foreclosures and evictions. They swarmed up the steps of the capitol building, into the rotunda, and there enthusiastically sang a version of the socialist theme song "Solidarity." The house and senate went into recess so their members could observe the group from the balcony. The delegates recruited spokesmen from the group to speak before both legislative bodies. Generally the legislators were sympathetic. However, they had passed a moratorium bill that provided for an additional year of redemption under certain conditions and they considered that adequate.

The U.F.L. leaders received even less response to their demands from the executive department in Pierre.[15] Application of relief measures in other states left much to be desired, but at least there were good intentions. Governor William Langer of North Dakota issued a proclamation forbidding the forced sale of farm properties. In Minnesota, numerous relief measures were adopted including a two-year moratorium on farm foreclosures. By comparison, relief legislation in South Dakota was lacking.

Facing collapse, South Dakota farmers continued to stave off foreclosures by their own means. Through 1933 the U.F.L. led the farmers of northeastern South Dakota in forcibly preventing such losses. The center of the power of the League had shifted from the Frederick area to Roberts County. By April 1933 the Sisseton branch boasted of the ability to gather fifteen hundred farmers in less than two hours.[16]

As the Depression continued, farmers in the Midwest became increasingly more militant. In Iowa a judge was dragged from his courtroom by angry farmers when he refused to agree to sign no more foreclosure orders. Throughout the nation there were parades and demonstrations by farmers demanding relief and in South Dakota, the U.F.L. continued to move to the left. The executive council of the League in Minneapolis issued a policy statement on the relationship of the organization to the so-called united front of American farmers. The council declared the U.F.L. to be "a left-wing organization within the farmers movement whose purpose is to unify the farmers struggles and develop those struggles toward the final aim of establishing a workers and farmers government."[17]

By the fall of 1933 the influence of the League was approaching its peak and, as a result, local officials were forced to become more accommodating toward the organization. Sheriffs in the northern section of the state came to expect to be met by hundreds of League-led farmers whenever they attempted to serve eviction notices. The U.F.L., nearly successful in its campaign to eliminate evictions, became a force in the lives of everyone connected with it. So efficient was the Roberts County branch that it became a model for the national organization.[18]

OPPOSITION TO THE U.F.L.

Though the League was at its height of power in South Dakota, opposition to it was beginning to strengthen. Thus, in 1934 an injunction was issued against the organization and eighteen of its members were arrested in Sisseton for riotous assembly. The arrests resulted from an incident in which the U.F.L. had removed a family from their home and replaced a former occupant who had been evicted. It was not just the individuals who were on trial, but the entire organization. The civil injunction prohibited the League from such basic activities as holding meetings or circulating literature. Publicity given the arrests by Attorney General Walter Conway contributed to the atmosphere of excitement that pervaded Sisseton. A special meeting of the ex-servicemen of the area unanimously voted for the upholding of law and order, and members pledged to support the local police officers.[19]

As the leaders of the U.F.L. sat in their cells, paranoia spread throughout Sisseton. Rumors of an intended League rally prompted

Attorney General Conway to mobilize members of the state constabulary. Heavily armed sheriffs and deputies from five counties along with agents of the state Department of Justice soon converged upon Sisseton. They were augmented by some fifty ex-servicemen. Sporting a submachine gun and a large supply of tear gas, the force, which now numbered nearly one hundred strong, prepared to defend the jail against a possible onslaught of angry farmers. While Sisseton became an armed camp, those U.F.L. members not in custody met at Browns Valley, Minnesota, some fifteen miles away. Fortunately, the streets of Sisseton remained quiet and deserted, for no attempt was ever made to free the prisoners.[20]

The trial of the U.F.L. leaders began in mid-June. States attorney Dana Babcock prosecuted the case for the state while Henry Paull, a representative of the International Labor Defense and the American Civil Liberties Union, Dewey Hanson of Omaha, M. C. Lasell of Aberdeen, and G. G. Lasell of Sisseton represented the defense.[21] The state produced about twenty witnesses and attempted to reconstruct the events of the eviction. In presenting the case to the jury, Babcock stressed that during the preceding year he and the sheriff had been confronted with mob resistance in Roberts County, and that under the incitement of the U.F.L., the protests had become vicious. Either this must end, maintained the prosecution, or the county would have to be put under martial law. Babcock concluded the case for the state with an appeal for "law and order."[22]

Henry Paull, young attorney for the defense, then rose to speak and the courtroom became quiet. The family that had moved onto the farm was a tool of the insurance companies, he argued. Pursuing this line of attack, he pointed out that 60 percent of the land that Roberts County farmers depended on for their living was already controlled by the insurance companies. Waving his arms back and forth in front of the jury, the Duluth lawyer concluded with these words:

> The conviction of these men will mean that thousands of Roberts County farmers, and many more farmers of the United States, will be driven from their homes into the vast army of unemployed job hunters. Many dispossessed farmers today are fighting for stand-

ing room in the breadlines of the big cities. The acquittal of these
men will establish the right of these seventeen farmers, and even
your right, gentlemen of the jury, to organize for the protection of
your homes.[23]

Silence greeted the end of Paull's summation, then a thunderous
applause shook the courtroom. The judge reached for his gavel, but
apparently realizing the futility of such a move, suffered the indignity
to the court.[24] This was not the first such insult of the trial, for every
day supporters of the defendants packed the courtroom and at numerous times clapped and yelled at Paull's attack of the witnesses of the
state. On several occasions the crowd rose en masse and rushed to the
front of the courtroom demanding dismissal of the action. Defense
attorney Paull added to the embarrassment of the court by referring
to state witnesses as "scabs and traitors."[25] The tension mounted as
the twelve men of the jury retired to determine the verdict.

After four hours of deliberation, the jury, made up primarily of
farmers, brought in a unanimous verdict of not guilty for all the defendants. The *Sisseton Courier* termed the verdict one of prejudice and
fear, and condemned the courtroom actions of the defense as
"un-American."[26] For the U.F.L. the outcome presented further proof
of the rightness of its cause and the ability of its leaders to outmaneu-
ver the "system."

Though the results of the trial seemed to represent a victory for
the League, just the opposite was true. The trial actually signified the
beginning of the end of the influence of the organization in South Dakota. During the trial it had become increasingly apparent that the
U.F.L. was receiving support from the Communist Party. Party organizers appeared in the Sisseton area to protest the indictments. Some
League leaders began to preach the inevitability of a socialist revolution. National directives instructed organizers of the Communist Party
to "show the face of the Party" in their efforts, and as a result, the
membership of the U.F.L. dropped sharply.

CONCLUSION

Though its influence was waning, the League indicated that it
would run a slate of candidates in the elections of 1934. C. H. Sharp

announced that he was running for Congress, Homer Ayres of Strool for lieutenant governor, and Knute Walstad for governor of South Dakota. However, before the elections took place, the League was attacked both verbally and physically by its opponents. In August 1934 the U.F.L. sponsored a "Farm School on Wheels" at Clear Lake, South Dakota. The school, which proposed to train farmers in organizational work, expected students from North Dakota and some ten counties of South Dakota. Courses offered included: History of the Farmers' Struggles in America, Course on Organization Work, Public Speaking, and Organizational Accounting. The U.F.L. leased the grounds at Clear Lake for the month of August, but the school's stay was to end shortly after its arrival.[27]

The citizens of the area, alarmed at what they believed to be the teaching of Communism at the school, prepared to take action. Led by local legion members, they raided the "School on Wheels" camp and viciously assaulted its members. The school moved to Veblen, South Dakota, where it remained for a short time before moving across the border into Minnesota.[28]

From this time on the U.F.L. exerted less and less influence in South Dakota. The election in the fall of 1934 pointed to the fact that the League represented only a small minority of the farmers in the state and that it was no longer the viable organization of protest it had been during the early years of the crisis. Soon the New Deal farm programs and public disapproval of the philosophical base of the U.F.L. joined to put an end to this incisive farm movement.

NOTES

1. Alan L. Clem, *Prairie State Politics—Popular Democracy in South Dakota* (Washington, D.C.: Public Affairs Press, 1967), pp. 26–27.
2. S. Dak. Bureau of Public Printing, *South Dakota Legislative Manual—1919* (Pierre: State Publishing Company, 1919), p. 412.
3. *Sisseton* (S. Dak.) *Courier*, 6 August 1931.
4. Ibid.
5. Ibid., 30 July 1931.
6. W. F. Kumlien, *A Graphic Summary of Relief in South Dakota: 1930–1935*

(Brookings: Agricultural Experiment Station, 1937), pp. 7–8. The percentage of the population of South Dakota engaged in agriculture in 1930 was one of the highest in the nation. Because of the lack of industry in the state, the farmer had little choice but to go on relief during periods of crop failure.

7. Henry Puro, "The Position of the American Farmer and the Tasks of the United Farmers League," *Report of the Executive Council to the First National Convention of the United Farmers League Held at Minneapolis, 22–25 June 1934* (Chicago: U.F.L. National Office, n.d.), pp. 1–2.

8. Plentywood (Mont.) *Producers News*, 27 November 1931. The *Producers News* became the official organ of the U.F.L. in 1932.

9. Ibid.

10. John L. Shover, *Cornbelt Rebellion—The Farmer's Holiday Association* (Urbana: University of Illinois Press, 1965), pp. 73–74.

11. U.S. Department of Agriculture, *Yearbook of Agriculture—1933* (Washington, D.C.: Government Printing Office, 1933), pp. 222–435.

12. S. Dak. Department of Agriculture, *South Dakota Agricultural Statistics—1934* (Pierre: State Publishing Company, 1934), p. 7.

13. *Aberdeen Evening News*, 19 February 1933.

14. *Producers News*, 24 February 1933.

15. Homer Ayres, Sturgis, South Dakota, interview on 10 April 1971.

16. *Aberdeen Evening News*, 1 April 1933.

17. *Producers News*, 7 April 1933.

18. Ibid., 12 January 1934.

19. *Sisseton Courier*, 22 February 1934.

20. *Sioux Falls Argus Leader*, 22 February 1934.

21. *Sisseton Courier*, 28 June 1934.

22. Ibid.

23. *Producers News*, 28 June 1934.

24. Ibid.

25. *Sisseton Courier*, 28 June 1934.

26. Ibid.

27. Ibid., 2 August 1934.

28. Ibid., 30 August 1934.

IV

Searching for Explanations
The Media Response

Throughout the Dust Bowl crisis, the media was used to rally farmers and the nation. Farmer organizations and political parties generally employed the print media through newspapers, journals, or pamphlets. The power of movies was just beginning to be felt, and the federal government sought to explain the disaster through documentary film, as well as other methods.

The media sometimes became the focal point for political action. This was the situation in Plentywood, Montana, where first the Non-partisan League and then the Communist Party subsidized and staffed the Producers News. *Charles Taylor, editor, made the local newspaper the primary organ for orchestrating a farmer-laborer party's successful countywide political campaign.* Producers News *provided the citizenry with leftist explanations for the Dust Bowl and the Depression and led the radical response to those catastrophes.*

A different tack came in 1939 with the preparation and presentation of The Plow That Broke the Plains. *This documentary, which brought together several nationally known artists, blamed the farmers' plight on the government and business and implied that solving the crisis would require the cooperation of all parties. The film proved very controversial and was banned until 1961. Even at the height of the disaster, Americans were not yet ready to face the task of inquiry.*

RADICAL RULE IN MONTANA
Charles Vindex

Plentywood, the seat of northeastern Montana's Sheridan County, is a busy, prosperous, sturdily growing, politically conventional town now approaching a population of 3,000. To a visitor in the 1960s, unaware of its history, it looks and sounds like any other vital American village. Yet in the 1920s when Plentywood had a thousand people or less, the town and country became widely known as the only American community actually governed by practicing "reds" who, far from concealing their radicalism, proclaimed it through the columns of a uniquely militant newspaper, the *Producers News*.

The reasons why this happened, and happened precisely where it did, can be stated only hypothetically. Geography entered into it, and local economic realities. Climate certainly played a part. But other western communities shared the climate and geography and endured the economic seesaw without going to ideological extremes. In Sheridan County special external influences coincided with special internal stresses at a difficult time. Perhaps there were also predisposing traits in the character of the populace. There were extensive settlements of people of the Scandinavian stocks, who already had a tradition of social experimentation together with fine organizing talent. Danish cooperatives at Dagmar, in the southeastern part of the county, had accumulated several years of successful operation before the radical period began.[1]

THE EVOLUTION OF SHERIDAN COUNTY

The word "red," as used by the participants themselves, meant anyone who subscribed to radical principles in politics or economics— specifically the principles enunciated by the local leadership in the

1920s and 1930s. Beyond that, the region had no single ideology to which all had to conform; it would be a mistake to suppose that this farm population ever consisted of political sophisticates. Some identified themselves as Social Democrats, some as "Debs Socialists"; many, having no clear conception of political realities, were merely dissatisfied and eager for change. So long as they followed the selected leaders, they were accounted "reds."

The leaders, too, were militant Socialists rather than Communists in 1918 and the early 1920s; after all, the success of genuine Communism was then a very new thing, even in Russia. Affiliation with the Communist party did not become widespread in Sheridan County until well along in the 1920s; it is unlikely that the actual membership ever grew much larger than the 575 who voted the ticket straight in 1932. The others, those who helped swell "red" majorities in the successful 1918–1926 elections, were persons under the influence of radical ideas in general, never disciplined Communists.

The region did not have even the beginnings of a land survey until 1906, when the homesteading era was approaching its end in the country at large. It had no railroad until 1910. Whites came late here, and came to a West that had left Wild West traditions behind. The country saw little of the bustle of ranching which had been—or had been made to seem— the pre-eminent western activity. The area was part of Valley County until 1913 and did not choose Plentywood as its seat until 1914.

This was a frontier of plowlands, not of herds; of group effort to solve group problems, not of gunsmoke and dubious heroics. Its familiar everyday figure was a farmer in blue bib overalls driving a team of nodding draft horses across a dusty field. Because of pressures created by frequent crop failures, its folk heroes would be politicians promising solutions.

The first influence bearing large implications for the future was a soil especially adapted to growing high-protein spring wheat that would later command premium prices. In a good year, such as 1912 or 1915, this land could and did reward six weeks' work in spring and fall with yields as high as 40 bushels of wheat to the acre.

Dry years tended to come in series and at the worst possible time— when war drove prices up. For six years following 1915 farmers here had almost nothing to sell, but because of adverse shipping rates, they paid higher than standard prices for everything they bought. Before they had harvested another good crop, the wheat market collapsed.

This demonstration of what they came to regard as settled injustice in the conditions of their lives became the second ruling influence to many in Sheridan County.

POLITICAL NONCONFORMITY

From the beginning, the region was politically nonconformist, though not yet "red." It started mildly by endorsing Theodore Roosevelt's split from the Republican party in 1912. During the bitter years of drought and failure, discontented persons organized Socialist groups throughout the county.

In 1917 the Nonpartisan League began spilling over from North Dakota. The League's platform included such planks as abolition of taxes on farm improvements and state ownership of terminal elevators and flour mills. These principles understandably appealed to an area which had great improvements still to make and desperately needed a fairer marketing system. Townspeople at first supported the new hopes, for when farmers lacked money the towns—which had prospered in 1912 and 1915—could only hang on the edge of disaster. Everyone felt the thing to do was spread the League gospel.

Early in 1918 the Socialist and League groups banded together in the People's Publishing Company to found a newspaper at Plentywood. Since no adequate editorial talent existed locally, an editor was chosen by League headquarters in Minnesota—a newspaperman of varied experience named Charles E. Taylor.

The people of the county found Taylor's abilities impressive. Later, when the *Producers News* called him "Sheridan County's most distinguished citizen,"[2] they accepted the judgment without reference to the fact that its source was a paper he edited.

Nevertheless, Taylor's qualities suited his immediate task. He knew how to put himself in the farmer's place, to see issues as the farmer saw them, to express the farmer's feelings as the farmer could not. Initially, at least, he seemed to be the best friend the farmer ever had.

CHARLES E. TAYLOR AND THE *PRODUCERS NEWS*

Taylor was born in Wisconsin in 1884, into a family of twelve. From his fifth year the family lived in a "poor quality log cabin" in central Minnesota. He walked three miles to "what was called a school" for three to five months each year until he was 12, when he began supporting himself. At 14 he took a job with a local newspaper and found his lifework.[3] Thereafter, he worked in printing plants in many places and in all capacities. In his twenties he briefly edited the Socialist *Border Call* at International Falls, Minnesota.

Taylor took a homestead near International Falls, studied law by correspondence, and in 1908 won election as judge in Koochiching County. Then his health failed. He gave up his homestead and Minnesota career and spent six years in Wyoming recovering from tuberculosis.

In 1918 he offered his services to the Nonpartisan League, which had set up the Northwestern Service Bureau to sponsor three dozen new publications. It sent him to Plentywood in March, with authority to launch the *Producers News* and wage Montana's first League campaign.

That first year the Leaguers elected every official on the county ballot except state senator and superintendent of schools. The *Producers News*, starting on April 19, outstripped already established local papers of a dozen communities and won almost total circulation in the county, although many recall that the paper was mailed to hundreds who never really subscribed but from whom the *Producers News* later tried to collect. Nine months of circulation success, however acquired, established a Taylor legend, an almost superstitious faith in his capacities. Even his enemies swore he could solve any problem, outargue any man.

The fact is that Charles E. Taylor was, by the record of his own printed words and in the memory of many still living, an alternately brilliant and oddly unstable man. He had great personal charge but with overtones of such chameleon-like qualities that he was a difficult editorial and political foe.

In one of his earliest editorials upon assuming editorship of the *Producers News* [P.N.], he went to considerable length to set forth his own patriotism. Printed on May 10, 1918, it was in response to some remarks about Socialism printed by rival editor Joseph F. Dolin of the Plentywood *Pioneer Press*:

> If he [Dolin] wants to attack the Socialist, it's alright with us. Most of them are used to it anyway. However, for the benefit of any person interested, the editor would like to remark that he comes from pretty old American stock; in fact his ancestors, several of them, fought with General Washington, also in the second war for Independence, and that they helped save the Union in '61, that many of the family were in the Spanish War and that he is the only member of his own immediate family old enough that is not with the colors and before this thing [World War I] is fought out very likely he will be with them. He also owns a Liberty Bond and helps the Red Cross as much as his means will allow. He is also a citizen of the United States . . . his ancestors were neither Tories nor Hessians.[4]

As time went on, Taylor's editorials became more vigorous, if not faultlessly worded. He once called a rival paper "that nauseous rag that emits itself once a week from its sty down the street."[5] Caught up in the excitement of political argument, he wrote sentences that became paragraphs and touched on a dozen subjects before they reached a full stop. In a statement called "The Policy of the *Producers News*," the paper declared:

> A group of class-conscious socialists in Sheridan County, then composing what is now Roosevelt, Daniels, and Sheridan counties, Montana, conscious of the great struggle existing between the classes, the exploited and the exploiters; the farmers and workers in one class whose labor produces all of the wealth, and the bosses and bankers in the other class, who produce nothing but grow rich and mighty on the loot plundered from the workers in the fields and factories, and conscious that this struggle existing throughout the world and nation also was just as ruthless here in Sheridan County and Montana as elsewhere, and understanding fully that farmers must organize to win in the struggle with these class enemies, and realizing that the press, large and small, supported and defended the exploiters and their system, the capitalist profit system, and consistently and consciously fought the working and producing class

in the interest of the robbers and the looters, and especially that the local press, dominated by the bankers and bosses through their local agents, were especially vicious and unreliable and misleading, and feeling the necessity of the local paper, owned and controlled by the farmers and workers, to support the cause of the farmers and workers in the great class struggle and to print the news, including the news which the ruling class suppressed, and interpret it from the workers' point of view so that the workers understand the significance, and just as important, to lead and direct them in their daily struggles with their exploiters; this group of socialists organized the People's Publishing Company, selling the small denomination shares widely among farmers and workers of the area, and finally in the spring of 1918 launched the *Producers News* in a modest way, as a class struggle paper.[6]

But Charles Taylor used words with infectious enjoyment, and knew how to deflate pretensions by burlesquing them. When a Plentywood lawyer advertised himself as a *Norsk advokat* (Norwegian attorney), hoping to win the Norwegian settlers as clients, Taylor took to mentioning him as the *Norsk abekat* (Norwegian monkey). The Norwegians were convulsed; the idea of Taylor making effective use of Norwegian terms struck them as the height of humor.

A controversial thinker since boyhood, Taylor soon made no secret at all of his Communist convictions. He thoroughly believed in the "dictatorship of the proletariat," the ultimate magic of the Communists of the period. Known as "Red Flag" Taylor, he hailed Marx and Lenin as prophets of the inevitable. At the same time he delighted in H. L. Mencken's all-enveloping scorn of prophets.

On a public platform he was a compelling figure, approximately six feet tall and massively handsome, with a tendency to put on weight. Since his conquest of pulmonary illness, his voice had developed great power and was well adapted to open-air exhortations in the days before speaker systems.

1920s PLENTYWOOD POLITICS AND LIFE

The Nonpartisan League ran its candidates on whatever ticket seemed convenient—in 1918, the Republican. But unsettling changes took place within its ranks almost at once. In its home state its troubles culminated in the recall of Governor Lynn J. Frazier in 1921; in Minnesota and Montana it was transformed into the Farmer-Labor party.

Plentywood leaders had not been content with the League system of handling funds. Members paid annual dues of $16 each, which, with a membership including virtually every farmer in the region, meant a lot of money in those days. Now, with the League disintegrating and the new party not disposed to police its members' other affiliations, the Taylor group saw a chance to keep the contributions of money in local hands. Using the Farmer-Labor name for their candidates they began adopting for their county machine an earlier organization, the Progressive Farmers' Club, which under their direction became a "brotherhood" with oaths, grips, passwords, and every device commonly used by such groups.

They elected all their candidates in 1922, easily repeated the performance in 1924, and almost repeated it in 1926, losing only the county superintendent of schools.

A Socialist force limited to a small region necessarily modified its objectives. The original platform was all but forgotten by the mid-1920s. In place of abolition of taxes on farm improvements, the region settled in 1922 for the honor system of assessments: i.e., each taxpayer himself assessed his taxable property. Instead of control of terminal markets, farmers had to be content with radical-minded men as managers of local grain elevators.

Taylor saw the task of exposing current wrongs as no less vital than that of propagandizing for the future. This crusading function did sometimes mobilize public opinion and correct abuses: e.g., in its first year the *Producers News* told the full story of a seed-grain swindle by which farmers, after a total crop failure, were sold seed which contaminated new ground with noxious weeds.

Some traits of the leadership were but little known to the local population. After 1922, when Rodney Salisbury, Taylor's lieutenant, was elected sheriff, Sheridan County became a secure haven for laborers who moved with the harvest. Many were "wobblies"—members of the International Workers of the World—determined men who carried red cards and took the rights of Labor seriously. In a sense an

American underground, "wobblies" were repeatedly subjected to murderous attack—as in Butte on August 1, 1917, when Frank Little was lynched, and in Centralia, Washington, November 11, 1919, when the IWW hall was mobbed and several persons killed.[7]

The regime gave almost equal consideration to bootleggers—with the approval of most of the public. The sheriff's men occasionally raided a saloon and captured or destroyed a few bottles of fluid; but surviving old-timers swear that not one raid came without ample warning. The county was, in fact, wide open. Saloons offered a choice of gambling games and devices which in Outlook (population 200) included an improbable roulette installation. Every hamlet had at least one illegal joint, Plentywood half a dozen. Enemies of the regime, however, were subject to raids by authorities, duly reported by the *Producers News*, which stated on Sept. 16, 1927: "Cases against several persons who were alleged to be operating slot machines in Sheridan County were tried before Justice John McElroy on the complaints of Sheriff Rodney Salisbury." Apparently the laws could be enforced, if the cause was right for the administration.

The 1920s were generally good years for farmers. In 1927 and 1928, wheat was so heavy that teamsters hauled smaller loads to spare wagons and horses during threshing time. Region and regime prospered together, although the latter's luck began and ended a bit sooner.

Business boomed in towns of the region. Scobey expressed its exuberance in 1925 by hiring scandal-ridden Chicago White Sox players such as Happy Felsch and Swede Risberg to help in its baseball rivalry with Plentywood. Old-timers recall that Plentywood, which had hired the famed colored pitcher, John Donaldson, went down to defeat twice to Scobey that year, betting enthusiasts winning several thousands of dollars from rival fans.

PRODUCERS NEWS EDITORIAL POLICIES

Meanwhile, the *Producers News* created a continuing sensation. The informed air of much of what was printed about the larger world and world issues gave its front page and sometimes its editorial page the quality of a much bigger publication. This was a matter which

Taylor himself oversaw. Usually he saw it with a judicious, measuring eye.

The exception was the Russian experiment. He held steadfastly to the view that Communist good faith was the rock on which humanity's future could be founded. " 'Soviet' Means Honesty," said the headline over one of his editorials as early as March 21, 1919.

Of 18 weeklies established in the county, only three survived the circulation blitz of the *Producers News*—the Plentywood *Herald*, the Medicine Lake *Wave*, and the Redstone *Review*. One by one, the others failed. Only three seriously attempted to fight Taylor—the Plentywood *Pioneer Press*, the *Sheridan County Farmer*, and from 1928 to the end, the Plentywood *Herald*.

In the first ten years Taylor made no attempt to please businessmen. With his paper in virtually every home in the county and with facilities for blanketing wider areas at will, he felt no need to solicit advertising. He let advertisers come to him. His attacks on businessmen began when the paper began. "Small Town Kaisers Get Some Jolt From Organized Farmers," said a headline in his second issue, April 26, 1918. He took it as axiomatic that businessmen on whatever scale cared little for their country, much for their own profits. Farmers, on the other hand, he characterized as selfless patriots who planted wheat "to help feed the country in its hour of terrible ordeal."[8]

It is impossible to tell the story of the *Producers News* without some attention to its attacks on individuals; for, though the least attractive of its features, they were by no means the least influential, especially on the paper's own career. During its 19 years it launched campaigns of out-and-out criminal libel against dozens of persons, of whom many had no means of striking back. These attacks maintained constant and widespread fear in the area, a feeling of absolute certainty that any man who opposed or offended the Taylorites would be abused and possibly destroyed.

Most of the early attacks had some intelligible motive involving politics or group advantage. The *Producers News* denounced the Anaconda Copper Mining Company mercilessly, calling it "the enemy of popular government."[9] Many Montana officials were portrayed with a copper collar. It seems ironic that the Anaconda Company ran a series of ten large advertisements called "Taxation Talks" in late 1921 and early 1922. The issue after the last ad appeared, the scathing denunciations began.

Candidates for office and rival newspapermen were the most consistent victims, however. Joseph F. Dolin, who published the Plentywood *Pioneer Press* until its suspension and then continued publishing the Medicine Lake *Wave*, bore ten years of frequent assault[10] and retaliated by denouncing Taylor as "Chief Bolshevist" of a "socialistic red-flag, IWW organization."[11] But as time went on, Taylor's shafts lost whatever precision of aim they might once have had and struck woundingly at obscure men whose pain served no end.

From that welter of slander one can cite only a few examples within the scope of an article:

1. When the manager of the Plentywood restaurant withdrew his advertising from the *Producers News* in August 1927, he received brutal publicity. Front-page stories asserted that cockroaches had been found in the food at the Elgin Cafe. Finally an emissary of the paper chose a busy hour to display a well-cooked mouse which he swore had just been served to him in his soup. References to the "mouse in the soup" continued in the paper for at least two years and became a boomerang in the 1928 election campaign.
2. Lawrence S. Olson, an early Taylorite who resembled Taylor in silhouette, left the group to join the staff of the Plentywood *Herald*. Thereafter the *Producers News* called him only Lard S. Olson, with the initial universally understood to be drawled. It charged that he had been caught crawling out of some belle's bedroom window; and when Olson cried "character assassination!" it declared its regrets: "Wonder where he keeps his character. No one ever dreamed that old baboon had any such thing."[12]
3. A Plentywood surgeon who had spoken out on some forgotten issue found himself accused—though never in legal form—of kidnapping a patient from a hospital in another town and directly causing his death.[13]
4. After an Outlook resident demanded payment of money he had loaned to the People's Publishing Company, the *Producers News*

sought to fix upon him the moral responsibility for two deaths in his family, and in effect suggested that he be mobbed and manhandled if not lynched. There was neither proof nor charge against him; but the malignity of the attacks, following soon after a family disgrace and tragedy, left him broken. "The *Producers News* refuses to howl with the pack," Taylor wrote in an editorial which managed to repudiate the pack while boasting of his own incitement of it, "but this might be an appropriate time to call attention to the fact that many cocky fellows have howled before they got through trying to wreck the *Producers News*."[14]

An inevitable accumulation of resentment hastened the movement's fall. Few people had at that time developed deep convictions hostile to its ideology; indeed few understood its ideology.

A few of Taylor's followers voiced their opinions loudly, however. In a letter to the editor, one U.F.L. [United Farmers League] member warned: "The capitalists are coming out with all the dirty lies they can think of against the Communist Party, but the truth will prevail. The Communist Party stands for humanity, truth, and hard-boiled facts. In that they are closer to God Jehovah than the capitalists, whose God is money, power, and greed. Don't let the Capitalists confuse you. They are bigger liars than Jim Crow, and he was kicked out of hell."[15]

OPPOSITION

Had the leadership possessed the judgment to check its aggressions, to refrain from pushing its advantage too far, it might have stayed in favor and in power. As it was, all that was needed to give hostile sentiment swift growth was a pretext for a campaign on grounds that could be represented as moral.

A pretext offered itself at the end of November 1926. After a day of heavy tax receipts, County Treasurer Eng Torstenson and Deputy Anna Hovet were preparing to leave the office. Masked bandits burst in, locked them in the vault, and made off with a reported $106,000 in cash and bonds.

If not a perfect crime, it was a competent one: the professional investigators failed to solve it. To enemies of the regime, however, it was simple. That winter and the following spring and summer they discussed it endlessly and solved it easily in every saloon and on every street corner: Taylor and Salisbury, they said, had committed the robbery by prearrangement with Eng Torstenson, who had unlawfully kept large sums in his office for the raid. The insurance company's three-year refusal to pay the county's claim was cited in support of this thinking.[16]

Harry E. Polk, a North Dakotan, bought the Plentywood *Herald* and led the 1928 campaign on more sober issues. With the whole record since 1918 to draw upon, he showed, for example, that the *Producers News*, which for ten years had accused Joseph F. Dolin of padding bills for county printing, had in fact padded its own bills. He showed that Salisbury—headlined as the "marathon sheriff"—had collected mileage for distances he could not possibly have traveled in six years. He cited the "mouse in the soup" as a convenient symbol of *Producers News* irresponsibility and hammered relentlessly at the rule by blackmail which the region had endured.

When the votes were counted, two Farmer-Laborites survived in office. The whipped candidates airily staged a "banquet" in honor of the winners and pretended to feature a real crow as their own share.

The *Producers News*, however, showed the real depth of discouragement. For the first time in its career it spoke of a "boost Plentywood policy" and tried to conciliate the business community. It repudiated its old political affiliations and declared itself independent. This phase lasted only long enough for Taylor to learn that nobody believed a word of his new policies. He resumed his support of the radical party. In 1930, the year the Depression really began to make itself felt, he was rewarded with nomination to the U.S. Senate on the Farmer-Labor ticket.

In northeastern Montana, Depression meant not just one thing. Disasters haunted the region following the economic crash. Drought and dust storms returned year after year; there were overwhelming insect infestations; wireworms destroyed potatoes; grasshoppers and army worms struck in such force in many localities that they hid every green thing with their bodies and left nothing behind, not even weeds, when they passed on. Farmers who owned reserves of wheat saw the price fall to 50 cents a bushel, then to 25 cents.

COMMUNISM

Revolutionists believed this to be the chance for which they had been waiting. Capitalism, they insisted, had demonstrated its fatal weaknesses. Radical ideas were spreading everywhere. Surely here, in the one American community where radicals had governed for a decade, there could be no doubt of success. Once more the leaders rebuilt their machine and created a new organization: The United Farmers League or UFL.

But something had been irretrievably lost. Faith in the leaders was dwindling; the leaders, as if under compulsion to hasten the end, blamed and denounced one another. The *Producers News*, its advertising falling off, was cut in May 1930 from its usually eight or more pages to a single sheet of four pages. As its appearance declined, so did its circulation and, by an odd corollary, its interest as reading matter. The extravagant Taylor devices which had made the paper entertaining, even when abusive, departed from it. It no longer had room for anything but propaganda in a style which depended chiefly on reiteration for its effects and seemingly sought to exhaust rather than persuade. Party release followed party release, spaced by exclamatory upper case fillers: SUPPORT THE UFL! DEFEND THE SOVIET UNION!

Its original slogan was "A paper of the people, for the people, by the people," but this was soon changed to "An official organ of the United Farmers League." Eventually a slogan in line with Communist ideology was chosen when the *Producers News* was proclaimed "The Paper of the oppressed and exploited."

It was, in fact, being kept alive by direct contributions of Communist party funds. In return the party demanded direct supervision. Taylor was suddenly not radical enough. Under suspicion as a "revisionist and renegade," he was quietly eased out; Erik Bert of New York took his place. Eventually Taylor separated from the party—

"expelled," say old-timers. Taylor's version is that he "left the party in June 1935, about the time the informers were joining."[17]

Certain that cumulative disasters had brought a truly revolutionary mood, the new leaders ignored the popular scruples that Taylor had tried to conciliate and behaved more and more like citizens of a soviet state. They established a quasi-military young Communist training center in the Farmer-Labor Temple, the auditorium which everyone in the movement, radical or less so, had helped build in 1924. They organized their children as Young Pioneers, the red model for all later political training groups for children.

When Rodney Salisbury's 14-year-old daughter Janis died, they gave her a "Bolshevik funeral"—so named in the *Producers News*—which deeply shocked church-going adherents by its blunt exclusion of religious rites. Hundreds turned against the movement when ideological saboteurs whispered that members of the UFL would thenceforth have to be buried in the same way.

In the following thirty years, radicals in the county and elsewhere adopted the defensive pretence that this funeral never really happened;[18] but the *Producers News* for March 11, 1932, reported every detail of the catastrophic blunder.

The windows and stage of the Farmer-Labor Temple, it said, were covered with red and black draperies decorated with hammer and sickle emblems. The Young Pioneers followed the coffin to the front of the hall, bearing a red flag which they draped over the flowers on the coffin. People attending were required to stand and sing "The Internationale." Leading Communists spoke; then the Pioneers sang "Red Flag," described as "Janis's song." At the grave on the Salisbury homestead they repeated this song as the coffin descended, then recited the Pioneer pledge: "I pledge allegiance to the workers' red flag and to the cause for which it stands. One aim throughout our lives—freedom for the working class." A prominent party member dropped the girl's Pioneer scarf into the grave, with "a few final words."

During the campaign of 1932 the *Producers News* announced that its candidates would run on the Communist ticket. It turned against all the things it had been before. Socialists, Nonpartisans,

Farmer-Laborites, and all liberals were frauds who existed only to "split the Communist vote."[19]

Election day, 1932, fell on November 8. On November 11 the *Producers News* acknowledged defeat for its candidates but boasted that 575 citizens had voted the Communist ticket straight. Next time, it promised, the total would be larger.

It was wrong. Open, avowed Communism had passed its crest in Sheridan County. Now it could only recede.

A RADICAL NEWSPAPER'S STRUGGLE TO SURVIVE

"We didn't have enough paper for this issue. Comrades, come to our rescue!" said the *Producers News* in September 1932. Flax wheat would be accepted in payment for subscriptions.[20] It would be a dreadful day for farmers and workers, coaxed the editor, when the *Producers News* was no longer there to fight their battles.

On February 3, 1933, Charles Taylor's name reappeared on the masthead. A partial revolt had taken place within the People's Publishing Company. The Trotskyites, or Taylorites, had won a point— the return of Taylor—but in other respects the Stalinist wing held control. For a year Taylor labored to breathe life into the dull pages; then he was out again. Alfred Miller, a refugee from Nazi Germany, took over.

Soon a curious notice appeared on the editorial page. Someone had organized a "Save the *Producers News* Club," using Taylor's name freely in club publicity. The party felt, it muttered ominously, that Taylor had no knowledge of this.[21] In a May 4, 1934, editorial entitled "A Back Stabbing Attempt," Editor Miller blasted the so-called club for its use of Taylor's name.

Seven weeks later Rodney Salisbury, Plentywood's sturdiest old Bolshevik, was denounced as a renegade because he had come out for a "so-called United Front ticket" for 1934—two years or more before the ideas became the official party line.[22] A dozen members, along with Salisbury, were expelled for this grave offense.

Meanwhile the county survived its only experience with "force and violence." Early in 1933 a small group of militants trained by the

Young Communist school raided the Red Cross office and seized a supply of winter clothing. The *Producers News*, stimulated by this success, began announcing frequent "demonstrations" and "mass meetings." For May Day, 1934, it planned a big demonstration in the streets of Plentywood. A band of angry citizens met it with fire hoses and pick handles and broke it up.

The radicals continued demonstrating in the countryside—often with the sympathy of other groups—against foreclosures and repossessions of farm machinery. But interest and attendance waned. At length the Plentywood *Herald* shrugged it all off with the comment, "Two is company, three is a crowd, and four is a Communist mass meeting."[23]

"The Communist party," cried a *Producers News* editorial on August 2, 1934, "leads the struggle toward the final solution—a Soviet America!" But this aggressive tone, once so typical, was beginning to give way to something milder. Faithful members now concentrated their efforts on merely rescuing the dying movement. On September 27 Taylor, in a letter given a three-column display, pleaded with the "renegades" to come back and submit to the party's discipline.

The 1934 red vote reached only half its 1932 total. The *Producers News*, in a mood for understatement, said, "A number of people believe the election resulted in a defeat for communism."[24]

Editor Alfred Miller alone still refused to compromise with anything less than the hard party line; but early in 1935 conservative forces lent practical-minded local reds a hand by starting deportation proceedings against him.

Columns of *Producers News* were full of the Miller deportation case, in which the editor was charged with "activities to overthrow the government by force and violence." But on July 26, 1935, Taylor again took over the paper, hinting at corruption in the staff during Miller's editorship. No further mention of Miller's deportation case was made in the paper.

At this juncture, the *Producers News* published a review of its own history which blandly concluded that it was not a Communist paper at all, never had been, "nor never pretended to be." It had simply supported the Communist party in the absence of any other working class party.[25] "The paper will support the idea of a mass labor party . . . and fight for the producers," the paper said, "but in a . . . more tolerant and less sectarian way."[26] In his final return, Editor Taylor came as peacemaker and healer.

It was too late. Within six months the paper's single sheet was cut to tabloid size; then it began to miss its publication day. On September 12, 1936, Taylor's house burned with most of its contents. Thereafter there was only trouble. The issue that reported Roosevelt's 1936 reelection was dated October; a notice to readers explained that it was "two weeks behind"—actually three weeks—and blamed breakdowns and inadequate help.

Working almost alone with failing plant and resources, Taylor managed throughout that winter to keep bringing out the single folded sheet equivalent to the front page and page 2 of the old-time *Producers News*. On March 6, 1937, he published the issue of February 19— two weeks and one day late. On the front page of this issue a boxed story announced:

READERS ATTENTION!

In the next issue of the *Producers News* a brilliant expose [sic] of the fakery of the late Moscow trials and executions will be presented by Max Schactman.

Mr. Schactman is a widely known writer and lecturer who has devoted his exceptional talents to the cause of the working class.

Don't fail to read the next issue.

The next issue was never published. The following week the plant stood silent.

THE END OF THE *PRODUCERS NEWS*

Sheridan County people at first could hardly take in the fact that the *Producers News* was gone, their revolution over, the chapter closed. To some the paper had meant hope, challenge, the excitement of purposeful action, to others an object of apoplectic hate; but for everyone its absence left an unaccustomed quiet, a sense of vacancy. Each of

them had been personally concerned; nobody had ever been indiffer-
ent to the *Producers News*. Nobody would be apt to see its like again.
The real significance of the Plentywood experience, indeed, may lie in
the certainty in the minds of those who lived through it that nothing
of its kind can be repeated. These people took the measure of the ideological assault in their own lives, not without pain, but inevitably. Today, if the term "Communist threat" makes timid persons elsewhere
hide under the bed, it evokes only skepticism in Sheridan County,
Montana.

CONCLUSION—EPILOGUE BY AN EDITOR

We can think of no more appropriate way of ending this treatment of a strange, difficult period in the history of a corner of Montana than to publish portions of a column which appeared in the May
25, 1967, issue of the *Daniels County Leader* of Scobey, Mont., soon
after the death of Charles E. Taylor. It was written by Burley Bowler,
publisher of this weekly newspaper. By personal association and
long-time journalistic encounter, Mr. Bowler knew the mercurial Taylor as well as or better than any person living. In spite of many years
of contention, it is obvious that Bowler's judgment of his fellow editor
was touched, after the passage of more than 50 years, with warmth
and no little understanding. We were informed of Publishers Bowler's
death Dec. 18, just as we go to press.

> An old friend, a bitter opponent, a colorful character, and one of the
> most talked-about, abused, and abusive scribes of his day passed on
> a few weeks ago in his 80th year. Of course we refer to Charley
> "Red Flag" Taylor, the first and long-time editor of the defunct *Pro-
> ducers News* at Plentywood.
>
> Charley was no ordinary country editor. He was more than bril-
> liant at times, and quite often ridiculous. He used his talents to ca-
> jole, to abuse, to extort and frighten his followers as well as his
> enemies and detractors. I knew the real Charley much better, per-
> haps, than those who served as his stooges or those who threatened
> him. I worked as a printer for several months in 1920 in the *Produc-
> ers News* shop.

Charley had come to Plentywood as editor for the old Non-Partisan League, which endorsed candidates on both party tickets. But Charley was far ahead of that early day Townley organization in his thinking.

One evening when we were alone at the shop he told me, "This Non-Partisan set-up is a face that will not last. It has got to follow the Lenin-Trotsky line and become part of the world revolutionary line. But I can't tell these dupes that or it would scare them to death."

It was several years later before he tipped his hand. He and Bill Dunne of Butte finally conceived the idea of organizing the Farmer-Labor party, fore-runner of the Communist party which got on the ballot for a couple of elections in several counties of Montana—including Daniels, Sheridan, and several others.

The Bolshevik revolution in Russia had thrilled Charley but when Stalin succeeded Lenin and exiled Trotsky, Charley was jolted. "Stalin is no Communist," Charley wailed, "he will have Trotsky killed." He was right in that. Stalin arranged for Trotsky to be assassinated by a servant in his home in Mexico.

For some time Stalin's New York organization had been keeping a close tab on Taylor and eventually sent Mother Bloor to Plentywood and she deposed him as editor of the *P.N.*, for by this time the Communist party had gained control of the paper, although the mortgage was held by the late Bill Haas, prosperous Outlook farmer.

After the Sheridan County treasury was "robbed," Haas and Charley became bitter enemies. Just a few hours before the robbery took place Bill Haas was warned to go to the treasury and retrieve his diamonds and a few thousand dollars he had stored there for safe keeping.

"I knew something was brewing," Haas told me later, "so I paid attention to the warning." This information, relayed to the defense counsel, upset a $100,000 snap judgment against the old *Helena Independent* for libel.

Bill Haas told me about his dispute on one of his several trips to Scobey trying to induce me to take over the *Producers News*. "I will foreclose the mortgage and give you the plant. If you make good you can pay me as you can; if you can't make anything of it I am no worse off as it is going to close anyway and become worthless."

I was not interested. At that time I owned 52 percent of the Plentywood *Herald* corporation which I later sold to Harry Polk of Williston.

The *Producers News* closed. Charley Taylor and some more of the reds left for Seattle. Charley returned months later and retrieved the *P.N.* press and trucked it west. The Communists failed there, however, and Charley eventually took a job as proof reader with the daily *Seattle Post-Intelligencer,* a job he held for more than 22 years. He retired in 1962 with his union pension and social security and returned to Minnesota.

Often I have wondered about how a man with a brilliant streak such as Charley showed at times could possibly become as warped as he did in his thinking. When he used to tell me how Communism would eventually engulf the world and remedy all its ills, I would try to convince him that Americans cherished their liberty and constitutional rights too much to be deceived by impractical and despotic Communist leaders. Charley would come back with the argument that "these poor dupes around here are just like all other Americans; once they understand the principles of Communism they will swing into line." I would remind him that Communists had no principles, no honesty, no practical plans. Then I would have to listen to another half hour oration as Charley waxed eloquent on the beauty of the world under Communist direction.

In the more than 50 years since I first met Charley I have never known a more impractical man. With more customers than he could serve, Charley couldn't run an ice cream stand successfully. He had no business sense whatever. Big hearted, he would dole out money to anyone who asked for it when he was flush. But he was usually broke and borrowing where he could without a thought of repayment. At times he would go to one of the banks, demand money on his plain note and the threat that if not accommodated he would have the county treasurer withdraw county funds deposited there.

One of the saddest cases was when he induced an old retired bachelor farmer to withdraw a few thousand dollars from the bank— "as they are going broke anyway" he told him—and Charley gave the old fellow his note for the case. The old fellow died broke, unable to collect from Charley. I have photostats of those unpaid notes.

Volumes could be written on this subject. Away from his politics and troubles, Charles was a charming and brilliant conversationalist, a big, happy-go-lucky fellow whose varying attitudes were never understood by anyone—not even himself—a character not easily forgotten. I never knew another comparable to him.

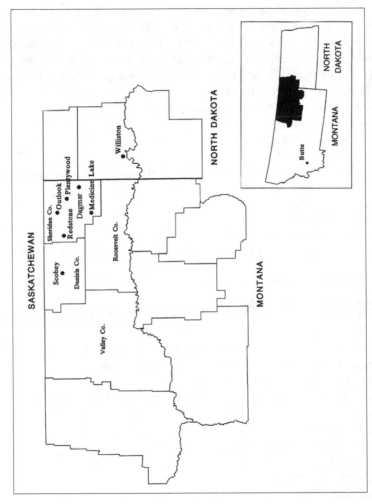

Radical farmers in northeastern Montana turn to the printed word to voice their concerns. Map by Robert Watrel.

NOTES

1. "Historical Data," Plentywood *Herald*, September 24, 1936.
2. This or similar language was used whenever Taylor ran for office, which was frequent in the 1920s. He was elected to the State Senate as a Republican, serving in the 18th Assembly in 1923. He ran on the Farmer-Labor ticket thereafter, and served in the 19th, 20th, and 21st Assemblies. His crowning political achievement was [his] nomination to the U.S. Senate on the Farmer-Labor ticket in 1930, opposing Democrat Thomas J. Walsh and Republican Albert J. Galen.
3. Taylor to author, September 20, 1965.
4. P.N., May 10, 1918.
5. P.N., November 17, 1922.
6. P.N., April 15, 1935.
7. William D. Haywood, *Bill Haywood's Book*. International Publishers, New York. 1929. pp. 301 and 352–358.
8. P.N., April 19, 1918, et. seq.
9. February 1922, et seq.
10. P.N., early 1918 at least to 1928.
11. Plentywood *Pioneer Press* editorial defiantly reprinted in P.N., April 18, 1919.
12. P.N., February 7, 1930.
13. P.N., November 17, 1923, et seq.
14. P.N., June 27, 1930.
15. P.N., May 27, 1932.
16. The claim was paid by the National Surety Company in August 1929, increased to $126,000 by accumulated costs and interest.
17. Taylor to author, September 12, 1965.
18. Everett Luoma, "Montana Socialist Continues Fight," *The Militant*, May 3, 1965.
19. P.N., November 2, 1932.
20. P.N., September 2 and 9, 1932.
21. P.N., May 4, 1934.
22. P.N., June 21, 1934.
23. Plentywood *Herald*, September 13, 1934.
24. P.N., November 9, 1934.
25. P.N., April 5, 1935.
26. P.N., July 26, 1935.

THE PLOW THAT BROKE THE PLAINS:
FILM LEGACY OF THE GREAT DEPRESSION
Vernon Carstensen

The Plow That Broke the Plains, a documentary film produced by an agency of the federal government, was intended to tell the story of the drought and dust storms on the Great Plains in the 1930s. In doing this it reflects many of the then-current views of the reasons these calamities were visited upon this land and the people living there. The sparse, impressionistic, and often poetic language of the commentary, the eloquent music, and the striking photography all serve to intensify the sense of despair and desperation felt by farmers and their families caught up first in the economic disaster of the Depression and then, particularly in 1934 and 1936, beset by widespread drought accompanied by devastating, punishing, even lethal dust storms—the black blizzards of the 1930s.

PLAINS FARMING

Dust storms and periods of drought are a fixed part of the Great Plains environment, but human memory is short, and by 1930 the farmers' experience in the region had spanned only two or three generations at most.[1] Few settlers had made farms in the lands west of the Missouri River before 1870, but in the years that followed—despite heat waves, drought, dust storms, blizzards, tornadoes, prairie fires, plagues of grasshoppers, high freight and interest rates, and low prices for wheat and corn—farms had multiplied in the Great Plains states with marvelous abandon.

In 1870 the federal census reported 116,172 farms in those states that lie wholly or in part within the Great Plains as film director Pare Lorentz pictures the area: North and South Dakota, Montana, Nebraska, Wyoming, Kansas, Colorado, Oklahoma, New Mexico, and Texas. The number of farms had grown to over 800,000 by 1900 and to 1.2 million by 1930. In 1850, when the census first counted American farms, 1.4 million were reported in the nation, the fruit of almost 250 years of land settlement. In the 60 years between 1870 and 1930, an almost equal number had been planted on the lands of the Great Plains or nearby.

This vast rush of settlers to the unoccupied land west of the Missouri flowed from a combination of many elements. Federal and state land policies, ranging from the Homestead Act to huge grants to railroads and grants to the states, created a situation in which acquisition of land by settlers was relatively easy. Dramatic advances in farming, transportation, and food processing technology, coupled with the development or discovery of cereals and other plants that seemed able to thrive in this subhumid land, promised or seemed to promise that settlers could raise good crops that would be carried to a constantly growing market in the United States and abroad.[2]

THE SELLING OF FARMING

The rapid occupation of the farmlands west of the Missouri was preceded and accompanied, as all American land settlement had been, by a vast outpouring of propaganda urging settlement. Indeed, in 1588, two decades before the first permanent English settlement was planted on the Atlantic shore, Thomas Heriot (also Hariot) published a book in London titled *A briefe and True report of the new found land of Virginia: of the commodities there found and to be raysed, as well marchantable, as others for victuall, building, and other necessarie uses for those that are and shalbe the planters there* . . . in which he corrected "false" statements that had been made about the productivity of Virginia and set down an account of what was produced there and what could be raised, which he said would "enrich planters who went thither."[3]

After Heriot, state and local governments, corporations, companies, and individuals produced books, pamphlets, and articles by the thousands in many languages to invite and entice land seekers to the perennially new lands of the United States. Some spoke the truth, some did not.[4]

In the propaganda designed to encourage settlers to come to the trans-Missouri country, Jay Cooke's hired writers pictured the lands along the route of the Northern Pacific Railroad in such exuberant terms as to win for this region of the Dakotas and eastern Montana the sardonic rubric "Jay Cooke's banana belt." Local boosters proclaimed the Red River Valley as the Nile of the North. In Nebraska in the 1870s, a series of wet years and good crops accompanied the settlers on their westward march into normally drier lands. In these circumstances and with boosterism rampant, perhaps it is not surprising that some concluded that farm making changed the climate to suit human needs. Thus, in 1879 a professor of natural sciences at the recently established University of Nebraska wrote, "As pioneers take up the government lands and encroach upon the plains, the line of abundant rainfall also marches west." These words, discovering a new and pleasant truth, were published by the state of Nebraska.[5] Drought in the mid-1880s destroyed this new truth, at least briefly, but it did not destroy the hope and expectation that control or modification of climate could occur.

Both the propaganda urging settlers to take up farms on the Great Plains and advances in technology that promised that the land would produce good crops were supported by the federal and state governments. In 1862 Congress established the United States Department of Agriculture (USDA) whose business it would be to identify and distribute among the American people useful agricultural information. That same year Congress passed the first Morrill Act to provide land grants to the states for the establishment of colleges of agriculture and mechanical arts.

By the 1880s these new institutions were beginning to "bring science down out of the sky and hook it to a plow," as one farmer had declared they should. Both the USDA and the land grant colleges were ardently committed to the proposition that all land fit for farming should be farmed and that the great and enduring purpose of all farmers, on new land and old, must be to make "two blades of grass grow where one grew before." The colleges, largely through the experiment stations that began to take shape in the 1880s, and the USDA, through its various departments, sought to find or develop new strains of plants and animals and better methods of tillage and harvest, all aimed at producing bigger, better crops on more and more land. The countless pamphlets and reports issuing from the colleges and the USDA blended with the propaganda of railroads and other corporations, companies, and individuals to encourage more settlement.[6]

But it was not easy to make a farm on the subhumid and semiarid lands of the Great Plains. It took three crops of settlers, some said, before one crop took root on the treeless, windswept land. Moreover, in the late 1880s and well into the 1890s, drought, low prices for wheat and corn, and high freight and interest rates led farmers in wheat country to join with cotton farmers, urban reformers, silver producers, and others to organize the Populist Party. The Populists' bid for national power failed with the presidential defeat of William Jennings Bryan in 1896.[7]

PRELUDE TO DISASTER

Before the nineteenth century had run out, farmers saw the slow return of modest prosperity. Although in the opening years of the twentieth century many farmers failed to prosper and President Theodore Roosevelt organized a Country Life Commission to study farm problems, many farmers did enjoy prosperity to the extent that the years 1910–1914 were later regarded as the golden years of American farming. The rise of the Farmers' Union, the Society of Equity, and the appearance of "night riders" in the tobacco lands, however, told anyone who would listen that many farmers were unhappy. The organization of the Non-Partisan League in North Dakota in 1916 indicated that not all wheat farmers prospered equally from the European war. But the war years spelled prosperity, often fabulous prosperity. In 1913 wheat sold for a dollar a bushel; by 1918 it had reached $2.75 and even higher.

When the United States entered World War I, farmers responded to the call of both profit and patriotism. They raised as much wheat and other produce as they could. It is estimated that during the war years croplands were increased by nearly 12 percent, but in the face of this headlong expansion and prosperity nobody made plans to retire the additional lands when the war ended. Then in 1920, farm prices began to collapse. Wheat dropped again to a dollar or less a bushel, but the cost of taxes, interest, transportation, farm machinery, seeds, and fertilizer—all of which had grown with farmers' prosperity—was slow to follow suit; so were farm mortgages, which were written in dollars rather than in bushels of wheat or corn. The secretary of agriculture reported that in consequence of the collapse of farm prices, one quarter of American farmers either went bankrupt or became insolvent during the years 1920 to 1923.[8]

The 1920s are often called the Decade of Prosperity, but farmers did not share equally in that prosperity. To meet fixed charges with lower prices for farm produce, most farmers did what seemed to them the only thing possible: They sought to produce more and more at a time when changes in diet and the loss of foreign markets reduced demand. They drove prices down still further and created a nearly permanent farm surplus. Early in the 1920s, farmers complained of the lack of purchasing power of the "farm dollar," and in some quarters there were demands that Congress take steps to obtain "parity" for farmers in the marketplace. What was sought under the banner of parity was a program that would assure a fairly constant ratio between the value of what a farmer had to sell and what he had to buy. For example, if in 1910 three hundred bushels of wheat would pay for a grain binder, that should also hold in 1925.

From the early 1920s until Herbert Hoover entered the White House as president, parity was sought by farmers and farm organizations, primarily through the McNary-Haugen farm bills that passed Congress twice, only to be vetoed by President Calvin Coolidge. The Hoover administration sought to deal with the vast farm surplus through the Agricultural Marketing Act, which was supposed to attain the ends sought by the McNary-Haugen Act but in a more effective way. Hoover's Federal Farm Board, charged with removing the surplus from the market, had barely come into operation when the stock market collapse of October 1929 signaled the arrival of the deepest economic depression into which the Republic had ever fallen.[9]

Whatever factors lay behind this Great Depression, it was a major catastrophe marked by a perverse irony because it struck in the
first year of Hoover's presidency. Hoover had campaigned in 1928 amid
claims that the United States had attained a new high plateau of prosperity. He bore the reputation as a great humanitarian for his work as
director of Belgian Relief during World War I and later for aiding
victims of flood and famine. His presidency saw the richest nation on
earth in disarray. The number of unemployed multiplied until one of
every five workers had no job, and the pay of those who had jobs was
reduced by as much as 60 percent. Private charities virtually collapsed,
bread lines formed in all major cities, the reduced number of freight
trains often carried hundreds of homeless men and boys, the hobo
jungles of earlier days grew and were renamed Hoovervilles, food
rotted in the fields, cotton went unsold, lumber remained unsawed,
and machines and workers stood idle.

THE HUMAN RESPONSE

Politicians and business leaders first sought to reassure themselves and the public by asserting—almost in chorus—that the American economy was "fundamentally sound," but the Depression deep-
ened, business and farming bankruptcies continued to increase, and a
host of panacea seekers came into view with schemes to lure prosperity to return by reforming or transforming American society. Some
tried direct action. In 1932, a reported 15,000 veterans of World War I,
seeking early payment of a promised bonus, migrated to Washington
and urged Congress to take action; the hungry marched on Washington, and so did farmers in pickup trucks and battered tin lizzies from
as far west as Oregon to plead for help from Congress. Meanwhile, in
the Midwest there were farmer strikes, milk strikes, and a "cow war"
in Iowa, and farmers organized to block farm mortgage foreclosure
sales. In the eyes of some observers, the entire country seemed in the
process of collapse during the grim fall, winter, and spring of 1932–
1933.

Meanwhile, the Franklin Roosevelt administration had come to
power in March 1933, and it moved boldly to deal with the widespread

disaster with a host of programs aimed, it said, at providing relief, recovery, and reform. In late April, less than two months after Roosevelt took office, incidents in the Midwest seemed to suggest that law and law enforcement were on the verge of breaking down. On April 26, 3,000 schoolteachers "rioted" in Chicago. The next day, farmers in Le Mars, Iowa, entered the courtroom of a sitting judge and demanded that he promise not to sign any more farm mortgage foreclosure papers. When the judge refused, he was dragged from his courtroom, taken into the country, threatened with hanging, treated roughly, and then released. On April 28 the governor of Iowa declared martial law in the county and sent in state militia.

That same day the U.S. Senate passed the Agricultural Adjustment Act (AAA), which, after being approved by the House, was signed by the president on May 12. The act proclaimed

> That the present acute economic emergency being in part the consequence of a severe and increasing disparity between the prices of agricultural and other commodities, which disparity has largely destroyed the purchasing power of farmers for industrial products, has broken down the orderly exchange of commodities and has seriously impaired the agricultural assets supporting the national credit structure, it is hereby declared that these conditions in the basic industry of agriculture have affected transactions in agricultural commodities with a national public interest, have burdened and obstructed the normal currents of commerce in such commodities, and render imperative the immediate enactment of Title I of this act.

This act, which was the first AAA, sought to create the machinery that would establish and maintain balance between production and consumption of agricultural commodities and to reestablish farmers' purchasing power to what it had been in the golden years, 1910 to 1914. The surplus in most commodities was to be dealt with by reducing production and paying farmers for what they had not raised. Hurried arrangements were made to reduce acreage in cotton, corn, wheat, and other crops, either by not planting or by destroying what had been planted. In the face of a predicted 1.2 billion pound surplus in pork, a program was launched in August 1933 to "remove" from the market 4 million young pigs and 1 million sows scheduled to farrow in the fall. The final report of this venture claimed that 6,188,717 light hogs and pigs had been destroyed and 222,149 sows slaughtered and their meat distributed through welfare agencies.[10]

The great "plow-up" and the wanton slaughter of the "little pigs" were widely denounced for political, sentimental, and humane reasons. All pigs under 70 pounds or so were destroyed on the fatuous claim that their meat was not usable—this in a country where roast suckling pig had wide literary, if not actual culinary, standing. To destroy food in such large quantities when millions were hungry, one cabinet officer remarked with wan irony, must be the mark of a highly "civilized" people. Indeed, no "primitive" nation would serve its economic institutions so well and its hungry people so badly. But whatever the complaints, the New Deal farm checks, autumn markets, and other factors resulted in a slight improvement in farm prices and farm income in 1933.

CLIMATIC CHAOS

Whatever promise of better times for farmers the New Deal programs held, those promises were mocked by the weather in 1934. Some areas had suffered from drought in 1931, 1932, and 1933; it would later be seen that those years marked the beginning of a dry weather cycle. The spring of 1934 produced signs of a bad crop year in the northern wheat country. There were high winds and dust storms in April, and early in May winds and spring drought produced a dust storm unmatched in the recorded history of the United States. From May 9–12, dust rode the northwest winds from Montana east to the Twin Cities, to Chicago, and on to blanket both New York and Washington and then out a hundred miles or more over the Atlantic Ocean. Dust was so thick that airplane flights from Chicago had to be canceled, street lights were turned on at midday, and wheat prices advanced frantically in the Chicago grain market. In Washington, Hugh H. Bennett is reported to have made dramatic use of the dust storm to support his argument for the establishment of an independent soil conservation service that would tie down the topsoil on the Plains.

The storm made front-page headlines in the eastern papers, and the *New York Times* reported that this one vast dust storm reached from Montana to New York and Washington to as far south as Nashville, crediting the Associated Press with the statement that 300 million tons of top soil had blown away in the storm. That figure, surely a literary device rather than a scientific measure, was promptly sanctified and appeared again and again in references to the great dust storm. In Washington, full reports were impossible because the Weather Bureau machinery used to measure dust was not working the day the big storm struck the national capital. For many, the storm was an omen of the evil days ahead; for farmers in the northern Plains, it was a prelude to ruin. The year 1934—marked by extensive drought, more dust storms, and widespread crop failure—was simply too much for many farmers to bear. The extent of drought damage is revealed in the stark figures compiled by the U.S. Department of Agriculture (Table 3).

The newly organized Progressive Party of Wisconsin spoke to this bleak situation in the first plank of its 1934 platform. "Modern capitalism," the Progressives said, "has failed." Led by Philip LaFollette, the Progressives captured the Wisconsin governorship in the fall election.

In 1934, dusted-out, broken farmers migrated from the northern Plains. Lois P. Hudson, in her novel *The Bones of Plenty* (1962) and in occasional pieces brought together in *Reapers of the Dust* (1965), tells of what this calamity did to the people who endured it. Her books should be read in conjunction with Lawrence Svobida, *An Empire of Dust* (1940), the story by a Kansas farmer of his losing battle against drought and dust; Vance Johnson, *Heaven's Tableland: The Dust Bowl Story* (1947); and John Steinbeck, *Grapes of Wrath* (1939), which deals with migrants from the southern Plains, where dust storms and drought were the most intense in 1936.

THE FILM

It is against this background of the uneasy and sometimes tragic march of the plowmen onto the Great Plains, as well as the Depression,

TABLE 3

Impact of the 1934 Drought on the Harvest in Selected States

	North Dakota		South Dakota		Nebraska		Kansas		Oklahoma	
	1929	1934	1929	1934	1929	1934	1929	1934	1929	1934
Cropland harvested (acres)	21.2	9.3	17.9	4.9	21.3	12.2	24.4	16.7	15.6	12.3
Crop failure (acres)	0.85	9.9	0.58	9.8	0.36	8.2	0.97	7.4	0.70	2.9
Cropland idle or fallow (acres)	2.4	5.2	0.56	2.7	0.58	2.3	1.3	3.8	1.1	1.8
Wheat threshed (acres)	10.0	2.9	3.5	0.15	3.7	2.3	12.0	8.3	4.6	3.5
Value of wheat crop (dollars)	97.5	17.3	33.5	0.67	53.6	14.6	151.0	72.7	49.8	30.4

Source: U.S. Government, *United States Census of Agriculture: 1935. Reports for States With Statistics for Counties and a Summary for the United States*, vol. I (Washington, D.C.: U.S. Government Printing Office, 1936).

dust storms, and drought of the 1930s, that Pare Lorentz made *The Plow That Broke the Plains*. The film was shown first to President Franklin Roosevelt and his guests at the White House in March 1936. On May 10, 1936, it was given a full dress premier at the Mayflower Hotel in Washington, D.C., at a program sponsored by the Museum of Modern Art. At both showings the film was received with enormous enthusiasm. Three years later it was withdrawn from circulation and was essentially withheld from public view until 1961.

The *Plow* is one of the first government-sponsored documentary films ever made. In some ways its production could be described as an accident that resulted from bringing together such ingredients as the New Deal, the great drought and dust storms of the mid-1930s, James D. LeCron, Henry A. Wallace, Rexford Tugwell, a somewhat flexible U.S. budget officer, and Pare Lorentz.

Lorentz was born in West Virginia in 1905.[11] He attended West Virginia Wesleyan University and the University of West Virginia, although he left to find work in New York before taking a degree. His first job in New York was that of editor of the *Edison Mazda Lamp Sales Builder*. He was interested in movies and soon became the film critic for *Judge* and other publications. In 1930 he collaborated with Morris Ernst on a book about the movies titled *Censored: The Private Life of the Movies*. In 1934 he published a picture book, *The Roosevelt Year, 1933*, begun apparently as a script for a documentary on the first year of the New Deal.

In June 1935, James LeCron and Henry A. Wallace talked with Lorentz about making a documentary film on the Dust Bowl, and Wallace arranged for Lorentz to talk with Rexford G. Tugwell, chief of the Resettlement Administration. Lorentz agreed to serve as the consultant on motion pictures for the Resettlement Administration and to make recommendations for documentaries. He urged, and Tugwell agreed, that the organization make one good picture that would attract public attention, and others would then follow. In August 1935, the Bureau of the Budget approved the expenditure of $6,000 in federal funds for a documentary. Since no experienced director-producer could be found, Lorentz agreed to produce the film on the great drought. Lorentz hired a three-man camera crew, all with experience making documentaries, and set out to make the picture, apparently with only the scantiest outline of what he would do. But he read everything he could on the subject.

The crew began shooting in Montana in September and moved south to Wyoming, Colorado, western Kansas, and then into the Texas Panhandle, where they were enveloped in a dust storm. There was trouble with the camera crew—some technical, some ideological—but the shooting on the Plains was completed. Lorentz went to Hollywood and, with difficulty, obtained some footage he wanted to fill out his picture. While there, he hired a crew to take pictures of migrants arriving in California. He then returned to New York to complete the film. He hired Virgil Thomson to write the music, and Thomson helped to persuade Alexander Smallens to conduct the score with about 20 members of the New York Philharmonic Orchestra. Lorentz is reported to have completed the work by fitting his shots to the music. The film cost almost $20,000.

THE MUSIC

The music to *The Plow* is distinctive and has received critical acclaim. According to William Bergsma, a distinguished and well-known composer, Lorentz divided *The Plow That Broke the Plains* script into nine coherent sections with a momentary break in the last section. Lorentz's delay of the final editing to match Thomson's music was a "rare and gratifying procedure" for a composer. Thus, a collaborative artistic mesh, rather than confrontation, resulted. The film became a model for documentaries.[12]

A writer of film music knows to "Mickey-Mouse" (verb, intransitive), which means to create an image of physical action. Thomson avoided Mickey-Mousing except at the end of the sixth part. There the orchestra sounds like a train when a train comes across the screen. Bergsma observed:

What he does, and what makes the music an active commentator, equal in importance to the verbal commentary, is to juxtapose appropriate cowboy songs in banjo and guitar, hymn tunes, popular styles (blues and tango), and the trends and tendencies of WPA

[Works Progress Administration] realistic art of the thirties, together with the sardonic jazz techniques of Brechtian theatre, to what we see on screen and are told in the narration. The tornado sequence, for instance, while properly agitated, is basically a wry misharmonization of "Praise God From Whom All Blessings Flow." The prior sequences showing the expansion of food production because of World War I start with a trumpet call, continue with "When Johnny Comes Marching Home Again" and "Mademoiselle From Armentiers." God is praised again when the jalopies move to California, a martial rhythm changing into a tango which grows more and more Mexican accompanying it in clear social comment. The one false note in this approach, to my ears, comes at the very end: the music ends triumphantly, a la MGM fadeout. Why? But at his best the composer as social critic has added a dimension otherwise unobtainable to a film of great artistic and historic importance.[13]

Supposedly Virgil Thomson was the twelfth composer Lorentz approached, but Thomson knew the Plains. A Kansas City background served Thomson well. Lorentz rejected his first eleven composers allegedly because he felt they wanted to write symphonies rather than music appropriate to his subject matter. The suite Thomson extracted from his music to *The Plow That Broke the Plains*—his first film music—remains one of his strongest and most frequently played works. Thomson, like Lorentz, was the right person in the right place at the right time.[14]

CENSORSHIP

Although the film won immediate and often rhapsodic praise, there was some difficulty getting it distributed to first-run movie houses. These obstacles were eventually overcome, and *The Plow* received widespread critical and popular approval except from some Plains states' politicians and boosters. In August 1938, the film was made available for educational distribution and continued to enjoy enormous popularity.

The Farm Security Administration prepared a fifty-page booklet, "Study Guide for U.S. Documentary Film *The Plow That Broke the Plains*," to be used when the film was shown. The booklet included a discourse on the problems of the Great Plains, suggested readings to stimulate further discussion, the full text of the commentary, a section on the use and misuse of the land, a multiple choice examination, a list of topics for discussion, and a bibliography of useful publications. In 1940, as an educational film *The Plow* had almost 6,000 bookings—5,694 is the government figure for the period August 1938 to sometime in April 1939.

Despite the popular and critical approval, *The Plow* came under increasing attack from Plains politicians. The attack climaxed in February 1939, when Representative Karl E. Mundt of South Dakota, a former debate coach at General Beadle State Teachers College and operator of a loan and investment company in Madison, South Dakota, rose in the House to denounce *The Plow*. "From beginning to end," he said, "it is a drama of distress." Mundt charged, among many other things, that "the continued exhibition of this picture cannot be considered as anything less than a direct effrontery to the fine American citizens who are enjoying this area as their homeland and who are constantly working to make it a happier and a more attractive place in which to live." Mundt demanded that the film be withdrawn from circulation, and he was supported by the South Dakota Editors Association.[15] The attack was successful.

On April 18, 1939, the film was withdrawn from circulation to be revised "in the light of improved agricultural conditions." Memos from within the USDA add a little more information. One memo states that the U.S. Film Service had "made an informal commitment to Congressman Mundt of South Dakota to withhold *The Plow* from circulation until it could be revised."[16] Funds for the "revision" were sought but could not be obtained, and *The Plow* went into hiding.

In 1961, *The Plow* again became available. As Robert L. Snyder put it, "Prints may be ordered from the National Archives and Records Service after obtaining clearance from the Department of Agriculture." The film's container bore a solemn warning: "To be used for study as an art form only. Because subject matter is long obsolete it is not to be used for public showing."[17] In 1972, through a cooperative arrangement between the American Historical Association and the

National Archives, the film was made easily accessible to instructors and students of American history.

CONCLUSION

Explanations assessing the causes and the blame for the Dust Bowl proved controversial. *The Plow That Broke the Plains*, a New Deal intellectual treatment, did not sit well with some members of American society, and they were able to ban the film for twenty-two years.

In many ways this censorship is an ironic event, for during the Hitler years, Congressman, and later Senator, Mundt refused to allow this film to be shown. What was considered so controversial, so dangerous to national security? Perhaps it was the nature of the crisis. Never before had so many U.S. citizens been so misled. The federal government had encouraged the expansion of farming onto marginal lands in the Great Plains, and this expansion, in turn, had resulted in the destruction of farm markets and a natural disaster that exposed a lack of proper planning. All of this contributed to the Dust Bowl. Farmers were leading the way in forming a partnership with the American system, and it spawned a calamity of enormous proportions. Such mistakes were bound to shake people's confidence.

But the power of truth and the media was strong. America's First Amendment beliefs would not allow the censors to prevail. An essential part of the recovery from the Depression was the need to explore all possible explanations to prevent a similar disaster from ever occurring. Out of this need came the Agricultural Adjustment Act, the National Recovery Act, the Public Works Administration, other New Deal programs, and ultimately *The Plow That Broke the Plains*.

NOTES

1. James C. Malin tells the story of dust storms on the Great Plains, 1850–1900, in three articles in the 1946 *Kansas Historical Quarterly*—14 (May 1946): 129–144; 14 (August 1946): 265–296; and 14 (November 1946): 391–413.
2. For a brief account of the movement of farmers into the trans-Missouri

country, see Gilbert C. Fite, *The Farmers' Frontier, 1865–1900* (New York: Holt, Rinehart, and Winston, 1966).

3. Reprinted under title, Thomas Hariot, *A Brief and True Report of the New Found Land of Virginia,* introduction by Randolph G. Adams (Ann Arbor: Clements Library Associates, 1951).

4. David M. Emmons, *Garden in the Grasslands: Boomer Literature of the Great Plains* (1971), provides an excellent account of the various propaganda employed to lure land seekers to the Great Plains.

5. Henry Nash Smith, "Rain Follows the Plow: The Notion of Increased Rainfall for the Great Plains, 1844–1880," *Huntington Library Quarterly* 10 (February 1947): 169–193, provides a very interesting account of the development and collapse of the notion that rain would follow the plow westward with the settlers.

6. Earle D. Ross provides a useful account of the founding and rise of the colleges of agriculture in *Democracy's College: The Land-Grant Movement in the Formative Stage* (Ames: Iowa State College Press, 1942). The annual reports of the Secretary of the Department of Agriculture, beginning in 1863, reflect the work of the department. In 1894 yearbooks began to be issued annually and were widely viewed as one of the ways in which farmers could keep up to date on improvements in farming.

7. Everett Dick, *The Sod House Frontier, 1854–1890* (New York: D. Appleton-Century, 1937), and Mari Sandoz, *Old Jules* (Boston: Little, Brown, 1935) are two of many books that tell of the hardships and difficulties of farm making on the Plains. John D. Hicks, *The Populist Revolt: A History of the Farmers' Alliance and the People's Party* (Minneapolis: University of Minnesota Press, 1931), and Robert L. Morlan, *Political Prairie Fire: The Non-Partisan League, 1915–1922* (Minneapolis: University of Minnesota Press, 1955), exhibit attempts by unhappy farmers to take political action.

8. See Henry C. Wallace, *Our Debt and Duty to the Farmer* (New York: Century, 1925), for a brief description of the economic collapse following World War I.

9. The arrival and course of the Depression are sketched in such volumes as Frederick Lewis Allen, *Since Yesterday: The Nineteen Thirties in America* (New York: Bantam Books, 1940); Dixon Wecter, *The Age of the Great Depression, 1929–1941* (New York: Macmillan, 1948); Broadus Mitchell, *Depression Decade: From New Era Through New Deal, 1929–1941* (New York: Rinehart, 1947); John K. Galbraith, *The Great Crash, 1929* (Boston: Houghton Mifflin, 1972); David A. Shannon, ed., *The Great Depression* (Englewood Cliffs, N.J.: Prentice-Hall, 1960); and Lester V. Chandler, *America's Greatest Depression, 1929–1941* (New York: Harper and Row, 1970).

10. U.S. Department of Agriculture, "A Report on the Administration of the Agricultural Adjustment Act, May 1933 to February 1934" (Washington, D.C.: U.S. Government Printing Office, 1934).

11. For a full account of Lorentz, see Robert L. Snyder, *Pare Lorentz and the Documentary Film* (Norman: University of Oklahoma Press, 1968). Most of the material presented in the following paragraphs rests on Snyder.

12. Manuscript, William Bergsma to author, n.d. Bergsma was professor of music at the University of Washington and was elected to the National Institute of Arts and Letters.

13. Ibid.

14. Ibid.

15. U.S. Congress, *Congressional Record, 76th Congress, 1st Session,* February 16, 1939, p. 1322.

16. Personal information supplied to the author by Wayne D. Rasmussen, U.S.D.A., n.d.

17. Snyder, *Pare Lorentz,* p. 79.

V

Historical Overviews

Historians disagree frequently, and this is certainly the case for any assessment of the Dust Bowl experience. Two basic questions have been the subject of considerable inquiry and divergent approaches. One concerns the nature of the human response of residents of the Great Plains to the Depression and the Dust Bowl disaster; farmers revolted against traditional politics and status quo solutions. Another question considers causal factors of the environmental catastrophe. Historians have pondered the extent to which nature, government institutions, and individual farmers should shoulder responsibility.

William C. Pratt defines the insurgency, stressing the complicated, nonmonolithic nature of the farm revolt. For Pratt, many questions remain, and those questions already answered might require additional consideration. Such analysis will demand a painstaking, county-by-county approach. Pratt believes we do not know exactly who participated in the insurgency. He identifies at least four farm revolt groups that have been ignored by historians: women, local business leaders, law enforcement personnel, and fascists. The factors that ended the farm revolt also have been inadequately explained.

Donald Worster explores the causal factors behind the Dust Bowl. He shows how maladaptation by farmers of the Great Plains led to an environmental crisis of record proportions. In some ways Worster is in harmony with The Plow That Broke the Plains *thesis. To fully explain the Dust Bowl, detailed, interdisciplinary investigations of the environment need to be combined with probing discussions of cultural elements of Plains peoples. According to Worster the most prominent historian of the Dust Bowl, James C. Malin, understood portions of causation but missed the mark on its totality. For Worster, it was capitalism that encouraged the Dust Bowl by promoting land as a commodity, private wealth as a social ethic, and risk as a positive value.*

Harry C. McDean concludes the section by surveying recent and past analyses of the Dust Bowl. He notes the schizophrenic nature of historical treatments and tries to identify why there has been so much confusion. Basic issues, he argues, have been misunderstood—issues such as the geography, economy, and politics of the Dust Bowl. McDean concludes by considering the strengths and weaknesses of the most recent works covering the Dust Bowl experience.

There is some common ground. Everyone agrees that much remains to be discovered about the Dust Bowl experience.

Rethinking the Farm Revolt of the 1930s
William C. Pratt

The northern Plains witnessed the last great farm revolt in its history during the 1930s, when a flood of protest spilled across the region, fed by the springs of hard times and earlier insurgencies. The countryside, for one last moment, forced itself upon the rest of the country and demanded attention for its plight. After a period of high visibility, these efforts receded in the wake of New Deal programs that seemingly undercut the rural revolt. Many of the protesters arrived at an accommodation with the new regime, accepting "half-a-loaf now" in terms of wheat allotment checks and refinanced mortgages instead of "pie-in-the-sky" dreams of "cost-of-production" and the "cooperative commonwealth." Some, of course, continued to resist the sirens of expediency and accommodation, at least a bit longer.[1] But most observers agreed that Depression era insurgency peaked in 1933 and had pretty much wound down by the 1936 election.

This article examines several aspects of the farm revolt that need further elaboration. What I have attempted here is not a new interpretation but a new way of exploring the topic. It is based upon pursuing hints in a range of sources, and at places I suggest a new departure for the study of rural insurgencies in this region. Some of my assertions and generalizations are based upon explorations at the county level in northwestern North Dakota and northeastern South Dakota, two sections with extended histories of agrarian activism. While most of the discussion is limited to the northern Plains, a number of the points have applicability to the study of the 1930s farm revolt elsewhere.

This movement was not monolithic, and an examination of its efforts in individual locales frequently shows important divergences.

Organized Farmers Have the Power

Just Another Farm Fake. Cartoon from *Farmers' Holiday Weekly*, 30 January 1933.

Farm protest was not simply struck from one mold but was shaped by local history and custom and by local personalities. All too often historians seem to rush to a judgment that obscures such differences and, as a result, obstructs our understanding of this rural insurgency both at the regional level and at the grassroots. To counter this tendency requires a close look at the local history of farm revolt, utilizing weekly newspapers, interviews with participants or their kin, and other tools sometimes relegated in historians' minds to antiquarians and genealogists. A walk in a graveyard, for instance, may turn up a clue unavailable elsewhere.

Such research leads the historian to reformers who had links with earlier radical causes such as the Socialist Party (SP) and the Nonpartisan League (NPL), the most important twentieth-century agrarian political movement in the upper Midwest. At the same time, many participants had ties to more conservative efforts, including taxpayers' groups and the Townsend movement, which sought old age pensions for the elderly. The study of this and many other topics requires an appreciation of complexity and nuance. What happened in one locale was not always reenacted in others, and insurgents did not always resemble or behave like their counterparts elsewhere. The following discussion demonstrates that there were important local variations in the farm revolt of the 1930s and argues that an appreciation of such differences is crucial for an understanding of the movement as a whole.

THE FARMERS' HOLIDAY AND THE UNITED FARMERS' LEAGUE

Many historians assume that the story of 1930s agrarianism is the story of the Farmers' Holiday, which called for farm strikes, picketed roads leading to market centers, and attempted to prevent foreclosure sales. In reality, however, it includes the efforts of other groups, particularly the Communist-led United Farmers' League (UFL). The Holiday did not appear in the Dakotas until the late summer of 1932, but the UFL had a presence in eastern Montana and western North Dakota before then. UFL speakers, including "Mother" Ella Reeve Bloor, appeared in many communities in the northwest counties of North Dakota, and UFL locals were formed in several towns.[2]

By the time the Holiday started up in the Dakotas, a vocal minority of UFL adherents was already in place. In some locales, its prior agitation prepared the way for the more acceptable Holiday.[3] On the other hand, sometimes the UFL was not established until after the 1932 farm strike broke out. Whatever the particular case, however, the UFL was sometimes an ally and sometimes a rival to the Holiday. The farm revolt peaked on the northern Plains in 1933 and 1934, and the UFL dissolved in 1935, urging its members to join the Holiday association. This step was in accord with the popular front strategy embraced by the Communist Party (CP) at the time. By the end of 1937, the Holiday itself closed up shop, merging into the Farmers' Union.[4] In North Dakota, however, a separate Holiday organization persisted at least through 1938.[5] Unquestionably, there was a much lower level of activity from 1935 on, but some county units continued to meet. As late as July of 1938, a small number of Holiday members met in Bowbells, North Dakota, to elect new officers for the Burke County organization.[6]

It is generally recognized that the Holiday movement was a Farmers' Union–sponsored effort. One South Dakota activist recently referred to it as "the army and the navy of the Farmers' Union [FU]."[7] Milo Reno, the titular head of the Holiday, had been the real leader of the Iowa Farmers' Union since the early 1920s, and national FU president John Simpson was a strong backer of the cause until his death in 1934. In the Dakotas and to some extent in Nebraska, the Holiday emerged with the blessing of the state union. Yet the dynamic element of the Nebraska Holiday was outside the official FU orbit and even hostile to the state Holiday organization.[8] And, in numerous places, the local Holiday developed its own leadership or assumed a somewhat independent stance in relation to the state Holiday leadership. For example, in Brown County, South Dakota, John Sumption became president of the county Holiday. He was a member of the UFL and a Communist.[9]

Many participants in the 1930s' insurgency were veterans of agrarian movements other than the FU. Centers of farm protest in the Depression era, particularly northwestern North Dakota and perhaps to a somewhat lesser extent northeastern South Dakota, often had an earlier radical past. Williams County, North Dakota, elected Socialist sheriffs on three separate occasions and one Socialist county commissioner prior to U.S. entry into World War I, while Burke County had been carried by the SP presidential candidate Eugene Debs in 1912.[10] Roberts County, situated in the extreme northeastern corner of South Dakota, had at one time been that state's strongest NPL county and was in the 1930s one of the region's most militant areas. There, after the League and its Farmer-Labor Party successor faded, the insurgent nucleus ran an independent ticket behind the presidential candi-

dacy of William H. "Coin" Harvey in the 1932 election.[11] Perhaps the
most unusual antecedent to the Depression era farm revolt in this
region was found in the Wilmot area of the same county. There, according to one report, former members of the Ku Klux Klan (organized in the 1920s) joined the CP in the 1930s. One native of northeast
South Dakota recently quipped: "Farmers in Roberts County will try
anything once or twice."[12] The linkage of the farm revolt of the 1930s
to this region's extended radical past is apparent in terms of both geography and personal biography.

Obvious continuities with earlier insurgencies, not to mention simi-
larities in rhetoric and imagery, however, should not lead us to con-
clude that the 1930s revolt was simply "twentieth century Populism"
or some other similar characterization. The Holiday (as well as the
UFL) was more a direct action movement than any other agrarian
uprising on the northern Plains. Unlike earlier economic movements,
the Holiday did not promote cooperatives or other enterprises. And,
unlike earlier agrarian political movements, it did not attempt to become a vehicle to gain public office. While some of its participants did
benefit politically through their involvement, the Holiday itself did
not become a partisan political machine. No other farm movement in
the region's history proved to be as decentralized and subject to local
direction. National and state leaders might recommend a course of
action, but county units were virtually autonomous and decided themselves what should be done in given situations.[13]

In their substantial investigations of farm revolt, scholars have
paid little attention to the identity of its participants. The most detailed account to date is Rodney D. Karr's profile of thirty-five Plymouth County, Iowa, activists who had been arrested in the famous
Le Mars episode, in which a mob threatened to lynch a county judge.
Karr found, in contrast to other studies and impressions, that the participants tended to be in their mid-thirties and did not own their own
farms. Rather, they worked on their parents' farms and feared (so
Karr speculates) that their inheritance was at stake.[14]

In many locales, though the names of leaders are available, the
numbers are insufficient to construct a similar sample. To be sure,
there were other episodes where a sizable group was named. In Wells

County, North Dakota, forty-five were charged with illegally inter-
fering with a sale.[15] The largest single number I have found, however,
is in Roberts County, South Dakota, where the state brought an injunction against ninety-two individuals. While this list is somewhat
misleading, including non-participants and even some opponents of
the insurgents, it offers a potentially useful base for a quantitative
study. Seventy-two defendants gave affidavits, and fifteen of them
later were brought to trial. Here I have been struck with the number
of names that were those of early settlers of the area. Most of Roberts
County was not opened to white settlement until the 1890s, and key
figures in the UFL in this county were among the first settlers or, in
some cases, sons of first settlers residing with or near their parents.[16]

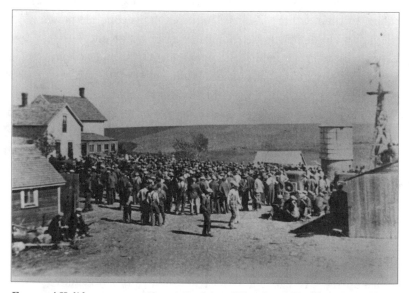

Farmers' Holiday penny auction at the farm of Mrs. Irene Von Bonn, near Elgin,
Nebraska, 1932. This was apparently the first such auction held in Nebraska. (Courtesy Nebraska State Historical Society.)

WOMEN IN THE FARM REVOLT

The involvement of women in the Depression era farm revolt is a
much neglected topic. In fact, a survey of the existing published scholar-

ship might suggest that historians had never considered the subject. Aside from the exploits of Mother Bloor, the Communist matriarch, there is almost no mention of women's participating in the rural uprising of the 1930s.[17] Yet two strong backers of the insurgency were women newspaper publishers. They were Alice Lorraine Daly, who operated the Aberdeen-based *Dakota Free Press*, and Marie Weekes, who published the *Norfolk* [Nebraska] *Press*. Both of them had enlisted in the farmer's cause at the time of the Nonpartisan League. In 1920, Weekes was an NPL Congressional candidate. Two years later Daly became the first woman in the region to run for governor. She was a long-time associate and companion of Tom Ayres, and together they were the mainstays of the NPL and Farmer-Labor party in South Dakota. With his death in 1932, she took over the paper and backed efforts to push the insurgency in a left-wing direction.[18] Weekes, on the other hand, was more conservative. Although she ran for Congress as an NPL candidate in 1920 and later provided broad support for the Holiday, there are hints that she was a sympathizer of Father Coughlin, the fiery "radio priest" who acquired an unsavory reputation as an anti-Semitic demagogue.[19]

Left-wing farm papers such as the *Producers News* and the *Farmers National Weekly* did devote some attention to the involvement of women, many of whom were active in selling subscriptions to the movement press. Some wrote for it as well. One of the most active women in the northern Plains was Effie Kjorstad of Williams County, North Dakota. The daughter of Norwegian immigrants, she was raised in a radical household. Her father had passed through the Socialist and NPL movements and had been the Communist candidate for sheriff in 1932. She herself ran for Congress in 1934 and state senate in 1936. A very energetic individual, she sold large numbers of subscriptions to the left-wing farm press and was a frequent speaker at protest meetings in the county. She was elected secretary-treasurer of the county Holiday organization at least twice and often was a delegate to Holiday, Farmers' Union, and anti-war conventions. In neighboring Mountrail County, women members of the left-wing Husa clan also were quite active.[20]

Most women participants in the farm struggles of the 1930s, of course, like their male counterparts, were anonymous rank-and-filers. They showed up for "penny auctions" and "Sears-Roebuck sales," fattening the crowd and adding to the volume of the protest.[21] One male observer recently noted that women often were more vocal than men at these sales. While they were not as inclined to direct action, some of them were quite willing to stand up to the sheriff and curse him for his role.[22] Students of women's involvement in farm movements on the northern Plains must actively look for references to women and ask questions about them. A substantial amount of information probably is out there; we simply have not hunted for it.

BUSINESS MEN AND LOCAL AUTHORITIES

At the time of the 1932 farm strike, it was not uncommon for local newspapers and business men to enlist as backers of the movement. Holiday leaders in the Dakotas sought business support, and numerous merchants came forward. In Ward and Williams Counties, North Dakota, for example, businessmen ran ads endorsing the strike.[23]

The left-wing UFL attracted business support as well. In Mountrail County, the movement was spearheaded by the Husa clan, who ran the community store in the hamlet of Belden.[24] While it was unusual for shopkeepers to assume such a leadership role, both the *Producers News* and the *Farmers National Weekly* featured advertisements paid for by a number of businesses.

The attitude of local authorities also was important. The popular image is that of embattled farmers facing armed sheriffs, and there are numerous such confrontations that are documented. On the other hand, some local law enforcement officials acted in collusion with Holiday activists and made themselves "unavailable" in crucial situations. In Adams County, North Dakota, the sheriff reportedly arranged for the protesters to grab the papers out of his hand, thus stopping the proceedings. Harry Lux of the Nebraska Holiday tells of a $50 contribution made to him by a sheriff and of the report about another in Colorado that he was going hunting at the time of a proposed farmers' action.[25] And we should note that local authorities were sometimes thwarted by their inability to line up a sufficient number of deputies. One of the region's most explosive episodes occurred at Milbank, South Dakota, in the summer of 1933. There, a forced sale of a farmer's equipment and livestock was attempted at the county fairgrounds. A large number of Holiday and UFL activists from South Dakota and Minnesota showed up. When protesters attempted to prevent a deputy sheriff from bidding, he pointed his gun at someone, and in the melee that followed, the gun was fired and struck the victim in the face with a tear gas shell. Upon seeing one of its number shot (and perhaps believing him killed), the crowd disarmed the deputies and then proceeded to conduct a "Sears-Roebuck sale." The state of South Dakota eventually brought an injunction against the United Farmers' League and the Unemployed Council and some ninety individuals, and prosecuted fifteen of them for participation in this episode and others. The case was brought in Roberts County, and all defendants were from there as well. After a dramatic trial in Sisseton, they were acquitted by the local jury.[26]

In some respects, Herbert Gutman's analysis of labor disputes in small nineteenth-century communities seems applicable here.[27] When outside financial interests sought to foreclose or evict a neighbor, much of the community interceded. We also have many examples where that did not occur and, over time, a conservative backlash developed, particularly against the UFL. American Legionnaires adopted vigilante tactics in Britton, South Dakota, in the summer of 1934, and the sheriff reportedly was a leader of a mob which beat several men, including a disabled World War I veteran. Neither local nor state authorities intervened, and no arrests were made.[28]

THE ROLE OF INDIVIDUAL COMMUNITIES

The rural upheaval of the 1930s is first and foremost the story of a grassroots movement. Accordingly, the best vantage point from which to study this episode is at the individual community level. It is, of course, helpful to examine the papers of key national and regional figures and to survey the daily and farm press. On the other hand, I suggest that it is also important to explore the particular settings in which this episode occurred. Each community that took part in the farm revolt of the 1930s has its own distinct history. The story of this insurgency is different in Roberts County, South Dakota, from that of Williams County, North Dakota. But then it is also different in Williams County from that of neighboring Mountrail County. And, to make the task even more complicated, the story in Bossko Township may be significantly different from that in Springdale, even though they both are in Roberts County. Such differences may be of real importance, yet existing published accounts usually do not consider them.

What is required, I suggest, is a thorough historical exploration of individual communities in which this revolt took place. My own preference involves an examination of the area's political and cultural history, before, during, and after the insurgency. That the UFL was apparently stronger in Roberts County than the Holiday may be explained by earlier historical developments. This same county also had three or four Communist Party locals into the 1940s, suggesting that it was very different from anywhere else in South Dakota.[29] Is that difference explained primarily by events prior to the Depression or by more recent ones? The farm revolt of the 1930s, like earlier rural movements, consisted of numerous local reports. Here, neighbors often organized and mobilized neighbors, people with whom they had a background of association over a period of time. With outside help on occasion, these men and women worked with others whom they already knew or knew about. Together they protected what they had and perhaps enhanced it as well. Different approaches and appeals worked in different places, and the only way to learn about such matters is through a close examination of diverse and separate communities. Such local studies may force us to qualify long-accepted generalizations such as John Shover's assumption that the farm revolt of the 1930s was more prevalent in corn-hog sections and John Miller's conclusion that the Holiday in South Dakota was more conservative than in neighboring states.[30]

PROTEST AND ANTI-SEMITISM

In important respects, the 1930s era insurgency is more akin to contemporary farm protest than to any earlier effort. That being the

Anybody Want to Bid? Cartoon from *Farm Holiday News*, 23 June 1923.

case, it may be useful to examine the seamier side of Depression farm revolt. In the 1950s some social scientists turned their attention to "exposing" the crankiness of Populism. This discussion sometimes touched upon twentieth century midwestern figures, including William Lemke, the North Dakota Congressman who ran for president in 1936 on Father Coughlin's Union Party ticket. Few dispute Coughlin's anti-Semitic credentials, and Lemke's reputation never has recovered from this episode. Still, we should note that Lemke's biographer, while treating Lemke's shortcomings, makes a good case that the North Dakota Congressman was not anti-Semitic.[31] Other evidence demonstrates that many Lemke backers in 1936 were not Coughlinites but rather reformers who were alienated from Roosevelt and his "brain-trusters" and who were determined to continue their fight for "cost-of-production," which they were convinced was a better basis for a farm program.[32] It also should be pointed out that not all support for Coughlin can properly be characterized as anti-Semitic. Initially, the "radio priest" backed FDR, and only over a period of time did his public positions become more extreme. In 1933 and 1934, his anti-banker rhetoric was not that different from traditional farm insurgents and normally was not openly anti-Semitic.[33]

All this said, however, there was anti-Semitism in the countryside, and it spilled over into the protest of the 1930s. Sometimes it was obvious and explicit. Perhaps the single most dramatic example occurred at the Nebraska state capitol in February of 1933. There, approximately 3,000 to 4,000 demonstrators gathered to pressure the legislature for relief. The group photograph on the steps of the building shows a placard that reads:

THE JEW SYSTEM OF BANKING
YEARS OF APPARENT PROSPERITY

It is illustrated with a large rattlesnake.[34]

Demonstration on the capitol steps, Lincoln, Nebraska. This photograph is a cropped version of one that originally appeared in the *Lincoln State Journal*, 18 February 1933. (Courtesy Nebraska State Historical Society.)

A closeup of the scene, showing the lettering on the rattlesnake placard. (Courtesy Nebraska State Historical Society.)

How we interpret this episode is extremely important. If we see the gathering as a group of anti-Semites, that certainly will color our view of the Depression-era insurgency. Within the Nebraska Holiday movement, there was an ongoing struggle between the Madison County group, which was close to the Communist Party and had a following in other parts of the state, and a group that was close to Milo Reno and the state Farmers' Union.[35] The Madison County group organized the capitol demonstration, but anybody could attend and no one took roll. That Coughlinites or other Jew-baiters were in the crowd that day does not tell us very much, but the anti-Semites who did show up have left an indelible mark on the historical record. Anti-Semitism surfaced elsewhere in Nebraska as well. Harry Lux recalled a man in northeast Nebraska who "claimed he was an attorney yes and he was the fella that brought that . . . Anti-Jewish leaflet with a picture of a rattlesnake on it." Another Nebraska Holiday supporter railed at "Communist Jews" and praised Hitler's persecution of them.[36] The depth of anti-Semitism in the 1930s farm revolt warrants further research, particularly in light of contemporary reports of anti-Jewish sentiment in rural areas of the northern Plains.

THE COMING OF THE NEW DEAL

It has become a cliché to say that New Deal programs ultimately destroyed the appeal of the 1930s-era farm insurgency. In November of 1933, an aide to Harry Hopkins wrote about the unsuccessful Holiday strike:

> Apparently one thing that is contributing largely to its failure is the arrival of wheat allotment checks. I have that from a chap named McCandless, farm reporter for the *Omaha World Herald*. I believe our CWA [Civil Works Administration] program will also do a lot to calm them down. Quite a few farmers will be getting jobs out of it. It will give them something to do and a little money.[37]

Even UFL leaders who denounced New Deal allotment programs signed up for them.[38] Reform had taken its toll, so to speak, as government programs eroded the earlier appeal of insurgency.

OTHER FACTORS

Yet there were other factors at work as well. Many farmers in the region had not had a real crop since 1930, and substantial numbers either lost their farms or quit before they did. A large exodus from the region dates to at least 1934, and it included militant activists. Burke County UFL leader James Pearson moved his family to Washington state in late 1934.[39] Numerous other radicals were among the North Dakota "Okies" who ended up on the west coast. South Dakota militants felt compelled to leave as well. Clarence Sharp, former Communist Party state secretary, remembers a number of Party members in the Frederick area leaving by 1935.[40] Whatever their destination, their departure from the Dakotas diluted the ranks of militants in the region.

Radical forces were also depleted by internal strife and factionalism. Key UFL figures in both North and South Dakota defected or were expelled from the Communist Party by 1935, with negative consequences for the left wing of the insurgency. Perhaps the case of "Red Flag" Charlie Taylor, long-time editor of the *Producers News* and former national UFL secretary, and Ashbel Ingerson, a prominent activist from Burke County, was most important. Both of them broke with the Party in 1935 and affiliated with the Trotskyists. Their departure from UFL ranks proved disruptive in much of eastern Montana and northwestern North Dakota.[41] On a more local scale, the expulsion of Helge Tangen from the Communist Party in Frederick, South Dakota, had a similar effect in the immediate area, and perhaps as many as one-third of the Party members dropped out.[42]

More disruptive overall was the growing anti-Communist sentiment on the northern Plains. In some cases, it grew out of publicity identifying particular farm activists as Communists. The 1934 trial in Sisseton and vigilante episodes in Marshall County, South Dakota, marked the beginning of a long retreat for radicalism in northeastern South Dakota. More than a year earlier, a similar "red scare" had developed in Nebraska in the wake of the Holiday march on the state capitol. Much of it was provoked by the pro-Reno element as it sought to discredit the more radical Madison County group. The day after the demonstration, an insurgent leader noted: "The red scare is something awful in this state."[43]

The diffusion of energies into other causes also played a role in undercutting the rural insurgency. While some leaders obtained government positions, others enlisted in the Workers Alliance (a labor organization for federal relief project workers) or the Townsend movement. The latter cause, which promised not only old age pensions but a substantial boost to the economy, attracted impressive numbers in some communities. It was popular in Burke County, where long-time activist L. L. Griffith took up its banner in 1935. There, several Townsend groups were formed, and Griffith was elected as a county commissioner. Townsend Clubs met on a regular basis while the Holiday faded into inactivity, though it continued to elect county officers.[44] More research into the place of Townsend efforts on the northern Plains is needed. Holiday leaders like North Dakota state president Usher Burdick were strong proponents, and earlier assessments of this movement as a conservative development probably should be qualified. It attracted progressive elements to its colors in the region and at least in some communities stood side by side with the Holiday and the Farmers' Union.[45]

CONCLUSION

Overall, the 1930s insurgency dramatized the plight of the farmer, protected many from eviction and foreclosure, and forced politicians to develop new programs to address the needs of rural America. Of course, it was not a complete success. "Cost-of-production" never was obtained, and many farm families were uprooted from their communities and forced to start over again somewhere else. Still, it must be said that the revolt bought time for a large number of farmers on the northern Plains, and that is not an insignificant achievement. In some sections, such as northeastern South Dakota, the Farmers' Union got its second wind, and it emerged from the Depression as a stronger force than before. New recruits from the earlier insurgency signed on and helped remake the national union into a modern progressive group.[46] This, too, is a partial legacy of the struggles of the 1930s. The Communist Party also recruited a number of farmers to its cause during the Depression era insurgency. While some quickly dropped out, others signed up for the long term. Enclaves of Communist farmers persisted in several Dakota communities well into the 1940s (and sometimes longer), resulting in FBI surveillance for two decades or more.[47]

The farm revolt of the 1930s was the last major agrarian outburst on the northern Plains. While a number of radicals lived on and hints of radicalism surfaced from time to time, the era of large scale farm protest in this region had passed. Yet, when the National Farmers' Organization (NFO) emerged a generation later, it drew support from sections that had risen up in revolt in the 1930s.[48] And even now, some farm activists link their efforts with those of the Depression era protest. Insurgents of that time helped shape the historical contours of the region, and further research into their activities is warranted.

NOTES

1. An earlier version of this essay was read at the Northern Great Plains History Conference at Sioux Falls, South Dakota, October 1987. The author wishes to thank the referees for their comments on the manuscript. John Shover, *Cornbelt Rebellion: The Farmers' Holiday Association*

(Urbana: University of Illinois Press, 1965); Lowell K. Dyson, *Red Harvest: The Communist Party and American Farmers* (Lincoln: University of Nebraska Press, 1982). See also Lowell K. Dyson, "The Farm Holiday Movement," Ph.D. diss., Columbia University, 1968.

2. Dyson, *Red Harvest*, provides a detailed account of the UFL and its antecedent, the United Farmers' Educational League. See also Allen Mathews, "Agrarian Radicals: The United Farmers' League of South Dakota," *South Dakota History* 3 (Fall 1973): 408–421. The *Bowbells Tribune*, the official paper of Burke County, ran numerous stories on UFL meetings in that county in 1931.

3. Other efforts in the background of the North Dakota Holiday were a "$1 Wheat" campaign and local taxpayers' groups. For the "$1 Wheat" movement, see Larry Remele, "The North Dakota Farm Strike of 1932," *North Dakota History* 41 (Fall 1974): 5–8. An unsympathetic story on the Burke County taxpayers' group is found in *Columbus Reporter*, 24 December 1931.

4. Dyson provides the most detailed treatment of the various maneuvers of the UFL and the Holiday. See Dyson, *Red Harvest*, pp. 67–82, 99–147. To simplify the discussion, I have not mentioned the Farmers' National Committee for Action (FNCA), another Communist-led group, which also was active on the northern Plains. It represented a somewhat more flexible tendency and sponsored several farm relief conferences. See Dyson, *Red Harvest*, and Harvey Klehr, *The Heyday of American Communism: The Depression Decade* (New York: Basic Books, 1984), pp. 141–145. As a practical matter, at the grassroots level, individuals who worked with the FNCA also were UFL members.

5. For the North Dakota Holiday, see James William Dodd, "The Farmer Takes a Holiday," M.S. thesis, North Dakota Agricultural College, 1960; Larry Remele, "The Public Reaction to the North Dakota Farmers' Holiday Association," M.A. thesis, University of North Dakota, 1969. For the South Dakota Holiday, see John E. Miller, "Restrained, Respectable Radicals: The South Dakota Farm Holiday," *Agricultural History* 59 (July 1985): 429–447.

6. *Bowbells Tribune*, 29 July 1938. The Burke County Holiday apparently had not been as active as the Williams County organization in recent years, however.

7. Author's interview with Oscar Brekke, Clinton, Minn., 26 September 1987. Brekke was president of the Grant County (S. Dak.) Holiday and then president of the South Dakota organization.

8. Gilbert C. Fite, "John A. Simpson: The Southwest's Militant Farm Leader," *Mississippi Valley Historical Review* 35 (March 1949): 563–584; John L. Shover, "The Farm Holiday Movement in Nebraska," *Nebraska History* 43 (March 1962): 53–78.

9. *Dakota Free Press*, 28 October 1932; author's interview with Clarence H. Sharp, Minneapolis, Minn. Sharp is a native of South Dakota and was the state secretary of the South Dakota CP from late 1932 until 1940. I have had several interviews and numerous conversations with him which have dealt (among other things) with topics discussed in this article.

10. *Williston Graphic*, 7 November 1912; 9 November 1916; *1913 Legislative Manual* (Devils Lake, N.D.: Journal Printing Company, 1913), 262–264. For a survey of Socialist efforts in the region, see William C. Pratt, "Socialism on the Northern Plains, 1900–1924," *South Dakota History* (forthcoming).

11. The most detailed account of the UFL in Roberts County is Gordon Smith, "History of the United Farmers' League in Roberts County" (unpublished manuscript in author's possession). See also Mathews, "Agrarian Radicals" and "The History of the United Farmers' League of South Dakota, 1923–1936: A Study in Farm Radicalism," M.A. thesis, University of South Dakota, 1972.

12. Author's interviews with Clarence H. Sharp, Minneapolis, Minn.; author's interview with James O. Monson, Sisseton, S. Dak., 13 August 1986.

13. Usher L. Burdick, former Holiday president in North Dakota, wrote: "The power of the Holiday rested with the Grass Roots. The county organization determined when to stop a foreclosure and the State organization had nothing to do with that. I could advise them, which I often did, but I could not control any county organization." (Quoted in Dodd, "The Farmer Takes a Holiday," p. 102.) See also Miller, "Restrained, Respectable Radicals," p. 429.

14. Rodney D. Karr, "Farmer Rebels in Plymouth County, Iowa, 1932–1933," *Annals of Iowa* 47 (Winter 1985): 637–645. This article is drawn from a larger unpublished study. See Rodney D. Karr, "The Farmers' Holiday Movement, Plymouth County, Iowa: 1932–1933," M.A. thesis, University of Nebraska at Omaha, 1980.

15. *Producers News*, 7 June 1935.

16. *State of South Dakota vs. United Farmers' League et al.*, Case File 6800, Roberts County Court House, Sisseton, S. Dak. Of those offering affidavits, twelve denied membership in either the UFL or the Unemployed Council, eleven admitted their affiliation with the latter group, and approximately fifty belonged to the left-wing farm group. Knute Walstad and his son Julius were key figures in the Roberts County UFL. Fifty-five years old in 1934, Knute had immigrated from Norway and homesteaded in the northwestern part of the county in the 1890s. See Smith, "History of the United Farmers' League of Roberts County." Other UFL influentials involved in these proceedings were Leonard Ruckdaschel and his son Ralph. The elder Ruckdaschel had moved to the area as a boy in 1909 and

was in his mid-fifties at the time of the injunction case. Elmer Eddy was another Roberts County pioneer who was enjoined for his alleged UFL activities. In 1898, he had homesteaded in the county. Before moving to his permanent farm site, Eddy also had operated a store and a post office in the northwestern part of Roberts County. He was 59 in 1934. Gilbert Gilbertson moved to the area with his parents in 1900. At the time of the injunction case, he was 47. C. S. Christianson, a UFL activist in the southern part of the county near Wilmot, farmed near his father's homestead. He was 48 when he was enjoined for his alleged deeds. Another UFL figure was Orville Monson. Although he had participated in the Milbank episode, he was not named in either the injunction or the riot case. His father had been an early settler just across the Roberts County line. The above information is taken from obituaries, recent interviews with children of these individuals, and tombstones.

17. One of the very few published historical studies treating women in any farm movement on the northern Plains is Karen Starr, "Fighting for a Future: Farm Women of the Nonpartisan League," *Minnesota History* 48 (Summer 1983): 255–262. The most focused account on Bloor is Thomas L. Edwards, "Ella Reeve Bloor: Urban Radical in the Upper Midwest 1930–1936," unpublished paper, Northern Great Plains History conference, Grand Forks, N. Dak., 29 September 1983. See also Dyson, *Red Harvest*; and William D. Rowley, "The Loup City Riot of 1934: Main Street vs. the 'Far-Out' Left," *Nebraska History* 47 (September 1966): 295–327.

18. *Dakota Free Press*, 10 June 1932; telephone interview with Homer Ayres, Sturgis, S. Dak., 9 March 1986. She continued publishing the paper until late 1935. For Coughlin, see Charles J. Tull, *Father Coughlin and the New Deal* (Syracuse: Syracuse University Press, 1965); David H. Bennett, *Demagogues in the Depression: American Radicals and the Union Party, 1932–1936* (New Brunswick: Rutgers University Press, 1969); Alan Brinkley, *Voices of Protest: Huey Long, Father Coughlin, and the Great Depression* (New York: Alfred A. Knopf, 1982).

19. Marie Weekes and her paper are discussed in James A. Stone, "Agrarian Ideology and the Farm Program in Nebraska State Politics With Special Reference to Northeast Nebraska, 1920–1933," Ph.D. diss., University of Nebraska, 1960; David Kathka, "The Farmers' Holiday Association in Madison County, Nebraska: 1932–1934," M.A. thesis, Wayne State College, 1966; and Burton W. Folsom, Jr., "Immigrant Voters and the Nonpartisan League in Nebraska, 1917–1920," *Great Plains Quarterly* 1 (Summer 1981): 159–168. Harry Lux, a key figure in [the] Nebraska Holiday, later reported that Weekes liked Father Coughlin and believed in the Protocol of the Elders of Zion. John Shover interview with Harry Lux, 1 March 1962, transcript, Nebraska State Historical Society, Lincoln, Ne-

braska. For Coughlin, see Charles J. Tull, *Father Coughlin and the New Deal* (Syracuse: Syracuse University Press, 1965); David H. Bennett, *Demagogues in the Depression: American Radicals and the Union Party, 1932–1936* (New Brunswick: Rutgers University Press, 1969); Alan Brinkley, *Voices of Protest: Huey Long, Father Coughlin, and the Great Depression* (New York: Alfred A. Knopf, 1982).

20. This sketch of Effie Kjorstad is based on a survey of the *Williams County Farmer Press*, the *Farmers National Weekly*, and the *National Farm Holiday News*. Numerous references to Ellen and Lillian Husa are found in the *Stanley Sun, Producers News*, and the *Farmers National Weekly*. Mother Bloor had presided at their grandmother's funeral. That provoked a great deal of local attention. See *Minot Daily News*, 3 January 1931 ("Mrs. Husa's Funeral Will Be Without Clergy"); *Ward County Independent*, 8 January 1931 ("No Minister at Rites for Belden Woman"). Other women who were mentioned by name often were related to prominent male participants in the 1930s-era insurgency. This tendency is found in other movements as well. See William C. Pratt, "Women Socialists and Their Male Comrades: The Reading Experience, 1927–1936," in *Flawed Liberation: Socialism and Feminism*, ed. Sally M. Miller (Westport, Conn.: Greenwood Press, 1981), pp. 145–178.

21. The protesters either sought to block a sale altogether or to arrange that the farm or livestock and equipment were sold to friendly bidders at a nominal price. In the latter case, the debt was satisfied at a loss to the creditor, and the farm or chattels were returned to the original owner. An action protecting the farm itself was called a "penny auction"; a "Sears-Roebuck sale" protected chattels. See John L. Shover, "The Penny Auction Rebellion," *The American West* 2 (Fall 1965): 61–72.

22. Author's interviews with James O. Monson, Sisseton, S. Dak., 13 August 1986; Veblen, S. Dak., 23 September 1987. Yet Irene Paull reports that a key UFL figure in northeastern South Dakota later told her: "Women took charge of evictions. They came over with boxes of pepper. They faced the sheriff and told him if he comes, he'll face a barrage of pepper." Paull manuscript on Julius Walstad, Irene Paull Papers, Minnesota Historical Society, St. Paul, Minnesota.

23. A headline in a Williston, N. Dak., paper reads: "Williston Business Men Add Their Approval to That of Minot and Jamestown" (*Williams County Farmers Press*, 18 August 1932). See Remele, "The North Dakota Farm Strike of 1932," pp. 14–15; Miller, "Restrained, Respectable Radicals," p. 444.

24. Members of this family were often mentioned in the *Stanley Sun*, the *Producers News*, and *Farmers National Weekly*. W. J. Husa operated the community's only store.

25. Author's telephone interview with Homer Ayres, Sturgis, S. Dak., 9 March 1986; John L. Shover interview with Harry Lux, 1 March 1962.

26. Author's interviews with Clarence H. Sharp, Minneapolis, Minn.; and Oscar Brekke, Clinton, Minn., 26 September 1987. For accounts of the trial, see Smith, "History of the United Farmers' League of Roberts County," and Mathews, "History of the United Farmers' League of South Dakota."

27. Herbert G. Gutman, *Work, Culture, and Society in Industrializing America: Essays in American Working-Class and Social History* (New York: Vintage, 1977).

28. For this episode, see Smith, "History of the United Farmers' League of Roberts County"; and Mathews, "History of the United Farmers' League of South Dakota." Almost sixteen years earlier, A. C. Townley, the major figure in the formation of the NPL in North Dakota, had been prevented from speaking in Britton. See Gilbert C. Fite, "Peter Norbeck and the Defeat of the Non-Partisan League in South Dakota," *Mississippi Valley Historical Review* 33 (September 1946): 230. It was unlikely that mob action of the Britton variety could have occurred in Sisseton or Milbank, S. Dak., or Williston or Stanley, N. Dak.

29. According to an FBI document, a local Communist reported in 1941 "that there are three branches of the CP in Roberts County with a total membership of about 50 members. He stated that the Mother Bloor Local Branch has ten members but he refused to give the names of any Party members." [deleted], 18 May 1953, FBI File 100-28935-38. At its peak in 1934, the CP may have had as many as one hundred members in Roberts County. Author's interviews with Clarence H. Sharp, Minneapolis, Minn.

30. In *Cornbelt Rebellion*, Shover assumes rather than demonstrates that the farm revolt was most active in the corn-hog sections. Yet as Smith has pointed out, that description does not fit Roberts County, and evidence from the Dakotas to date suggests that corn-hog production is not the sine qua non for this farm revolt. Miller's thesis about the conservative nature of the South Dakota Holiday probably will be revised as historians come to a more complex understanding of Emil Loriks, a key figure who served as executive secretary-treasurer of the South Dakota organization. On one hand, he promoted a conservative image for the Holiday and clearly sought business backing. On the other hand, he actively participated in "stirring up" the farmers. (Author's interview with Oscar Brekke, Clinton, Minn., 26 September 1987.) The extensive correspondence between Loriks and Homer Ayres also suggests that this "restrained, respectable radical" had a working relationship with less "respectable" elements in the farm movement. Ayres was active in the UFL and ran for Lieutenant Governor in 1934 on the Communist-backed United Front ticket. Ayres was a Loriks ally in several of the battles of the late 1930s.

The personal relationship between the two men was cordial, and they respected one another. (Loriks Papers, American State Bank, Oldham, S. Dak.) A recent popular biography of Loriks follows Miller's "restrained, respectable" thesis on the South Dakota Holiday. See Elizabeth E. Williams, *Emil Loriks: Builder of a New Economic Order* (Sioux Falls: Center for Western Studies, 1987).

31. Daniel Bell, *The Radical Right: The New American Right* (Garden City: Doubleday, 1963); Edward C. Blackorby, *Prairie Rebel: The Public Life of William Lemke* (Lincoln: University of Nebraska Press, 1963). For Coughlin, see n. 18, above.

32. L. C. Miller, editor of the *Bowbells Tribune*, backed Lemke in 1936 but had voted for Norman Thomas, the Socialist Party presidential candidate, in 1928 and 1932.

33. Apparently Emil Loriks was somewhat sympathetic to Coughlin at least as late as 1935. Wrote one observer: "Loriks made several bad blunders. He said that the fascist[s] Father Coughlin and Huey Long were men like old Thomas Jefferson." (*Farmers National Weekly*, 26 July 1935.) See also Elizabeth Evenson Williams, "A South Dakota Agrarian's Views of Huey Long," *Midwest Review* 8 (Spring 1986): 40–55.

34. The anti-Semitic placard was first called to my attention in a discussion with Michael Farrell and William Locke during the making of the 1985 Nebraska Educational Television Network documentary, "Plowing Up a Storm: The History of Midwestern Farm Activism."

35. Shover, "The Farm Holiday Movement in Nebraska"; Kathka, "The Farmers' Holiday Association in Madison County."

36. John L. Shover interview with Harry Lux, 1 March 1962; Dyson, *Red Harvest*, p. 132. According to a *Farmers National Weekly* account, Milo Reno told the 1934 National Farmers' Union convention: "The New Deal ought to be called the Jew Deal." See Lem Harris, "National Convention of Union Avoided Actions Called for in Speeches," *Farmers National Weekly*, 7 December 1934.

37. Quoted in Richard Lowitt and Maurice Beasley, eds., *One Third of a Nation: Lorena Hickok Reports on the Great Depression* (Urbana: University of Illinois Press, 1981), p. 97.

38. Most of the UFL leaders in Roberts County enrolled in the 1934 wheat allotment program (Smith, "History of the United Farmers' League of Roberts County"). In Burke County, N. Dak., that also apparently was the case. See *Bowbells Tribune*, 7 December 1934.

39. *Bowbells Tribune*, 7 December 1934.

40. Author's interview with Clarence H. Sharp, Minneapolis, Minn.

41. Taylor had a long history of involvement in the left wing of the farm movement. See Dyson, *Red Harvest*; and Charles Vindex, "Radical Rule

in Montana," *Montana: The Magazine of Western History* 18 (January 1968): 2–18. After he left the Party, Taylor maneuvered a takeover of *Producers News*, and, as a result, the paper no longer covered the left-wing farm movement outside of Montana nor sympathized with the CP. Ingerson also had been a key UFL figure. An FBI report dated 1941 asserted that the Trotskyists in Plentywood, Montana (Taylor's old stronghold in the extreme northeastern part of the state), "have driven the Stalinists back as far as Belden, North Dakota." ("Communist Activities in the State of Montana," 16 June 1941, FBI File 100-3-51-16.) Though this comment is an exaggeration, the Taylor/ Ingerson defection had serious consequences. The *Bowbells Tribune* editor answered an Ingerson criticism in 1938: "As a matter of fact, Ash, you have become so famous over Burke County as disorganizer No. 1 that you are almost considered infamous, even among your old friends, who saw you destroy the Communist Party because it would not bend to your will" (*Bowbells Tribune*, 16 September 1938).

42. *Dakota Free Press*, 3 November 1933; author's interviews with Clarence H. Sharp, Minneapolis, Minn. Sharp has repeatedly said that Tangen's expulsion "was a terrible mistake."

43. Quoted in Shover, *Cornbelt Rebellion*, p. 132. The publicity surrounding the so-called "Loup City Riot" the following year had a devastating impact as well. See Rowley, "The Loup City Riot of 1934."

44. The *Bowbells Tribune* provided a substantial amount of attention to the local Townsend movement between 1935 and 1938.

45. The then left-wing *Williams County Farmers Press* seemingly gave the Townsend movement and the Holiday equal billing in 1936. That year the county Townsend leader joined the presidents of the local Holiday, Farmers' Union, and relief workers organization in endorsing this paper in the forthcoming election for official county newspaper (*Williams County Farmers Press*, 29 October 1936).

46. For an overview of the Farmers' Union, see John A. Crampton, *The National Farmers' Union: Ideology of a Pressure Group* (Lincoln: University of Nebraska Press, 1965). This organization on the northern Plains is treated in Robert S. Thompson, "The History of the South Dakota Farmers' Union, 1914–1952," M.A. thesis, University of South Dakota, 1953; and Charles and Joyce Conrad, *50 Years: North Dakota Farmers' Union* (North Dakota Farmers' Union, 1976).

47. Clarence Sharp served as a CP traveling representative in the Dakotas during the 1940s and 1950s (Author's interviews with Clarence H. Sharp, Minneapolis, Minn.). His travels in the region were monitored by the FBI. In 1959, for example, six FBI agents participated in the surveillance of one of Sharp's trips in the Dakotas ("M.H.," 30 September 1959, FBI File 100-390741-7; "V.C.F.," 24 September 1959, FBI File 100-38183-12). Some

party members continued to pay dues, subscribe to the *Daily Worker* or the *Worker*, and visit with Sharp when he made his rounds, but there was little Communist activity in these states by the late 1940s.

48. Author's interview with James O. Monson, Veblen, S. Dak., 23 September 1987. Monson, the son of a 1930s activist, reported that some former UFL members joined the NFO in the 1960s. Though undercut by the prosperity of the next decade, the NFO had considerable success in northeastern South Dakota (Roberts, Marshall, and Brown counties). I have personal knowledge of a former UFL activist who later was involved in [the] NFO in McHenry County, N. Dak., and sons of earlier insurgents who participated in the newer movement in Burke and Williams counties, N. Dak., and Madison County, Nebraska.

THE DIRTY THIRTIES: A STUDY IN
AGRICULTURAL CAPITALISM
Donald Worster

"The history of any land begins with nature, and all histories must end with nature," J. Frank Dobie once wrote.[1] He was eloquently right, but until very recently such a view was not regarded seriously by academic historians, who commonly took nature for granted, beginning and ending their studies with an air of human omnipotence. That attitude, however, is becoming harder to maintain in innocence, as a group of ecologically informed historians challenge it. It is now more acceptable to say, with Dobie, that nature has played a stage-center role in the making of history—the making of its setbacks and tragedies as well as its progress and triumphs. Whether defined as climate, as vegetation, as the presence or absence of water, as soil and topography, or more compositely as ecosystem and biosphere, nature has been a force to be reckoned with in social evolution. Many geographers and anthropologists have long acknowledged that fact. And now historical thinking, if it wants to be taken seriously, must to some extent also become ecological.[2]

There have been some important exceptions to the historians' neglect of environmental perspectives. Strikingly, those exceptions have come mainly out of the Great Plains. Dobie was a well-known son of this region, growing up and teaching here. So was his University of Texas associate, Walter Prescott Webb, who stitched history and environment together in his writings.[3] And so was the man who, more than any other, anticipated the emerging ecological synthesis in history: James Malin of the University of Kansas. As far back as 1950 Malin was envisioning history as a process of "ecological adaptation" and was promoting the grasslands as an ideal laboratory for tracking that process.[4] These scholars, particularly Webb and Malin, were not always clear about what they meant by adaptation—whether it was a process of yielding to natural exigencies or of surmounting them by means of technology—but they were all convinced of the profound importance of the human dialogue with nature. The Great Plains have uniquely had an impact on the historical imagination because conditions of settlement there have presented so stark a contrast with those in more humid American environments. But in the case of Malin there was another, more specific influence at work, riveting his attention on the earth. During the 1930s he found himself directly in the midst of the Dust Bowl, as dramatic an example of maladaption as any in human ecological experience. Anyone who lived through the "dirty thirties" or the subsequent echoes of it, as he did, could hardly fail to be impressed by the relevance of environmental health to human welfare and happiness. The Dust Bowl made emphatically clear the consequences nature can have for people, the surprises she can bring to those who leave her out of their calculations.

In the traumatic years of the Dust Bowl, the Great Plains offered at once a stimulus to the rise of an ecologically oriented history and a compelling subject for historians to grapple with. My main purpose here is to move toward a cultural explanation for this disaster, one that will, when complete, be adequate to its significance and alert to its complexity. Such an explanation cannot be the work of any single individual, for it demands what no individual alone can achieve: first, a detailed, interdisciplinary investigation of the special environmental conditions of the Plains—their cycles of weather and climate, of drought and rainfall, their grassland ecosystems as a force for moderating and buffering those cycles—and, second, a probing interpretation of the cultural elements introduced here. Of course, the rubric of culture in that account will encompass the tools, the agricultural techniques, devised to make a living from nature, but more basically it must be seen to refer to the values, world views, classes, and institutions active on the Plains. Those social and mental structures have created the tools and determined how they have been used. Finally, it is in the swirling interaction of all these agencies that an adequate explanation of the Dust Bowl is to be found. Ecological history is not monocausal. It assigns neither to nature nor to culture a sole, exclusive authority over the past, its rhythms and events.[5]

JAMES MALIN AND THE CAUSES OF THE DUST BOWL

James Malin, an early advocate of the field of ecological history, attempted an explanation of the Dust Bowl experience. Or rather, he suggested a couple of explanations, both of them fragmentary and not entirely compatible with each other. Part of their weakness as history comes from Malin's bias and provinciality, which prevented him from taking a detached view of the culture he was seeking to understand. Their value, on the other hand, is that they make any simplistic alternative impossible to sustain. Though I will argue that his explanations do not satisfy the tests of evidence or logic, whether taken singly or in tandem, they still have their supporters and so require some attention.

In the first place, Malin argued that the Dust Bowl was essentially the work of nature, being caused by conditions of severe drought; that therefore it was an inevitable disaster and the Plains people its victims, not its perpetrators. In 1946 he published in the *Kansas Historical Quarterly* a series of three articles arguing that dust storms "are a part of the economy of nature and are not in themselves necessarily abnormal."[6] Painstakingly, he tried to show that, long before there was white settlement and plowing of the native sod, dust storms had blown across the region. Some of the dust storms in his examples may in fact have been due to drought and others to prairie fires, both events being capable of destroying natural vegetation and freeing the soil to move. Severe, prolonged drought can ruthlessly destroy the grassland ecosystem; it certainly did so in the distant past, might have done so to some degree in the thirties, and undoubtedly will do so again in the future. Unfortunately, however, Malin could not, from his travelers' reports and newspaper notes, establish conclusively that drought had been the sole and sufficient cause of the pre–Dust Bowl storms. Nor could he demonstrate that any of the earlier storms matched those of the 1930s in intensity or scope, though he did make it incontestable, if anyone doubted the point, that not every puff of dust had a human origin. In arguing that case, he must grant the critical point that dust storms are evidence of ecological disturbance and disequilibrium, whatever the cause. The difficulty he faced was how to assign all, or even most, of that disturbance to natural factors—and he could not, as an historian working with archival evidence, surmount it.

Scientists, climatologists, and ecologists in particular may one day be able to tell the historian why droughts happen. They may eventually be prepared to trace their contribution to wind erosion acre by acre, square mile by square mile, county by county. But neither in the thirties nor in the decade or two after was science able to give a clear, reliable answer as to whether humans or nature was responsible for the Dust Bowl. More recently, however, photographs taken from orbiting earth satellites have begun to supply the kind of data that Malin lacked—and it has not been strong for his case against nature. In the late winter of 1977, when the Plains were roiled again by high winds and dirt, when Oklahoma was stunned by its worst dust storm in twenty years, the meteorologist Edwin Kessler demonstrated precisely, with the aid of the new high-level cameras, that the source of the dust was West Texas farms, plowed and planted to seed, while neighboring New Mexico lands left in grass remained stable.[7] The dust could actually be seen picking up from one side of a fence, the plowed side, and streaming eastward. Aerial cameras have documented that it was not the ragged, pervasive specter of drought but the human mind and its ill-considered land practices—a mind marking its presence by straight fence lines—that was the main culprit in the 1970s; and the cameras show persuasively that the same was probably true in the 1930s. There can hardly be any doubt now that the destruction by plow of the grass cover on vulnerable lands—semiarid lands where the soil is loose and the horizon flat and open to winds—has been the leading reason for the devastating scale of dust storms in the twentieth century.

Malin seems to have realized, even as he was writing, the inadequacy of blaming nature for the Dust Bowl. There was clearly something more at work—in the culture of Plains people and the nation. Here is what he wrote at the end of his dust storm series:

The worst manifestations of soil blowing as related to agricultural operations occurred during the pioneering process. The country was new, the population was not settled-in on a firm and stabilized foundation in harmony with the new environment. . . . The older and better established communities usually kept their soil fairly well under control. In recent times, because of the technological revolution in agriculture and as the result of the initial exploitive stage of power farming, the period of the late 1920s was analogous in a sense to pioneering. In the light of that experience and well considered conservation measures, the worst features of those eras need not be repeated. There is no reason to assume that dust storms can be prevented altogether, because without question they were frequent and severe prior to white settlement and the plowing of the sod, but the damage incident to agricultural operations should and can be minimized by careful soil management.[8]

This conclusion took most of the wind, and much of the dust, out of his earlier argument. It was an almost backhanded way of admitting that there had been, after all, significant cultural forces at work creating the Dust Bowl disaster.

Malin's second thesis, when closely examined, had problems of its own. It began with the claim that ecological disequilibrium on the Plains and the dust storms it generated was due not merely to nature, but to the culture of a "pioneer" people. The settlement of the region was going through a youthful phase when the land was still unfamiliar to its new inhabitants. As newcomers, they did not understand what their environmental limits were nor have the techniques to overcome them. Added to their lack of knowledge was an instability in their social organization; things generally, the soil included, were out of their control. That primitive phase would give way, Malin was sure, to one of "better established communities," when the population would stay put, when farm turnover would come to an end, when generation would begin to follow generation on the same piece of land. The erosion (except for what was natural and inescapable) would come to an end. In later writings, Malin would do pathbreaking work on the phenomenon of frontier instability; in 1946 he associated such instability with the land destruction of the thirties. But there was some uncertainty in his reasoning; he was not at all sure what he meant by "pioneering." Modern power farming in the form of the tractor and the mechanized harvester had appeared on the Plains, he pointed out, immediately before the major dust storms—a state of affairs hardly found on the archetypal American frontier or in classic pioneer life. He described the plainsmen as going through an early "exploitive stage" with that technology; their culture in the late 1920s was only "analogous in a sense to pioneering."[9] With this sentence Malin shifted the terms of his indictment. Advanced technology now became the culprit, undermining at least temporarily the good judgment embedded in a traditional agronomy. But the tractor was not forever to be a bad influence, for once the revolution was assimilated a new plateau of civilization would be reached. Thus no matter what he meant by pioneering, whether he had in mind the entering of a new land or the adoption of a new technology, Malin remained optimistic. The Dust Bowl episode was a brief spot of darkness and chaos on the road to order, and nothing like it would happen again.

In the passage quoted above, conservation appears as a normal activity of a culturally mature region. It is defined not as the preservation of grassland ecosystems but as a regime of "careful management" of the soil, and it will arrive, Malin asserts, with time, with affluence, with more (not less) technology, with population equilibrium. The confidence behind these assurances resembles closely that of the so-called Progressive conservationists, as described by Samuel Hays.[10] Like Malin, they maintained that environmental destruction was a result of a pioneering culture—of poor, ignorant, unsettled people—and that it would disappear with progress. But unlike the Progressive conservationists, for whom the state was the proper agency to assume active command and move the society beyond its pioneering crudities, Malin denied that government was needed to enforce conservation. Careful management would come about inevitably with further development of the private economy.

ANOTHER EXPLANATION

Was Malin right in this confidence? Was the Dust Bowl merely a passing stage in the Plains region's cultural maturing? And is environmental adaptation a product of progress and prosperity? The answer to all those questions must be a qualified no. The "dirty thirties" were largely the outcome of a well-established, long-maturing economic culture, that of agricultural capitalism. Moreover, its recent apotheosis as agribusiness has not made it a more adaptive or stable culture, nor more preservation-minded. To be sure, in the aftermath of the thirties it has been placed under some restraint by other, countervailing forces in American culture; nonetheless, agricultural capitalism remains the dominant agency on the Plains today, and the prospect is less reassuring than Malin wanted us to believe.

Any attempt to understand the cultural roots of the Dust Bowl must begin with a scrutiny of Great Plains rural society in the late 1910s and the 1920s. Before that time there were, of course, forays by farmers into the fragile shortgrass country, the lands lying beyond the hundredth meridian; there was precedent for both agricultural settlement and widespread ecological disruption. And there was a recurrent pattern of crop disaster and farm failure, of retreating to ground representing less risk. But in the teens and twenties there occurred the critical assault on the grasslands that some have called "the Great Plow-up."[11] A brief summary of the history of those years will tell us much about how and why there was a Dust Bowl.

World War I put the American wheat farmer into a happy dither. As the Turks cut off shipments of grain from Russia, the largest producer and exporter of wheat in the world, Europeans turned to the United States, to the Great Plains, for their food supply. Wheat, it was said in Washington and in the western provinces, would help win the war by feeding the Allies and toughening their resolve. When the war ended, Europe for a while still needed food imports, and by 1919 America, under government-set goals, harvested 74 million acres of wheat—yielding 952 million bushels in all, a 35 percent increase over the 1909–1913 average, and providing 330 million bushels for shipment abroad. Most of this gain came in winter wheat, the standard variety grown over most of the southern Plains, which [was] planted in the fall and cut in the following midsummer. From 1914 to 1919, Kansas, Colorado, Nebraska, Oklahoma, and Texas had expanded their wheatlands by 13.5 million acres, mainly by plowing up 11 million acres of native grass.[12]

The Great Plow-up, initially provoked by the wartime mobilization of the national economy, might have been expected to pass with victory. Such was not to be the case. The war integrated the Plains farmers more thoroughly than ever before into the national economy— into its network of banks, railroads, mills, implement manufacturers, energy companies—and, moreover, integrated them into an international market system. When the war was over, none of that integration loosened; on the contrary, Plains farmers in the 1920s found themselves more enmeshed than ever, as they competed fiercely with each other to pay off their loans and keep intact what they had achieved. By the mid-twenties that integration did begin to pay off; having squeezed through the postwar depression, many Plains farmers began to rake in substantial fortunes. There was, for instance, Ida Watkins, the "wheat queen" of Haskell County, Kansas, farming two thousand acres; in 1926, she made a profit on her wheat of $76,000, more than President Coolidge's salary. Down in the Texas Panhandle the movie mogul Hickman Price set about to show plainsmen what modern commercial farming could really do, how it could apply the large-scale business methods of Henry Ford to the mass production of wheat. His factory farm stretched over fifty-four square miles and required twenty-five combines at harvest time. In every part of the Plains there were pacesetters like this man and woman who fervently believed in capitalistic enterprise and sought to apply it to the unproductive grasslands. These two were among the largest and most successful entrepreneurs; the less aggressive were forced by the competitive marketplace to follow their lead.[13]

The mobility of Malin's machines not only allowed these large-scale enterprises to develop but also encouraged widely dispersed holdings. It was now possible to drive one's equipment to another county or even to another state, plant wheat, return home in a few weeks, and wait until the next spring before visiting the land again—in other words, to become a "suitcase farmer." This was particularly attractive to wheat speculators, many of whom were city bankers, druggists, or teachers; they put in their seed, went back to their regular work, and waited to see what would happen to the Chicago grain futures. In a year of high prices they might make a killing, paying for an entire farm with one crop, then selling the land at a tidy sum to another fast-buck chaser. Not all suitcase farmers were looking for such quick returns; some of them were more concerned about their investment's long-range security.[14] But the machine made possible, as it made common, an exploitative relationship with the earth—a bond predominately commercial—so that the land became little more than a form of capital that must be made to pay as much as possible.

All across the flat open spaces the tractors steadily plowed away, especially in the second half of the twenties and up until the very eve of the dust storms. Occasionally they even worked at night, their headlights moving like fireflies in the grass. Near Perryton, Texas, H. B. Urban, an altogether typical wheat farmer of the day, arrived in 1929 and cranked up his two International tractors; each day he and his hired man broke out twenty acres of native prairie, until virtually his whole section of land was stripped of its grama and buffalo grass. In thirteen southwestern Kansas counties, where there had been two million crop acres in 1925, there were three million in 1930. Altogether in that period farmers tore up the vegetation on 5,260,000 acres in the southern Plains—an area nearly seven times as large as Rhode Island. Most of the freshly plowed ground went into wheat, so that over the decade of the twenties the production of that cereal jumped three hundred percent, creating a severe glut by 1931. That, in sum, was the environmental history immediately preceding the dirty thirties. When the black blizzards began to roll across the region in 1935, one-third of the Dust Bowl region—thirty-three million acres—lay naked, ungrassed, and vulnerable to the winds.[15]

This Great Plow-up was not dictated by Malthusian population pressures, which in many parts of the world have been responsible for decisions to put marginal land into food production. Nor was it exclusively or primarily drought that disrupted the ecological system of the Plains; it was humans and the economic culture pushing them ahead. Nor was their push carried out in ignorance or inexperience. For over a century men had been coming into the shortgrass country, observing it, and writing about its risks. For a half-century before the Dust Bowl, cattlemen had trailed their animals to railheads there, and farmers had repeatedly tried breaking the sod to make houses and crops, leaving a record of devastating reverses as well as some years of bounty. Furthermore, by the second and third decades of the twentieth century the region could by no means be labeled an intellectual frontier; an extensive scientific literature was available on it, and the hard realities of the country had permeated widely into common consciousness.[16] All of this information was almost studiously disregarded in the 1920s plow-up. To describe those who did that disregarding as backward, primitive folk, as a hard-living rabble of frontiersmen, simply will not do. On the contrary, they were, especially the leaders among them, people with access to capital and expertise; some of them were in fact men and women of education and broad sophistication. The historical problem to be solved is why such people used their capital as they did, why they demanded and quickly deployed the new machinery, why they chose to hear what they did from the past and present, shutting out what did not appeal to them—what, in other words, they were after and why. If we call them hungry, then we must be careful to specify what they were hungry for. If we call them pioneers, then we must go further to distinguish them from other pioneers in national and world history.

PLAINS ENTREPRENEURIALISM

Essentially, the Great Plow-up was the work of a generation of aggressive entrepreneurs, imbued with the values and world view of American agricultural capitalism. They smelled an opportunity to create a profit on the Plains and, in the classic way of entrepreneurs, they charged out to create that profit—to derive from the land both personal wealth and status. No matter that others had failed or that the risks were high; these entrepreneurs were convinced they would succeed, as indeed they did in the short run. For a few years at least they made the region say money instead of grass. Throughout the twenties a scattering of reporters came to watch them succeed, writing up their achievements in glowing prose for newspapers and magazines. Many of these farmers had once been lowly clodhoppers; now they were making their mark on the world, were getting celebrated as "kings" and "queens" of wheat. And justly so, for the food that

poured from the erstwhile grasslands was, if the environmental costs
are disregarded, a positive gain for the nation and the world as well as
for the entrepreneurs. They heard little criticism. Standing behind
them all the way, trumpeting their contribution to humanity repeatedly so that it was not lost on the American public or on the farmers,
was a vast chorus of bankers, millers, railroad executives, and government officials, all of them looking forward themselves to sharing
in the abundance being created. It is, of course, the nature of entrepreneurs, in agriculture as in industry, to disregard the voices of caution and criticism, to show themselves venturesome where others have
been ruined, and to court disaster.

Entrepreneurialism was not a new cultural innovation on the
Plains. It had been around, gathering force, seeking territory for its
expression, for several centuries—indeed it had been the animating
ethos of the economic culture of capitalism since its rise to hegemony.[17]
Out of that imported cultural heritage we can single out several influential ideas about nature and farming, all of them endlessly reiterated
and repeatedly acted on by Europeans and Americans long before
anyone had contemplated plowing the high Plains. Each of these would
be an idea with bleak consequences in the 1930s.

First, the agricultural entrepreneur stood for the idea that the
land's true and only end was to become a commodity—something to
be used, bought, and sold for human gain. The land itself, divided into
property and made an object of speculation, was the first part of nature to be commodified by this culture, then came its products. That
drive toward commodification was never uncontested or universally
accepted. On the Plains there were, as there had been elsewhere, many
rival cultural values present; often these had been brought over from
Old World farming or religious traditions, or from some obscurely
intertwined, peasant-grounded combination of the two.[18] These rivals
for moral authority found their way into much of the literature and
art of the region; into, for example, the novels of Willa Cather, who
spoke often of the mysterious spiritual power of the Plains—of an
indwelling presence in nature there, one particularly accessible to many
women and to recent immigrants.[19] But it is safe to say that the typical wheat entrepreneur did not read Cather or put much stock in peas-

ant modes of thought. None of that, he was quick to insist, was ratio-
nally compatible with his drive to dominate and commodify.

Second, entrepreneurialism was part and parcel of the social ideal
of economic individualism. It deliberately made, with no end of para-
dox, the pursuit of private wealth into a social ethic. The implications
in that individualism for the ecological communities of the Plains were
predictable: farmers would not be expected to accommodate their
ambitions to the whole of nature, or recognize and use those ecological interdependencies for their own survival. Likewise, they would,
and did, reject any restraint on their economic freedom to get what
they could from the Plains in their own terms now, in their own generation. All others, future and present, must look out for themselves.
Here again Malin was simply wrong; it was the entrepreneurial culture, not frontier life, that was destructive to communal bondedness
and social stability.[20]

Third, risk was treated in this economic culture almost as a positive value, as a needed spur to success. Without risk, there could be
no gain. This idea has been emphasized earlier; what should be added
now is the insistent search by the bearers of entrepreneurial culture
to find ways to pass the risks on to someone else. Since they saw
themselves as taking chances that, if profitable, would enrich the entire society, entrepreneurs hoped that others would pay some of their
costs. In the case of the Dust Bowl those costs included the damage
that the dust storms did to health and property and the rehabilitation
they necessitated. More than two billion dollars was spent by New
Deal agencies in the thirties to keep the farmers of the Plains region
in business.[21] As risk-spreaders, these federal programs signified the
maturation of the national capitalist economy: the coming of a new era
when entrepreneurial drives need not entail such severe penalties for
failure. Back in the 1890s, when little outside assistance had existed,
the Plains settler had learned that he had either to adapt to nature or
leave. The generation that came to plow in the twenties and ate their
own dust in the thirties successfully evaded much of that disciplining.
They lived in a more humane and protective age that allowed them
considerable economic freedom while removing some of the old anxiety and the bitterness of defeat.

Bring these ideas, this economic culture, into a volatile environment where intermittent drought was a fact of life—and the outcome could hardly be anything different from the dirty thirties. That such an outcome would seem to be unavoidable is clear in the famous government report, *The Future of the Great Plains* (1936). Its chief author, the economist Lewis Cecil Gray of the Resettlement Administration, one of the country's leading agricultural historians, made an analysis of the cultural roots of the Dust Bowl similar to the one suggested here, of "the attitudes of mind" inherent in an expansionary, entrepreneurial society.[22] The evidence was clear to Gray that the disaster could not be wholly laid at the door of nature, of imperfect technique, of inadequate knowledge, or of "frontier society." As in the case of that other great tragedy of the decade, the Depression, the Dust Bowl was a crisis made and delivered by socially destructive forces in modern American culture.

CONCLUSION

In 1946 James Malin vigorously rejected Gray's cultural analysis of the Plains debacle, and he was not alone. His was a common response in the region, somewhat so in the thirties and unabashedly so by the time he wrote. A resurgent national economy, a new war raging in Europe, the success of the federal relief programs in helping people hang on until better times—all these elements made deeper critical inquiry unpopular. Most important of all, nature contributed to the renewal of self-assurance. The return of rains, accompanied by bumper wheat crops in the early 1940s, demonstrated that the environmental damage had not been permanent—and, indeed, it has been difficult until the present nuclear age for humans anywhere to inflict irreversible destruction on the earth and its fabric of life. Nature has extraordinary powers of recuperation, a fact that has been proved many, many times in the long geological history of the Great Plains. When the healing comes, it is easy and altogether human to suppress the memory of misjudgment and loss; to revert to old, familiar ways and deny responsibility. That was precisely what Malin hoped would happen: a renewal of faith in the culture of entrepreneurial farming.

Any effort to find a different path for the Plains he harshly identified with "totalitarianism."[23]

Despite assurances that the Plains would achieve a mature, agricultural capitalism in the post–World War II period; that the land and society could come under firm, enlightened control; that no radical reform in the culture would be necessary, the region's recent ecological history has seen some disturbing chapters. High crop prices and great profit expectations have again and again produced waves of profit-seeking enterprise when grasslands have been destroyed to make more crops. In the aftermath of each of those waves have come new cycles of dust storms, some of them as grueling as anything in the thirties. Then, so the familiar pattern goes, the blowing dust brings in its train warnings from federal soil scientists, larger budget requests from federal agencies, and talk of new state and national laws to reform the culture. Perhaps these frequent replays of the thirties have produced a cumulative reform of the culture. One might argue, though not precisely in the terms Malin did, that the capitalistic agriculture has in fact been substantially altered since the 1930s; that it no longer enjoys the power and influence it once held in the region; that today it is strictly hedged about with governmental authority; and that these reforms, these countervailing pressures, have successfully prevented another Dust Bowl from occurring.[24] It will take a few serious, prolonged droughts to test thoroughly the accuracy of such an argument. Very recent evidence, however, indicates that the entrepreneur is still around, still sitting tall in the tractor seat—and the old danger is not over.

In the late spring and early summer of 1983 the national news again announced the impending threat of western wind erosion. For example, *Time* reported that wheat operators had torn up the sod on 6.4 million acres of marginal grasslands in Montana and Colorado. Depressed livestock prices and favorable federal wheat support programs were responsible for this frenzy. "I want to make a buck," was the way one Montanan expressed his motives to *Time*. He and his neighbors had broken 250,000 acres of grazing land over the preceding decade. "We face the possibility of another Dust Bowl," said the executive vice president of the Montana association of conservation districts. So serious was the threat that the conservative senator from Colorado, William Armstrong, with backing from the Reagan administration and the Montana Stockgrowers' Association, introduced a "sod-buster" bill that would deny federal payments of any kind for crops grown on highly erodible land. And a Colorado county began contemplating the issuing of permits by its commissioners before any more sod could be plowed up.[25] Unmistakably, leaders of the region were being forced to admit that they did not yet have sufficient public authority to restrain risk-taking entrepreneurs, nor could they depend on capitalistic maturity to achieve soil conservation. Whether they now had the will to establish that authority remained to be decided.

The ecological history of the future Great Plains is still to be accomplished, still to find its historians. When they come to write it, they will have a subject of international significance, for these days the dry lands of the earth are everywhere under pressure and scrutiny. In that future history, as in past accounts, we may expect the key issue to be the fit of the Plains's economic culture to its environment. And we can predict that historians will return often to the dirty thirties to understand what that culture has been and what it is in the process of becoming.

NOTES

1. Quoted in David A. Dary, *The Buffalo Book* (New York: Avon, 1974), p. 4.
2. This sentence is a paraphrase of Lewis Mumford, *The Power of the Pentagon* (New York: Harcourt, Brace, Jovanovich, Harvest ed., 1970), p. 393. For a discussion of the new ecological history, see my article, "Nature as Natural History: An Essay on Theory and Method," *Pacific Historical Review* 53 (February 1984): 1–19.
3. Both of Walter Prescott Webb's major works, *The Great Plains* (Boston: Ginn, 1931) and *The Great Frontier* (Boston: Houghton Mifflin, 1952), are landmark studies in the environmental impact on culture.
4. James C. Malin, "Ecology and History," *Scientific Monthly* 70 (May 1950): 295–298.

5. A useful discussion of this problem is in John Bennett's *The Ecological Transition: Cultural Anthropology and Human Adaptation* (New York: Pergamon, 1976), esp. 162–167, 209–242.

6. James C. Malin, "Dust Storms: Part One, 1850–1860," *Kansas Historical Quarterly* 14 (May 1946): 129–144.

7. Edwin Kessler, Dorothy Alexander, and Joseph Rarick, "Duststorms From the U.S. High Plains in Late Winter 1977—Search for Cause and Implications," *Proceedings of the Oklahoma Academy of Science* 58 (1978): 116–128.

8. James C. Malin, "Dust Storms: Part Three, 1881–1890," *Kansas Historical Quarterly* 14 (November 1946): 391–413.

9. Ibid. The distinction between pioneering and entrepreneurialism is commonly obscured in American historical writing as it is in popular mythology; indeed, they are often conflated, especially in the West, producing a "cowboy capitalism." Malin's writing is replete with the confusion.

10. See Samuel Hays, *Conservation and the Gospel of Efficiency: The Progressive Conservation Movement, 1890–1920* (Cambridge: Harvard University Press, 1959).

11. See, for example, Vance Johnson, *Heaven's Tableland: The Dust Bowl Story* (New York: Farrar, Straus, 1947), chap. 12.

12. A. B. Genung, "Agriculture in the World War Period," in U.S. Department of Agriculture, *Farmers in a Changing World* (Washington, [D.C.: U.S. Department of Agriculture], 1940), p. 280–284; Lloyd Jorgenson, "Agricultural Expansion Into the Semiarid Lands of the West North Central States During the First World War," *Agricultural History* 23 (January 1949): 30–40; *Kansas City Star*, 19 April 1935.

13. Johnson, *Heaven's Tableland*, 136–137; *Topeka Capital*, 3 August 1926; *Panhandle Herald* (Guymon, Okla.), 13 December 1928. See also Garry Nall, "Specialization and Expansion: Panhandle Farming in the 1920s," *Panhandle-Plains Historical Review* 47 (1974): 66–67. The largest operator of all on the Plains was located in Montana: see Hiram Drache, "Thomas B. Campbell—The Plower of the Plains," *Agricultural History* 51 (January 1977): 78–91. Campbell's ambition was to be a "manufacturer of wheat"; he farmed, with House of Morgan backing, over 100,000 acres, most of it on Indian reservations.

14. Leslie Hewes, in *The Suitcase-Farming Frontier: A Study in the Historical Geography of the Central Great Plains* (Lincoln: University of Nebraska Press, 1973), gives a thorough accounting of this phenomenon, and one strongly supportive of its entrepreneurial characteristics.

15. H. B. Urban, transcribed interview, 15 June 1974, Panhandle-Plains Historical Museum, Canyon, TX; *The Dust Bowl*, U.S. Department of Agriculture, Editorial Reference Series No. 7 (Washington, D.C.[: U.S. De-

partment of Agriculture], 1940), 44; Clifford Hope, "Kansas in the 1930s," *Kansas Historical Quarterly* 36 (Spring 1970), 2–3; Johnson, *Heaven's Tableland*, 146.

16. A number of excellent studies of popular understanding of the Plains have been published by geographers and historians; see, for example, Brian Blouet and Merlin Lawson, eds., *Images of the Plains: The Role of Human Nature in Settlement* (Lincoln: University of Nebraska Press, 1975).

17. Entrepreneurialism is essential to all forms of agricultural capitalism, whether it be potato farming in Maine or rice growing in California. But the strength of this drive may, of course, vary from time to time and place to place. Not all of American agriculture had been so unstable or risk-taking as that of the semiarid Plains.

18. Frederick Luebke, "Ethnic Group Settlement on the Great Plains," *Western Historical Quarterly* 8 (October 1977): 405–30.

19. One thinks, for example, of the Swedish immigrant Alexandra Bergson in Willa Cather's *O Pioneers!* (Boston: Houghton Mifflin, 1913). Though eager to acquire more and more property, Bergson responds to the land with a powerful love and yearning. "It seemed beautiful to her," writes Cather, "rich and strong and glorious. Her eyes drank in the breadth of it, until her tears blinded her" (p. 65).

20. A provocative discussion of this set of ideas is C. B. Macpherson's *The Political Theory of Possessive Individualism: Hobbes to Locke* (Oxford: Oxford University Press, 1962).

21. This figure includes, in addition to ecological restoration efforts, all programs of farm price supports, rural relief, and public works expenditures.

22. Great Plains Committee, *The Future of the Great Plains*, U.S. House Document 144, 75th Congress (Washington, D.C.[: U.S. Government Printing Office], 1937), 63–67.

23. James C. Malin, *The Grassland of North America: Prolegomena to Its History* (Lawrence, Kansas: privately published, 1956), p. 335.

24. As John Borchert has written, the flurry of federal soil and water conservation programs since the thirties has "encouraged a widespread belief that, though there will be future droughts, there need be no future dust bowl." See "The Dust Bowl in the 1970s," *Annals of the Association of American Geographers* 61 (March 1971): 13.

25. *Time* (27 June 1983): 27.

DUST BOWL HISTORIOGRAPHY
Harry C. McDean

In the late 1930s, Undersecretary of Agriculture Milburn Lincoln Wilson organized "Travelling Great Plains Schools," culminating three decades of research and reform work in the Great Plains. The schools brought hundreds of rural social scientists together with scores of federal and state policymakers. The schools were broken into two sections, one dedicated to the southern Plains and the other to the northern. Those who attended spent several weeks making their way through the Plains, with care taken to differentiate problems particular to each of the two regions. In the southern Plains, the school spent several days examining the problems specific to the Dust Bowl area that Wilson's staff clearly delineated on maps provided the students. As the maps showed, the term *Dust Bowl* designated a specific region in the Great Plains, including northeastern New Mexico, southeastern Colorado, southwestern Kansas, and the panhandles of Texas and Oklahoma.[1]

The schools were aided by agronomists, who demonstrated to the students the difference between the soils in the Dust Bowl and those found elsewhere in the Plains. Here were soil groups whose configuration was distinctive: most notably, the Dust Bowl had extensive reddish-chestnut soils that bordered upon brown soils. Although both soil groups were susceptible to depletion, erosion, and blowing, the reddish-chestnut soils were especially sensitive to cultural mistreatment.

At the schools, historians and rural sociologists also informed the students of their research in the Dust Bowl. The work of Jesse T. Sanders, Robert T. McMillan, and Otis Duncan in the social and the agricultural history of the Dust Bowl especially explained why its soils were mistreated and how that mistreatment generated the great dust storms of the 1930s. Although this history was complex, the students learned how cultural traits of Dust Bowl residents encouraged excesses by many of its farmers in the 1920s. For while other Great Plains farmers worked radically to revise their farm operations in order to conserve the soil, those in the Dust Bowl area thoughtlessly devised dry farming techniques that allowed them to put under the plow those soils with high susceptibility to windblowing. As a result, new dry farming techniques were applied in the 1920s, destroying the natural, regenerative process that had kept Dust Bowl soils fertile and intact.[2]

Students also learned from the social scientists that the application of the new destructive farming techniques was furthered by several socioeconomic phenomena peculiar to the Dust Bowl in the 1920s. One was the tendency of townsfolk to buy or lease raw land and use the new dry farming techniques to cultivate it. They planned to farm only as long as it was profitable to do so, hoping that all would go well. Another farming development distinctive to the Dust Bowl area in the 1920s was the migratory nature of much of its population. Wage and day laborers routinely took up tenant farming during slack times. Viewing such "farming" as interim employment, they were willing to farm land that was susceptible to depletion. Although they did not destroy the land wherever they went—for they ranged into Plains areas whose soil was not so sensitive and routinely wandered into non-Plains states like Arkansas—they helped to create the farming culture that violated the tenuous soils of the Dust Bowl.

Social scientists like Duncan, Sanders, and McMillan provided the students of the schools with several possible reasons why these developments were peculiar to the Dust Bowl area during the 1920s. One was that only in the southern Plains was there considerable part-time mining, lumbering, and oil work available in the 1920s—hence the migratory nature of much of its population. Because this transient population felt no sense of permanence or belonging, it expressed little interest in the application of soil conservation measures designed to create a permanently successful farm population in the region. Another reason was that other Great Plains states had opened their land to cultivation in an earlier day and those settling it had failed and abandoned their land during the great northern Plains drought of the 1917–23 era. Hence, northern Plains townsfolk already knew what their counterparts in the Dust Bowl region would learn in the 1930s—that farming of sensitive soil groups can have disastrous consequences during times of drought.

The goal of the "Travelling Great Plains Schools" was to pinpoint problems specific to precise areas within the Plains and to suggest resolutions to them. Since they were traveling schools, subsequent meetings were organized. These brought together leading economists, farm management experts, historians, rural social scientists, meteorologists, climatologists, astronomers, astrophysicists, geologists, ecologists, dendrochronologists, anthropologists, archaeologists, and geographers. Their mission was to study "to what extent science can produce a program for land use" in specific areas of the Plains, "which, if put into operation, will bring harmony between man and nature."[3]

DUST BOWL SCHIZOPHRENIC HISTORIOGRAPHY

The extent to which these experts succeeded in this mission is difficult to assess. Indeed, the question proves the subject of lively debate among modern scholars, especially historians, who write on the Dust Bowl. Yet, in spite of the robustness of the debate, modern Dust Bowl historians have accurately captured in their works most of the aforementioned facts about the Dust Bowl. Unfortunately, one cannot say the same about some of those who write survey textbooks in American history, for they fail to grasp even the most elementary facts about the Dust Bowl.

As a result, modern Dust Bowl history is schizophrenic. Even the most basic characteristic of the Dust Bowl—its geographic boundary—has two different compositions. The textbook writers locate the Dust Bowl in a variety of places where the Dust Bowl history books do not: in the Great Plains generally, or in states outside the Plains, or often anywhere that the dust blew in the thirties. Most commonly, these writers locate the Dust Bowl by backtracking the "Okies" to their origins, at least insofar as they were described by John Steinbeck in *The Grapes of Wrath*.[4]

Such inaccurate and vague boundary descriptions become more pronounced when the textbook writers seem automatically to associate drought conditions with the Dust Bowl. Bernard Bailyn and associates tell their readers that improved prices for farm goods in the mid-1930s were "caused by a cruel drought on the Great Plains, choking the farmers in vast clouds of topsoil that swept across the region." Others say that the drought and its corresponding dust storms were even more pervasive. Stephen Thernstrom contends that farm price increases in the mid-thirties "were partly the result of the great droughts and windstorms and turned many wheat fields into little Saharas." Arthur Link and associates never find a Dust Bowl in their text, contending instead that "a severe drought in the Middle West and Southwest cooperated with the AAA [Agricultural Adjustment Act] to reduce farm production." More surprising is the text of George B. Tindall, which covers with precision the regional planning aspects of the New Deal but fails to find a Dust Bowl. Indeed, in the absence of any appraisal of this area, he contends that the creation of the Soil Conservation Service in 1935 "went far to heal the scars of erosion and the plague of dust storms," wherever they were.[5]

Obviously, these historians live in a different world from that of M. L. Wilson. They seem to view Great Plains regions differently than either Wilson or the specialists in Dust Bowl history. Worse yet, these same historians miss the most important point made by both contemporary social scientists of the 1930s and recent Dust Bowl historians—that the Dust Bowl was not a natural disaster; it was a disaster caused by what people did to nature.

Although every old-timer in the Great Plains realizes that dust has blown there since only God knows when, both the contemporary rural social scientists and recent Dust Bowl historians have shown that a special set of conditions caused the dust to blow massively during one particular time in an exact location. The intent of their work, in fact, was to reveal the complexity of natural, human, and technical events that combined to cause the great dust storms in the Dust Bowl.

Clearly, our textbook writers are ignorant of their conclusions. Why is this? There are several possible explanations.

One reason might be that they have been deceived by books or articles that have Dust Bowl in their titles but whose texts cover other subject matter. One such study was favorably reviewed in spite of its misleading title: Walter Stein's *California and the Dust Bowl Migration*.[6] Stein neither tells his reader where the Dust Bowl region was nor does he distinguish its problems or its migrants from those in the other areas. To add to the mystery, Stein contends that the migration was but part of a larger migration from the Great Plains which began in the 1920s. To him, "The Great Plains tier of the United States embraces five states from the Dakotas on the north to Texas on the South."[7] One wonders which of the remaining seven Great Plains states are recognized as such by Stein. Stein also views the migrants from a perspective different from that of contemporary rural social scientists and recent Dust Bowl historians. For although he concedes that the dust storms were "a man-made catastrophe," he sees a network of natural, economic, technical, and political conditions converging to create victims—poor, defenseless, Dust Bowl migrants who fled to California.[8] In fact, it was Stein's and Steinbeck's "victims" who did the victimizing; at least some of them helped form the farming culture that created the ecological disaster called the Dust Bowl.

In defense of Stein and more certainly of Steinbeck, one must understand that their works appeared before most of the recent histories on the Dust Bowl were published. Although these two authors could not benefit from that research, our recent textbook writers could have. Why have these historians failed to balance off the work of Stein and Steinbeck against these recently published Dust Bowl histories? Perhaps their inability to do so stems from misperceptions about the region encouraged by the specialists' varied approaches to it.

For example, most historical treatments of the drought of the 1930s fail to distinguish the Dust Bowl from other drought areas. Here, historians of the drought tend to lump all problems, issues, policies, and programs into one package; and treat them as a whole. Therefore, for anyone but a specialist in Great Plains studies, reading such work can only suggest that any conclusions that apply in one area of the Plains necessarily apply in another. Several otherwise superior articles on the drought in the thirties encourage the thought that wherever one looks in the Great Plains one encounters similar problems and issues. C. Robert Lambert's "The Drought Cattle Purchase, 1934–35: Problems and Complaints," Van L. Perkins's "New Dealers and the Drought of 1934," and Mary Hargreaves's "Land-Use Planning in Response to Drought: The Experience of the Thirties"—all stress the federal policies designed to meet problems widespread in the drought areas at the expense of highlighting problems peculiar to specific areas in the Plains.[9]

Of course, this tendency has been counterbalanced by work that does distinguish the problems of particular areas in the Plains. For example, as early as 1979, Theodore Saloutos, in his article "The New Deal and Farm Policy in the Great Plains," notes that "in the Dust Bowl of the southern Great Plains there was a great need for checking wind erosion, especially on nuisance lands owned by absentee owners."[10] Still, Saloutos's work and that of others suffers from the possibility of misinterpretation.[11] True, these works do distinguish clearly the areas in the Plains that they are about. Yet their purpose was to examine the origins and the character of broad federal policies and programs in the Great Plains. Thus it is fair to say that recent "drought" and Great Plains histories tend to dim the distinctive features in the Dust Bowl.

But there is yet another possible reason why our textbook writers misunderstand the Dust Bowl. Perhaps it is because the bias of some Dust Bowl historians has helped create misperceptions about it in the minds of the textbook writers.

PAUL BONNIFIELD'S DUST BOWL

In fact, a major misconception of Stein and Steinbeck provides the basis upon which Paul Bonnifield—the author of the first of three major histories on the Dust Bowl to appear in recent years—builds his work.[12] Although this book should not misguide anyone interested in the region's boundaries (it provides accurate maps of the area), it advances vigorously one of Stein's misinterpretations: that those who left the Dust Bowl were victims of government policy. It even goes beyond Stein to maintain that those who remained in the Dust Bowl were also victimized by the government. This prejudice against the policies of the federal government is argued in an unusual but nonetheless compelling way. Bonnifield maintains there is ample evidence to indicate that, had the migrants not been forced off their farms by government policy, they would have worked out farming systems to prevent future Dust Bowls while earning standards of living comparable to those of other Americans.

Bonnifield's approach is intriguing. He begins by showing his readers that not only is drought commonplace in the history of the Plains, but so is the dust storm. Bonnifield dates dust storms back to the 1850s, noting that the editor of the *Kansas Free State* believed there was a "normal blowing season" in Kansas that "makes anyone exposed to it as 'sooty' as a collier." In discussing subsequent droughts and dust-blowing situations in the true Dust Bowl region, Bonnifield shows that those who didn't leave the region "adapted to the new conditions and continued their business." Moreover, there always existed "a few hardy souls who moved in to continue the task of opening the country."[13]

With this stage in Dust Bowl history set in place, Bonnifield is able to uncover a historical plot. Arguing that "hard times were not new to the old-timers," Bonnifield shows how in the 1930s Dust Bowl "farmers were making genuine efforts to meet the crisis caused by wind and drought." He finds farmers like Charles T. Peacock, who designed a machine that formed "a lister row and placed check dams at regular intervals." These and similar farm innovations demonstrate, says Bonnifield, that "the people of the dust bowl were not defeated, poverty-ridden people without hope. They were builders for tomorrow. During those hard years they continued to build their churches, their businesses, their schools, their colleges, their communities. They grew closer to God and fonder of the land. Hard years were common in their part, but the future belonged to those who were ready to seize the moment."[14]

Given these conditions and attitudes, why then did anyone leave the Dust Bowl? Because "despite statements to the contrary, the federal government was involved in removal and steps were being taken to force people out. It was planned to return the majority of the land to grazing under government control." And who specifically designed this plot? Apparently, the schemers were Lewis C. Gray of the National Resources Board, Hugh Bennett of the Soil Conservation Service, and M. L. Wilson of the USDA [U.S. Department of Agriculture]. Bonnifield particularly blames Wilson who, as undersecretary of agriculture, "had several years' experience in promoting his program [and] was in a position to carry out his concept of [a] rational land-use program on a grand scale."[15]

What was Wilson's most lethal weapon in the scheme? The Soil Conservation Districts Act, which, says Bonnifield, the farmers in the Dust Bowl viewed as a "scheme of reorganizing their society and drastically changing their land ownership." The result, he said, was that "they dealt a big blow to the scheme . . . by voting down the proposed Soil Conservation Districts." This was important, says Bonnifield, in part because it was the chief weapon in Wilson's arsenal to redesign life in the Dust Bowl. The districts, had they been created, would also have given the Soil Conservation Service greater power in the Dust Bowl, and no sensible farmer wanted that. It would have been particularly bad, says Bonnifield, because "not a single new implement or technique of preventing wind erosion was developed by the Soil Conservation Service." What farmer would want to work with that organization? More important, "The advancements by the farmers in developing new implements and techniques were not emulated by the Soil Conservation Service." Finally, their methods were costly.[16]

Anyone who finds Bonnifield's conclusions convincing is cautioned to read other recently published articles and books on the Dust Bowl as well as studies from the thirties.[17] Should Bonnifield himself read this body of work, he would then understand that Wilson believed that federal, state, and local experts needed to work closely with local farmers to recognize and resolve problems specific to their farm area. To the extent there was any grand design, in the Soil Conservation Districts Act, that was it.

Bonnifield's conspiracy theory aside, the strength in his book builds from its detailed discussion of how "the farmers did take unnecessary chances and in general were careless about protection against wind erosion" in the Dust Bowl. In spite of the advances in "scientific dry-land farming [that] were designed to conserve moisture," Bonnifield shows why "the dry surface of moist soil will blow" anyway. Therefore, to stop the blowing "it was necessary to develop techniques and technology aimed specifically at wind erosion."[18] Thus, even the harshest critic of New Deal planning agrees with other recent Dust Bowl historians on one point: the great Dust Bowl of the thirties was created by people, not by drought and wind.

DONALD WORSTER'S DUST BOWL

Although Donald Worster's history of the Dust Bowl, the second of three major books to appear in recent years, agrees with Bonnifield on this one point, it does so for reasons that stem from a bias antithetical to Bonnifield's.[19] It is Worster's belief that the Dust Bowl grew out of, and was worsened by, the inability or unwillingness of the federal government to curtail the exploitive tendencies of capitalist farmers.

It is possible that Worster's bias unwittingly contributed to our textbook writers' misconception of the Dust Bowl. For all the merits of his book, which won the Bancroft Prize, Worster blurs the distinctiveness of the Dust Bowl region through his strenuous effort to convince his reader that American culture created the people who caused the Dust Bowl. As Worster puts it, there "are ecological values taught by the capitalist ethos." These values, he says, created the Dust Bowl. "It came about because the expansionary energy of the United States had finally encountered a volatile, marginal land, destroying the delicate ecological balance that had evolved there." What did it was not the people's plows, but their "social system, a set of values, an economic order," or "those elements of capitalism."[20]

This proposition is perhaps the most engaging of any presented by recent Dust Bowl historians. And the history Worster weaves around this line of reasoning is presented so compactly that one feels compelled to believe it. Yet Worster's panoramic view of American culture and the value it places on exploitation tends to compromise

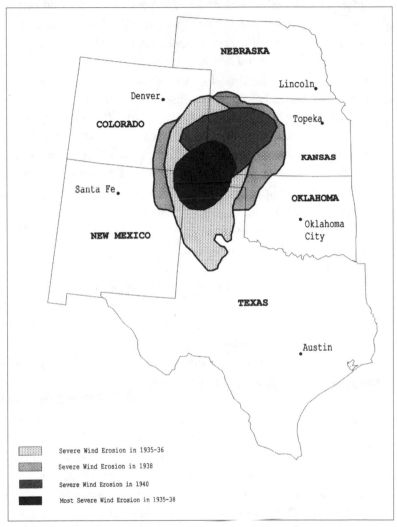

Extent of the Dust Bowl, 1935–1940. From Donald Worster, *Dust Bowl*, 1988. Map by Michael Shambaugh-Miller.

his work. For he carries his message beyond the boundaries of his study and encourages the thought that Dust Bowls might occur virtually anywhere, regardless of the character of the people and of the land.

Worster's cataclysmic view of American culture is pushed relentlessly upon the reader. Contending that Americans have "a greater
resource hunger than others, greater eagerness to take risks, and less
capacity for restraint," Worster concludes that they made a marginal
land into a Dust Bowl. The Dust Bowl was "the inevitable outcome of
a culture that deliberately, self-consciously, set itself that task of domi-
nating and exploiting the land for all it was worth. The entirety of the
Great Plains is threatened: "the region," warns Worster, "may be in
the most serious ecological trouble it has ever seen." And anyone who
thinks he is safe because he farms not only outside the Great Plains
but outside the United States altogether should take heed of this warning: the expansion of American farming culture "to other nations has
already begun to create a new chain of environmental disasters."[21]

Worster's forebodings aside, his approach persuades his readers
to overlook the fact that in the Dust Bowl there were natural conditions specific to that area. Moreover, it does not permit the reader to
understand that these natural conditions encountered a particular farm
culture—likewise specific to the area—in the 1920s and the 1930s.
And that, together, they created the Dust Bowl.

Rather, Worster's approach leads the reader to ask: "Why study
the Dust Bowl at all?" After all, is not American farm culture headed
toward the "inevitable," the creation of wide-spread dust bowls and
"ecological disasters"? For, as Worster himself says, the purpose of
the book is "to explain why the world is facing a future of dust bowls."[22]

Yet this conclusion ignores some of the research done in the Plains
by rural social scientists during the 1920s and early 1930s.[23] For example, in Oklahoma these researchers found a phenomenon that pro-
foundly affected the farm economy of their state—a "culture of
migratoriness." As Sheila Manes describes this phenomenon, it was a
"peculiar [to this specific area], impoverishing system . . . that moved
mostly locally, but also in slightly wider circles, back and forth" among
several southwestern states, including the area that became the Dust
Bowl.[24] Not only was it made up of numerous workers who viewed
farming as part-time or interim employment, but its volume ebbed
and flowed with the tide of nonagricultural work in the area. Hence,

Manes's work (and that of others) shows how this migratoriness combined with other cultural traits peculiar to those who farmed in this region to help create the ecological disaster called the Dust Bowl; farm conditions in the Dust Bowl were not only peculiar to this one specific area but also to a specific period in time, roughly between the two World Wars.[25]

Moreover, these conditions and the farming practices that created them were clearly out of step with the vanguard of farming systems being developed elsewhere in the Plains by the pure scientists and social scientists who worked for the experiment stations, the agricultural colleges, or the USDA itself. Their scholarly publications during the twenties and thirties help to explain why a Dust Bowl never occurred elsewhere in the Plains. They demonstrate clearly how some Plains states were far more attentive than others to recognizing and resolving their specific farm problems.[26]

Montana was especially advanced in making significant reforms in land conservation and management. The publications of M. L. Wilson, Elmer Starch, E. J. Bell, and Dwight Sanderson are among the many that explain how Montana's public institutions cooperated closely with both federal and private agencies (like the Rockefeller Foundation) to recognize and resolve the particular problems of farmers and farming areas in Montana.[27] These efforts resulted in new soil conservation technologies—like the duckfoot cultivator that formed a clod rather than a dust mulch, furrow drills that listed wheat, shelter belts, dry land irrigation systems, strip farming, and farm diversification. As Montana historian Robert G. Dunbar points out, these soil conservation techniques were widely adopted in the north-central part of the state when the drought of the thirties came.[28]

Additionally, scholars might look closely at the efforts of the Bureau of Agricultural Economics [BAE] to persuade the Great Plains states to address their problems. For example, early in the 1920s the BAE sought to identify "pathological farming areas" in the Great Plains.[29] This was official jargon for "diseased" areas—those with a combination of natural and human factors at work creating a sick farming culture.

Perhaps the BAE should have picked a better phrase than "pathological farming areas," for some states resented its application to certain of their sections. The agricultural college in Kansas so resented
these designations that it steadfastly refused during the 1920s to co-
operate with the BAE in recognizing problems peculiar to these areas in Kansas and in seeking to solve any recognized problems. In
fact, William Jardine—who served as director of the agricultural experiment station, as dean of the college of agriculture, and finally as
president of Kansas State College—was made secretary of agriculture in March 1925 in part because President Calvin Coolidge and
Secretary of Commerce Herbert Hoover knew that Jardine would
relish firing Henry C. Taylor, the man who directed the BAE and
launched the "pathological farming area" efforts.[30]

One should not belabor the point that separates Worster from
Manes and the rural social scientists who lived in and studied the culture of Dust Bowl area residents in the 1920s and 1930s. But this commentary does suggest another reason why our textbook writers and
other scholars continue to believe that the drought created the Dust
Bowl: It is quite possible that they have not read this body of work, or
at least have not read it carefully.

R. DOUGLAS HURT'S DUST BOWL

This suspicion is furthered by the fact that the third book-length
history of the Dust Bowl to appear in recent years—that of R. Douglas Hurt—has no discernible bias running through it.[31] Hurt provides such a well-balanced and straightforward account that one cannot read it and fail to understand the character and causes of the Dust
Bowl.

Yet in spite of Hurt's work, not only do the misconceptions of the
survey text writers persist, but even specialists in western history
provide accounts of the Dust Bowl that continue to present misconceptions of the Dust Bowl, their declarations implying knowledge of
Bonnifield, Worster, and Hurt not withstanding. Here, a recent book
by Richard Lowitt, *The New Deal and the West*, comes to mind.[32]
Lowitt devotes two chapters to the Great Plains, yet the Dust Bowl

does not appear until near the end of the second of these chapters. One encounters it in an unusual way. Lowitt explains that throughout the Plains "the wind whipped the topsoil into great drifts," often causing minor streams to disappear "and major ones, such as the Red River along the eastern boundary of the Dakotas," to become "hardly more than a creek." But, says Lowitt, "the brunt of these storms fell on western Kansas, eastern Colorado, western Oklahoma, the Texas panhandle, and parts of New Mexico. This area soon became known as the Dust Bowl, but dust swirled over the entire area of the Great Plains."[33]

Lowitt's choice of words here ("these storms fell on") betrays his lack of understanding of the Dust Bowl. It is his view that identical forces were at work throughout the Great Plains; it is just that the Dust Bowl got the worst of them. Throughout the thirty pages of text dedicated to the Great Plains, Lowitt fails to find any problems that were unusual to the Dust Bowl area. Save for one brief paragraph where he dedicates a few sentences to soil conservation practices applied in the Dust Bowl area, Lowitt makes no effort to review the natural or the human conditions that were specific to that area.

Because Lowitt views the problems in the Dust Bowl and the Plains as one and the same, he is led to draw some peculiar conclusions. He says that throughout the Plains there were "conditions and practices fostering erosion and drought." Just which conditions and practices fostered drought we are never told. But Lowitt does explore those that fostered erosion. Apparently, he agrees with the report of the Great Plains Drought Area Committee, which he quotes as saying "the basic cause of the present Great Plains situation is our attempt to impose upon the region a system of agriculture to which the Plains are not adapted or to bring into a semi-arid region methods which are suitable, on the whole, only for a humid region." In fact, Lowitt contends that this assumption became "official New Deal Gospel." Having coined a phrase, Lowitt then proceeds to show how it resulted in only "fragmented reforms" in the Plains, another phrase of Lowitt's whose meaning one wonders about. After all this, one is not surprised when he ends his chapters on the Plains by asking if the "historic cycle . . . of adequate rainfall and drought would begin anew."[34]

It is difficult to understand how Lowitt arrived at such conclusions in view of his statement in a footnote that "the best, most balanced and most comprehensive study is by R. Douglas Hurt, *Dust Bowl*," for Hurt's book does not support Lowitt's contentions.[35] Hurt begins by carefully delineating the Dust Bowl area. Having clearly established the boundaries, he then shows how dust blowing occurred throughout the Plains as far back as recorded settlement reveals. This being the case, Hurt closes his first chapter by observing that in the Dust Bowl area these storms were exacerbated by "the adoption of a *new* [my emphasis] agricultural technology."[36] In the second chapter, aptly titled "Causes of the Dust Bowl," Hurt takes great care to iden- tify the "composition" of the "major soil groups specific to the area that, together with the settlement of man, were responsible for the creation of the Dust Bowl."

Only after carefully examining the Dust Bowl's soils and the spe- cial new agricultural technologies employed there during the 1920s does Hurt move on to provide a view of broader issues, such as the climate of the Plains in general and the federal homesteading policies. Even here, Hurt provides insights into agricultural techniques pecu- liar to the Dust Bowl area. For instance, he draws upon Leslie Hewes's work on suitcase farming to explain how this type of farmer was en- demic to the Dust Bowl area. He had "flexibility. If a crop failed, a suitcase farmer still had another income, and his livelihood did not depend upon him remaining on the land. If a wheat crop did not look profitable, a suitcase farmer could abandon his field to the mercy of the wind. When suitcase farmers abandoned their land, they seldom returned to apply the proper soil conservation techniques to keep it under control."[37] Hurt then proceeds to provide a detailed analysis of how, beginning in the late 1930s, farmers worked with federal, state, and local officials to create particular agricultural technologies de- signed to meet problems specific to the Dust Bowl area. By the 1950s, says Hurt, "the Dust Bowl farmers understood the relationship be- tween soil conservation and successful farming."[38]

CONCLUSION

As a result of Hurt's study—and of others discussed above—we now have a clear understanding of the parameters and causes of the

Dust Bowl of the 1930s. Those who write textbooks of American history and monographs on the Great Plains need only to take heed of their contributions. Beyond that, scholars might also want to note that recent Dust Bowl histories provide instruction in the problem of marginality in modernizing societies: they show us how marginal people operate in a marginal economy. Here are people whose abilities do not square with the needs of modernizing societies—their abilities do not fit into the emerging technostructure. They are therefore left to carve out for themselves a life in the margins—those areas of the ecostructure where modern economic institutions do not choose to venture. These are usually areas where the returns are small and the risks are high—such as in the Dust Bowl.

NOTES

1. M. L. Wilson to President C. A. Lory, Colorado State College, 21 July 1939, in the National Archives, Record Group [hereafter cited as NA RG] 16, Washington, D.C.; M. L. Wilson, memorandum for Dr. E. C. Auchter, 1 July 1939, NA RG 54.
2. Wilson, Memo for Dr. Auchter, NA RG 54; Philip M. Glick to Morris L. Cooke, Chairman, the Great Plains Committee, 23 November 1936, in NA RG 83; M. L. Wilson to Dr. V. Bush, President, Carnegie Institution, 14 June 1939, NA RG 16.
3. "Conference on Man and Nature in the Great Plains . . . September 1939," in M. L. Wilson, Speeches and Papers, in the files of the History Section, U.S. Department of Agriculture, Washington, D.C.; M. L. Wilson, Memorandum to Mr. C. A. Taeusch, Program Planning Division, Bureau of Agricultural Economics, 7 February 1939, in NA RG 16.
4. Joseph Conlin, *The American Past, Part II: A Survey of American History Since 1865* (San Diego: Harcourt Brace Jovanovich, 1984), p. 699; John M. Blum, Arthur Schlesinger Jr., William S. McFeely, Kenneth M. Stampp, Edmund S. Morgan, and C. Vann Woodward, *The National Experience, Part Two: A History of the United States Since 1865* (San Diego: Harcourt Brace Jovanovich, 1985), p. 688; Mary Beth Norton, David M. Katzman, Paul D. Escott, Howard P. Chudacoff, Thomas G. Paterson, William M. Tuttle, and William J. Brophy, *A People and a Nation: A History of the United States, Vol. 2, Since 1865* (Boston: Houghton Mifflin, 1984), p. 393.

5. Bernard Bailyn, David Brion Davis, David Herbert Donald, John L. Thomas, Robert Dallek, and Gordon S. Wood, *The Great Republic: A History of the American People*, 3rd ed., vol. 2 (Lexington, Mass.: D.C. Heath, 1985), p. 738; Stephen Thernstrom, *A History of the American People, Vol. 2, Since 1865* (San Diego: Harcourt Brace Jovanovich, 1984), p. 645; Arthur S. Link, Robert Remini, Douglas Greenberg, and Robert C. McMath Jr., *The American People: A History, Vol. 2, Since 1865* (Arlington Heights, Ill.: Harlan Davidson, 1984), p. 415; George Brown Tindall, *America: A Narrative History* (New York: W. W. Norton, 1984), p. 1072.

6. Walter Stein, *California and the Dust Bowl Migration* (Westport, Conn.: Greenwood Press, 1973).

7. Ibid., pp. 4, 6–7.

8. Ibid., pp. 8–32.

9. Lambert's piece is in *Agricultural History* 45 (April 1971): 85–93; Perkins's was delivered to the meeting of the Organization of American Historians in Los Angles, April 1970; Hargreaves's is in *Agricultural History* 50 (October 1976): 561–582.

10. Saloutos's work appeared in *Agricultural History* 43 (July 1979): 345–355.

11. Harry C. McDean, "Social Scientists and Farm Poverty in the North American Plains, 1933–1940," *Great Plains Quarterly* 3 (Winter 1983): 17–29; "Federal Farm Policy and the Dust Bowl: The Half-Right Solution," *North Dakota History: Journal of the Northern Plains* 40 (Summer 1980): 21–31; see also n. 16.

12. Paul Bonnifield, *The Dust Bowl* (Albuquerque: University of New Mexico Press, 1979).

13. Ibid., pp. 13, 18, 20–38.

14. Ibid., pp. 87, 153, 155, 202.

15. Ibid., pp. 152, 170.

16. Ibid., pp. 155–156, 166–167.

17. Harry C. McDean, "M. L. Wilson and the Origins of Federal Farm Policy in the Great Plains," *Montana: The Magazine of Western History* 34 (Autumn 1984): 50–59; Philip M. Glick, "The Soil and the Law," *Journal of Farm Economics* 20 (May 1938): 430–47; "The Soil and the Law," *Journal of Farm Economics* 20 (August 1938), 606–640; "The Federal Subsistence Homesteads Program," *Yale Law Journal* 44 (June 1935): 1324–1379.

18. Bonnifield, *The Dust Bowl*, pp. 39–60, 44–45, 153, 155.

19. Donald Worster, *Dust Bowl: The Southern Plains in the 1930s* (New York: Oxford University Press, 1979), p. 6. Notice that even this title could mislead the casual reader.

20. Ibid., pp. 5, 6.

21. Ibid., pp. 4, 239, 240. Worster contends elsewhere that the disasters of

the thirties did advance the application of ecological concepts in agricultural development. See his "Grass to Dust: The Great Plains in the 1930s," *Environmental Reviews* 3 (1977): 2–13.

22. Worster, *Dust Bowl: Southern Plains*, p. 242.
23. Guides to these publications are offered by the experiment stations in each of the Great Plains states. For example, see "List and Indexes of Montana Agricultural Experiment Stations Bulletins and Circulares, 1894–1958" (Bozeman: Montana Agricultural Experiment Station, 1959), pp. 1–70.
24. Sheila Manes, "Pioneers and Survivors: Oklahoma's Landless Farmers," in *Oklahoma: New Views of the Forty-Sixth State*, ed. Anne Hodges Morgan and H. Wayne Morgan (Norman: University of Oklahoma Press, 1982) pp. 93–132.
25. Harry C. McDean, "The 'Okie' Migration as a Socio-Economic Necessity in Oklahoma," *Red River Valley Historical Review* 3 (Winter 1978): 77–92; see also McDean, "Dust Bowl," cited in n. 11.
26. See n. 23.
27. Edward J. Bell, Jr., "Montana Agriculture and the State University, 1893–1968" (mimeo, Department of Agricultural Economics, Montana State University, Bozeman, 1967), pp. 1–19, and "Montana State University: Instruction, Research, and Extension in Economics and Sociology, 1893–1968" (mimeo, Department of Agricultural Economics, Montana State University, Bozeman, 1968), pp. 1–43. The effort to plan agriculture and conservation in Montana during the twenties was both general and specific. For an example of the general, see "An Agricultural Program for Montana," Montana Extension Service Bulletin no. 84 (May 1927), pp. 4–45. For an example of the specific, see "A Program for the Development of Agriculture in Fergus County, Montana" (Lewistown, Mt., July 1927), pp. 1–45. For an overview of these efforts, see Roy E. Huffman, "Montana's Contributions to New Deal Farm Policy," *Agricultural History* 33 (October 1959): 164–167. One of the most exhaustive testimonies of the work done in Montana is deposited in Archives of the Center for Great Plains Studies, Lincoln, Nebraska. It is the book manuscript of Elmer Starch, "The Saga of a Sage."
28. Dunbar kindly lent his manuscript "Agriculture in Montana" to the author. Dunbar's assessment of Montana's land conservation practices appears on pages 17–20 of this manuscript.
29. M. L. Wilson to E. A. Duddy, 12 May 1924, in the Papers of M. L. Wilson, Montana State University Library, Bozeman, Montana; M. L. Wilson to H. R. Tolley, 25 October 1924, NA RG 16.
30. "H. C. Taylor's Conference With Secretary Jardine, April 30, 1925"; "typescript of hand written notes found on Dr. Taylor's desk, after 4:30 April

19, 1925"; W. E. Grimes, professor of agricultural economics, Kansas State Agricultural College, to H. C. Taylor 17 November 1923; H. C. Taylor to Hon. Herbert Hoover, 16 August 1934, all in the Papers of Henry C. Taylor, Wisconsin State Historical Society, Madison, Wisconsin.

31. R. Douglas Hurt, *Dust Bowl* (Chicago: Nelson-Hall, 1981).

32. Richard Lowitt, *The New Deal and the West* (Bloomington: Indiana University Press, 1984).

33. Ibid., p. 57.

34. Ibid., pp. 62, 42–46, 55–63.

35. Ibid., p. 232.

36. Hurt, *Dust Bowl*, pp. 15–16, 30.

37. Ibid., pp. 26–29. The reference is to Leslie Hewes, *The Suitcase Farming Frontier: A Study in the Historical Geography of the Central Great Plains* (Lincoln: University of Nebraska Press, 1973).

38. Hurt, *Dust Bowl*, p. 154.

MODERN BIBLIOGRAPHY OF THE DUST BOWL
Jay H. Buckley

Billions of tons of blowing dirt from millions of acres of land sym-
bolize the Dust Bowl and Depression of the 1930s. These black blizzards that swept over the Great Plains region were not caused by a
natural disaster but by what adherents to an economic tradition did to
intensify a natural occurrence during drought years. During the past
60 years, historiography has both elucidated and obscured the causes
and effects of this recurrent phenomenon in analyzing the complexi-
ties of natural, human, and technical events that resulted in a tremendous displacement of earth, most of it from the Great Plains states.
This bibliography lists the most recent articles and books associated
with the Dust Bowl as well as providing a selection of some time-worn
classics.

ARTICLES

Anderson, Clifford B. "The Metamorphosis of American Agrarian Idealism
in the 1920s and 1930s." *Agricultural History* 35 (October 1961): 182–188.
Ankli, Robert E. "Farm Income on the Great Plains and Canadian Prairies,
1920–1940." *Agricultural History* 51 (January 1977): 92–103.
Arrington, Leonard J. "The New Deal in the West: A Preliminary Statistical
Inquiry." *Pacific Historical Review* 38 (August 1969): 311–16.
———. "Western Agriculture and the New Deal." *Agricultural History* 44
(October 1970): 337–353.
Bauer, Patrick B. "Farm Mortgage Relief Legislation in Iowa During the
Great Depression." *Annals of Iowa* 50 (Summer 1989): 23–62.
Beddo, James B. "Depression and New Deal: Letters From the Plains." *Kan-
sas Historical Quarterly* 43 (Summer 1977): 140–153.
Benson, Jackson J. " 'To Tom Who Lived It': John Steinbeck and the Man
From Weedpatch." *Journal of Modern Literature* 5 (April 1976): 151–224.
Blackorby, Edward C. "William Lemke: Agrarian Radical and Union Party

Presidential Candidate." *Mississippi Valley Historical Review* 49 (June 1962): 67–84.

Borchert, John R. "The Dust Bowl in the 1970s." *Annals of the Association of American Geographers* 61 (1970): 1–22.

Brown, Lorne A. "Unemployment Relief Camps in Saskatchewan, 1933–1936." *Saskatchewan History* 23 (Autumn 1970): 81–83.

Bryant, Keith L., Jr. "Oklahoma and the New Deal." In John Braeman, Robert H. Bremner, and David Brody, eds., *The New Deal*. Columbus: Ohio State University Press, 1975.

Burbank, Garin. "Agrarian Socialism in Saskatchewan and Oklahoma: Short-Run Radicalism, Long-Run Conservatism." *Agricultural History* 51 (January 1977): 173–180.

Cantor, Louis. "A Prologue to the Protest Movement: The Missouri Sharecropper Roadside Demonstration of 1939." *Journal of American History* 50 (March 1969): 804–822.

Carey, James C. "The Farmer's Independence Council of America, 1935–1938." *Agricultural History* 35 (April 1961): 70–77.

Case, H.C.M. "Farm Debt Adjustments During the Early 1930s." *Agricultural History* 34 (October 1960): 173–181.

Choate, Jean. "Debt, Drought, and Depression: South Dakota in the 1930s." *Journal of the West* 31 (October 1992): 33–44.

———. " 'We Want Our Money Back': The National Farmers' Process Tax Recovery Association in Minnesota and Iowa." *Minnesota History* 52 (Fall 1990): 100–111.

Coffee, Marilyn. "The Dust Storms of the 1930s." *Natural History* 87 (February 1978): 81.

Conway, J. F. "The Prairie Populist Resistance to the National Policy: Some Reconsiderations." *Journal of Canadian Studies* 14 (Autumn 1979): 77–91.

Curtis, James C. "Dorthea Lange, Migrant Mother, and the Culture of the Great Depression." *Winterthur Portfolio* 21 (1986): 1–20.

Dodd, James W. "Resolutions, Programs, and Policies of the North Dakota Farmers' Holiday Association, 1932–1937." *North Dakota History* 28 (April–July 1961): 107–117.

Doerr, Arthur H. "Dry Conditions in Oklahoma in the 1930s and 1950s as Delimited by the Original Thornthwaite Climatic Classification." *Great Plains Journal* 2 (Spring 1963): 67–77.

Drache, Hiram M. "Thomas B. Campbell—The Plower of the Plains." *Agricultural History* 51 (January 1977): 78–91.

Dyson, Lowell K. "The Red Peasant International in America." *Journal of American History* 58 (March 1972): 958–973.

———. "Radical Farm Organizations and Periodicals in America, 1920–1960." *Agricultural History* 45 (April 1971): 111–120.

————. "Was Agricultural Distress in the 1930s a Result of Land Speculation During World War I? The Case of Iowa." *Annals of Iowa* 40 (1971): 577–584.

Easterlin, Richard. "Population Change and Farm Settlement in the Northern United States." *Journal of Economic History* 36 (March 1976): 45–75.

Fabry, Judith K. "The Surplus Farm Population: Agricultural Policy-makers and the Program for Older Rural Youth, 1935–1940." *Journal of the West* 31 (October 1992): 26–32.

Faragher, John Mack. "History From the Inside-Out: Writing the History of Women in Rural America." *American Quarterly* 33 (Winter 1981): 535–557.

Fausold, Martin L. "President Hoover's Farm Policies, 1929–1933." *Agricultural History* 51 (April 1977): 362–377.

Fearon, Peter. "From Self-Help to Federal Aid: Unemployment and Relief in Kansas, 1929–1932." *Kansas History* 13 (Summer 1990): 107–122.

Feder, Ernest. "Farm Debt Adjustments During the Depression—the Other Side of the Coin." *Agricultural History* 35 (April 1961): 78–81.

Fink, Deborah. "Sidelines and Moral Capital: Women on Nebraska Farms in the 1930s." In Wava G. Haney and Jane B. Knowles, eds., *Women and Farming: Changing Roles, Changing Structures.* Boulder: Westview, 1988, 55–70.

Fite, Gilbert C. "Farmer Opinion and the Agricultural Adjustment Act, 1933." *Mississippi Valley Historical Review* 48 (March 1962): 656–673.

————. "Great Plains Farming: A Century of Change and Development." *Agricultural History* 51 (January 1977): 244–256.

Flamm, Michael W. "The National Farmers Union and the Evolution of Agrarian Liberalism, 1937–1946." *Agricultural History* 68 (Summer 1994): 54–80.

Folsom, Burton W., Jr. "Immigrant Voters and the Nonpartisan League in Nebraska, 1917–1920." *Great Plains Quarterly* 1 (Summer 1981): 159–168.

Forsythe, James L. "Clifford Hope of Kansas: Practical Congressman and Agrarian Idealist." *Agricultural History* 51 (April 1977): 406–420.

Fossey, W. Richard. "Talkin' Dust Bowl Blues: A Study of Oklahoma's Cultural Identity During the Great Depression." *Chronicles of Oklahoma* 55 (Spring 1977): 12–33.

Foster, Donald, and Colin Read. "The Politics of Opportunism: The New Deal Broadcasts." *Canadian Historical Review* 60 (Fall 1979): 324–349.

Friedberger, Mark. "The Farm Family and the Inheritance Process: Evidence From the Corn Belt, 1870–1950." *Agricultural History* 57 (1983): 1–13.

Guth, James L. "The National Cooperative Council and Farm Relief, 1929–1942." *Agricultural History* 51 (April 1977): 441–458.

Hargreaves, Mary W. M. "The Dry Farming Movement in Retrospect."

Agricultural History 51 (January 1977): 149–165.

———. "Land Use Planning in Response to Drought: The Great Plains Experience of the Thirties." *Agricultural History* 50 (October 1976): 561–582.

Hart, John F. "The Middle West." *Annals of the Association of American Geographers* 62 (1972): 258–282.

Heathcote, R. L. "Perception of Desertification on the Southern Great Plains: A Preliminary Inquiry." In R. L. Heathcote, ed., *Perception of Desertification.* Tokyo: The United Nations University, 1980.

Hecht, Alan D. "Drought on the Great Plains: History of Societal Response." *Journal of Climate and Applied Meteorology* 22 (January 1983): 51–56.

Hendricksen, Kenneth E. "The National Youth and the New Deal, 1935–1943." *South Dakota History* 9 (Spring 1979): 131–151.

———. "The Civilian Conservation Corps in South Dakota." *South Dakota History* 11 (Winter 1980): 1–20.

Hewes, Leslie. "Early Suitcase Farming in the Central Great Plains." *Agricultural History* 51 (January 1977): 23–37.

Hope, Clifford R. "Kansas in the 1930s." *Kansas Historical Quarterly* 36 (Spring 1970): 1–12.

Horn, Michael. "Frank Underhill's Early Drafts of the Regina Manifesto 1933." *Canadian Historical Review* 54 (December 1973): 393–418.

Horowitz, David A. "The Perils of Western Farm Politics: Herbert Hoover, Gerald P. Nye, and Agricultural Reform, 1926–1932." *North Dakota Quarterly* 13 (Fall 1985): 92–110.

Hurt, R. Douglas. "Agricultural Technology in the Dust Bowl, 1932–40." In Brian W. Blouet and Frederick C. Luebke, eds., *The Great Plains: Environment and Culture.* Lincoln: University of Nebraska Press, 1979.

———. "Federal Land Reclamation in the Dust Bowl." *Great Plains Quarterly* 6 (Spring 1986): 94–106.

———. "The Dust Bowl." *American West* 14 (July–August 1977): 22–27, 56–57.

———. "The National Grasslands: Origin and Development in the Dust Bowl." *Agricultural History* 59 (April 1985): 246–259.

———. "Letters From the Dust Bowl." *Panhandle-Plains Historical Review* 52 (1979): 1–13.

———. "Return of the Dust Bowl: The Filthy Fifties." *Journal of the West* 18 (October 1979): 85–93.

Isern, Thomas D. "How to Kill a Chinch Bug: The Folk Technology of Farming on the North American Plains." *Journal of the West* 31 (October 1992): 45–50.

Jellison, Katherine. "Women and Technology on the Great Plains, 1910–40." *Great Plains Quarterly* 8 (Summer 1988): 145–157.

Johnson, William R. "National Farm Organizations and the Reshaping of Agricultural Policy in 1932." *Agricultural History* 37 (January 1963): 35–42.

Karr, Rodney D. "Farmer Rebels in Plymouth County, Iowa, 1932–1933." *Annals of Iowa* 47 (Winter 1985): 637–645.

Kearny County Historical Society. "Diaries of Iman C. Wiatt." In *History of Kearny County, Kansas.* Vol. 2. North Newton, Kansas: Mennonite Press, 1973.

Kirkendall, Richard S. "Commentary on the Thought of Henry A. Wallace." *Agricultural History* 41 (April 1967): 140–141.

———. "Corn Huskers and Master Farmers: Henry A. Wallace and the Merchandising of Iowa Agriculture." *Palimpsest* 65 (May–June 1984): 82–93.

———. "Henry A. Wallace's Turn Toward the New Deal, 1921–1924." *Annals of Iowa* 49 (Winter–Spring 1988): 221–239.

———. "The Mind of a Farm Leader." *Annals of Iowa* 47 (Fall 1983): 138–153.

———. "Reflections of a Revolutionary on a Revolution." *Journal of the West* 31 (October 1992): 8–14.

———. "The Second Secretary Wallace." *Agricultural History* 64 (Spring 1990): 199–206.

Kirschner, Don S. "Henry A. Wallace as Farm Editor." *American Quarterly* 17 (Summer 1965): 187–202.

Koerselman, Gary H. "Secretary Hoover and National Farm Policy: Problems of Leadership." *Agricultural History* 51 (April 1977): 378–395.

Lambert, C. Roger. "Slaughter of the Innocents: The Public Protests AAA Killing of Little Pigs." *Midwest Quarterly* 14 (April 1973): 247–254.

———. "Texas Cattle and the AAA, 1933–1935." *Arizona and the West* 14 (Summer 1972): 137–154.

———. "The Drought Cattle Purchase 1934–1935: Problems and Complaints." *Agricultural History* 45 (April 1971): 85–93.

———. "Want and Plenty: The Federal Purchase Relief Corporation." *Agricultural History* 46 (July 1972): 390–400.

Larson, T. A. "The New Deal in Wyoming." *Pacific Historical Review* 38 (August 1969): 249–274.

Lawton, Alma. "Relief Administration in Saskatoon During the Depression." *Saskatchewan History* 22 (Spring 1969): 42.

Lewis, Michael E. "National Grasslands in the Dust Bowl." *Geographical Review* 79 (April 1989): 161–171.

Lockeretz, William. "The Dust Bowl: Its Relevance to Contemporary Environmental Problems." In Merlin Lawson and Maurice E. Baker, eds., *The Great Plains: Perspectives and Prospects.* Lincoln: University of Nebraska Press, 1981, 11–31.

———. "The Lessons of the Dust Bowl." *American Scientist* 66 (1978): 560–569.

Logsdon, Guy. "The Dust Bowl and the Migrant." *American Scene* 12, no. 1. Tulsa: Gilcrease Institute of American History and Art, 1971.

Lookingbill, Brad. "'A God-forsaken Place': Folk Eschatology and the Dust Bowl." *Great Plains Quarterly* 14 (Fall 1994): 273–286.

Loriks, Emil. "The Great Depression: The Early Thirties and the National Farm Holiday Movement." In *Selected Papers of the First Nine History Conferences, 1969–1977*. Madison: Dakota State College, 1981.

Lowitt, Richard. "George W. Norris and the New Deal in Nebraska, 1933–1936." *Agricultural History* 51 (April 1977): 396–405.

Luebke, Frederick. "Ethnic Group Settlement on the Great Plains." *Western Historical Quarterly* 8 (October 1977): 405–430.

———. "Regionalism and the Great Plains: Problems of Concept and Method." *Western Historical Quarterly* 15 (January 1984): 19–38.

Malone, Michael P. "Montana Politics and the New Deal." *Montana: The Magazine of Western History* 21 (January 1971): 2–11.

Manes, Sheila. "Pioneers and Survivors: Oklahoma's Landless Farmers." In Anne Hodges Morgan and H. Wayne Morgan, eds., *Oklahoma: New Views of the Forty-Sixth State*. Norman: University of Oklahoma Press, 1982, 93–132.

Mathews, Allan. "Agrarian Radicals: The United Farmers League of South Dakota." *South Dakota History* 3 (Fall 1973): 408–421.

May, Irvin, Jr. "Cotton and Cattle: The FSRC and Emergency Work Relief." *Agricultural History* 46 (July 1972): 401–413.

———. "Marvin Jones: Agrarian and Politician." *Agricultural History* 51 (April 1977): 421–440.

McDean, Harry C. "Dust Bowl Historiography." *Great Plains Quarterly* 6 (Spring 1986): 117–126.

———. "Federal Farm Policy and the Dust Bowl: The Half-right Solution." *North Dakota History* 47 (Summer 1980): 21–31.

———. "M. L. Wilson and the Origins of Federal Farm Policy in the Great Plains." *Montana: The Magazine of Western History* 34 (Autumn 1984): 50–59.

———. "The 'Okie' Migration as a Socio-Economic Necessity in Oklahoma." *Red River Valley Historical Review* 3 (Winter 1978): 77–92.

———. "Social Scientists and Farm Poverty in the North American Plains, 1933–1940." *Great Plains Quarterly* 3 (Winter 1983): 17–29.

———. "Western Thought in Planning Rural America: The Subsistence Homesteads Program, 1933–1935." *Journal of the West* 31 (October 1992): 15–25.

McKinzie, Richard. "Cultural Life During the Great Depression." In James E. Wright and Sarah Z. Rosenberg, eds., *The Great Plains Experience:*

Readings in the History of a Region. Lincoln: University of Nebraska Press, 1978, 405–411.

McMath, Robert C., Jr. "Populism in Two Countries: Agrarian Protest in the Great Plains and Prairie Provinces." *Agricultural History* 69 (Fall 1995): 517–546.

Miller, John E. "McCarthyism Before McCarthy: The 1938 Election in South Dakota." *Heritage of the Great Plains* 15 (Summer 1982): 1–21.

——. "Restrained, Respectable Radicals: The South Dakota Farm Holiday." *Agricultural History* 59 (July 1985): 429–447.

Nall, Garry. "Dust Bowl Days: Panhandle Farming in the 1930s." *Panhandle-Plains Historical Review* 47 (1975): 42–63.

——. "Specialization and Expansion: Panhandle Farming in the 1920s." *Panhandle-Plains Historical Review* 47 (1974): 46–67.

Nash, Gerald D. "The West in the Great Depression, 1929–41." In Nash, ed., *The American West in the Twentieth Century: A Short History of an Urban Oasis.* Englewood Cliffs, N.J.: Prentice-Hall, 1973; reprint, Albuquerque: University of New Mexico Press, 1977, 139–159.

Neth, Mary. "Building the Base: Farm Women, the Rural Community, and Farm Organizations in the Midwest, 1900–1940." In *Women and Farming: Changing Roles, Changing Structures,* eds. Wava G. Haney, and Jane B. Knowles. Boulder: Westview, 1988, 339–355.

Nielsen, Kim E. "Who Were These Farmer Radicals? The Douglas County Farm Holiday Association." *Minnesota History* 51 (Fall 1989): 270–280.

Norrie, Kenneth. "Dry Farming and the Economics of Risk Bearing: The Canadian Prairies, 1870–1930." *Agricultural History* 51 (January 1977): 134–148.

Opie, John. "The Drought of 1988, the Global Warming Experiment, and Its Challenge to Irrigation in the Old Dust Bowl Region." *Agricultural History* 66 (Spring 1992): 279–307.

——. "100 Years of Climate Risk Assessment on the High Plains: Which Farm Paradigm Does Irrigation Serve?" *Agricultural History* 63 (Spring 1989): 243–269.

O'Rourke, Paul A. "South Dakota Politics During the New Deal Years." *South Dakota History* 1 (Summer 1971): 232–234.

Oyos, Lynwood W. "Labor's House Divided: The Morrell Strike of 1935–1937." *South Dakota History* 18 (Spring–Summer 1988): 67–88.

Parfit, Michael. "The Dust Bowl; Half a Century Ago, Parts of the Great Plains Blew Away, and the Question Now Is: Could It Be Happening All Over Again?" *Smithsonian* 20 (June 1989): 44–56.

Patterson, James T. "The New Deal in the West." *Pacific Historical Review* 38 (August 1969): 317–328.

Pool, Carolyn Garrett. "Reservation Policy and the Economic Position of

Wichita Women." *Great Plains Quarterly* 8 (Summer 1988): 158–171.

Popper, Deborah Epstein, and Frank J. Popper. "The Great Plains: From Dust to Dust." *Planning* 53, 12 (December 1978): 12–18.

Pratt, William C. "Farmers, Communists, and the FBI in the Upper Midwest." *Agricultural History* 63 (Summer 1989): 61–80.

———. "Radicals, Farmers, and Historians: Some Recent Scholarship About Agrarian Radicalism in the Upper Midwest." *North Dakota History* 52 (Fall 1985): 12–24.

———. "Rethinking the Farm Revolt of the 1930s." *Great Plains Quarterly* 8 (Summer 1988): 131–144.

———. "Rural Radicalism on the Northern Plains, 1912–1950." *Montana: The Magazine of Western History* 42 (Winter 1992): 42–55.

———. "Socialism on the Northern Plains, 1900–1924." *South Dakota History* 18 (Spring–Summer 1988): 1–35.

———. "Where Do We Go From Here? Historians and Farm Movements on the Northern Plains." *Journal of the West* 31 (October 1992): 59–70.

———. "Women Socialists and Their Male Comrades: The Reading Experience, 1927–1936." In Sally M. Miller, ed., *Flawed Liberation: Socialism and Feminism*. Westport, Conn.: Greenwood, 1981, 145–178.

———. "Workers, Unions, and Historians on the Northern Plains." *Great Plains Quarterly* 16 (Fall 1996): 229–250.

Purdy, Virginia C., ed. "Dust to Eat [by Caroline A. Henderson]." *Chronicles of Oklahoma* 58 (Winter 1980): 440–454.

Quinten, B. T. "Oklahoma Tribes, the Great Depression, and the Indian Bureau." *Mid-America* 49 (January 1967): 29–43.

Rasmussen, Wayne D. "The Impact of Technological Change on American Agriculture." *Journal of Economic History* 20 (December 1962): 578–591.

Remele, Larry. "The North Dakota Farm Strike of 1932." *North Dakota History* 41 (Fall 1974): 5–18.

Riebsame, William E. "The Dust Bowl: Historical Image, Psychological Anchor, and Ecological Taboo." *Great Plains Quarterly* 6 (Spring 1986): 127–136.

———. "Managing Drought Impacts on Agriculture: The Great Plains Experience." In Rutherford H. Platt and George Macinko, eds., *Beyond the Urban Fringe: Land Use Issues of Nonmetropolitan America*. Minneapolis: University of Minnesota Press, 1983, 257–272.

Riley, Glenda, and Richard S. Kirkendall. "Henry A. Wallace and the Mystique of the Farm Male, 1921–1933." *Annals of Iowa* 48 (Summer–Fall 1985): 32–55.

Riney-Kehrberg, Pamela. "From the Horse's Mouth: Dust Bowl Farmers and Their Solutions to the Problem of Aridity." *Agricultural History* 66 (Spring 1992): 137–150.

————. "Hard Times, Hungry Years: Failure of the Poor Relief in South-western Kansas, 1930–1933." *Kansas History* 15 (Autumn 1992): 154–167.

————. "In God We Trusted, in Kansas We Busted . . . Again." *Agricultural History* 63 (Spring 1989): 187–201.

————. "Separation and Sorrow: A Farm Woman's Life, 1935–1941." *Agricultural History* 67 (Spring 1993): 185–196.

Risser, James. "A Renewed Threat of Soil Erosion: It's Worse Than the Dust Bowl." *Smithsonian* 11 (March 1981): 120–131.

Rowley, William D. "The Loup City Riot of 1934: Main Street vs. the 'Far Out' Left." *Nebraska History* 47 (September 1966): 295–327.

Russell, P. A. "The Co-operative Government's Response to the Depression, 1930–1934." *Saskatchewan History* 24 (Autumn 1971): 81.

Sage, Leland L. "Rural Iowa in the 1920s and 1930s: Roots of the Farm Depression." *Annals of Iowa* 47 (Fall 1983): 91–103.

Saloutos, Theodore. "The New Deal and Farm Policy in the Great Plains." *Agricultural History* 43 (July 1969): 345–355.

————. "New Deal Agricultural Policy: An Evaluation." *Journal of American History* 61 (September 1974): 394–416.

Sannes, Erling N. "Gas Sunday: Organizing Fargo, North Dakota, Teamsters in 1935." *Journal of the West* 35 (April 1996): 29–32.

————. " 'Make Sioux City a Good Place to Live': Organizing Teamsters in Sioux City, 1933–1938." *Annals of Iowa* 50 (Fall 1989–Winter 1990): 214–240.

————. " 'There Is Power in a Union': Organizing Fargo's Milk-Wagon Drivers in 1934." *North Dakota History* 54 (Spring 1987): 3–12.

————. " 'Union Makes Strength': Organizing Teamsters in South Dakota in the 1930s." *South Dakota History* 18 (Spring–Summer 1988): 36–66.

Schapsmeier, Edward L., and Frederick H. Schapsmeier. "A Prophet in Politics: The Public Career of Henry A. Wallace." *Annals of Iowa* 39 (Summer 1967): 1–21.

————. "Henry A. Wallace: Agrarian Idealist or Agricultural Realist?" *Agricultural History* 41 (April 1967): 127–137.

Schuyler, Michael W. "Drought and Politics in 1936: Kansas as a Test Case." *Great Plains Journal* 15 (Fall 1975): 3–27.

————. "Federal Drought Relief Activities in Kansas, 1934." *Kansas Historical Quarterly* 42 (Winter 1976): 403–424.

————. "Great Plains Agriculture and the New Deal." In James E. Wright and Sarah Z. Rosenberg, eds., *The Great Plains Experience: Readings in the History of a Region*. Lincoln: University of Nebraska Press, 1978, 375–386.

————. "New Deal Farm Policy in the Middle West—A Retrospective View." *Journal of the West* 33 (October 1994): 52–63.

Schwieder, Dorothy. "Rural Iowa in the 1920s: Conflict and Continuity." *Annals of Iowa* 47 (Fall 1983): 104–115.

Schwieder, Dorothy, and Deborah Fink. "Plains Women: Rural Life in the 1930s." *Great Plains Quarterly* 8 (Spring 1988): 79–88.

Shover, John L. "The Communist Party and the Midwest Farm Crisis of 1933." *Journal of American History* 51 (September 1964): 248–266.

———. "The Farm Holiday Movement in Nebraska." *Nebraska History* 43 (March 1962): 53–78.

———. "The Penny Auction Rebellion." *American West* 2 (Fall 1965): 64–72.

———. "Populism in the Nineteen-Thirties: The Battle for the AAA." *Agricultural History* 39 (January 1965): 17–24.

Sillars, Malcolm O. "Henry A. Wallace's Editorials on Agricultural Discontent, 1921–1928." *Agricultural History* 26 (October 1952): 132–140.

Sinclair, Peter R. "The Saskatchewan CCF: Ascent to Power and the Decline of Socialism." *Canadian Historical Review* 54 (December 1973): 419–433.

Soth, Lauren. "Henry Wallace and the Farm Crisis of the 1920s and 1930s." *Annals of Iowa* 47 (Fall 1983): 195–214.

Starr, Karen. "Fighting for a Future: Farm Women of the Nonpartisan League." *Minnesota History* 48 (Summer 1983): 255–262.

Swain, Donald C. "The Bureau of Reclamation and the New Deal, 1933–1940." *Pacific Historical Quarterly* 61 (July 1970): 137–146.

———. "The National Park Service and the New Deal, 1933–1940." *Pacific Historical Review* 41 (August 1972): 312–332.

Taylor, Leslie A. "Femininity as Strategy: A Gendered Perspective on the Farmers' Holiday." *Annals of Iowa* 51 (Winter 1992): 252–277.

Vindex, Charles. "Radical Rule in Montana." *Montana: The Magazine of Western History* 18 (January 1968): 2–18.

Wagner, Jonathan F. " 'The Greatest Thing I Ever Did Was Join the Union': A History of the Dakota Teamsters During the Depression." *Great Plains Quarterly* 8 (Winter 1988): 16–28.

Wall, Joseph F. "The Iowa Farmer in Crisis, 1920–1936." *Annals of Iowa* 47 (Fall 1983): 116–127.

Ware, James. "The Sooner NRA: New Deal Recovery in Oklahoma." *Chronicles of Oklahoma* 54 (Fall 1976): 339–351.

Warrick, Richard A. "The Possible Impacts on Wheat Production of a Recurrence of the 1930s Drought in the U.S. Great Plains." *Climatic Change* 6 (1984): 5–26.

Warrick, Richard A., and Martyn J. Bowden. "The Changing Impacts of Droughts in the Great Plains." In Merlin Lawson and Maurice E. Baker, eds., *The Great Plains: Perspectives and Prospects*. Lincoln: University of Nebraska Press, 1981, 111–140.

Weller, Kay Ellen. "The Dust Bowl as Place to Western Kansas Women."
Social Science Journal 32 (April 1995): 213–218.

Wertsch, Douglas. "Wallaces' Farmers' Crusade Against Rural Crime in the
1920s." *Annals of Iowa* 50 (Spring 1990): 375–388.

Wessel, Thomas R. "Roosevelt and the Great Plains Shelterbelt." *Great Plains
Journal* 8 (Spring 1969): 57–74.

Whisenhunt, Donald. "The Texas Attitude Toward Relief, 1929–1933."
Panhandle-Plains Historical Review 46 (1973): 94–112.

White, Gilbert F. "The Future of the Great Plains Revisited." *Great Plains
Quarterly* 6 (Spring 1986): 84–93.

Wickens, James F. "The New Deal in Colorado." *Pacific Historical Review*
38 (August 1969): 275–292.

Wilhite, Donald A. "Government Response to Drought in the United States:
With Particular Reference to the Great Plains." *Journal of Climate and
Applied Meteorology* 22 (1983): 40–50.

Williams, Elizabeth Evenson. "A South Dakota Agrarian's Views of Huey
Long." *Midwest Review* 8 (Spring 1986): 40–55.

Wilson, Joan Hoff. "Hoover's Agricultural Policies, 1921–1928." *Agricultural
History* 51 (April 1977): 335–361.

Winters, Donald L. "Ambiguity and Agricultural Policy: Henry Cantwell
Wallace as Secretary of Agriculture." *Agricultural History* 64 (Spring
1990): 191–198.

———. "The Hoover-Wallace Controversy During World War I." *Annals of
Iowa* 34 (Spring 1969): 586–597.

Worster, Donald. "Grass to Dust: The Great Plains in the 1930s." *Environmental Review* 3 (1977): 2–11.

———. "The Dirty Thirties: A Study in Agricultural Capitalism." *Great
Plains Quarterly* 6 (Spring 1986): 107–116.

Yoder, Frank. "Stay on the Farm: Surviving the Great Depression in an Iowa
Township, 1920–1950." *Annals of Iowa* 51 (Summer 1991): 53–78.

Zahavi, Gerald. " 'Who's Going to Dance With Somebody Who Calls You a
Mainstreeter': Communism, Culture, and Community in Sheridan County,
Montana, 1918–1934." *Great Plains Quarterly* 16 (Fall 1996): 251–286.

BOOKS

Adams, Willena, ed. *Texas Cities During the Great Depression.* Austin: Texas
Memorial Museum, 1973.

Allen, Richard, ed. *A Region of the Mind: Interpreting the Western Canada
Plains.* Regina: Canadian Studies Centre, University of Saskatchewan, 1973.

Andryszewski, Tricia. *The Dust Bowl: Disaster on the Plains.* Brookfield,
Conn.: Millbrook, 1993.

Armitage, Katie. *Making Do and Doing Without: Kansas in the Great Depression.* Lawrence: University of Kansas, Division of Continuing Education, 1983.

Bader, Robert Smith. *Hayseeds, Moralizers, and Methodists: The Twentieth-Century Image of Kansas.* Lawrence: University Press of Kansas, 1988.

Baldwin, Sidney. *Poverty and Politics: The Rise and Decline of the Farm Security Administration.* Chapel Hill: University of North Carolina Press, 1968.

Bennett, David H. *Demagogues in the Depression: American Radicals and the Union Party, 1932–1936.* New Brunswick: Rutgers University Press, 1969.

Bennett, John. *The Ecological Transition: Cultural Anthropology and Human Adaptation.* New York: Pergamon, 1976.

Bird, Caroline. *The Invisible Scar.* New York: David McKay, 1966.

Blackorby, Edward C. *Prairie Rebel: The Public Life of William Lemke.* Lincoln: University of Nebraska Press, 1963.

Blouet, Brian W., and Merlin Lawson, eds. *Images of the Plains: The Role of Human Nature in Settlement.* Lincoln: University of Nebraska Press, 1975.

Blouet, Brian W., and Frederick C. Luebke, eds. *The Great Plains: Environment and Culture.* Lincoln: University of Nebraska Press, 1979.

Bonnifield, Paul. *The Dust Bowl: Men, Dirt, and Depression.* Albuquerque: University of New Mexico Press, 1979.

Bremer, Richard G. *Agricultural Change in an Urban Age: The Loup Country of Nebraska, 1910–1970.* Lincoln: University of Nebraska Press, 1976.

Brinkley, Alan. *Voices of Protest: Huey Long, Father Coughlin, and the Great Depression.* New York: Alfred A. Knopf, 1982.

Burbank, Garin. *When Farmers Voted Red: The Gospel of Socialism in the Oklahoma Countryside, 1910–1924.* Westport, Conn.: Greenwood, 1976.

Campbell, Christiana M. *The Farm Bureau and the New Deal.* Urbana: University of Illinois Press, 1962.

Card, Brigham Y. *The Canadian Prairie Provinces From 1870 to 1950: A Sociological Interpretation.* Toronto: J. M. Dent and Sons, 1960.

Cochrane, Willard W. *The Development of American Agriculture: A Historical Analysis.* Minneapolis: University of Minnesota Press, 1979.

Conrad, Charles, and Joyce Conrad. *50 Years: North Dakota Farmers' Union.* North Dakota Farmers' Union, 1976.

Crampton, John A. *The National Farmers' Union: Ideology of a Pressure Group.* Lincoln: University of Nebraska Press, 1965.

Cumberland, William H. *Wallace M. Short: Iowa Rebel.* Ames: Iowa State University Press, 1983.

Curtis, James. *Mind's Eye, Mind's Truth: FSA Photography Reconsidered.* Philadelphia: Temple University Press, 1989.

Danbom, David B. *The Resisted Revolution: Urban America and the Industrialization of Agriculture, 1900–1930.* Ames: Iowa State University Press, 1979.

Dubofsky, Melvin, and Stephen Burwood, eds. *Agriculture During the Great Depression.* New York: Garland, 1990.

Dyson, Lowell K. *Farmers' Organizations.* New York: Greenwood, 1986.

———. *History of Federal Drought Relief Programs.* Washington, D.C.: U.S. Department of Agriculture, 1988.

———. *Red Harvest: The Communist Party and American Farmers.* Lincoln: University of Nebraska Press, 1982.

Farris, John. *The Dust Bowl.* San Diego: Lucent, 1989.

Fearon, Peter. *The Origins and Nature of the Great Slump, 1929–32.* Atlantic Highlands, N.J.: Humanities, 1979.

Fink, Deborah. *Agrarian Women: Wives and Mothers in Rural Nebraska, 1880–1940.* Chapel Hill: University of North Carolina Press, 1992.

———. *Open Country, Iowa: Rural Women, Tradition, and Change.* Albany: State University of New York Press, 1986.

Fite, Gilbert C. *American Farmers: The New Minority.* Bloomington: Indiana University Press, 1981.

Fleischhauer, Carl, and Beverly W. Brannon. *Documenting America, 1935–1943.* Berkeley: University of California Press, 1988.

Francis, R. Douglas, and Herman Ganzevoort, eds. *The Dirty Thirties in Prairie Canada.* Vancouver: Tantalus Research, 1973.

French, Warren. *A Companion to the Grapes of Wrath.* New York: Viking, 1963.

Frieson, Gerald. *The Canadian Prairies: A History.* Toronto: University of Toronto Press, 1984.

Ganzel, Bill. *Dust Bowl Descent.* Lincoln: University of Nebraska Press, 1984.

Garraty, John A. *The Great Depression: An Inquiry Into the Causes, Course, and Consequences of the Worldwide Depression of the Nineteen-thirties, as Seen by Contemporaries and in the Light of History.* San Diego: Harcourt Brace Jovanovich, 1986.

Grant, H. Roger, and L. Edward Purcell, eds. *Years of Struggle: The Farm Diary of Elmer G. Powers.* Ames: Iowa State University Press, 1976.

Green, Donald E. *Land of the Underground Rain: Irrigation on the Texas High Plains, 1910–1970.* Austin: University of Texas Press, 1973.

Gregory, James N. *American Exodus: The Dust Bowl Migration and Okie Culture in California.* New York: Oxford University Press, 1989.

Guither, Harold D. *Heritage of Plenty: A Guide to the Economic History and Development of United States Agriculture.* Danville, Ill.: Interstate Printers and Publishers, 1972.

Guthrie, Woody. *Dust Bowl Ballads* (sound recording FH 5212). New York: Folkway Records, 1964.

Ham, George E., and Robin Higham, eds. *The Rise of the Wheat State: A History of Kansas Agriculture, 1861–1986*. Manhattan, Kansas: Sunflower University Press, 1987.

Hamilton, David E. *From New Day to New Deal: American Farm Policy From Hoover to Roosevelt, 1928–1933*. Chapel Hill: University of North Carolina Press, 1991.

Hazell, H. Don. *Midnight at Noon: A Pictorial Review of the Dust Bowl.* Kansas City: Mindon Cards, 1969.

Hesse, Karen. *Out of the Dust.* New York: Scholastic, 1997.

Hewes, Leslie. *The Suitcase Farming Frontier: A Study in the Historical Geography of the Central Great Plains.* Lincoln: University of Nebraska Press, 1973.

Hudson, Lois P. *The Bones of Plenty.* Boston: Atlantic Monthly, 1962.

———. *Reapers of the Dust: A Prairie Chronicle.* Boston: Little, Brown, 1964.

Hurley, F. Jack. *Portrait of a Decade: Roy Stryker and the Development of Documentary Photography in the Thirties.* Baton Rouge: Louisiana State University Press, 1972.

———. *Russell Lee, Photographer.* Dobbs Ferry, N.Y.: Morgan and Morgan, 1978.

———. *Marion Post Wolcott: A Photographic Journey.* Albuquerque: University of New Mexico Press, 1989.

Hurt, R. Douglas. *The Dust Bowl: An Agricultural and Social History.* Chicago: Nelson-Hall, 1981.

Jellison, Katherine. *Entitled to Power: Farm Women and Technology, 1913–1963.* Chapel Hill: University of North Carolina Press, 1993.

Kirkendall, Richard S. *Social Scientists and Farm Politics in the Age of Roosevelt.* Columbia: University of Missouri Press, 1966.

Klehr, Harvey. *The Heyday of American Communism: The Depression Decade.* New York: Basic Books, 1984.

Koerselman, Gary H. "Herbert Hoover and the Farm Crisis of the Twenties: A Study of the Commerce Department's Efforts to Solve the Agricultural Depression, 1921–1928." Ph.D. diss., Northern Illinois University, 1971.

Lang, James B. "The Shelterbelt Project in the Southern Great Plains—1934–1970—A Geographical Appraisal." Master's thesis, University of Oklahoma, 1970.

Leuchtenberg, William. *Franklin D. Roosevelt and the New Deal, 1932–1940.* New York: Harper and Row, 1963.

Low, Ann Marie. *Dust Bowl Diary*. Lincoln: University of Nebraska Press, 1984.

Lowitt, Richard. *The New Deal in the West*. Bloomington: Indiana University Press, 1984.

Lowitt, Richard, and Maurice Beasley, eds. *One Third of a Nation: Lorena Hickok Reports on the Great Depression*. Urbana: University of Illinois Press, 1981.

Malin, James C. *History and Ecology: Studies of the Grassland*. Robert P. Swierenga, ed. Lincoln: University of Nebraska Press, 1984.

Mathews, Allan. "The History of the United Farmers League in South Dakota." Master's thesis, University of South Dakota, 1972.

McDaniel, Marylou, ed. *God, Grass, and Grit: A History of the Sherman County Trade Area*. Hereford, Tex.: Pioneer, 1971.

McDean, Harry C. *A Preliminary List of References for the History of American Agriculture During the New Deal Period, 1932–1940*. Davis: University of California–Davis, Agricultural History Center, 1968.

Nail, David. *One Short Sleep Past: A Profile of Amarillo in the Thirties*. Canyon, Tex.: Staked Plains, 1973.

Nall, Garry L. "Agricultural History of the Texas Panhandle, 1880–1965." Ph.D. diss., University of Oklahoma, 1972.

Neth, Mary. "Preserving the Family Farm: Farm Families and Community in the Midwest, 1900–1940." Ph.D. diss., University of Wisconsin–Madison, 1987.

Olsen, James C., and Ron Naugle. *History of Nebraska*. 3rd ed. Lincoln: University of Nebraska Press, 1997.

Opie, John. *Ogallala: Water for a Dry Land*. Lincoln: University of Nebraska Press, 1993.

Ottoson, Howard, et al. *Land and People in the Northern Plains Transition Area*. Lincoln: University of Nebraska Press, 1966.

Pelieu, Claude. *Dust Bowl Motel Poems*. Paris: C. Bourgois, 1977.

Perkins, Van L. *Crisis in Agriculture: The Agricultural Adjustment Administration and the New Deal, 1933*. Berkeley: University of California Press, 1969.

Pewe, Troy L., ed. *Desert Dust: Origin, Characteristics, and Effect on Man*. Boulder: Geological Society of America, 1981.

Raven, Margot. *Angels in the Dust*. Mahwah, N.J.: Bridgewater, 1997.

Rees, Goronwy. *The Great Slump: Capitalism in Crisis, 1929–1933*. New York: Harper and Row, 1970.

Reid, Robert L. *Picturing Minnesota, 1936–1943*. St. Paul: Minnesota Historical Society Press, 1989.

Riney-Kehrberg, Pamela. *Rooted in Dust: Surviving Drought and Depression in Southwestern Kansas*. Lawrence: University Press of Kansas, 1994.

Robinson, Elwyn B. *History of North Dakota*. Lincoln: University of Nebraska Press, 1966.

Rogers, Earl M. *A List of References for the History of Agriculture in the Great Plains*. Davis: Agricultural History Center, University of California–Davis, 1976.

Rosenberg, Norman J., ed. *North American Droughts*. Boulder: Westview, 1978.

Rutland, Robert Allen. *A Boyhood in the Dust Bowl, 1926–1934*. Niwot: University Press of Colorado, 1995.

Rylance, Daniel F. *Years of Despair: North Dakota in the Depression*. Grand Forks: Oxcart, 1973.

Saarinen, Thomas F. *Perception of Drought Hazard on the Great Plains*. Department of Geography Research Paper no. 106. Chicago: University of Chicago Press, 1966.

Sage, Leland L. *A History of Iowa*. Ames: Iowa State University Press, 1974.

Saint-Etienne, Christian. *The Great Depression, 1929–1938: Lessons for the 1980s*. Stanford: Hoover Institute Press, 1984.

Saloutos, Theodore. *The American Farmer and the New Deal*. Ames: Iowa State University Press, 1982.

Schapsmeier, Edward, and Frederick Schapsmeier. *Henry A. Wallace of Iowa: The Agrarian Years, 1910–1940*. Ames: Iowa State University Press, 1968.

Schell, Herbert S. *History of South Dakota*. Lincoln: University of Nebraska Press, 1969.

Schlebecker, John T. *Whereby We Thrive: A History of American Farming, 1607–1972*. Ames: Iowa State University Press, 1974.

Schruben, Francis W. *Kansas in Turmoil, 1930–1936*. Columbia: University of Missouri Press, 1969.

Schulz, Constance B., ed. *Bust to Boom: Documentary Photographs of Kansas, 1936–1949*. Lawrence: University Press of Kansas, 1996.

Schuyler, Michael W. *The Dread of Plenty: Agricultural Relief Activities of the Federal Government in the Middle West, 1933–1939*. Manhattan, Kansas: Sunflower University Press, 1989.

Shannon, David, ed. *The Great Depression*. Englewood Cliffs, N.J.: Prentice-Hall, 1960.

Sheridan, David. *Desertification of the United States*. Washington, D.C.: Council on Environmental Quality, 1981.

Shindo, Charles J. *Dust Bowl Migrants in the American Imagination*. Lawrence: University Press of Kansas, 1997.

Shortridge, James R. *The Middle West: Its Meaning in American Culture*. Lawrence: University Press of Kansas, 1989.

Shover, John L. *Cornbelt Rebellion: The Farmers' Holiday Association*. Urbana: University of Illinois Press, 1965.

Snyder, Robert L. *Pare Lorentz and the Documentary Film.* Norman: University of Oklahoma Press, 1968.

Stanley, Jerry. *Children of the Dust Bowl: The True Story of the School at Weedpatch Camp [CA].* New York: Crown, 1992.

Stein, Walter J. *California and the Dust Bowl Migration.* Westport, Conn.: Greenwood, 1973.

Stock, Catherine McNicol. *Main Street in Crisis: The Great Depression and the Old Middle Class on the Northern Plains.* Chapel Hill: University of North Carolina Press, 1992.

Stryker, Roy. *In This Proud Land: America 1935–1943 as Seen in the FSA Photographs.* Greenwich, Conn.: New York Graphic Society, 1973.

Trachtenberg, Alan. *Reading American Photographs: Images as History, Mathew Brady to Walker Evans.* New York: Hill and Wang, 1989.

Turner, Ann Warren. *Dust for Dinner.* New York: HarperCollins, 1995.

Ware, James Wesley. "Black Blizzard: The Dust Bowl of the 1930s." Ph.D. diss., Oklahoma State University, 1977.

Warrick, Richard A. *Drought on the Great Plains: A Case Study of Research on Climate and Society in the USA.* Worchester, Mass.: Clark University, Center for Technology, Environment, and Development, 1980.

Wee, Herman van der, ed. *The Great Depression Revisited: Essays on the Economics of the Thirties.* The Hague: Nijhoff, 1972.

Wessel, Thomas R., ed. *Agriculture in the Great Plains, 1876–1936.* Washington, D.C.: Agricultural History Society, 1977.

Westin, Jeane. *Making Do: How Woman Survived the '30s.* Chicago: Follett Publishing Company, 1976.

Wilhite, Donald A., and Richard O. Hoffman, eds. *Drought in the Great Plains: A Bibliography.* Lincoln: University of Nebraska–Lincoln, Institute of Agriculture and Natural Resources, 1980.

Williams, Elizabeth E. *Emil Loriks: Builder of a New Economic Order.* Sioux Falls, S.D.: Center for Western Studies, 1987.

Winters, Donald L. *Henry Cantwell Wallace as Secretary of Agriculture, 1921–1924.* Urbana: University of Illinois Press, 1970.

Wolfert, Ira. *An Epidemic of Genius.* New York: Simon and Schuster, 1960.

Wood, Nancy. *Heartland: New Mexico Photographs From the Farm Security Administration, 1935–1943.* Albuquerque: University of New Mexico Press, 1979.

Wooten, Hugh H. *The Land Utilization Program, 1934 to 1964.* Agricultural Economics Report No. 85. Washington, D.C., 1965.

Worster, Donald. *Dust Bowl: The Southern Plains in the 1930s.* New York: Oxford University Press, 1979.

———. *Rivers of Empire: Water, Aridity, and the Growth of the American West.* New York: Pantheon, 1985.

Yass, Marion. *The Great Depression.* London: Wayland, 1970.

Yurchenco, Henrietta. *A Mighty Hard Road: The Woody Guthrie Story.* New York: McGraw-Hill, 1970.

Zielinski, John M. *Unknown Iowa: Farm Security Photographs, 1936–1941.* Kalona, Iowa: Photo-Art, 1977.

SELECTED CLASSICS

Allen, Frederick Lewis. *Since Yesterday: The Nineteen Thirties in America.* New York: Bantam, 1940.

Alsup, Frances McNeil. "A History of the Panhandle of Texas." Master's thesis, University of Southern California, 1943.

Archie, David E. "Times of Trouble: The Cow War." *Iowan* 7 (April–May 1959): 28–35, 52–53.

Asch, Berta, and A. R. Magnus. *Farmers on Relief and Rehabilitation.* WPA, Division of Social Research, Research Monograph 8. Washington, D.C.: Government Printing Office, 1937.

Baker, William. "A History of Cimarron County." *Chronicles of Oklahoma* 31 (Autumn 1953): 255–267.

Bell, Earl H. *Culture of a Contemporary Rural Community: Sublette, Kansas.* Rural Life Studies, vol. 2. Washington, D.C.: USDA, Bureau of Agricultural Economics, September 1942.

Benedict, Murry R. *Farm Politics of the United States, 1790–1950.* New York: Twentieth Century Fund, 1953.

Bennett, Hugh Hammond. *Report of the Great Plains Drought Area Committee.* Washington, D.C.: Government Printing Office, 1936.

———. *Soil Conservation.* New York: McGraw-Hill, 1939.

Blum, John M. *From the Morgenthau Diaries: Years of Crisis, 1928–1938.* Boston: Houghton Mifflin, 1959.

Borland, Hal. *High, Wide, and Lonesome.* Philadelphia: Lippincott, 1956.

Brink, Wellington. *Big Hugh: The Father of Conservation.* New York: Macmillan, 1951.

Brown, Earle, Selma Gottlieb, and Ross Laybourn. "Dust Storms and Their Possible Effects on Health." *U.S. Public Health Reports* 50 (4 October 1938): 1369–1383.

Burrill, Meredith F. "Geography and the Relief Problem in Texas and Oklahoma." *Southwest Social Science Quarterly* 17 (December 1936): 294–302.

Carey, James C. "William Allan White and Dan D. Casement on Government Regulation." *Agricultural History* 33 (January 1959): 16–21.

Chase, Stuart. *Rich Land Poor Land: A Study of Waste in the Natural Resources of America.* New York: McGraw-Hill, 1936.

Cronon, Francis D. *Droughts: Areas of Intense Drought Distress, 1930–1936.* Social Research Bulletin, series 5, no. 1. Washington, D.C.: Works Progress Administration, 1937.

Dawber, Mark A. "Churches in the Dust Bowl." *Missionary Review of the World* 62 (September 1939): 394–397.

Dileva, Frank D. "Attempt to Hang Iowa Judge." *Annals of Iowa* 32 (July 1954): 337–364.

———. "Frantic Farmers Fight Law." *Annals of Iowa* 32 (October 1953): 81–109.

———. "Iowa Farm Price Revolt." *Annals of Iowa* 32 (January 1954): 171–202.

Edwards, Anthony D. *Influence of Drought and Depression on a Rural Community: A Case Study in Haskell County, Kansas.* USDA Social Research Report 7. Washington, D.C.: Government Printing Office, 1939.

Faulkner, Edward H. *Plowman's Folley.* Norman: University of Oklahoma Press, 1943.

Feder, Ernest. "Farmer-Debtor Relief: A Case Study." *Journal of Farm Economics* 39 (May 1957): 451–467.

Finnell, H. H. "The Plow-up of Western Grasslands and Its Resultant Effect Upon Great Plains Agriculture." *Southwest Social Science Quarterly* 32 (September 1951): 94–100.

Fite, Gilbert C. *George N. Peek and the Fight for Farm Parity.* Norman: University of Oklahoma Press, 1954.

———. "John A. Simpson: The Southwest's Militant Farm Leader." *Mississippi Valley Historical Review* 35 (March 1949): 563–584.

———. "Peter Norbeck and the Defeat of the Non-Partisan League in South Dakota." *Mississippi Valley Historical Review* 33 (September 1946): 230.

———. "Some John A. Simpson–Franklin D. Roosevelt Letters on the Agricultural Situation." *Chronicles of Oklahoma* 26 (Autumn 1948): 336–345.

Floyd, Fred. "A History of the Dust Bowl." Ph.D. diss., University of Oklahoma, 1950.

Genung, Albert B. "Agriculture in the World War Period." In *Farmers in a Changing World.* Washington, D.C.: U.S. Department of Agriculture, 1940.

Glick, Philip M. "The Soil and the Law." *Journal of Farm Economics* 20 (May 1938): 430–447; 20 (August 1938): 606–640.

Gray, Lewis C. "Federal Purchase and Administration of Submarginal Land in the Great Plains." *Journal of Farm Economics* 21 (1939): 123–131.

Great Plains Committee. *The Future of the Great Plains.* U.S. House Doc. 144, 75th Cong., 1st Sess., 1935. Washington, D.C.: Government Printing Office, 1936.

Guthrie, Woody. *Bound for Glory.* New York: Dutton, 1943.

Hargreaves, Mary W. M. *Dry Farming in the Northern Great Plains, 1900–*

1925. Cambridge: Harvard University Press, 1957.

Henderson, Caroline A. "Letters From the Dust Bowl." *Atlantic Monthly* 157 (May 1936): 540–551.

Henson, Edwin R. "Borrowed Time in the Dust Bowl." *Land Policy Review* 3 (October 1940): 3–7.

Huffman, Roy E. "Montana's Contributions to New Deal Farm Policy." *Agricultural History* 33 (October 1959): 164–167.

Humphreys, William Jackson. *Rain Making and Other Weather Vagaries.* Baltimore: Williams and Wilkins, 1926.

Jacks, Graham Vernon, and Robert Orr Wyhte. *Vanishing Lands: A World Survey of Soil Erosion.* New York: Doubleday, Doran, 1939.

Jamieson, Stuart. *Labor Unionism in American Agriculture.* U.S. Department of Labor Statistics Bulletin no. 836. Washington, D.C.: Government Printing Office, 1945.

Joel, A. H. *Soil Conservation Reconnaissance Survey of the Southern Great Plains Wind-Erosion Area.* U.S. Department of Agriculture Technical Bulletin no. 556. Washington, D.C.: Government Printing Office, 1937.

Johnson, Ole E. *Trials and Tribulations: A Story of the Farmers Economic Struggle.* 1954.

Johnson, Vance. *Heaven's Tableland: The Dust Bowl Story.* New York: Farrar, Straus, 1947.

Jorgenson, Lloyd. "Agricultural Expansion Into the Semiarid Lands of the West North Central States During the First World War." *Agricultural History* 23 (January 1949): 30–40.

Kifer, Russell S., and H. L. Stewart. *Farming Hazards in the Drought Area.* WPA, Division of Social Research, Research Monograph 16. Washington, D.C.: Government Printing Office, 1938.

Knight, Harold V. *Grass Roots: The Story of the North Dakota Farmers Union.* Jamestown: North Dakota Farmers Union, 1947.

Kramer, Dale. *The Wild Jackasses: The American Farmer in Revolt.* New York: Hastings House, 1956.

Kraenzel, Carl Frederick. *The Great Plains in Transition.* Norman: University of Oklahoma Press, 1955.

———. "New Frontiers of the Great Plains: A Cultural Approach to the Study of Man-Land Problems." *Journal of Farm Economics* 24 (August 1942): 571–588.

Kumlien, W. F. *A Graphic Summary of Relief in South Dakota: 1930–1935.* Brookings, S.D.: Agricultural Experiment Station, 1937.

Lange, Dorothea, and Paul S. Taylor. *An American Exodus: A Record of Human Erosion in the Thirties.* New York: Reynal and Hitchcock, 1939; rev. ed., New Haven: Yale University Press, 1969.

Lauber, Patricia. *Dust Bowl: The Story of Man on the Great Plains.* New York: Coward-McCann, 1958.

Link, Irene. *Research Bulletin: Relief and Rehabilitation in the Drought Area.* Washington, D.C.: WPA, June 1937.

Lipset, S. M. *Agrarian Socialism: The Cooperative Commonwealth Federation in Saskatchewan.* Berkeley: University of California Press, 1950.

Lord, Russell. *Behold Our Land.* Boston: Houghton Mifflin, 1938.

———. *The Wallaces of Iowa.* Boston: Houghton Mifflin, 1947.

Malin, James C. "The Adaptation of the Agricultural System to Sub-Humid Environment." *Agricultural History* 10 (July 1936): 118–141.

———. "Dust Storms, 1850–1900." *Kansas Historical Quarterly* 14 (May, August, November 1946): 129–144, 265–296, 391–413.

———. "Ecology and History." *Scientific Monthly* 70 (May 1950): 295–298.

———. *The Grasslands of North America: Prolegomena to Its History.* Lawrence, Kansas: p.p., 1956.

———. "The Turnover of Farm Population in Kansas." *Kansas Historical Quarterly* 4 (November 1935): 339–372.

Manfred, Frederick. *The Golden Bowl.* St. Paul: Webb, 1944; reprint, Brookings: South Dakota Humanities Foundation, 1992.

Martin, Robert F. *Income in Agriculture, 1929–1935.* New York: National Industrial Conference Board, 1936.

May, Henry F. "Shifting Perspectives on the 1920s." *Mississippi Valley Historical Review* 43 (December 1956): 405–427.

McCune, Wesley. *The Farm Bloc.* Garden City, N.Y.: Doubleday, 1943.

McMillian, Robert T. "Farm Families in the Dust Bowl." *Land Policy Review* 1 (September–October 1938): 14–17.

McWilliams, Carey. *Factories in the Field: The Story of Migratory Farm Labor in California.* Boston: Little, Brown, 1939.

Mitchell, Broadus. *Depression Decade: From New Era Through New Deal, 1929–1941.* New York: Rinehart, 1947.

Morlan, Robert L. *Political Prairie Fire: The Nonpartisan League, 1915–1922.* Minneapolis: University of Minnesota Press, 1955.

Norris, Ada Buell. "Black Blizzard." *Kansas Magazine* (1941).

Osburn, Fairfield. *Our Plundered Planet.* Boston: Little, Brown, 1948.

Parks, William Robert. *Soil Conservation Districts in Action.* Ames: Iowa State College Press, 1952.

Patton, James G. *The Case for the Farmers.* Washington, D.C.: Public Affairs Press, 1959.

Perkins, Ralph. "Relief Work in a Dust Bowl Community." *Sociology and Social Research* 23 (July–August 1939): 539–545.

Pfister, Richard. "A History and Evaluation of the Shelterbelt Project." Master's thesis, University of Kansas, 1950.

Public Works Administration. *Report of the Mississippi Valley Committee.*
    Washington, D.C.: Government Printing Office, 1934.
Resettlement Administration. *The Plow That Broke the Plains.* Documen-
    tary film by Pare Lorentz, 1936.
Rowell, Edward J. "Drought Refugee and Labor Migration to California in
    1936." *Monthly Labor Review* 43 (December 1936): 1355–1363.
Saloutos, Theodore, and John D. Hicks. *Agricultural Discontent in the Middle
    West, 1900–1939.* Madison: University of Wisconsin Press, 1951; reprint,
    *Twentieth-Century Populism: Agricultural Discontent in the Middle West,
    1900–1939.* Lincoln: University of Nebraska Press, 1964.
Sanderson, Dwight. *Research Memorandum on Rural Life in the Great De-
    pression.* New York: Social Science Research Council, 1937.
Schickele, Rainer. *Agricultural Policy.* New York: McGraw-Hill, 1954.
Schmidt, Carl Theodore. *American Farmers in the World Crisis.* New York:
    Oxford University Press, 1941.
Sears, Alfred B. "The Desert Threat in the Southern Great Plains: The His-
    torical Implications of Soil Erosion." *Agricultural History* 15 (January
    1941): 1–11.
Sears, Paul B. *Deserts on the March.* Norman: University of Oklahoma Press,
    1935.
———. "The Black Blizzards." In Daniel Aaron, ed., *America in Crisis.* New
    York: Knopf, 1952.
Seibert, Victor C. "A New Menace to the Middle West: The Dust Storms."
    The Aerend 8 (Fall 1937): 209–226.
Sheldon, Addison E. *Land Systems and Land Policies in Nebraska.* Lincoln:
    University of Nebraska Press, 1936.
Slichter, Gertrude Almy. "Franklin D. Roosevelt and the Farm Problem, 1929–
    1932." *Mississippi Valley Historical Review* 43 (September 1956): 238–
    258.
Smith, Henry Nash. "Rain Follows the Plow: The Notion of Increased Rain-
    fall for the Great Plains, 1844–1880." *Huntington Library Quarterly* 10
    (February 1947): 169–193.
Smith, Wilda Maxine. "Reactions of Kansas Farmers to the New Deal Pro-
    gram." Ph.D. diss., University of Illinois, 1960.
Stegner, Wallace. *Beyond the Hundredth Meridian.* Boston: Houghton Mifflin,
    1954.
Steinbeck, John. *The Grapes of Wrath.* New York: Viking, 1939.
Stephens, P. H. "Why the Dust Bowl?" *Journal of Farm Economics* 19 (1937):
    750–757.
Svobida, Lawrence. *An Empire of Dust.* Caldwell, Idaho: Caxton, 1940; re-
    print edition, *Farming the Dust Bowl: A First-hand Account From Kan-
    sas.* Lawrence: University Press of Kansas, 1986.

Taeuber, Conrad, and Carl C. Taylor. *Research Bulletin: The People of the Drought States*. Washington, D.C.: WPA, March 1937.

Talbot, Ross B. "The North Dakota Farmers Union and North Dakota Politics." *Western Political Quarterly* 10 (December 1957): 880–885.

Tannehill, Ivan Ray. *Drought: Its Causes and Effects*. Princeton: Princeton University Press, 1947.

Taylor, Paul S., and Tom Vasey. "Drought Refugee and Labor Migration to California, June–December 1935." *Monthly Labor Review* 42 (February 1936): 312–318.

Trombley, Kenneth. *The Life and Times of a Happy Liberal: A Biography of Morris Llewyllyn Cooke*. New York: Harpers, 1954.

Tucker, William P. "Populism Up-to-Date: The Story of the Farmers Union." *Agricultural History* 21 (October 1947): 198–208.

U.S. Department of Agriculture. *The Dust Bowl*. Editorial Reference Series no. 7. Washington, D.C.: Government Printing Office, 1940.

———. *Farmers in a Changing World: The Yearbook of Agriculture, 1940*. Washington, D.C.: Government Printing Office, 1940.

U.S. Natural Resources Board. *Soil Erosion a Critical Problem in American Agriculture*. Part 5. Washington, D.C.: Government Printing Office, 1935.

U.S. Treasury Department, Public Health Service. *Dust Storms and Their Possible Effect on Health*. Washington, D.C.: Government Printing Office, 1935.

Vestal, Stanley. *Short Grass Country*. New York: Duell, Sloan, and Pearce, 1941.

Wallace, Henry A. *The Causes of the World Wide Depression of 1930*. Des Moines, Iowa: Wallace's Farmer, 1931.

Webb, Walter Prescott. *The Great Plains*. New York: Ginn, 1931; reprint, Lincoln: University of Nebraska Press, 1981.

Wecter, Dixon. *The Age of the Great Depression, 1929–1941*. New York: Macmillan, 1948.

Wee, Herman van der, ed. *The Great Depression Revisited: Essays on the Economics of the Thirties*. The Hague: Nijhoff, 1972.

Wehrwein, George S. "Appraisal of Resettlement." *Journal of Farm Economics* 19 (February 1937): 190–202.

White, Roland A. *Milo Reno: Farmers Union Pioneer: The Story of a Man and a Movement*. Iowa City: Athens, 1941.

Young, Forrest A. "The Repercussions on the Economic System of the Great Plains Region of Kansas of Mechanization of Agriculture." Ph.D. diss., State University of Iowa, 1938.

CONTRIBUTING EDITORS

JOHN R. WUNDER is professor of history and former director of the Center for Great Plains Studies at the University of Nebraska-Lincoln. He is the author of *"Retained by the People": A History of American Indians and the Bill of Rights* (New York: Oxford University Press, 1994) and editor of *At Home on the Range: Essays on the History of Western Social and Domestic Life* and *Working the Range: Essays on the History of Western Land Management and Environment* (Westport, Conn.: Greenwood Press, 1985). He is coeditor, with Ralph H. Virgil and Frances W. Kaye of *Spain and the Plains: Myths and Realities of Spanish Exploration and Settlement on the Great Plains* (Niwot: University Press of Colorado, 1994).

FRANCES W. KAYE is former editor of the *Great Plains Quarterly* and professor of English at the University of Nebraska-Lincoln. She has published numerous articles about Great Plains literature, especially about the contrasts between Canadian and American themes. She is the author of *Isolation and Masquerade: Willa Cather's Women* (New York: Peter Lang, 1993). She has coedited *Mapping the North American Plains: Essays in the History of Cartography* (Norman: University of Oklahoma Press, 1987), with Frederick C. Luebke and Gary E. Moulton, and *Spain and the Plains*.

VERNON CARSTENSEN was professor emeritus of history at the University of Washington. He is the author of *Farms or Forests: Evolution of a State Land Policy for Northern Wisconsin, 1850–1932* (Madison: University of Wisconsin College of Agriculture, 1958) and the editor of *The Public Lands: Studies in the History of the Public Domain* (Madison: University of Wisconsin Press, 1963) and *Farmer Discontent, 1865–1900* (New York: Wiley, 1974).

INDEX

AAA. *See* Agricultural Adjustment Act
Adams County FHA, resolution by, 209
Agrarian activism, 141, 325
Agricultural Adjustment Act (AAA), 19, 91, 177, 190, 254, 309, 369; corn loan program of, 192; *Plow* and, 317; Supreme Court decision on, 104–5; wheat crop and, 88
Agricultural capitalism, 355, 358, 362, 365n17
AHA. *See* American Historical Association
Albion News, The, 129
Allen, Tom: moratorium law and, 188
Allen, W. Murray: Hagen and, 209
Allotment plan, 56, 190, 346n38
AMA *See* American Medical Association
Amarillo Globe-News, 162
American Historical Association (AHA), ix, 316
American Legionnaires, 269; vigilante tactics of, 333
American Medical Association (AMA), Baker and, 28–29
American Telephone and Telegraph Company, 29

Amlie, Thomas R., 70
Anaconda Copper Mining Company, criticism of 289–90
Annals of Iowa, ix, 148n1
Antelope County Holiday Association, Clasey farm and, 51
Anti-Communist sentiment, 339
Antisemitism, 334–37, 346n34
"Anybody Want to Bid?" (*Farm Holiday News*), 335
Apocalypse, dust storms and, 163, 164
Apostolic Faith Church, 157
Armstrong, William: sod-buster bill and, 363
Aronson, Ole, 214
Assemblies of God, 157
Associated Press, on dust storms, 83, 311
Auctions. *See* Penny auctions
Ayres, Homer, 275, 345n30
Ayres, Tom, 331

Babcock, Dana: prosecution by, 273
BAE. *See* Bureau of Agricultural Economics
Bailyn, Bernard, 369
Baker, Norman, 5; Cow War and, 28–29, 30, 33
Baker, William, 168